The Gold Standard

A Fifty-Year History

of the CFA Charter

A Fifty-Year History of the CFA Charter

The Gold Standard

NANCY REGAN

The objective distinction of a trade association is
the enhancement of the welfare of its members.
The goal of a profession is selfless service to society.

—M. Harvey Earp, CFA, *Standards of Practice Handbook*, 1982

CFA Institute

Charlottesville   New York   Hong Kong
London   Brussels   Buenos Aires

Copyright © 2012 CFA Institute

All rights reserved. No part of this publication may be reproduced or transmitted in any form or by any means, electronic or mechanical, including photocopy, recording, or any information storage and retrieval system, without permission of the copyright holder. Requests for permission to make copies of any part of the work should be mailed to: CFA Institute, Permissions Department, P.O. Box 2083, Charlottesville, VA, USA 22902-2083.

CFA®, Chartered Financial Analyst®, AIMR-PPS®, GIPS®, and Financial Analysts Journal® are just a few of the trademarks owned by CFA Institute. To view a list of the CFA Institute trademarks and a Guide for the Use of the CFA Institute Marks, please visit our website at www.cfainstitute.org.

CFA Institute is a nonprofit corporation devoted to the advancement of investment management and security analysis. Neither CFA Institute nor its publication's editorial staff is responsible for facts and opinions contained in articles in this publication.

Unless otherwise specified, photographs and exhibits are reprinted courtesy of CFA Institute archives.

Disclaimer: References in this publication to specific individuals being CFA charterholders or CFA Institute members are for historical purposes only; these representations may or may not reflect the individual's current status as a CFA charterholder or member in good standing. Questions regarding the current charterholder or membership status of an individual mentioned in this publication should be directed to cmservices@cfainstitute.org.

Library of Congress Control Number: 2011929671
ISBN 978-0-938367-43-7

Design and production by BW&A Books, Inc.
Printed in China
First edition, first printing, 2012

This book is dedicated to the thousands of men and women who have earned the CFA designation. Their hard work and ongoing commitment to knowledge and ethical behavior have made the CFA charter the gold standard of their profession.

Contents

Appendices

Preface

*A*s the current chair of CFA Institute, I have the honor and privilege of providing a brief preface to this wonderful account of the 50-year-old CFA Program. As in any good history book, the events, milestones, and anecdotes convey the complex narrative that is our heritage at CFA Institute. Candidates of today and tomorrow will be amazed at the simple beginnings of the program and the wonderful foresight the founders of the CFA Program had when they began this certification process. Who could have imagined how successful this program would become—with roughly 200,000 candidates enrolled in 2011 to take the exam at 266 exam sites in 90 countries around the world?

As discriminating analysts taught to uncover hidden value and capture it, we must ask a question: What has driven this value creation? What is the "secret sauce" that makes the CFA Program the gold standard of certifications? Simply put, it is the passion and dedication of our people. As you read about the program, try to imagine the depth and breadth of the commitment of the volunteers and CFA Institute staff members who carried this program over the decades. For more than 50 years, this ever-expanding and dedicated group of people has guarded the program's success with their work ethic, intellects, and professional reputations. During many years as a CFA Institute volunteer, I have been continually amazed at the passion and dedication that I see among our volunteers and staff as they support the work of CFA Institute and the CFA Program. This dedication to maintain the highest standards for a global practitioner's exam and continuing education is the bedrock of the organization's long and continued success. And although the industry (and with it the curriculum and the format of the exam) has changed dramatically over the decades, what has not changed has been the volunteer passion and dedication that allows this program to remain the global gold standard for investment management certification.

In addition to the passion of our members who built the CFA Program and continue to maintain it, we must not forget the passion and resolve of the candidates, who work hard to take and pass the three exams. Many of their stories are

Although men are accused of not knowing their own weakness, yet perhaps few know their own strength. It is in men as in soils, where sometimes there is a vein of gold which the owner knows not of.

—Jonathan Swift

Daniel S. Meader, CFA, CFA Institute chair for 2011–2012.

told in these pages. I recently heard the following story from a candidate facing an incredible challenge simply making it to the exam site:

> I am from (Dhaka) Bangladesh, and on the day of the exam, there was a planned strike by the main opposition party. We were expecting a major showdown, and there was a chance that the exam would be cancelled. The night before the exam, around 20 buses were burned by the opposition activists who called the strike. CFA Institute offered candidates deferment or a refund option, which about half of the candidates chose to accept— but I did not. Many of us who chose to take the exam found a novel way to the exam center. We learned that ambulance traffic was able to move throughout the city, so many of us traveled in ambulances to the exam. I came back home in a small ambulance that I shared with nine other candidates!

This book has been some years in the making. *The Institute of Chartered Financial Analysts: A Twenty-Five Year History* told the history of the CFA Program until the book's publication in 1987. Much has happened since that time. For this 50th anniversary commemoration, we wanted a volume that would not only accurately capture the history of the CFA Program but also provide a sense of the personalities who drove that history.

As you turn the pages of this book to learn the history of the CFA Program, I hope you will sense the passion of our countless volunteers, staff, and candidates —and realize the enormous value of their efforts. The gold standard is alive and well at CFA Institute.

DANIEL S. MEADER, CFA
Southlake, Texas, USA
June 2011

Acknowledgments

A writer who revisits a subject that she has not considered for a quarter-century can find herself in a fast moving stream, especially if the topic she revisits is dynamic. Few investment professionals who have lived through the last 50 years—or even the last 10 years—would deny the dynamism of this profession. It is reflected in the extraordinary changes that took place at CFA Institute between 1985 and 2011. When I began work on the history of the Institute of Chartered Financial Analysts in 1985, there were 17 people on staff. It took me less than two weeks to recognize all of them by sight and know most of them by name. We worked in one little building just west of Charlottesville. It looked like a house (Pete Morley's office had a fireplace in it) and felt like a family.

In 2009, when I stepped back into the world of the CFA Program, I found just that—the world. Clocks showing the time in eight world cities line the lobby. CFA Institute is still a family, but now it is a large, multigenerational family whose members are spread across the globe. Its staff numbers in the hundreds; its charterholders and candidates, in the hundreds of thousands. Yet, despite all the changes, there is a comforting familiarity to what I have seen. Now, as then, dedicated people work hard to make the CFA Program the gold standard in financial education that it is. Now, as then, there are three exams, a continuing education program, a very helpful staff, and leaders who travel all over the world.

It is probably against the rules to write an acknowledgments section as long as the book itself, but I could. Numerous volunteers and CFA Institute staff members have graciously helped me understand events, locate documents, set up interviews, and run equipment. If I have met, called, or written to you in the last two years—you have helped me, even if your name is not mentioned here. I can honestly say that everyone I have encountered in connection with the CFA Program has aided this project.

My deepest thanks go first to the members of the Leadership Team, who reviewed every chapter, corrected my misunderstandings and outright errors, and sagely suggested cuts: John Rogers, Jeannie Anderson, Ray DeAngelo, Bob

Johnson, and Tom Robinson. They waded through every draft with good grace and came up with unfailingly good advice.

Following them on this journey through chapter drafts were historical reviewers, who blessed me with their knowledge. For incomparable insights into the early days of the CFA Program, I especially thank Ray Smith, Harvey Earp, and John Gillis. These three gentlemen guided my way with their candor, sharp insight, and extraordinarily good memories. For perspectives on the "middle years" of the CFA Program, I am very grateful to George Troughton, John Maginn, Jim Vertin, Charley Ellis, Ted Muller, B. Millner, George Noyes, Joe Dabney, Katy Sherrerd, Jeff Diermeier, Nitin Mehta, and Ashvin Vibhakar. Don Tuttle was part of this illustrious group but deserves individual thanks. In addition to reviewing chapters for historical accuracy, he also helped me understand events and ideas and patiently answered my many questions. I deeply appreciate his thoroughness, his generosity, and his calm good humor.

Through oral or written reminiscences or correspondence with me, the following board chairs of CFA Institute and its antecedents have given me a much better understanding of its history: Ted Aronson, Gary Brinson, Dwight Churchill, Abby Joseph Cohen, Monique Gravel, Mike McCowin, Bernadette Murphy, Rossa O'Reilly, Frank Reilly, Philippe Sarasin, Fred Speece, Chuck Tschampion, Gene Vaughan, Jay Vawter, Tom Welch, Eliot Williams, and Brian Wruble.

I thank especially some friends of the CFA Program abroad who provided their insights: Gentaro Yura of Japan, George Teo of Singapore, Beat Gerber of Switzerland, John Stannard and Nicola Ralston of the United Kingdom, Burin Kantabutra of Thailand, and Lee Kha Loon and Joanne Sugiono of Hong Kong.

If it is true that everyone I encountered at CFA Institute helped me in some way, it is also true that some helped me significantly. Many of them received the dreaded "quick question" e-mail from me time and again—and always answered. Warm thanks to them all: Nancy Dudley, Peter Mackey, Colleen Anderson, Jan Squires, Bob Luck, Joe Lange, Chris Koppel, Tina Sapsara, Wanda Lauziere, Derik Rice, Shirley Terrell, Clay Bretz, Matt Johnson, Matt Hepler, Dennis McLeavey, Steve Horan, Charles Appeadu, Heather Packard, Jon Stokes, Betty Crutchfield, Annette Abbott, Mary-Kate Hines, Abby Pratt, and Mary Whalen.

I reserve special appreciation for those involved in the editing of this manuscript: first to Wendy Conklin, who saw every chapter in its roughest form and helped to smooth each, then to Maryann Dupes, who helped to organize the review process, and especially to Elizabeth Collins for the final careful editing. Thank you for making me look much better than I deserve.

A quick but deep thanks to my husband, Jonathan Kates, and my daughters, Ellie, Adrienne, and Sylvia, who have witnessed me at my most witless, struggling to get chronologies correct or find a document mysteriously gone missing. For their affectionate tolerance and their love, I am eternally grateful.

Two persons stand apart as my indispensable guides. The first is Tom Bowman, who was determined to see the history of the CFA Program brought up to date. I appreciate his faith in my ability to do that and thank him especially for the countless hours he spent giving me his perspective on events and guiding me to others who might have seen things differently. The second person without whose help I could not have written this history is Wendi Ruschmann, archivist and historian at CFA Institute. Wendi has been a reliable and dedicated resource; she has found every document I needed—and then some. She has also been a keen historical reviewer of every chapter, and thus saved me from numerous mistakes. We had many a good laugh and shared many excited moments looking at old photographs and documents. When crunch time came and deadlines flew at us like bats in a 3-D horror movie, we somehow managed to keep our composure and get the work done. She has been a true colleague, and I am very grateful to her.

Everyone named in these acknowledgments has worked diligently to ensure the accuracy of this book. Any inaccuracies that remain are my responsibility alone.

NANCY REGAN
Charlottesville, Virginia, USA
14 April 2011

Introduction

This history is a happy success story—a story that is well begun. But the success of "professionalization" was not assured at the beginning and is far from done.

Seeing the global strength of the CFA Program today, the reader may have some difficulty imagining the uncertain, on-again/off-again pathway of the CFA Program from Benjamin Graham's original 1940s proposal to its present stature. Nobody would have anticipated the broad acceptance of the importance of professional learning and exam-based certification of gifted young people with admirable career aspirations to serve the needs of investors in more than 100 countries. Moreover, in those early years, Canada and the United States felt surprisingly comfortable when declaring as "international" their fragile joint venture in "professionalizing" the then-underpaid work they found so fascinating and challenging.

Skeptics were abundant—and articulate. In this delicate period, charters were being placed with pride on the walls of successful passers of the early examination—note the singular because, to attract as many practitioners as possible, the first class of candidates had to take only one exam to become qualified.

Today's numbers tell a great story: As of November 2011, 118,610 have earned their CFA charters since 1963. In June 2011, 115,027 sat for the exams, and candidates included 13,787 in China, 10,515 in India, 3,658 in South Korea, and 680 in Brazil.

But these compelling data do not tell the very *human* story of the CFA Program's history—in particular, the story of great and enduring friendships, new and old, of many individuals. These friends shared a set of beliefs, hopes, and aspirations for their profession and for the careers of young people who would join with them in serving the needs and interests of individual investors who depend on us. This book tells how and why so many investment professionals have committed so much time as students, as teachers, as exam graders, and as leaders of our—I repeat, *our*—CFA Program.

The success of investment professionals has great importance for workers' retirement security, education for children, and our educational, cultural, health care, and religious institutions, whose fiscal strength comes from endowment investments and the financial contributions of successful investors. Fair dealing in our capital markets depends on informed investors having accurate information. Mergers, initial public offerings, stock options, and the investment of savings by millions of people depend on fair pricing in deep and resilient capital markets. These favorable factors depend on widespread and well-understood knowledge of industries and companies in every major nation and investors' confidence in the fairness of their securities markets.

Central to the great responsibilities for fairness and integrity in the financial world is the work of hundreds of thousands of people of many ages in many countries with the skills, self-discipline, and integrity of investment professionals. Serving these aspiring professionals with education is a splendid mission. And central to that mission are two parts: certification through the CFA Program and continuing education so that analysts can keep up with the steady proliferation of new knowledge. The challenge that arises out of the proliferating knowledge is for all CFA charterholders to commit to continuing the journey of lifelong learning that is the ultimate hallmark of all great learned professions.

Charles D. Ellis, CFA, served as ICFA president for 1983–1984 and AIMR chair for 1993–1994.

Over much of CFA Institute history, numerous worries—in retrospect, hilarious worries—have arisen about the continued success of the CFA Program, which allows CFA Institute to meet its fiscal commitments. Many have foreseen a time when, "inevitably," demand for the charter will have peaked and begun to decline. Another worry has been that the charter will not find acceptance in other countries. But the charter has found widespread acceptance. The CFA Program has been challenged to work its way through various political issues and develop appropriate relationships with various nations' regulators. Happily, most of our once-distressing concerns have faded away because of the hopes and aspirations being fulfilled by our vibrant CFA Program and the strong, ongoing educational programs of CFA Institute.

This history tells how much our "forefathers" have done for us and our profession. The history of our professional community described here invites us to join in the community of investment experts and enjoy the pleasure of friendships within the mission of continuing to develop our profession. The book also reminds us of the challenge the founders of our profession faced and we face in determining, articulating, and living by high standards, by ethical principles. We need to remember always that the great test of our principles is when we live by them even when doing so costs us money.

No matter what the success of the CFA Program so far, the history of true success will be told when investment professionals worldwide have embraced the importance of continuing education and accepted the discipline of continuing to study and learn. The continuously expanding body of knowledge is what makes our work so fascinating, difficult, and professionally and personally rewarding.

The "Dean" of our profession, Ben Graham, would be so very pleased and hopeful at this juncture—pleased by our progress and hopeful that we will continue advancing. We should make our future progress worthy of a history as inspiring as this one.

CHARLES D. ELLIS, CFA
New Haven, Connecticut, USA
June 2011

Prologue

Judging by the current global prominence of the CFA Program, one could easily assume that it has always been an impressive, international organization. Holders of the Chartered Financial Analyst designation work on every continent except Antarctica, in 134 countries, and at thousands of financial and educational institutions around the world. CFA charterholders speak dozens of languages—even though English is the language in which every CFA examination has been printed. The CFA Program has spread so far and so clearly become the gold standard for financial education that its existence seems almost eternal—certainly, inevitable. Stacked on top of each other, booklets from the CFA exams taken in 2009 alone would reach half a mile (approximately 1,000 meters) into the sky, higher than the tallest building on any continent.

Fifty years ago, however, not even two CFA exam booklets could be piled on top of each other, because until the early 1960s, no exams were being given on the discipline of financial analysis anywhere in the world. An analyst from that era would probably have laughed at the notion that 148,000 people would take a financial analyst exam *in a single year*, as they did in 2009. All but the most forward thinking among them would have considered radical the idea that *any* analyst would sit for a certifying examination.

Toward the closing years of World War II, however, and especially in the middle decades of the 20th century, just such a radical idea began to take shape, in part because the role of the financial analyst was changing. As more and more information on companies and corporations became available in the wake of Depression-era financial reforms, financial analysts, whose work feeds on information, emerged from the back rooms of brokerage houses. The nature and status of their work was changing, as were their job titles: from "statistician" to "security analyst" to "financial analyst." "The development of the financial analyst as a personality and as an adviser to the general public closely parallels the popular acceptance of common stocks as an investment medium," a commissioner of the U.S. Securities and Exchange Commission once observed.[1] That acceptance came about when "the public corporation began to cast off the mantle of se-crecy and corporate financial information began to become generally available." When companies kept their data as private as possible, analysts were starved for information and few of them were employed. But when, in the 1940s and 1950s, data became more widely available, analysts had a banquet.

The role of the financial analyst changed even more when World War II was over. Countries of the world began to rebuild, economies expanded, and money poured into capital markets from both individual and institutional investors. Se-curity analysts found themselves with not only more information but also more responsibility and, eventually, more influence. The same SEC commissioner noted that analysts had become "persons of influence and responsibility" in North American financial markets. What they lacked was the kind of formal, pro-fessional training and recognition that other professions—accounting, medicine, law, even insurance underwriting—had.

Without a doubt, the person who first expressed the need for the profes-sional certification of analysts was Benjamin Graham, the acknowledged "Dean of Wall Street," a man with a vision of what financial analysis should be and the intellectual ability to articulate it. Guided by Graham's urging, and by industry leaders dedicated to making his idea a reality, the analyst communities in the United States began, in the early 1940s, to consider whether their work qualified as a profession, whether it rested more on knowledge than on judgment, and whether it could be tested at all.

More than 20 years were needed for this conversation to come to a fruit-ful conclusion. In those 20 years, the world changed dramatically—in financial markets and beyond. Between 1941 when the first conversations began and 1963 when the first CFA exams were given, the United Nations was formed, the U.S. Office of Price Administration was created to control inflation, and the S&P 500 Index was introduced. In those same years, the war-ravaged economies in Europe and Asia were rebuilt, and a long period of great economic expansion began.

This 20-year conversation among analysts took place in the cities of North America—in Chicago and Los Angeles, in Toronto and Montreal, in Boston and Philadelphia, and most of all, in New York. During those years, conversations about the training of analysts also began abroad, notably, in London and Tokyo. But the impulse for *certification* arose specifically within North America. Perhaps the idea of certifying analysts first took root there because of the dominance of Wall Street in the financial markets of the time. Other financial centers were recovering from the devastating war during the period and rebuilding. "After the second world war, New York was indisputably the world's leading financial cen-tre," one financial historian has noted.[2] Of course, New York was also where Ben Graham worked, taught, theorized, invested—and prodded his fellow analysts.

Whatever the determining factor, the soil in which the seed of an idea for certifying analysts was planted was decidedly North American. Within a few decades, that seed sprouted and flourished within the United States and Canada, and soon thereafter, its roots spread throughout continents and across oceans—until in the present day, the CFA Program finds itself truly international. How the lively discussion begun in North America in the 1940s resulted in the 116,981 CFA charters that have hung on walls in 134 countries worldwide is the story this book will tell.

part one

Establishing
a Profession:
1941–1982

Since security analysis is essentially a vocation of ideas and
expert knowledge, it is a service of a high order. But service
is more than mere honesty. Service means honesty plus
knowledge, and the knowledge aspect is being recognized
more and more by the intelligent public.

—Shelby Cullom Davis, CFA, Report of the Subcommittee
on Certified Security Analyst Proposal, 31 March 1953

From Idea
to Institute:
1941–1963

*E*arly in the 1940s, security analysts, as they were then called, began a debate among themselves about the wisdom and necessity of obtaining a "professional rating." Some believed their work was an art and, therefore, could not be tested. Others felt there was no need for testing, even if an exam could be devised; everything was fine just as it was. Still others held that without a measurable standard, security analysis could never truly be considered a profession.

Professions, by common understanding, possess certain attributes. Although most forms of work require particular skills, professional work requires more—not only accepted practices but also a specialized body of knowledge, the mastery of which practitioners demonstrate by passing examinations. Professional work, moreover, is typically characterized by the capacity "to render judgments with integrity under conditions of both technical and ethical uncertainty." In other words, a code of ethical behavior guides a profession.[1] Perhaps the most telling characteristic of a profession, however, is that its work is performed in the service of others: clients, in particular, and society as a whole. As one scholar put it, "The great promise of the professions has always been that they can ensure the quality of expert services for the common good."[2] By these criteria, could financial analysis be deemed a profession? In the 1940s and 1950s, many of those practicing it in the United States and Canada were determined to find out.

THE FIRST SEED IS PLANTED

The idea of certifying security analysts as professionals is justly attributed to Benjamin Graham, considered by many to be the "greatest intellectual" of the emerging profession of financial analysis.[3] Unlike some of his peers, Graham opposed the view that analysts "should rely on art rather than science" and posited, instead, that financial analysis requires "the aid of well-established methods and of specialized knowledge and experience."[4] Graham loved the work of security analysis and took great pride in it. He realized, however, that financial analysis

My present purpose is not to compliment . . . but rather to summon you to deeper efforts and wider accomplishments.

—Benjamin Graham, "Towards a Science of Security Analysis," speech in the Proceedings of the 5th Annual Convention of the NFFAS, August 1952

THE FATHER OF FINANCIAL ANALYSIS

"Ben Graham developed the idea of our profession just as surely as Sir Robert Peel created the idea of an effective policeman, and just as certainly as the London constables are still called Bobbies in respect for Sir Robert's conceptualization of their mission and qualifications, those of us who serve in the profession as financial analysts are living out Ben's idea of what we might be able to do. We are, at least we aspire to be, adherents to the mission he originated."

—CHARLES D. ELLIS, CFA, 1982[7]

This portrait of Benjamin Graham was commissioned by his student, Warren Buffett, was presented to the Financial Analysts Federation in 1963, and hung for years in the Harris Bank in Chicago. Today, it adorns the headquarters of CFA Institute in Charlottesville, Virginia, USA. Jan Hoowij, artist

would never attain the status of a profession, unless its practitioners submitted themselves to a testing program. Graham argued that earning a proficiency rating would "put qualified analysts on a par with accountants, attorneys and other professions."[5] According to his biographer, Graham, not usually a quarrelsome man, was driven by his passion for this idea and its defense and was willing to ruffle the feathers of "those who felt threatened by the prospect of being appraised by their peers."[6]

To conceptualize security analysis as a profession was a revolutionary way of thinking in the 1940s. During the first several decades of the 20th century, analysts had been called "statisticians" or "financial statisticians" and, according to one who practiced during that time, were barely more than "part-time librarians with a very limited inventory of books."[8] As another put it, "Analysts were statisticians with the professional rating and financial reward of third-class library clerks."[9] Slowly, however—and in no short measure because of Ben Graham—these statisticians began "to develop some techniques of security appraisal, to answer factual questions [and] give opinions about securities."[10] Theirs was certainly not a glamour job—that belonged to the bond salesmen of the era. According to the historians of one analysts society, "The job of the analyst in the financial institutions was more routine."[11] An analyst was "a back-office man who was expected to keep the salesmen posted on such information as bond ratings, earnings and interest coverage, and the tax collection record of government bodies which had bonds outstanding." Worse, their own job security was poor: "[Analysts] were considered overhead and were terminated quickly when trading volume declined."[12] Few companies employed analysts; fewer still employed many.

By the 1940s, however, this situation was changing. Legislation passed in the 1930s mandated the disclosure of financial information and "required companies to make public detailed information about their financial performance."[13] Soon, security analysts saw their limited "libraries" of financial data become vastly expanded. Brokerage houses began to establish large research departments staffed by analysts, a practice that was "quite unknown until the 1940s," according to one Wall Street historian.[14] The task of analysts in these newly established or expanded departments was "to turn out stock recommendations and market letters."

Around the same time, the work of security analysts was being analyzed, studied, and codified—by Ben Graham himself. Although he still maintained his business on Wall Street, in 1929, Graham began teaching an evening class called "Advanced Security Analysis" at his alma mater, Columbia University. The class was intended for Columbia undergraduate and graduate students, but being in the evening, it also allowed "those who worked on Wall Street" to enroll.[15] And enroll they did. Among Graham's students in night school, it is worth noting, was Sir John Templeton, later a distinguished CFA charterholder, known as a pioneer in diversified global investments.[16] Years later, Graham also taught and mentored Warren Buffett, another bright star in the investing firmament.

Benjamin Graham (left) and David Dodd (right) taken on the 25th anniversary of their book titled *Security Analysis*. Photo courtesy of Barbara Dodd

In 1934, after five years of teaching these night classes, Graham and his Columbia colleague David Dodd published *Security Analysis*. Based on Graham's methods of evaluating securities, as well as on the classes he was giving at Columbia, the book found a ready audience. By the late 1940s and early 1950s, it had become "almost required reading" among analysts, according to Richard W. Lambourne, president of the National Federation of Financial Analysts Societies (NFFAS) in 1953.[17] With the accumulation of information resulting from disclosure rules, and the development and dissemination of analytical methods like Graham's, security analysts were beginning to assemble techniques and some agreed-upon knowledge, and striding toward professional status.

These illustrations showing "Then," the roaring 1920s, and "Now," depicting the 1950s, were published in *The Exchange*, a New York Stock Exchange publication. Photo courtesy of the New York Stock Exchange Archives, NYSE Euronext

In this climate, the possibility of certifying security analysts was first given serious consideration. "Ben Graham and I first talked of professional standards for analysts as long ago as 1941," recalled Louis Whitehead, himself rising to prominence as an investment manager in wartime and post–World War II New York (and later a CFA exam grader).[18] Whatever the substance of their private conversations, Graham's first public mention of the idea came a year later, on 5 May 1942, when his proposal to establish a rating system for analysts was brought before

the New York Society of Security Analysts (NYSSA). According to fellow NYSSA member Lucien O. Hooper, "A letter was sent to the membership outlining the idea, and a meeting of the whole group was called to approve it and set the machinery in motion."[19] The rating system was to be limited to members of NYSSA, which, with 328 members, was the largest society of analysts at the time. The proposal stated that a Board of Qualifiers would confer the rating of Qualified Security Analyst upon applicants who met designated standards of character and education. Mention was also made of having to pass an examination. One observer of Graham's work noted that it was striking "how Graham emphasizes the element of 'good character'" in proposing a rating system for analysts, placing it ahead of "education and experience."[20] Given the essential position of ethics and professional conduct in the CFA Program that resulted from Graham's idea, his early emphasis on character is all the more salient.

As Graham argued, those who achieved the professional rating he was proposing would have the potential to grow in terms of employability, salary, and prestige. Investors who consulted such Qualified Security Analysts would know that the person they had chosen had demonstrated knowledge and competence.[21] At the May 1942 meeting, NYSSA members voted—90 to 6—in favor of Graham's idea "in principle." This result was not the ringing endorsement it appeared, however, for two-thirds of NYSSA members were not even present at the meeting and did not vote on the issue at all. Moreover, as Lucien Hooper slyly noted in his autobiography, although "only six members voted against it" (himself included), they were "a noisy minority."[22]

Three years later, Hooper and Graham brought the issue of rating analysts to a wider audience when they debated it in the inaugural issue of *The Analysts Journal*, published by NYSSA in January 1945.[23] The Qualified Security Analyst proposal they were considering displayed some recognizable elements of what later became the CFA Program but also some differences. A Board of Qualifiers was to be set up by the society and cooperating agencies —e.g., the Association of Stock Exchange Firms and insurance companies. The board would confer the rating upon applicants who met designated standards, including those relating to character, education and experience, and passing of an examination. This examination might "be waived for suitable reasons," the proposal noted cryptically.

As was to be expected, Ben Graham argued the affirmative case and Lucien Hooper, the negative. Defining a security analyst as "one whose function it is to advise others respecting the purchase and sale of specific securities," Graham acknowledged that "the field is wide" and probably would include "several thousand practitioners in the United States alone." The universe of "those giving advice or suggestions on security transactions" was clearly expanding, Graham acknowledged, and not everyone in it was equally well qualified. In such a mixed field, he argued, attaining the rating of Qualified Security Analysis (Q.S.A.) would

Lucien O. Hooper, CFA, class of 1963, served as president of NFFAS for 1949–1950.

confer benefits on both analysts and clients. Clients working with a Q.S.A. holder would know the analyst had met "certain minimum requirements in regard to knowledge of his field" and had "professional competence" and would have to "observe rules of ethical conduct." These, Graham noted, would "no doubt become increasingly definite and stringent" over time. In the same way, employers would benefit from hiring someone with the Q.S.A. designation. The Q.S.A. holder would benefit as well: He (in the 1940s, analysts were almost always men) would gain "prestige, improved ability to get a job, and the chance for higher pay." Moreover, Graham posited, he would be likely to have a "more professional attitude towards his work" and a "keener interest in maintaining and advancing the standards of his calling."

Graham anticipated possible objections, including the then-potent question of whether security analysis was an "art" rather than a "science" and thus based on judgment rather than "specific knowledge or technique." If security analysis were based solely on good judgment, one might argue, it could not be tested by examinations. Thus, establishing a rating system would be unnecessary and would not make sense. But the man who wrote the book on *Security Analysis* would not be persuaded by such an argument. After all, in his writings and speeches, Graham sought to convince colleagues and investors that "analyzing and evaluating securities should be regarded as a structured process patterned after the scientific method."[24] Although Graham acknowledged that "judgment plays an important role," he noted also that security analysis "requires the aid of well-established methods and of specialized knowledge and experience," both of which could, in fact, be tested.

To those who argued that holding a Q.S.A designation might mislead the public, Graham countered that it would "purport to guarantee only that the holder has met certain minimum tests—not that he possesses maximum abilities," any more than the possession of an MD guarantees that a doctor will be the best in his or her field. As for the notion that setting up a Q.S.A. rating system might create privilege, Graham acknowledged it might, but only in the desirable sense of excluding "unqualified practitioners." As time passed, moreover, "a constantly larger percentage of analysts" would have sat for the exam and the so-called privileged class would thus grow ever greater.

Graham recognized that administrative difficulties would necessarily arise. He asked, "Who would judge the competence of others and by what right? Who would give the necessary time to the task?" Graham suggested that this "hurdle" might be surmounted by "waiving the examination at the outset for those with practical experience of not less than 10 or 15 years." These experienced, even prominent, analysts would then be free to judge their peers without prejudice. As for who would take the time to develop and administer the proposed exams, Graham predicted that "public spirited analysts of reputation will devote time to this task as to other non-profit work." Given the extraordinary history of

GRAHAM IN ACTION

"Many years ago, I was working as a trainee in a credit department on Wall Street and taking evening banking courses. Inadvertently, I once walked into a classroom where a quick moving instructor was vividly discussing a topic whose meaning was floating high above my head. I left promptly and inquired about the lecturer and his subject. It was young Benjamin Graham teaching advanced security analysis . . . I thanked the Lord for not being a security analyst."

—NICHOLAS MOLODOVSKY, CFA
1964[25]

volunteerism associated with the CFA Program, Graham's words were certainly prescient.

Opposing Graham's Q.S.A. proposal was Lucien Hooper. The immediate past president of NYSSA, Hooper worked at W.E. Hutton and Company and was the author of a well-known market letter. He was not shy about expressing his opinions. "The life of an analyst is complicated enough," he complained, "without the addition of any unnecessary appurtenances." By "appurtenances," Hooper meant a self-imposed testing system, which, he argued, had *not* been greeted with "unremitting enthusiasm" by the majority of analysts but, rather, had been of interest only to a "comparatively small number of the more serious-minded members of the New York Society of Security Analysts." No matter that Hooper himself was probably one of those serious-minded fellows, he asserted that "no spontaneous response" had come from within the profession and found little call for such a system from outside the profession by those using security analysts. "It is not charged that the practices of the profession are honeycombed with abuses which need immediate and radical correction," he noted dryly. Dishonesty or shady ethical practices were not the problem, Hooper said. Rather, he continued, "Laziness is our exacting profession's most virulent enemy." Exams would not protect the public from those unwilling "to put in the required number of hours of work. . . ."

Moreover, Hooper argued, the increase in both the numbers *and* the professionalism of analysts during the last decade had been made without any self-imposed "regimentation." Considering the administration of the proposed rating program, Hooper worried that it would "naturally demand much of the time of many of our most competent and busiest members" and would, in addition, "involve a considerable financial expense." (He would be proven right about both.) Prefiguring the need for private self-regulation, Hooper argued that "the rating itself would be meaningless unless the rating authorities [were] able to enforce penalties"—much as lawyers can face disbarment and doctors lose their licenses for incompetence and malfeasance.

Among Hooper's most important reasons for not instituting a Q.S.A. program was timing: "Some of the members who have been most violently opposed to this proposal are now in the Armed Services and unable to voice their objections." These "younger members"—then away at war—"should be consulted." After all, Hooper noted, "this rating idea is more important to them than to established senior analysts." In fact, a good number of younger analysts were serving in the U.S. Armed Forces, and those who returned in the next few years would find themselves in a world of new political and financial realities. Ultimately, a program of analyst certification would mean more for their careers than for those of Hooper's generation. Yet, as we will see, certification would become a matter of prestige and importance for older analysts as well.

Hooper concluded with a telling point, one that would continue to challenge analysts for two decades to come: "We have no stated set of principles to which we may ask new analysts to conform." Indeed, security analysts as a group did not yet have a formal code of ethics and professional standards. "To establish a professional rating before . . . a code of professional principles," Hooper argued, would be like "placing the cart before the horse."

Looking back on this debate more than 60 years later, it is clear that Graham carried the future. But Hooper carried the day. The time was not, as he argued, "propitious" for instituting a certification program for financial analysts.

Discussion on the topic that Graham and Hooper took up in 1945 would occupy practitioners of security analysis for another 15 years. Not until 1959 would analysts agree to establish a certification program; not until 1963 would any analyst sit for the examination that Graham and the New York Society first discussed in the early 1940s.

STEPS TO PROFESSIONALISM

Following the published debate, discussion of whether security analysts could or should be certified would continue to wax and wane, but the process of professionalizing security analysis moved steadily forward. By the late 1940s, moreover, several analyst societies had created something that would mark both "an important milestone" and a "first step toward giving professional standing to analysts."[26] On 1 May 1947, leaders from the New York, Chicago, Boston, Providence (Rhode Island), and Philadelphia societies met at a restaurant in lower Manhattan and "spent a day getting acquainted and discussing mutual problems."[27] As Kennard Woodworth, Jr., reported in *The Analysts Journal*, these society representatives considered ways to get together more often and share ideas. After consulting with officers and members of their societies, representatives of the New York, Philadelphia, Boston, and Chicago societies gathered again in New York and, on 11 June 1947, adopted a constitution that "formally endorsed the idea of a national federation of autonomous societies." Rather than forming a single national society to which all analysts would belong individually, the societies themselves would confederate. Analysts would continue to join a local society where they worked or lived. That society, in turn, could decide to become part of the federation.

Calling themselves the National Federation of Financial Analysts Societies (NFFAS), the four original members were soon joined by societies from Los Angeles (1947), San Francisco (1948), Detroit (1949), Providence (1950), Saint Louis (Missouri) (1950), and Montreal (1950). By the end of the 1950s, 23 societies were federation members, including two in Canada—Montreal and Toronto; by the time the first CFA examination was given in 1963, 34 societies had affiliated.

Linking local analyst societies into a federation did not, in itself, bring about the CFA Program, of course, but it did set the stage because it helped to *nationalize* the discussion. One stated goal of the NFFAS was to help societies with their work in improving the professional standards and analytical techniques of their members. Individual societies continued to sponsor educational programs, but the NFFAS annual conferences (and, eventually, publications) made it possible for issues and ideas to receive an airing throughout the United States and Canada and for knowledge to be widely shared. In the work of two of its first standing committees—the Education and Training Committee and the [Professional] Ethics and Standards Committee—NFFAS directly addressed what would prove fundamental to making financial analysis a profession: *what to know* (an agreed-upon body of knowledge) and *how to act* (an agreed-upon code of ethics). From within these standing committees, moreover, would arise nearly all the individual leaders necessary for the establishment of a national certification program for analysts: A. Moyer "Abe" Kulp, M. Dutton Morehouse, George M. Hansen, William C. Norby, Shelby Cullom Davis, Marshall Ketchum, and Ragnar Naess. All were, in the words of one who knew them, "visionaries."[28] In the early 1950s, these men helped the movement toward certifying analysts progress both nationally and locally.

The prime motivation for pursuing certification, it should be noted, was to achieve recognized professional status. Unlike their counterparts in accounting or insurance underwriting, those practicing financial analysis did not, up to that point, have a means of establishing their professional credentials except by years of experience. Most U.S. and Canadian analysts held a bachelor's degree or higher, often in economics or finance, but there was no specific university program leading to a degree in "financial analysis." Nor was there any established program on Wall Street—or in any of the world's other capital markets, for that matter—specifying formal qualifications leading to professional certification. Local analyst societies held educational events, to be sure, but none had a formal testing program. And although research analysts at the supervisory level might have to pass a New York Stock Exchange examination, that step only allowed them to publish their research reports; it did not certify professional attainment to the level found in other professions.

At the time Graham's idea was beginning to gain momentum among analysts, two other business-related occupations, accounting and insurance underwriting, already tested and certified their members, and one of them had held professional status for a long time. Accountants had established their first professional group in 1854 in Great Britain (in Scotland). By the 1870s, similar certifying groups had emerged in other parts of the British Isles, and in the United States, such a group formed in 1887. Approximately 10 years later, the U.S. group administered its first examinations for certifying accountants, in New York State, and awarded the first Certified Public Accountant (CPA) designations in 1896. In the early 1900s, an examination program for the professional designation CPA existed in six states and, by 1923, in all of the United States. In England and other countries with British-derived accounting systems (such as Canada), accountants achieving professional status through examinations, society membership, and other criteria were known as Chartered Accountants (CAs). Although insurance underwriter programs were not as old as the accountancy certification programs, insurance underwriters in the United States also had a certification program. The American College of Life Underwriters, for example, administered its first examinations in 1928. Underwriters of other types of insurance had programs dating from the 1940s.

THE SEED SPROUTS

These older business certification groups served to some degree as models. Yet, those who took Ben Graham's idea and began to shape it into what eventually became the CFA Program were true pioneers. They justifiably considered themselves professional men and had an idea of what constituted a profession (knowledge, testing, ethics). Abe Kulp and the others were, nevertheless, plowing unbroken ground. Nothing like what they needed existed within any community of analysts.

In 1950, the serious work of gaining acceptance among analysts for the creation of a certification program began in earnest. The Professional Ethics and Standards Committee of NFFAS, under the chairmanship of Ragnar Naess of New York, investigated further the feasibility of certifying analysts. Naess reported in 1951 that NFFAS members seemed to have an awareness of the need for certification but that differences of opinion remained, especially in New York (which had the largest society by far), as to "whether this should be done at all, and as to what method should be followed if it is done."[29] Ironically, despite its apparent skepticism, NYSSA was proceeding with a program of its own to certify security analysts as Chartered Security Analysts—the first recorded use of the word "chartered" in regard to analyst certification.

This certification proposal received a "very high" favorable response among NYSSA members, according to their Standards Committee chair at the time, Walter K. Gutman.[31] Naess's NFFAS committee discussed the New York proposal among themselves, moreover, and sent it around to society presidents to see if it would garner national support. Interestingly, the New York proposal was felt to lack rigor. George Hansen, the federation's president from 1950 to 1951, found it "rather on the 'considerate' side." Also objectionable to those reviewing it was its local nature. If certification or chartering was to have true meaning, one committee member wrote, "the program should be administered on a national basis," not solely in New York.

In 1952, Naess appointed a subcommittee to consider the certified security analyst proposal. Its charge was to examine yet another NYSSA proposal, this one for a "Senior Security Analyst." Geographically balanced among societies, the subcommittee was composed of Shelby Cullom Davis (New York), William

WHAT'S IN A NAME?

Many misconceptions exist about the origin of the word "chartered" in the CFA designation. Some have asserted that it came from the British title, CA, for Chartered Accountant. Others have speculated that the organization's first director, C. Stewart Sheppard, who was a native Welshman, may have chosen it for its British-sounding resonance.

The truth is more mundane. When the NYSSA first used the title "Chartered Security Analyst," it was based on the existing professional designation of Chartered Life Underwriters used in the U.S. insurance industry. The leaders of NYSSA thought there might be an advantage "in having similar designations in these two large financial service businesses."[30]

William C. Norby, CFA, class of 1963, served as president of the Financial Analysts Federation for 1963–1964.

Held (San Francisco), William C. Norby (Chicago), and Herbert Wells (Providence). Its report was issued in 1953 and expressed serious reservations about this "senior" designation, which would have been awarded to those with 10 years of experience as an analyst once they submitted an analytical study of a security or group of securities. Even assuming that widespread support existed within the analyst community for the designation, the committee concluded that no program could be instituted until two main questions were answered: "What precisely are the standards?" (by which was meant both ethical standards and knowledge) and "Who does the examining?"[32] Moreover, the report reiterated, any designation "should be national in scope"—rather than local:

> [I]t would appear that a professional status for security analysts on a national basis is desirable, and that, if a degree indicating distinction be granted . . . it should be done by the leading security analysts of the United States acting jointly with leading educators in business and finance—all in accordance with a well-established program of examinations and standards.

While the federation waited for its members to signal a "more universal demand for professional status than is now apparent," members of local societies continued to move forward, with one society's activities coalescing around what ultimately would become a national certification program.

If the New York Society of Security Analysts was responsible for planting the seed that was to become the CFA Program, the Investment Analysts Society of Chicago (IASC) was responsible for nourishing its germination. The oldest of the analyst groups, the IASC was founded in 1925 and was originally called the Investment Analysts Club of Chicago. Like other analyst societies, the IASC was a means for exchanging information vital to the practice of security analysis. From luncheon meetings attended by "eight or ten people" in its early days, it had grown to a membership of 137 when it joined the NFFAS in 1947 and was the second largest society at the time.[33] The 1952–53 federation subcommittee that looked into the NYSSA Senior Security Analyst proposal had as one of its members William Norby, an investment analyst with Harris Bank and a Chicago society member.

Sometime in 1953, Norby, together with fellow IASC members Dutton Morehouse and J. Parker Hall III approached faculty at the University of Chicago's School of Business to discuss two significant ideas. They wished to have a faculty member draft a certification proposal, and they wished to establish an annual mid-year seminar for financial analysts. The latter idea would become the Beloit Seminar (later, the Financial Analysts Seminar), and the former would become the basis for the CFA Program.

By the middle of 1953, a "tentative proposal" for certifying security analysts was being circulated by Norby to the NFFAS Professional Ethics and Standards

(PES) Committee. According to the committee chair, Shelby Cullom Davis, "The proposal provided a framework for the systematic [annual] testing and recognition of professional competence" of financial analysts and would eventually be managed by an appointed "Committee on Education and Examinations."[34] To begin with, however, the proposal indicated that the major responsibility for setting standards and for writing and grading the examinations would be "undertaken by the [University of Chicago] School of Business" with examinations to be held once a year, simultaneously, in several of the larger centers and all papers to be forwarded "to [the University of] Chicago for grading." The proposal identified three levels of testing and achievement:

- *Preliminary*—approximating those of general college courses at the bachelor's level.
- *Associateship*—following four to six years of thorough professional experience, with the designation "A.S.F.A." after one's name.
- *Fellowship*—in the area of policy formation, with successful completion leading to an "F.S.F.A" designation.

Although it was ultimately deemed "too bookish," the tentative proposal did more than simply add another set of initials to an already crowded field. By proposing a three-stage series of examinations, it articulated in a rudimentary way the extensive program that obtaining the CFA designation would become.

Following the submission of the "tentative proposal," members of the PES Committee engaged in a "testy and somewhat confused correspondence."[35] A particularly thorny issue for them was the Chicago proposal's provision to exempt "some members of senior standing" from the first two exams and grant "honorary fellowship"—that is, full certification—to a "senior and select group" of federation members without an examination. This suggestion evoked hoots of derision from some committee members. Leonard Jarvis of New York warned that it would turn NFFAS into an "undemocratic oligarchy," and William Held predicted that analysts would react by wondering why to bother to "work along with the bookworms . . . when you can be a big political noise in the Federation and get an honorary award?" Also troubling to committee members was the stipulation that University of Chicago faculty members were to grade the exams for some unspecified period of time. Even those strongly in favor of a certification program did not wish to be judged by academics; they wished to judged by their peers.

The most important outcome of the Chicago proposal was not what it presaged but, rather, who was appointed to move it forward. Abe Kulp of the Philadelphia Society was asked to head the federation's 1954 Subcommittee on Certification. More than some others who had explored the issue before him, Kulp was a strong partisan of certification for analysts. A senior vice president at Wellington Management Company and director of the Wellington Fund, Kulp is

HISTORICAL SPOTLIGHT

Shelby Cullom Davis, CFA, who helped create the CFA Program, served as U.S. Ambassador to Switzerland from 1969 to 1975.

Shelby Cullom Davis, CFA, class of 1963. Jean Raeburn, photographer

remembered as "dogged" by C. Ray Smith, one of the first staff members of the CFA Program. "He was stubborn and deliberate and really hardworking," Smith recalled, and although Kulp didn't raise his voice much, he also "just didn't give up on anything."[36] According to PES Committee member Ragnar Naess, Kulp believed that "the integrity of financial analysts was of prime importance" and that "confidence in Wall Street" and in the "honesty and ability of financial institutions" would be greatly enhanced by means of an education and testing program.[37] In the long run, the confidence inspired by such a program could also protect analysts' ability to self-regulate. Knowledgeable, patient, and determined, Kulp was exactly the right person to see the analyst certification through to reality. As Smith put it, "I don't think there would have been a CFA, certainly not in our time . . . without Abe [Kulp's] tenacity."[38]

In April 1954, Kulp's subcommittee reported to the federation on its six months of intense work. They had examined conditions unique to analysts and those found in other professions that tested their members, the accounting and insurance professions among them, and concluded that much more work would have to be done before a creditable examination program could be undertaken. They were, according to Kulp, unanimous in their opinion that however the program evolved, the minimum standard must be challenging. "If certification is adopted," he wrote, "it should *mean* something."[39] [Emphasis added.] This approach was essential because "the only real purpose of certification" was not individual aggrandizement but "to improve the quality in standards in our field . . . because of the growing importance of the security analyst in financial affairs."

For the next few years, the PES Committee and its Subcommittee on Certification worked to refine the tentative proposal; they tackled, in particular, the perennially difficult problem of whether experienced senior analysts—many of them prominent in their fields—should be "grandfathered" in without testing or would have to take exams in order to be certified. They modified the original proposal so that the certification of analysts would be administered by "an independent organization of stature"—perhaps one patterned after the American Institute for Property and Casualty Underwriters. They did not want it overseen by a university, although being housed at one was acceptable. The subcommittee also looked into how such an independent organization or institute might be financed—by grants, community contributions, candidates' fees. The committee members' hope was that it might be operational as soon as the "fall of 1956."[40] Federation President M. Dutton Morehouse of Chicago accepted the report, calling it "the best ever submitted at an annual meeting" of the federation, and praising its thoroughness. His words may have been cold comfort against the fact that the federation's directors decided *not* to endorse the establishment of a certification program; rather, they exhorted the committee to prepare a report for the 1956 meeting "setting forth specific recommendations." The profession still did not have an agreed-upon body of knowledge or a stated code of ethics. Without these, what would certification mean?

Fortunately, President Morehouse and his Chicago Society colleague Bill Norby had an idea that would help delineate a body of knowledge. In 1955, they had proposed to the federation the establishment of a mid-year seminar for financial analysts to be held at Beloit College in Wisconsin. Begun in 1956 (and continuing today as the Financial Analysts Seminar), the Beloit Seminars brought leading analysts together to discuss issues facing their profession. As Norby recalled years later, the certification program "really got off dead center" at an evening meeting during the 1958 Beloit Seminar. He continued: "[I]t was Dutton Morehouse's idea to ask seminar lecturer Ezra Solomon, then at the University of Chicago . . . to draw up an outline of the basic or core of knowledge that underlay investment research and analysis and which might be the subject of examination."[41] As Norby remembered it, he, Morehouse, and Abe Kulp, together with members of the NFFAS Executive Committee, were involved in the discussion with Solomon, who agreed to prepare the outline.

Reporting to the NFFAS in August 1958, A. Hamilton Bolton of Montreal, one of the seminar's regents, noted that he, Morehouse, Norby, and Marshall Ketchum had also talked with Dean Alan Wallis of the Chicago Business School during the seminar about setting up a "modus operandi" for security analyst accreditation. Bolton reported that they had asked Ezra Solomon, who worked on the original project in 1953, to delineate this new project. Associate Dean James H. Lorie of the Chicago Business School presented a proposal for Solomon's project, which was accepted, and work began in earnest on a specific plan. Out of this project, a consensus would finally emerge to go ahead with certification.

The need to refine and expand the previous work on certification could not have been more urgent. Just prior to approaching Ezra Solomon at the Beloit Seminar in 1958, Abe Kulp and his committee had been dealt a serious blow by

M. Dutton Morehouse, CFA (class of 1963), NFFAS president (1952–1953), appeared on the cover of *Finance* in June 1954.

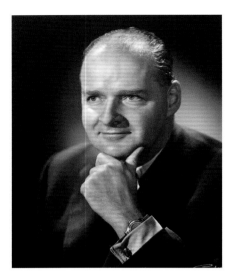

A. Hamilton Bolton, CFA (class of 1963), of Montreal, was president of the NFFAS for 1959–1960. Gaby, photographer

the federation's directors at their annual meeting, held in May of that year in Los Angeles. Submitting a report that expanded upon the tentative proposal of 1953, Kulp was seeking sanction to work toward "the selection of a suitable high-caliber education institution which would be interested in undertaking a [certification] program along the line of the Report."[42] Such an institution, the report declared, would "conduct the examinations, supervising and cooperating with other educational institutions, to set up the desired courses of study in various sections of the country." Kulp's committee also concluded that such a program could not succeed without "a suitable man to head it." They submitted a budget for the work that "would not be beyond [the federation's] ability to provide." After working for nine years and more, the PES Committee was ready to begin an analyst certification program.

No matter how hopefully Kulp's committee tendered its 1958 report, the NFFAS directors were still unready to proceed. Outgoing NFFAS President Gilbert H. Palmer of Cleveland maintained, "We all agree with the aim" of certification, yet some directors acted as if they had never heard of certification before. Others, like Lawrence R. Kahn of New York, evinced personal sympathy, perhaps even approval, for certification. As a representative of NYSSA, however, which had recently turned down a similar proposal, Kahn did not think he could vote to approve the report and set certification in motion. One person who expressed strong and perhaps surprising support for Kulp's committee was Lucien Hooper, Ben Graham's antagonist in the 1945 debate. Noting that it would be "extremely unfortunate to ask Abe Kulp to go ahead without a strong endorsement," Hooper suggested that Kulp's report be accepted in general principle and that money to fund further investigation be appropriated. Without such an endorsement, President Palmer warned, "We are in effect throwing out certification." In the end, Palmer solicited from the directors a vote of confidence telling Kulp to "go ahead and make his contacts." But the committee's report, and the certification program it contained, was not accepted.

"Let me tell you, it was a real shock when the proposal was tabled (and nearly killed) at the convention in Los Angeles in 1958," David D. Williams of the Detroit Society recalled many years later. "The hang-up," in Williams's opinion, "turned out to be grandfather rights for senior members of the business, who weren't about to spend nine hours writing an exam with uncertain results."[43] While the refusal to accept Kulp's report probably was based on more reasons than grandfathering, Williams was correct in thinking that this issue was very important. It was, in fact, one of the most important issues that Ezra Solomon and others would have to confront in order for the CFA Program to be established.

The potential grandfathering of senior analysts had dogged those trying to initiate a certification program for as long as there had been any thought of formalizing the profession of financial analysis. In 1945, for example, the introductory note preceding the Graham–Hooper debate had indicated that any proposed examination "might be waived for suitable reasons." Primary among those reasons was the notion that certain analysts should not have to take any examinations at all but should be grandfathered in because of their status or experience, and become—in the words of an early CFA Program staff member—"just sort of anointed and given the CFA charter."[44]

The stated purpose of a certification program, however, was to establish uniform professional standards. Whether someone might be deemed "certified" without taking an examination was thus a *very* thorny issue. On the one hand, the new designation would benefit from being held by senior analysts, some of whom were prominent in financial circles; on the other hand, it would be diminished by not setting the same standard (i.e., a test to pass) for all. Again and again, the issue of grandfathering was discussed by the PES Committee but remained unresolved. Although the committee's consensus by the mid-1950s was that grandfathering "would be undesirable" and "would cast some cloud on the whole program," the members did not stand firmly against it. Rather, they left the matter for "further study" time after time.[45] The time for firm stances, however, was coming.

In 1957, Abe Kulp had contacted Professor Willis Winn, then vice dean of the Wharton School at the University of Pennsylvania. Winn had experience with the Chartered Life Underwriters Program, including their decision against grandfathering. Sufficiently high standards, he argued, can be maintained only if "all those receiving the professional recognition be required to go over the same hurdles." It would be a great mistake, he cautioned Kulp, "to undertake such a program as you envisage" if it meant including people on the basis of their position. When Kulp's committee submitted its 1958 report putting forth a program for certifying analysts, it clearly stated that a "grandfather clause would be undesirable and would threaten the general acceptance of this whole proposal." For the first time, no need for "further study" was mentioned.

While Abe Kulp was grappling with the problem of grandfathering, Ezra Solomon at the University of Chicago was beginning to outline a certification program for analysts. Solomon was an interesting choice for the work. A professor of finance, Solomon had never practiced financial analysis. He had, however, addressed the issue of certification previously. Although there is no official record of who wrote the 1953 tentative proposal, Solomon was involved, as Hamilton Bolton asserted, and may have been its sole author. When he returned to the work in the middle of 1958, Solomon had three main problems to solve: the issue of grandfathering for senior analysts, the structure of the certification program and exam, and the issue of who would administer the program. His previous experience in looking at these issues helped, no doubt, yet what he achieved in terms of specificity during the six months he devoted to it was remarkable.

By mid-March 1959, Solomon had a proposal ready that addressed all of these issues and became the basis for the CFA Program. It included these key provisions:

A. Moyer "Abe" Kulp, CFA (class of 1963), served as the first ICFA (Institute of Chartered Financial Analysts) president, 1961–1964. Fabian Bachrach, photographer

Ezra Solomon, who wrote the first curriculum, later served on the Council of Economic Advisers to U.S. President Richard M. Nixon.

Ezra Solomon of the University of Chicago. Photo courtesy of Special Collections Research Center, University of Chicago Library

1. a recommendation that the NFFAS establish an "Institute of Chartered Financial Analysts";
2. a recommendation that an "Initiating Group" be formed to oversee the establishment of the institute;
3. a series of three sequential exams, the passing of which would entitle one to membership in the institute and the right to use the designation "CFA" after one's name;
4. a method for the partial grandfathering of senior analysts that allowed those born before 1915 who had been members of a society for at least six years to take only Exam III and those born before 1925 who had been members of a local society for six years to take only Exams II and III; and
5. an examination curriculum and suggested study materials.

The Solomon Proposal was like nothing that Abe Kulp and his committee had seen before. Here was a concrete, workable *plan* for certifying financial analysts. Those directors who had longed to have "specific standards" set forth the previous year or wanted "precise facts presented" would find them here. Kulp brought the proposal to the NFFAS Executive Committee one month later, where it was approved unanimously. The only hurdle remaining was the 1959 annual meeting of the NFFAS directors, scheduled for June in Montreal.

If the Solomon Proposal was remarkably complete—and clearly it was a rudimentary version of today's CFA Program—it was not perfect, as Kulp would realize in Montreal. Ironically, given the Canadian location of the 1959 annual meeting, the proposal made no provision for the different circumstances facing Canadian analysts—an omission the Canadians were quick to point out. Equally embarrassing was that some of the language in the proposal made it seem as if those chosen for the "Initiating Group" would be awarded the CFA designation *without* needing to take an exam. That appearance was not accurate, but the mistake in language raised the flag of "favoritism" among those inclined to wave it.

Abe Kulp's presentation to the directors began, inauspiciously, with a red-faced apology to the Canadian analysts for neglecting to consider circumstances unique to their country in the creation of a curriculum. Kulp followed this apology with a quick but firm explanation that the Initiating Group would *not* be exempt from the examination—and with instructions to the NFFAS directors to reverse the first two pages of the report (which had been stapled incorrectly and were hence incomprehensible).

Perhaps the most significant dispute arising among the directors was over the proper interpretation of the results from a survey of NFFAS members and whether majority support for certification existed among them. Armed with survey results showing that the analysts favored certification by a margin of 74 percent to 26 percent, Abe Kulp certainly thought support was there. Not all the directors agreed. William Bennett of San Francisco argued that because only

20 percent of members responded, one could as easily interpret the results to mean that fully 80 percent were uninterested in certification. Lawrence Kahn of New York noted that barely 16 percent of NYSSA members had responded and added that all those who had called him to express an opinion were unanimously *opposed*.

Patient as ever, Kulp listened to the arguments against a certification program go on and on, broken by only an occasional word of support. Charles E. Brown of Houston, for example, expressed a wish to "sit down and engage in the work that would be necessary" to obtain the proposed charter. "We have seen the history of other professions," he reminded his fellow directors. He was confident that the program put forth by Kulp's committee would raise "the standards of our societies along professional lines." Even more supportive was Dutton Morehouse of Chicago, whose remarks effectively ended the debate over how to interpret the survey results. Present as a committee chair (Government Relations) and not a director, he noted, "I don't think I have any official right to speak here." And then he spoke anyway. Addressing the issue of a low response rate (20 percent), Morehouse said:

> The hardest thing in the world I have ever tried to do is to get an expression of opinion out of this group of people. They just plain won't answer mail; they won't answer telegrams; they won't do anything; so that I think we are completely unjustified in trying to say that, because we have a small proportion of people who have answered a questionnaire, that other people are all against. I think we have to assume that the only people who have any interest either for or against have answered, because this group just will not answer a questionnaire; and I don't think that those who have not taken the trouble to answer deserve any consideration.

At least one director was persuaded by all this competence. Nathaniel Bowen of New York noted, "Before I came here, I had decided to vote against this . . . . However, I do think that the program outlined by Abe's Committee is a good one and it will mean a lot, I think, to the younger analysts coming along. . . ." He announced, "I'll vote for it."

President L. Hartley Smith put the matter to a vote, but not before Lawrence Kahn, mindful that they were "voting on a very important thing," called for an explicit, individual vote by each director. Even before NFFAS Secretary George Hansen had finished tabulating the votes, Smith declared the results: "I think there's no question but what the favorable vote received a majority." Hansen's final calculations confirmed this outcome: The report and its plans for a CFA Program passed 56 to 13. After nearly 20 years of debate, financial analysts had finally confirmed in June 1959 that their work was a profession, and had adopted a means of demonstrating that decision.

Abe Kulp took a brief moment to reflect on the enormity of what had just transpired. Addressing the directors who had passed his report and voted a certification program for analysts into being, Kulp noted, "This is a very sobering, as well as a very happy, moment. . . ." Their decision, he assured them, would not be divisive "in any way." The new program, he promised, would be given "the most careful consideration. . . ."

Dedicated and hardworking by nature, even Abe Kulp probably did not foresee just how much "careful consideration" would be needed to establish the CFA Program nor how much time that work would take.

THE INSTITUTE OF CHARTERED FINANCIAL ANALYSTS IS CREATED

After assembling the Initiating Group (159 past society presidents agreed to be in it) and then narrowing it down to a group of "not more than seven" to serve as its executive council, Kulp's first order of business was to find a director and choose a physical location for the new Institute of Chartered Financial Analysts (ICFA), most likely at a university. In a burst of optimism shortly after the CFA Program was approved, Kulp thought the first CFA exams could be given as soon as June 1960.

The Solomon Proposal had not explicitly provided for an executive director, but Ezra Solomon had suggested in a commentary that it might be desirable to get a "respected academician—either retired . . . or on leave of absence—to serve for a year as a full-time paid officer of the Institute." Such a person would be charged with "formulating the curriculum in detail, . . . explaining it to constituent societies," and developing "outlines, study guides . . . and sample questions."[46] In notes to himself made during the late 1950s, Abe Kulp had begun to specify what qualities he most wanted in the person who would run the program in its formative stages. He wanted an academician "on the staff of a widely-recognized business school," someone who liked people and had "promotional ability," someone who had sufficient academic contacts to elicit cooperation from colleges around the country, and someone who could be available to the ICFA "75 percent of the time."[47] Of all the qualities likely to exist in a single person, the last—a substantial amount of free time—was without a doubt the least probable attribute for a person highly prominent in both academia and finance.

At first, Ezra Solomon himself was considered, as was his colleague at the University of Chicago, Marshall Ketchum, a long-time member of the Investment Analysts Society of Chicago; Douglas Hayes of the University of Michigan was also mentioned. But all three had far too many commitments to consider taking the position. In his proposal for the creation of an institute, Solomon had hinted that someone like Ben Graham would be good for the job. Kulp put Graham on the list of those to approach and eventually contacted him. Kulp knew that he wanted a person whose feet were firmly planted in both worlds: someone who was sufficiently academic to be able to put together a creditable exam and, at the same time, who had either practiced financial analysis or could convince practitioners that he understood their world. Even though Graham had taught at Columbia and The New School—and later at the University of California at Los Angeles—he was truly a practitioner, not the academician whom Kulp sought. Moreover, Graham was retired, living in Beverly Hills, California—and, in his opinion, too distant from the center of things. He did not want the position. Interestingly, beyond contributing the seminal idea and nudging the analyst community ever forward toward professionalizing, Graham did not become involved in the formation of the ICFA or in the formation of the CFA Program, and he never received a CFA charter.

For the remainder of 1959 and into 1960, Kulp and NFFAS officer Jeremy C. Jenks of New York contacted deans of prestigious business schools: Harvard, Columbia, Chicago, and Wharton, among them. Although these contacts generated lists of possible candidates, they came with the caution that men with busy academic careers probably could not give "more than one day a week" to the ICFA.[48] The financial analysts working to organize the institute were already devoting more time than *one day* on a volunteer basis—despite their own demanding workloads. Kulp was head of the Wellington Fund; Dutton Morehouse was a manager at Brown Brothers Harriman; Gil Palmer was vice president at Cleveland First National City Bank; and Jeremy Jenks was at Cyrus Lawrence in New York. An executive director, even part time, would have to be able to give more than one day a week to the task or the first exams, already a year late according to Kulp's wishful projection, would never be given.

By October 1960, more than a year after the ICFA's creation was approved, Kulp changed his strategy. Instead of looking for a particular person, he decided to seek the right graduate school of business with which to affiliate and find his director that way. George Hansen, who was serving as treasurer to both the federation and to the fledgling ICFA, suggested to Kulp that he contact Charles C. Abbott, who had recently become dean of the University of Virginia's new Graduate School of Business Administration. Abbott had been a professor of banking and finance at Harvard Business School for many years and worked with Hansen at the Keystone Custodian Funds in Boston. Kulp took Hansen's advice and discovered that Abbott and the University of Virginia were interested in hosting the proposed institute. Abbott even had a few people in mind for the directorship.

Kulp, Hansen, and Jenks met with Abbott in Washington, DC, on 18 March 1961. Abbott believed that C. Stewart Sheppard, whom Virginia had recently hired away from Cornell University (where he was dean of the Graduate School of Business and Public Administration), might be a good candidate for the directorship of the ICFA. He also indicated that University of Virginia President Edgar F. Shannon, Jr., was disposed to have the institute at UVA, then positioning itself to

Professional Designations Due

Chartered Analysts Group Selects U. Va. Headquarters

The Graduate School of Business Administration at the University of Virginia has been chosen as the national headquarters of the Institute of Chartered Financial Analysts.

The decision to locate the headquarters in the Old Dominion was taken by the executive council of the institute, meeting here yesterday as part of the 14th annual convention of the National Federation of Financial Analysts Societies.

Jeremy C. Jenks, outgoing federation president, said the university would help develop and administer a program for chartering analysts, that is, giving them a professional designation that might be comparable to that for a certified public accountant (CPA).

Dr. C. Stewart Sheppard, who this fall will become professor of business administration at the University of Virginia, will serve as director of the institute.

QUALIFIED MEMBERS

Dr. Sheppard is now dean of the Graduate School of Business Administration at Cornell.

Jenks said the institute intends to charter qualified mem-

C. S. SHEPPARD
To Head Institute

G. M. HANSEN
Executive Secretary

bers rather than certify them because charters can be revoked or suspended for unethical performance, while certificates usually are lifetime awards.

A formal code of ethics for analysts will be adopted by the institute. For administering the program of the Institute of Chartered Financial Analysts, the university will receive financial support from the institute.

In other business transacted yesterday, directors of the national federation voted to change the name of the group to the Financial Analysts Federation.

26 ORGANIZATIONS

The board also admitted to the federation the Financial Analysts of Atlanta, Ga. Admission of the Atlanta society brings to 26 the number of component organizations now in the federation.

Organized in 1947, the federation has experienced continuous growth and now embraces some 6,800 analysts in the United States and Canada.

Directors elected new officers who will assume their posts on July 1.

George S. Kemp Jr. of Richmond, a general partner in the investment firm of Abbott, Proctor & Paine, was named president. David D. Williams, vice president and assistant trust officer of the National Bank of Detroit, was elected executive vice president.

If precedent holds, Williams will move up next year at the Detroit convention to the presidency.

HANSEN RE-ELECTED

Williams is also vice chairman of the Institute of Chartered Financial Analysts, or-

ganized last July to establish a program of standards and accreditation for professional analysts.

George M. Hansen of Keystone Custodian Funds, Boston, was re-elected executive secretary and treasurer. Hansen has been the federation's chief administrative officer for a number of years.

He was the third president of the federation, in 1950-51.

In regard to the chartering program for analysts, a spokesman said that the examinations for an analyst's charter would comprise three series.

There would be no grandfather clause, as such, but men now in the professions would not be required to pass the same examinations as future applicants.

"This is a growing up for the profession," the spokesman said. "As analysts have become more important in the financial life of the nation, it is natural that high and uniform standards be developed."

---

become a top-ranked U.S. university. Charlottesville, Virginia, certainly fulfilled the requirement that the ICFA be located away from the major financial centers. The group liked what they heard, visited the UVA grounds on 17 April, and met with Sheppard in New York three days later.

Before finalizing their decision, the Executive Council had another university to consider. The other main contender was the University of Michigan, which also had a potential director to offer and several active members of the federation on its faculty. Prime among them was Douglas Hayes. Executive Council member Gil Palmer, himself an advocate for Michigan, recalled, however, that although Michigan's business school had a greater reputation in the early 1960s, the very newness of the business school at Virginia worked in its favor. Those creating the ICFA wanted it to be an "important part of the institution it joined."[49] Whereas this aspect could not be guaranteed at the University of Michigan, becoming important to the new graduate school was a virtual certainty for the CFA Program if it went to the University of Virginia. So, although Michigan was attractive, the decision went in favor of Virginia. At the FAF annual meeting in Richmond in April 1961, the directors voted to accept the Initiating Group's recommendation that the ICFA be located at the University of Virginia's Graduate School of Business and that C. Stewart Sheppard be its first director.

THE FIRST EXAMINATIONS

Abe Kulp's hopeful prediction in 1959 that the first exams could be ready by 1960 was just one in a series of overly optimistic estimates of what creating the CFA Program would entail. In 1955, Kulp had believed that it would take about a year to begin examinations once certification passed. Six years later, optimism still prevailed, even in the face of all the time it had taken to win approval for the program. Announcing the hiring of Stewart Sheppard in the July/August 1961 *Financial Analysts Journal* (formerly, *The Analysts Journal*), Kulp indicated that Sheppard would devote his time to drawing up the "appropriate examinations which we hope to hold in the fall of 1962."[50]

If the first examinations did not take place until June

1963, it was not for want of effort. Stewart Sheppard did not formally join the UVA business school faculty until September 1961, and the ICFA did not formally incorporate until 31 January 1962, but the new director was busy with ICFA matters immediately following his appointment. In June 1961, Sheppard and Charles Abbott met with the ICFA's Executive Council to discuss the educational challenges involved in setting up an examination program.

The Executive Council charged Sheppard with devising sample questions and exams to submit to them for final approval. They also wished to make a substantial revision to the three-exam structure spelled out in the Solomon Proposal. Exams I and II, as delineated by Solomon, were to be combined into a single eight-hour test; Exam III would also be eight hours long. After some debate, the council decided that the "new" Exam II would not be an exam in the common sense but, instead, would be a thesis of "independent and original research" in an area related to "professional financial interest."[51]

Potential Level II candidates were doubtless relieved to know that the thesis requirement was short-lived. Consulting with the American Institute for Property and Life Underwriters about their certification program, Abe Kulp received a cautionary note from its president, Harry J. Loman. "You will probably find the administration of the thesis requirement a terrible headache," he warned. These were hard enough to administer well in a university setting, he reminded Kulp, and "to administer this type of program on a national scale, so that all persons will be treated in an equal manner will be most difficult."[52] Finding little enthusiasm for the thesis proposal at its February 1962 meeting, the Executive Council abandoned the idea and settled on an examination format close to that put forth in the Solomon Proposal, with the notable addition of an ethics question at Level III.

The work of helping Stewart Sheppard formulate examination questions was given to a group called the "Council of Examiners," an ICFA body that still exists today. Joining Sheppard and Charles Abbott in September 1961 were Marshall Ketchum of the University of Chicago and Douglas Hayes of Michigan. Within the year, Eric Kierans, president of the Montreal Stock Exchange, who advised on Canadian material, and Corliss Anderson, a retired practitioner who was also a lecturer at Northwestern University, completed the council roster. The participation of Kierans was particularly significant because, as a Canadian, he would help ensure that the exam content reflected the different regulatory environment and practices facing analysts in Canada. All members of the Council of Examiners agreed to waive their eligibility for the 1963 exam so as to ensure their disinterest in its construction.

Whatever doubts surrounded the timing, format, and extent of the first CFA exams, the Executive Council expressed no doubt about the person chosen to create and administer them. C. Stewart Sheppard, a native Welshman and naturalized U.S. citizen, is remembered by those who knew him as an idea man and a "visionary."[53] Sheppard held a doctorate in economics from Columbia and before

HISTORICAL SPOTLIGHT

In September 1961, Lewis Powell, an attorney working for a Richmond, Virginia, USA, law firm was asked to write the ICFA Articles of Incorporation and Bylaws. Powell later became a Justice of the United States Supreme Court.

going to Cornell had worked for many years at New York University, where he was an associate professor and later associate dean of the Graduate School of Business. Although his career had been primarily in academia, his time at New York University made him what Kulp was looking for: someone with Wall Street credibility as well as academic credentials. According to Ray Smith, who served as Sheppard's assistant director beginning in June 1962, he "knew some of the practicing people" as well as "a lot of academic people."

As an academic who appreciated what practitioners needed, Sheppard understood and could articulate why the program had to have a body of knowledge and a code of ethics and ethical standards. Equally important, Sheppard was a comfortable public speaker, a talent he used while visiting analyst societies nationwide to explain and promote the program. As George Hansen noted, getting the ICFA off the ground required "a bit of a selling job." As he remembered it, "There were people in large numbers who were a little bit nervous about who was giving it and what was being highlighted and how were their answers going to be judged. They didn't . . . think that there was any way that you could really measure ability, which was the most important thing."[54] Sheppard's promotional efforts must have been well received, for within the first two years of its operation, the ICFA administered exams to more than 2,000 financial analysts.

Sheppard also did well in choosing Ray Smith as his assistant. A recent graduate of the University of Virginia and a CPA, Smith had a one-year appointment in 1961 to do some teaching at Virginia and assist an accounting professor with the preparation of a book. Smith's office happened to be next to Sheppard's and, Smith recalled, "I saw everything that was going on with Stewart."[55] Early in 1962, Sheppard asked Smith if he would stay on for another year and work with him in the CFA Program. Smith agreed to do so "for a year." As with most estimates associated with the early CFA Program, this one was a little short: Smith worked for the ICFA until 1972.

Smith, 26 years old in 1962 to Sheppard's 45 years, was charged with working to set up the administration of the first CFA exams. He spent time selecting reading materials, helping organize study groups, and establishing examination centers. At the time Smith began this work, the plan to offer the first exam in 1962 was still in effect. "But," Smith recalled, "I think they realized real fast that that wasn't going to happen." That realization came, according to Sheppard, after a January 1962 visit he and Abe Kulp made to the American College of Life Underwriters (CLU) at Bryn Mawr, Pennsylvania. It was a sobering visit for the two men, who felt "very subdued" after the consultation, which showed them how much they had still to do. Sheppard was humbled: "Here we were, we had everything announced, and we weren't ready."[56] The examination horizon would need to be pushed back once more.

Not only was the date changing; the extent of the first administration was similarly influenced by Kulp and Sheppard's consultation with the CLU. Deter-

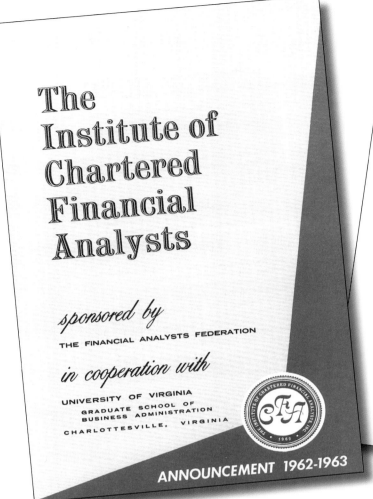

APPLICATION PROCEDURES
AND FEES

Registration and Examination Application forms may be received from:
THE INSTITUTE OF CHARTERED FINANCIAL ANALYSTS
Post Office Box 1523
Charlottesville, Virginia

Initial Registration

To be considered for C.F.A. candidacy, the applicant must first complete a detailed Registration form. This form together with all required supporting documents must be forwarded to the Institute *no later than November 1st preceding the year in which the applicant expects to take his initial examination.* Once the applicant has been accepted for candidacy, it will not be necessary for him to file another Registration form.

A fee of $10.00 must accompany the Registration form. If the application for candidacy is not approved the fee will be returned.

Application for Examinations

C.F.A. candidates must file applications for each separate examination. Examination Application forms must be forwarded to the Institute *no later than December 31st preceding the year in which the candidate expects to take an examination.*

The examination fee schedule is as follows:

EXAMINATION I	
EXAMINATION II	$25.00
EXAMINATION III	$50.00

Active C.F.A. Status $75.00

An annual fee of $25.00 will be charged the C.F.A. graduate to maintain active status in The Institute of Chartered Financial Analysts. Active members may expect to receive reports and other printed materials, and to participate in the formulation and maintenance of Institute objectives.

10

mined to make the CFA exam challenging, the two men now questioned "how many high quality tests" could be readied by the new date, early 1963. Recognizing the difficulty of preparing three comprehensive exams, the Executive Council voted in February 1962 to administer only Examination III, the grandfather exam for senior analysts—for which all the Executive Council members themselves were eligible.[57]

Before Smith arrived, Sheppard had used a consultant to help prepare questions and initially thought to use true/false and short-answer questions. But, as Smith remembers, they basically discarded everything and started from scratch again. They realized the type of question they had been considering "wasn't going to work for Exam III," where the emphasis would be on portfolio management and which required "a lot of judgment and reasoning."[58] Smith wrote a number of questions, and the Council of Examiners submitted many others.

The first comprehensive brochure about the CFA Program. Seen here are the cover and page 10.

*First
Board of Trustees
The Institute of Chartered Financial Analysts
1962–1963*

Left to right: C. Stewart Sheppard, Executive Director; M. Dutton Morehouse, CFA, Secretary; Grant Torrance;
A. Moyer Kulp, CFA, President; George M. Hansen, CFA, Treasurer; Howard C. Tharsing, CFA;
George Stevenson Kemp, Jr., CFA; David D. Williams, CFA, Vice President; E. Linwood Savage, Jr., CFA.
Not Shown: Gilbert H. Palmer, CFA.

Courtesy of Rip Payne Photography

Smith remembers that what came in varied considerably in quality and in format: "Some members would write questions out and you could almost use them the way they were," whereas others "would just sort of scratch down some ideas, and we had to write them." The process allowed for continual refinement in what types of questions to use, how to structure the wording, how to determine the amount of time that should be allotted for each—all the necessary steps of exam creation. Some questions were treated as samples. "We let people actually try to answer them so we could get a better handle on timing," Smith recalled.

By late 1962, a draft of the Level III exam was being readied. At the September meeting of the ICFA Board of Trustees (formerly known as the Executive Council but changed after incorporation), an extended debate took place between the trustees, who were practitioners, and the Council of Examiners, who were mostly academicians. The discussion centered primarily on appropriate content and the weighting of each question for grading. Also at issue was whether or not the trustees should take trial examinations—"not to test themselves, but to test the exam."[59] Sheppard expressed some concern that such a dry run, while advantageous in vetting the exam, might subject the trustees to the criticism of having some "special advantage" the following year when the actual Examination III was given. The trustees remained unconcerned, confident in their own integrity as long as the questions contained on the final examination were not known by them and all candidates for the examination also received sample questions. Sheppard concurred and, later that month, sent each trustee a series of sample questions together with a questionnaire that they were to fill out after taking the test under "simulated exam conditions"; all were to write in longhand and take no more than a half-hour for each of the eight questions.

The results led Sheppard to conclude that more work was in order. He, Smith, and the Council of Examiners constructed a full-fledged "dummy" exam, had it administered to a group of Canadian analysts in late 1962, and graded it "as if it were the actual test."[60] Canadians were chosen because of their homogeneity as a group and because their geographical distance would help ensure confidentiality. Sheppard was determined that no one connected with the ICFA would have even the *appearance* of advantage when the real examination was given. The trial-run test takers also filled out a questionnaire. Some thought it "excellent," whereas others had a negative reaction. With their comments in mind, Sheppard revised the "dummy" exam.

By February 1963, this revision had become the basis for "Examination III—Sample," which was made available to all candidates as part of a Study Guide. The review guide was based on a book of readings being readied by City University of New York faculty member Eugene M. Lerner and was a compilation of relevant articles from the *Financial Analysts Journal* on portfolio analysis and management. One month later, Sheppard sent to each of the Council of Examiners a copy of the preliminary draft of the actual exam; he sent it in the strictest confidence and replete with a serious warning: "Not to Be Discussed With Anyone Not on

HISTORICAL SPOTLIGHT

Although his or her name is lost to history, one exam taker in 1963 had a very unusual exam center: The RMS Queen Mary, which was traveling to England at the time of the first exam, 15 June 1963. The ICFA paid the ship's purser $50 to proctor the exam.

The Institute of Chartered Financial Analysts, Inc.	The Institute of Chartered Financial Analysts, Inc.
IDENTIFICATION AND ADMISSION TICKET	IDENTIFICATION AND ADMISSION TICKET
SECTION I	**SECTION II**
C.F.A. **EXAMINATION III**	**C.F.A.** **EXAMINATION III**
June 15, 1963, 9:45 a. m. - 12:00 Noon	June 15, 1963, 2:00 p. m. - 4:15 p. m.
REPORT TO:	REPORT TO:
Your Identification Number_____	Your Identification Number_____
THIS TICKET IS NECESSARY FOR ADMISSION	**THIS TICKET IS NECESSARY FOR ADMISSION**
Candidate Must Report To Exam Room By 9:30 a. m.	Candidate Must Report To Exam Room By 1:45 p. m.

1963 CFA Level III Exam Ticket.

the Council." Such confidentiality was essential. "We learned a lot from the CPA and the CLU," Smith acknowledged, "but one of the first things we ever learned is [that] everything had to be heavily secured."[61] By March 1963, the CFA Program had its first exam ready; it also had its first candidates. More than 300 senior analysts had registered to take the first CFA examination that coming June.

THE FIRST CANDIDATES: "A NERVOUS GROUP OF SUCCESSFUL INVESTMENT PROFESSIONALS"

Who took the first CFA exam in 1963? Two hundred and eighty-four candidates sat for the Level III exam. Two hundred and seventy-eight were men; six were women. Two hundred and sixty-eight were awarded CFA charters, a pass rate of 94 percent and a standard that has been equaled and surpassed only once, in 1964. The people taking these first exams were well established, successful, knowledgeable—and older than current candidates usually are. All candidates were—and had to be—born before 1915, making the youngest among them nearly 48; many were over 60. All had to have six years of experience in actual financial analysis. Among those sitting for the first CFA exam were more than a dozen past presidents of the National Federation of Financial Analysts Societies. Some of the first candidates were analysts who would later receive distinguished awards and analysts after whom awards would be named. Members of this first group had written countless articles and published dozens of books on financial

HISTORICAL SPOTLIGHT

The first exam was held at the following examination centers:

American University, Washington, DC, USA
Arizona State University, Arizona, USA
Case Western Reserve University, Ohio, USA
Emory University, Georgia, USA
Indiana University, Indiana, USA
Industrial National Bank, Rhode Island, USA
McGill University, Montreal, Quebec, Canada
New York University, New York, USA
Northeastern University, Massachusetts, USA
Richmond Professional Institute, Virginia, USA
Southern Methodist University, Texas, USA
University of Baltimore, Maryland, USA
University of California, Berkeley, California, USA
University of California, Los Angeles, California, USA
University of Chicago, Illinois, USA
University of Cincinnati, Ohio, USA
University of Denver, Colorado, USA
University of Houston, Texas, USA
University of Kansas City, Kansas, USA
University of Minnesota, Minnesota, USA
University of Pennsylvania, Pennsylvania, USA
University of Rochester, New York, USA
University of Toronto, Ontario, Canada
Washington University in St. Louis, Missouri, USA
Wayne State University, Michigan, USA

The Institute of Chartered Financial Analysts

The Board of Trustees of the Institute of Chartered Financial Analysts have conferred the designation of

Chartered Financial Analyst

upon

George Mossin Hansen

who has fulfilled all the requirements prescribed for this designation. In Testimony Whereof this Charter is issued under our hands and seal at Charlottesville, Virginia, this the fifteenth day of September A.D. 1963 and of this Institute the first.

Charter Number 1

Secretary

President

Executive Director

Charter Number 1, received by George M. Hansen, CFA, in 1963, hangs at CFA Institute headquarters in Charlottesville. Donated to CFA Institute by George M. Hansen II and George M. Hansen III.

topics. Lucien Hooper, nearly 67 years old when he sat for the exam, had 40 years' experience and a regular column in *Forbes*.

They were also, as several have since admitted, very apprehensive. Most had not taken an examination in more than 30 years. As Hooper put it in his autobiography, "Experienced analysts like myself, Ragnar Naess, and Joe Galanis, when we took the first exam . . . were really scared that we would not pass."[62] Naess, a member of NYSSA, recalled that people in his informal study group were "very nervous" and felt "there was really something at stake"—so much so, in fact, that many society members were reluctant to take the exam. Although determined to sit for the examination himself, Naess admitted his own concern: "I remember that I was worried about passing the exam. Some questions could be answered in more than one way and which to choose was not easy . . . ."[63] He recalled feeling very relieved when he passed.

George Hansen, who received CFA Charter No. 1, had similar memories of discomfort: "I think there was a certain amount of nervousness among people." Hansen remembered "sitting in a one-arm desk/chair type thing for three or four hours," and he remembered the result: "I'm sure that any one of us, who sat there in Boston taking it, sweat."[64] Hansen recalled that those in the Boston study group took the preparation "very, very seriously." There was a healthy competition among firms in Boston to see who would be most successful on the exam. Hansen and E. Linwood Savage, Jr., secluded themselves the weekend before the test and "asked questions back and forth." In Hansen's opinion, "it helped a great deal."

VOICES OF THE CLASS OF 1963

East Coast analysts were not the only ones who expressed concern. A Chicago exam taker, Fred J. Young, CFA, remembered well his thoughts on the day of the exam:

Fred J. Young, CFA, stands next to his 1963 charter for a 2009 photograph. Jennifer Girard Photography

> When [that] Saturday . . . came we all met at the University of Chicago for the exam. It was essentially an all day affair with a group of people, all of whom were born prior to 1915 and none of whom had taken an exam in many years. It was, indeed, a nervous group of successful investment professionals. Some of them stayed in their car[s] in the parking lot to the last minute still cramming for the exam. Nobody wanted to be a flunkee.[65]

Perhaps the reaction of a younger analyst from Chicago, Thomas N. Mathers, CFA, best illustrates how prominent those taking the first CFA exam really were:

I remember very vividly walking into the examination room at the University of Chicago and seeing the cream of the investment professionals in Chicago sitting there—Parker Hall . . . Harold Finley (the second highest IQ ever tested in Chicago). My thought remained with me ever since: "They've got to flunk somebody, and they can't flunk any of these people, so that leaves me."[66]

The initials after his name tell it all: He passed—as did the others he mentions.

Another Chicagoan, George H. Norton, Jr., CFA, had a particularly good reason to celebrate the day, as well as to remember the technology of the times:

George H. Norton, Jr., CFA, class of 1963. Photo courtesy of Dale H. Norton, CFA

I well remember the first CFA exam in 1963, for June 15 is my birthday. That day I picked up my good friend, Bill Norby, and we headed for the University of Chicago to spend the day in written examination. Many of us in the Chicago Society (the oldest) had been active supporters of Dutton Morehouse in his worthwhile effort to achieve an appropriate [accreditation] program. As we wrote our answers, I sat next to Al Bingham, Sr. V.P. and head of Trust Investments at Chicago Title and Trust Company. After doing a lot of "hand" calculating, Al finally turned to me and said, almost in frustration, "Give me that slide rule." In this present day and age . . . whoever heard of a slide rule? . . . I still have my pocket slide rule, which I purchased on entering the Investment Research Department of the Harris Bank, Chicago, 55 years ago.[67]

Although not all 284 of those taking the first CFA exam were as prominent as Lucien Hooper, they all did seem to share substantial anxiety. Some went to considerable length to protect themselves from a dreaded failure. In an interview many years later, one candidate, Robert Larson, CFA, reflected back on that experience:

I took the exam the first year. [I] was in Lake Placid, New York, for a meeting of the New York State Bankers Association when I heard about the examination, and I decided that I would go up to Toronto, Ontario, to take it. . . . I wanted to be as far away as I could if I failed. It was two or three hours' drive, . . . but I decided to go to Toronto, as I say, because I was fearful that I would fail it and I didn't want it to be too prominently on my record.[68]

The amount of material that had to be learned—or relearned—overwhelmed some, such as Harold A. Dulan, CFA:

I considered myself successful as an Investment Adviser and as a Professor of Finance so I had some soul searching to do about the examination, particularly since I did not know any of the people associated therewith, except Stewart Sheppard . . . I finally decided that if the exam was to be given I would take it.

My next shock and hurdle came when I received the material (books, articles, problems, etc.), as prerequisite study for the exam. It was voluminous. I tried to study the material. By the fall of 1962 I had only slightly penetrated the material the exams were to cover. The only thing I knew to do to break the logjam was to register in a motel ten miles from Fayetteville for two weeks and literally "hole up." I studied day and night. The rumor around the city was that Bess, my wife, and I were getting a divorce.[69]

Dulan stayed married—and he passed.

In St. Louis, where only three analysts had registered, Carl L.A. Beckers studied alone. Recalling his determination to pass, Beckers remarked, "I studied harder for that than for any exam in my life."[70] In Cleveland, former ICFA president Gil Palmer sat down with 12 or so other analysts, talking over what to study and reviewing exam-taking techniques. "We took this very seriously," Palmer recalled: "It was no joke: we were very much interested in passing it." Like Carl Beckers, those senior analysts in Cleveland, and others throughout the United States and Canada, prepared for their first exam in decades—feeling "proud and determined to pass." (The 1963 CFA exam morning session is reprinted in Appendix A.)

THE FIRST CFA CHARTERS ARE ACHIEVED

Once the exams were finished, gathered up, and returned to Charlottesville, the work of evaluating them began. As was true of the creation of the CFA exams, standards for grading were to be kept high. CFA exam graders were expected to be as "adamant on high standards," in Abe Kulp's phrase, as the Council of Examiners had been about designing the CFA exam itself.

From its second exam administration onward, the CFA Program was able to use charterholders among those grading exams, which reflected the founding intention that practitioners would be evaluated by those who worked in their profession, not only by academicians. Grading the first exam, however, presented unique challenges because those who might have been tapped to be graders had themselves been candidates. The first year the exam was given, Ray Smith and Stewart Sheppard used professors to grade—among them, UVA faculty members William Rotch and C.F. Sargent, and also Pierce Lumpkin, formerly of the Federal Reserve Board and then teaching at Richmond Professional Institute.

When the grading of the eight questions was completed in late July 1963, Sheppard and Smith reviewed all of the exams and the grades that had been assigned. "We wanted the first exam given . . . to set the right tone," Smith noted. "It needed to be challenging but practical."[71] Implicit in Smith's remarks was the perceived need for the first Exam III to be sufficiently challenging that even an experienced practitioner (a so-called grandfather in the profession) might fail if unprepared. In fact, as Smith noted, "we did fail people in the first year."

(left) Peter M. McEntyre, CFA, class of 1963, served as mayor of the City of Westmount, Montreal, for 1969–1971. He established anonymously the Westmount Essay Competition, which was renamed the McEntyre Writing Competition upon his death. Mr. McEntyre's portrait now hangs in the Westmount City Hall. Clive Horne, RCA, photographer

(right) Jane Ashby, CFA, class of 1963, member of the CFA Society of Colorado, was one of the first female charterholders. Photo courtesy of Smith College

Although pressure to reverse their grades sometimes came from those who failed, Sheppard, Smith, and the trustees held firm. More than the wrath of the unhappy grandfathers was riding on their steadfastness. Their willingness to maintain high standards had implications for the future of the entire CFA Program. As Smith put it, because some people failed the first exam—"and some of them big names"—the CFA Program set the right tone:

> The charter was not a giveaway; the program was serious. "There were going to be teeth in it, and we had high standards . . . [And] that turned out to be a very good thing."[72]

A TELEGRAM TALE

The 268 CFA candidates who passed the first exam were notified by telegram, but 1963 turned out to be the only year telegrams were used. As Ray Smith recalled, "It caused us a little problem." In one city, "the most prominent CFA candidate did not pass and thus did not get a telegram. The other candidates in his bank did get telegrams." Of course, Smith and Stewart Sheppard immediately got a telephone call asking what happened. "When we let the candidate know that he failed," Smith says, "we got lots of pressure to re-grade the paper, which we did not do." The prominent candidate in question took the exam again the next year and passed. As Smith notes, sticking to the failing grade served a good purpose: "It helped the industry understand that we did have standards and your 'name' did not get you the Certificate."[73]

1963 CFA CHARTERHOLDERS

All member societies at the time, with the exception of those newly admitted, had at least one candidate sitting for the Level III exam in 1963. Members sitting for the exam came from the following societies:

ATLANTA
George S. Vest
Norman S. Welch

BALTIMORE
Floyd W. Bousman
Luther C. Dilatush
Joseph F. Glibert
Samuel Hopkins
Walter H. Kidd

BOSTON
Theodore M. Abbot
Richard P. Barnard
Kenneth V. Berry
Robert L. Blair
Arthur L. Coburn, Jr.
Bertram H. Dubé
Vincent T. Estabrook
Andrew P. Ferretti
George M. Hansen
Robert L. Johnson
William Van H. Kip
Leon A. Lavallee
David S. Loveland
David R. Porter
E. Linwood Savage, Jr.
George M. Shannon
Felix C. Smith
Dudley F. Wade

CHICAGO
Lyndon O. Adams
Joseph A. Allen
Robert J. Avery
Philip C. Biggert
Albert Young Bingham
John M. Blair
Hartman L. Butler, Jr.
Roy C. Demmon
W. James Diltz
Lang Elliott

Harold M. Finley
F. Jack Foersterling
Sylvester M. Frizol
William D. Heer, Jr.
John W. Holloway
Bion B. Howard
Robert J. Kiep
Thomas N. Mathers
Wm. Walker McLaury
M. Dutton Morehouse
William C. Norby
George H. Norton, Jr.
Richard Carl Rasmussen
Richard H. Samuels
Joseph Sondheimer
Pericles P. Stathas
William W. Tongue
Robert H. Walter
Harry H. Wildeman
Fred J. Young

CLEVELAND
Robert M. Boyd
Albert G. Clark
Richard W. Cook
Calvin S. Cudney
Alan Homans
Charles A. Hoskin
J. P. Long
Richard E. Mayne
Edward W. McNelly
Gilbert H. Palmer
Lawrence S. Robbins
David G. Watterson
Loren M. Whittington

COLUMBUS
Leo D. Stone

DALLAS
Herbert M. Jones

DENVER
Jane Ashby
George B. Fisher
Walter Mac Stewart

DETROIT
Carroll S. Anderson
George R. Berkaw
Frank W. Hausmann, Jr.
Thomas N. Hitchman
Herbert Davis Hunter
Allen M. Lomax
George A. Nicholson, Jr.
Charles H. Schmidt
Robert W. Storer
Robert F. Taylor
David D. Williams

HOUSTON
James Anderson, Jr.
Richard L. Bradley, Jr.
Barney A. Bradshaw
Charles E. Brown
Jack Greer Taylor

INDIANAPOLIS
Anna E. Carpenter
Frank J. Travers

JACKSONVILLE
Allen C. Ewing

KANSAS CITY
William Wallace Cook
Grant Torrance
Charles G. Young, Jr.

LOS ANGELES
Ernest Ach
John Cecil Bessell
James R. Comeskey
George Fernandez
Allen D. Harper

Robert W. Houston
David C. Pearson
Foster B. Rhodes
Harlan B. Robinson
L. Hartley Smith
Raymond W. Treimer

MILWAUKEE
Elgin E. Narrin
George L. Struck

MONTREAL
Raymond W. Altimas
A. Hamilton Bolton
Willard S. Bush
Margaret E. Cameron
Philip R. Carrillo
Philip H. Davies
Etienne de Kosko
Alfred John Frost
Ross E. Fullerton
Leo Sterling Jackson
Frank S. Lamplough
Ernest H. McAteer
Peter M. McEntyre
William T. Moran
Thomas G. Sweeny

NEW YORK
A. John Adamiak
William W. Amos
T. Frank Bannon
Philip Bauer, Jr.
John R. Bennet
Raymond S. Bernhardt
Gordon L. Bishop
Julian G. Buckley
Richard M. Cantor
Glenelg P. Caterer
Ida Cepicka
James A. Close
James A. Collins

Thomas B. Comstock
G. Howard Conklin
William E. A. Davidson
Jerome G. Davis
Shelby Cullom Davis
Harold A. Dulan
Edgar R. Everitt
John W. Finley
Leslie Eugene Fourton
James P. Franklin
Alan Kenneth Gage
Joseph M. Galanis
James E. Gallagher
Victor B. Gerard
William W. Graves, Jr.
M. Mallory Gray
Arthur W. Gregory, Jr.
Raymond W. Hammell
Raymond J. Harter
Gordon L. Heimer
George A. Hellawell
Frederick A. Hesse
John Hinkle
Arno F. W. Hinze
Lucien O. Hooper
Roland P. Horton
E. Douglas Howard II
Jeremy C. Jenks
Irving Kahn
Daniel F. Kalczynski
Allan E. Kappelman
Stanley R. Ketcham
Thomas H. Lenagh
Charles E. Lobdell
E. Victor Margand
Philip R. Marvin
F. Kenneth Melis
Oswald E. D. Merkt
Charles N. Morgan, Jr.
Victor F. Morris
Ragnar D. Naess

Frederick W. Ohles
Joseph R. Paris
Donald H. Randell
Dillman A. Rash
Harry McHugh Reed
Robert E. Rich
John F. Roche
David Rosenberg
Walter J. Schloss
Lawrence W. Schmidt
Joseph L. Seiler, Jr.
James W. Squires
John Stevenson
Edna M. Thompson
Charles W. Walker
Volkert S. Whitbeck
Louis H. Whitehead
John W. Winthrop
Louis E. Zell, Jr.

OMAHA-LINCOLN
Fred S. Kuethe

PHILADELPHIA
Arthur D. Baker, Jr.
F. Harman Chegwidden
Martin W. Davenport
F. W. Elliott Farr
John D. Foster
Harry A. Gentner
Richard D. Hasse
Eugene M. Kaufmann, Jr.
A. Moyer Kulp
Russell Lamon
Clifford Lewis III
E. G. Rawson Lloyd
John E. Maus
Edwin D. McCauley
John G. Parsons, Jr.
J. Blaine Saltzer
William C. Trapnell

PHOENIX
Eugene F. Tompane
Paul M. Wilson

PITTSBURGH
Charles N. Berents

PROVIDENCE
Theron S. Curtis, Jr.
Ralph L. Fletcher, Jr.
William N. Owen
Willard B. Van Houten
Herbert C. Wells, Jr.

RICHMOND
Alex Armour
Thomas Kenneth McRae
Clifton M. Miller, Jr.
Joseph J. Muldowney
John B. Purcell
Edmund A. Rennolds, Jr.
Charles H. Wheeler III

ROCHESTER
George F. Butterworth III
John G. Ermatinger
Winthrop K. Howe, Jr.
Robert P. Larson
Bertrand H. Mallison
Lee J. Rusling

SAINT LOUIS
Carl L.A. Beckers
Edward E. Haverstick, Jr.
Henry F. Langenberg

SAN FRANCISCO
Hamilton Barnett
Alan V. Bartlett
W. Edward Bell
Ralph A. Bing
Patrick R. Byrne
John L. Davis
Hull P. Dolson
Herbert B. Drake
Eugene H. Gray
Richard W. Lambourne
James McNab
Marvin H. Miller
Spencer A. Murphy
Robert H. Perry
Rene L. Rothschild
Howard C. Tharsing

TOLEDO
Howard W. Wilson

TORONTO
Leonard E. Barlow
John R. Hall
Donald J. Rogers

TWIN CITIES
George L. Bedford
R. Austin Hume
John E. Hyre
Russell E. Laitala
F. Raymond Zech

WASHINGTON
Horace C. Buxton, Jr.
Francis R. Drake
Thomas L. Ferratt
Nathan Sameth

WILMINGTON
Richard V. King

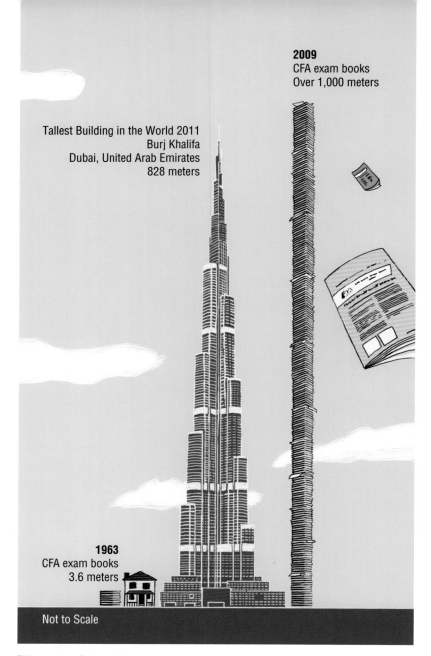

2009
CFA exam books
Over 1,000 meters

Tallest Building in the World 2011
Burj Khalifa
Dubai, United Arab Emirates
828 meters

1963
CFA exam books
3.6 meters

Not to Scale

Illustration: Robert Meganck

Stacked on top of each other, all the booklets from the first CFA exam—Level III, given in 1963—would barely reach to the second floor of a typical two-story house—a truly tiny pile compared with the half-mile-high tower the 2009 exam booklets would reach. The 1963 stack would be an impressive perch nonetheless. From it, we could see into the future of a program that has not only lasted but has also grown in scope and range and complexity—while always remaining true to its founding vision—for 50 years.

chapter two

Establishing Standards: 1964–1982

On 27 April 1964, the Institute of Chartered Financial Analysts held its first annual meeting for members. Eligible to attend were the 268 men and women who had passed the 1963 Level III CFA examination. Addressing them, C. Stewart Sheppard asked for their continued help in educating potential candidates about "the type of examination which they might expect" and, especially, "the extent of preparation required."[1] Outgoing Board of Trustees President A. Moyer "Abe" Kulp, CFA, also spoke; he reviewed the accomplishments of the previous year, the grading procedures, and upcoming examination cycle. "The year 1963–1964," he told the first class of charterholders, "will be the most significant in the history of the Institute."

Those who succeeded Abe Kulp at the helm of the CFA Program during the intervening 50 years might dispute his claim about the significance of the program's first full year. In some respects, however, Kulp was correct. The 1963–64 time period had been momentous. The administration of the first exams in 1963 had said, in effect, "We are here." A successful administration of all three levels in June 1964 would say, "We are here to stay." By the end of this *annus mirabilis,* those responsible for the CFA Program would have done even more than they dreamed: adopted a code of ethics, adjudicated the first case of its possible violation, established study groups throughout the United States and Canada, garnered considerable publicity, increased sixfold the number of exams given, doubled the staff, outgrew office space, and declined to accept a request from the warden of Sing Sing prison to enroll inmates "of previous importance on Wall Street" in the CFA Program.

In reporting to ICFA members in April 1964, Abe Kulp was facing a proud new reality. In addition to the 268 men and women now bearing the designation CFA after their names, another 1,997 had registered to take the upcoming exams, which would include all three levels for the first time. No longer were Kulp and the Council of Examiners struggling to bring certification to analysts. Instead, they were struggling to manage the program's growth. "The widespread and

We must be adamant on high standards.

—A. Moyer "Abe" Kulp, CFA, private papers, 1957

David D. Williams, CFA, class of 1963, served as president of the ICFA for 1964–1965.

enthusiastic acceptance" of the CFA designation had, Kulp noted with significant understatement, "exceeded all earlier expectations." In fact, the new program had exceeded every conceivable expectation, and by a wide margin. The institute's original bylaws had mandated that the Initiating Group serve until "200 persons" had received the CFA designation and assumed that result would take about 10 years. Yet, after only a single administration of the CFA exam, that number had been reached and surpassed. The "four-drawer file cabinet, not even new," whose purchase a determined Stewart Sheppard had persuaded a reluctant George M. Hansen, CFA, to authorize a year before, was already full.

How to account for this early success? No doubt, it helped that the program's supporters had done their best to make it known. Financial Analysts Federation (FAF) President William C. Norby, CFA, of Chicago, had been tireless in his active promotion of the CFA designation as "the standard for the investment community."[2] In January 1964, Norby, mindful that certain agencies wanted analysts to have credentials of some kind, began writing to regulatory bodies, including the U.S. Securities and Exchange Commission (SEC), to suggest that they adopt the CFA designation as a qualification for research personnel. Norby's efforts bore fruit. As Abe Kulp proudly reported to members in April 1964, "The S.E.C. and the New York Stock Exchange have endorsed the program in various ways. . . ."[3] Moreover, just one year after the CFA exams began, the New York Stock Exchange (NYSE) adopted Rule 344, which specified that supervisory research personnel could use the attainment of a CFA charter as one of three sufficient qualifications. In a speech before an accounting organization given in May 1964, SEC Commissioner Byron D. Woodside touted the achievement of analysts in instituting the new CFA Program, calling it "a very fine program which should receive the support and commendation it deserves" because it "fostered an educational program and established examination procedures by means of which those who qualify by study, and demonstrate fitness by meeting the required standards, can become Chartered Financial Analysts."[4]

The fledgling CFA Program had also received a fair amount of good publicity in the print media. A month before the first examinations, on 6 May 1963, the *Wall Street Journal* had run a long article featuring Lucien O. Hooper, CFA, a regular *Forbes* columnist, immersed in test preparation (see p. 40). In addition, the June 1963 administration of the first CFA exams had been noted in the *New York Times*, while the *Los Angeles Times* ran a picture in its business section of a roomful of analysts (none too young looking) hard at work on the Level III test. Announcements naming the candidates who passed the first exams appeared in both of these papers as well as in the *Chicago Tribune*, the *Washington Post*, and other U.S. and Canadian newspapers.

Even before the first exams were given, ICFA Vice President David D. Williams, CFA, of Detroit, had been quoted regarding the program in a widely syndicated column written for the *New York Daily News* by Sylvia Porter, an economist and

FINANCIAL ANALYSTS EXAM—Prof. David K. Eiteman of UCLA conducts the initial examination given by the Institute of Chartered Financial Analysts. Those who pass will receive degrees as Chartered Financial Analysts, equivalent to a CPA in accounting or CLU in insurance. The examination climaxes 10 years of effort by securities industry to professionalize status of financial analysts.
Times photo

Copyright © 1963. *Los Angeles Times.* Reprinted with permission.

business writer popular at the time. This attention delighted Abe Kulp. Soon after, Stewart Sheppard was featured in the *Wall Street Journal.* When the *Chicago Tribune* listed the names of successful local analysts, it also interviewed Bill Norby, who firmly stated his conviction that the CFA Program's purpose—to "make financial analysis a profession"—would be realized. Norby concluded with a bold prediction: "We believe that 10 years hence all research work in this field will be supervised by a C.F.A."[5] In September 1963, the *New York Times* ran an article about the CFA Program noting, "Security analysis appears to be on the verge of attaining recognition as a professional discipline."[6]

Articles about the upcoming CFA exams also appeared in the first half of 1964, some featuring more analysts studying hard. According to Abe Kulp, some financial houses (he does not say which) had begun to require that "entire research staffs" register for the CFA exam and finance departments in some business schools were "reorganizing curricula to conform to C.F.A. Study Guides."[7] As if to illustrate this assertion, the *New York Times* ran an article on 22 May 1964 headlined "27 Security Analysts Cram for Examination." It featured a picture of two "crammers," both of whom were from the investment firm Naess and Thomas. One of that firm's principals was, of course, Ragnar D. Naess, CFA, who was instrumental in the creation of the certification program for analysts and was one of those prominent candidates from the first class of CFA charterholders. Whether

New Testing Program Establishes Standards For Security Analysis

Institute Offers "CFA" Title To Qualified Practitioners; 300 Bone Up for First Exam

6 May 1963
THE WALL STREET JOURNAL
By Ed Cony—Staff Reporter

NEW YORK—Lucien Hooper of W.E. Hutton & Co., who has been analyzing securities for 44 years and writing market letters for 42 years, hopes to pass an exam June 15—on security analysis.

It would be astounding, of course, if Mr. Hooper failed the test. Nevertheless, he and some 300 other veteran security analysts around the country are taking the exam very seriously, many of them boning up at weekly seminars. "I suppose this would be the equivalent (in difficulty) of a bar exam," says Mr. Hooper.

That's precisely the reaction desired by the Financial Analysts Federation, an association of security analyst societies in 27 U.S. and two Canadian cities. The federation set up the Institute of Chartered Financial Analysts to make up the exam and bestow the title of Chartered Financial Analyst (CFA) on those who pass it.

The institute is trying to establish for the first time formal standards of ethics and competence for security analysts. These analysts work not only for brokerage houses, as Mr. Hooper does, but also for investment banking concerns, insurance companies, commercial banks, mutual funds and investment counseling firms. Institute officials hope that the CFA designation eventually will mean as much in the securities industry as the CPA title does in the accounting field.

Far From "The Street"

The CFA program is being developed far from the pressures of Wall Street at the University of Virginia, where C. Stewart Sheppard, the institute's executive director, is a professor at the Graduate School of Business Administration. The institute began operations last fall on the Charlottesville campus under a $75,000 grant to the university from the Financial Analysts Federation.

The institute's initial test in June comes on the heels of the Securities and Exchange Commission's Special Study of Security Markets. The study had harsh words about the qualifications and conduct of some of those who provide investment advice.

It noted a "lack of entry standards" for "analysts of all types." It charged that some brokerage houses assign "inexperienced analysts with little or no supervision to research tasks such as portfolio analysis." And it complained that the New York Stock Exchange "encourages its members to advertise their research and advisory activities without concerning itself with their ability to perform the services which they purport to perform."

The SEC examined the qualifications of new investment advisers, those who advise the public for a fee and who are required to register with the commission. It reported that 89 out of 141 advisers who registered during one three-month period had no prior experience in the securities business. And over 40% of them held no academic degree higher than a high school diploma.

The study cited as "an extreme situation" a daily investment advisory publication launched last year. Entitled The Trading Floor and priced at 50 cents a copy, it recommended for its readers 11 new stocks a day—six on the Big Board; five on the American Stock Exchange.

His Mother Helped

"The entire 'staff' and publisher of this ambitious undertaking turned out to be a 19-year-old boy," said the SEC. His experience in the securities industry: "Two months as a beginning clerk at Carl M. Loeb, Rhoades & Co., two months as a beginning clerk at Bache & Co." He cranked out The Trading Floor on a mimeograph machine in the kitchen of his family's Brooklyn apartment with an assist from his mother "who helped him collate and staple the pages."

Although the backers of the CFA concept are concerned about such "extreme situations," they have no illusions about acting as policemen for the entire industry. "It's the last thing we'd want to do," says Mr. Sheppard, the institute director. "We want to get at the policy makers in the industry, men who are conscious of the professional nature of financial analysis. We hope they'll recognize the importance of the CFA designation and pursue it voluntarily."

Can the voluntary approach effectively protect the public against the dangers of malpractice? The SEC is skeptical. In its special study the SEC dismissed the CFA concept as having "but limited public benefit." It criticized what it described as a "lack" of "power and determination to exclude unqualified persons from engaging in analytic activities without supervision."

But A. Moyer Kulp, vice president and director of the Wellington Fund, a big mutual fund, and an institute trustee, contends that the SEC report "greatly underestimates the significance of this movement." Mr. Kulp says: "The setting of standards is, in itself, very important. Employers will see to it that standards are followed," Mr. Kulp asserts, because firms which "choose to ignore the CFA will be at a competitive disadvantage."

The institute is laying considerable stress on ethical standards as well as competence. The institute's brochure states that "confidential reports" on each candidate's character will be obtained. And the CFA application blank, above the space for the applicant's signature, bears this sentence: "I further understand and agree that the CFA designation may be rescinded at any time in the event of violation of professional ethical standards."

When the testing program is fully implemented, a CFA candidate will have to take a series of three, four-hour examinations, no more than one in one year. He will have to be at least age 24 to take the first test, 26 for the second and 30 for the third. To be eligible for the final two exams the candidate will have to be a member of a security analysts society affiliated with the Financial Analysts Federation and to have had "work experience of a responsible nature in financial analysis."

Institute officials say they have been encouraged by the initial response to their program. They received 320 applications for the first test, about three times as many as they had expected. Fifteen applicants were rejected, most of them because they were engaged in the selling end of the business, rather than in analysis.

Those accepted are all at least [48] years old and have belonged to a security analyst society for at least eight years. The list of candidates includes Mr. Kulp of the Wellington Fund, David D. Williams, vice president of the National Bank of Detroit, and the six other members of the institute's board of trustees. Because of their experience, the first two exams are being waived for the members of this initial group.

But there's nothing easy about this test, says the institute's Mr. Sheppard, the former dean of Cornell University's Graduate School of Business and Public Administration. "It's going to be tough.

If a candidate relying on his experience comes in and tries to answer the questions off the top of his head, he's going to be in trouble."

A sample test prepared by the institute indicates that questions will be designed to determine such things as a candidate's grasp of fundamental economic issues, his concept of professional ethics, his method of evaluating securities and his ability to run a research department. Two examples from the sample test:

You are the manager of the research department of a firm that limits its research analysis primarily to common stocks. (A) How would you select the stocks you would analyze? (B) What instructions would you give a new junior analyst who is to prepare a research report on one of these stocks? (C) As manager of the department on what basis would you like your performance to be measured?

"The acceptance of Keynesian economics and the consequent commitments by Western Governments to 'full employment economics' made equity investment considerably safer in the postwar world; inflation made it much more desirable." (London Observer, Jan. 6, 1963) Discuss critically the above statement in the light of American experience.

Reprinted by permission of *Wall Street Journal*. Copyright © 1963 Dow Jones & Company, Inc. All Rights Reserved Worldwide.

Financial Post, Toronto(Ont)
SATURDAY, SEPTEMBER 26, 1963

18 Canadians Awarded CFA

CHARLOTTESVILLE, Va.— Eighteen students from Canada were among the 268 successful candidates who received the first awards of the professional designation of Chartered Financial Analyst (C.F.A.) from the Institute of Chartered Financial Analysts, University of Virginia.

Institute was organized in 1962 and is sponsored by the Financial Analysts Federation, which includes 8,250 members in 34 constituent societies in major cities of the U. S. and Canada. Institute is chartered to meet "the increasing need for high standards of technical and ethical performance in financial analysis."

Here are the Canadian graduates:

MONTREAL
Raymond W. Altimas, Jones Heward & Co.
A. H. Bolton, Bolton, Tremblay & Co.
Willard S. Bush, Du Pont of Canada.
Miss Margaret E. Cameron, McLean Budden Ltd.
P. R. Carrillo, Graymont, Ltd.
P. H. Davies, Canadian National Railways.
A. John Frost, Guaranty Trust Co.
Ross E. Fullerton, Royal Trust Co.
L. S. Jackson, Jackson, McFadyen Securities, Ltd.
Etienne Kosko, Bolton Tremblay & Co.
F. S. Lamplough, Collier, Norris & Quinlan.
Ernest McAteer, Oswald Drinkwater & Graham Ltd.
Peter M. McEntyre, St. Lawrence Sugar Refineries Ltd.
W. T. Moran, Greenshields Inc.
Thomas G. Sweeny, Bluenose Netting & Twine Ltd.

TORONTO
L. E. Barlow, McLeod, Young, Weir & Co.
John R. Hall, Manufacturers Life Insurance Co.
Donald J. Rogers, Equitable Securities Canada Ltd.

Reprinted from the *Financial Post*, Toronto, 26 September 1963.

Cleveland Financial "Quiz Kids"

Pictured here are the first 13 Clevelanders to be awarded the designation Chartered Financial Analysts. The new CFAs are (seated left to right) Alan Homans, National City Bank; David G. Watterson, Boyd, Watterson & Co.; Lawrence S. Robbins, Fahey, Clark & Co.; Dr. C. Stewart Sheppard, director of the Institute; L. M. Whittington, Society National Bank; E. W. McNelly, Union Commerce Bank, and Charles A. Hoskin, McDonald & Co. (Standing left to right) J. P. Long, Cleveland-Cliffs Iron Co.; Gilbert H. Palmer, National City Bank; Richard E. Mayne, Central National Bank; William C. Norby, president of the Financial Analysts Federation; Richard W. Cook, Prescott & Co.; Calvin S. Cudney, Cleveland Trust Co.; Robert M. Boyd, Boyd, Watterson, and Albert G. Clark, Central National Bank.   Plain Dealer Photo (William A. Wynne)

Used with permission of *The Plain Dealer*. © 1963. All rights reserved.

Naess "required" those working for him to register for CFA exams is not known, but it is fair to say that he set a compelling example.

By any measure, the CFA Program was taking off. Such early success, however, breeds its own kind of pressure. The tiny staff—Stewart Sheppard, C. Ray Smith, both still working only part time, two secretaries, and a registrar—was challenged by having to produce three exams, a new brochure, and study guides as well as setting up nearly twice the number of exam centers (more than 50 as opposed to 27). Even with the extraordinary willingness of key volunteers—the Council of Examiners (COE) and the Board of Trustees—this workload was demanding a lot from them.

According to Ray Smith, volunteerism then, as now, was significant in the program's success. Both the board and the COE were composed of "tremendously hard-working" individuals, tireless in their devotion to the advancement of the program. Because everyone involved—including Ray Smith and Stewart

Sheppard—had other work, weekend meetings were necessary. In his first year at the ICFA, Smith recalled, "I was working with the ICFA 50 out of 52 weekends...."[8] Most of the volunteers were older than Sheppard, who was 45 (Kulp was in his mid-60s, for example) and certainly much, much older than Smith, who was only 26. Yet, their stamina, their dedication to the profession, *and* their love for this volunteer work was unmatched. Smith recalled one time in particular:

> I think we were in New York. We'd been working since six o'clock in the morning. It was two o'clock the next morning. And I think it was Abe Kulp [who] said, "Well, we need to go get a drink." And I said, "I'm too young to die!"

No doubt a little levity was needed, for the challenge of readying the second year's examinations loomed large. As Sheppard remembered it, offering "all three examinations" in 1964 placed an "inordinate burden on the administrative staff and its physical facilities."[9] That there were nearly 2,000 registrations to process did not help things, although it certainly was pleasing to everyone to see the CFA Program taken up so quickly and so widely.

Beyond the effects of good publicity, much of the enthusiasm represented by the growth in candidate registrations was the result of promotion of the new CFA Program within individual societies and of Stewart Sheppard's ceaseless efforts in visiting societies around the United States and Canada to discuss the program. Ray Smith recalled one cogent example of Sheppard's oratorical talent:

C. Ray Smith (left) and C. Stewart Sheppard (right) were the first official ICFA staff members. Photo courtesy of Rip Payne Photography

> ... Stewart gave a speech; I think it was in Kansas City ... at the Financial Analysts Federation annual meeting. [It] was on ethics, and it was a great speech. [Afterwards], all these people came up, and the reporters came up, and they wanted a copy of his speech. So, Stewart said "I'll send it to you!" The truth was Stewart didn't have a written speech. He had just made that speech [up] on the way up there ... so, we had to come back to Charlottesville and write the speech that he had given in Kansas City. I'll never forget that.[10]

As David G. Watterson, CFA, of Cleveland, the institute's sixth board president recalled, the CFA Program owed a "great debt of gratitude to Stewart Sheppard" for visiting so many local societies in that initial year and generating interest for the program.[11] Leonard E. Barlow, CFA, of Toronto, who succeeded Watterson as ICFA president, thought the hiring of Sheppard was "a stroke of genius." Not only did his academic credentials and Wall Street connections help him create examinations both high in quality and pertinent to a practitioner, but Sheppard also possessed a gift for public speaking. He was "a real salesman," in Watterson's words. In 1963 and 1964, especially, Sheppard put this talent to work promoting those aspects of the CFA Program that specifically defined financial analysis as a profession: the CFA examination program, which required mastery of a body of knowledge, and the CFA ethical standards, which mandated trustworthy behavior.

For the first 10 years or so, those leading the ICFA were occupied with setting up the CFA Program's infrastructure and mapping it. Each of the elements that Sheppard promoted in his speeches, together with the exam-grading process, received careful attention: the code of ethics and how to enforce it; the examination content and how to grade it; and the body of knowledge and how to delineate it. The rest of this chapter examines the historical development of each of these elements—how each "structure" was established and how it was refined. As the chapter hopes to show, one could say of each structure: *This* is the essential element of the CFA Program.

A PUBLIC WARRANTY: CODIFYING ETHICAL STANDARDS

Certainly investors are entitled to expect some public warranty that those to whom they are entrusting their financial resources are individuals possessed not only with technical competency but also with a moral and ethical sense of responsibility.

—C. Stewart Sheppard, "The Professionalization of the Financial Analyst," 1967

In 1964, Stewart Sheppard delivered a speech to the Southwestern Finance Association in Dallas on "The Professionalization of the Financial Analyst." In it, Sheppard asserted that the "moral element" of a profession is of equal importance with "the mastery of a complex intellectual discipline."[12] Later revised and printed in the *Financial Analysts Journal* in 1967, the speech expressed what Sheppard continually emphasized throughout the CFA Program's formative years. High ethical standards, he maintained, were essential to the CFA Program and would serve as a public warranty to investors. The designation "CFA" had to indicate to clients and employers alike that the individuals who had earned it possessed not only knowledge but also a reliable sense of responsibility and sound ethical conduct.

Sheppard's early speeches to members and prospective candidates were as often on ethics as on exam content or preparation, which is not surprising. To Sheppard—as to those working to create a certification program in the 1950s—having a code of ethics for analysts was the *sine qua non* for establishing financial analysts as professionals. They considered codified ethical standards the hallmark of a true profession, equal in importance to delineation of a body of knowledge and the establishment of a series of examinations. Sheppard was a forceful spokesperson for this view.

As far back as the 1945 Graham–Hooper debate, moreover, codified ethics had been cited as a necessity if analysts were to be credibly viewed as professionals. Lucien Hooper had, in fact, used the absence of a formal code of ethics as a reason for not initiating a certification program; he asserted that "to adopt a professional rating before a code of ethics" would be an "ill-advised sequence."[13] Hooper and Graham's own society, the New York Society of Security Analysts (NYSSA), would remedy that lack in June of the same year (1945) by adopting its own printed code of ethics, the first for a society.

By the early 1960s, as the certification program for analysts was close to becoming a reality, the FAF set about creating a code of ethics for analysts. Dave Watterson of Cleveland, chair of the FAF Professional Ethics and Standards Committee, was charged with writing this formal code. To that end, he assembled several distinguished analysts on his committee. Watterson remembered Douglas Hayes, CFA, of the University of Michigan and Leonard Barlow, CFA, of the Toronto Society as being particularly helpful.[14] Watterson made a number of drafts of an ethics code, the final version of which was approved, without change, at the FAF Annual Conference in Detroit in May 1962.

Watterson was also at this time chair of the ICFA Ethical Standards Committee. He collaborated with Stewart Sheppard to create a set of standards appropriate for charterholders. Keeping the FAF code and guidelines essentially the same, Sheppard and Watterson drafted seven guidelines pertinent to charterholders, including the proper use of the CFA designation, and distributed them, together with copies of the FAF Code of Ethics, to the ICFA Board of Trustees at its March 1964 meeting, where the guidelines were adopted unanimously as the ICFA Code of Ethics. Because ethics questions were to appear on all three exams in slightly more than two months, passage of the Code of Ethics came at a critical time.

To help candidates prepare for the 1963 CFA examinations, nine articles on ethical issues had appeared in the 1963 Study Guide, including one, "How Ethical Are Businessmen?" by Raymond C. Baumhart, S.J., a Jesuit ethicist who held a doctorate in business administration from Harvard University. Despite material of this caliber, and despite the professional prominence of the first CFA class— who no doubt had handled ethical issues correctly numerous times—the 1963 candidates did not do as well on the ethics questions as had been expected.

This outcome surprised both the ICFA trustees and the examiners because, as Sheppard put it, "It was felt by many, including myself, that [ethics problems] would be give-away questions."[15] Their presence on the exams was expected to be useful mostly in demonstrating the "importance of proper moral conduct to the C.F.A. holder." Instead, the ethics questions, which concluded the first CFA examination, challenged the candidates, "who either failed to detect the ethical problem or were unable to provide alternative solutions." In reflecting on how to remedy this situation, Council of Examiners member Charles Abbott of Virginia suggested that the ethical question "which by and large received the poorest answers, be put first" in the afternoon section of the Level III exam. In future years,

EXAM STORY: TECHNOLOGY UPS AND DOWNS

A longtime exam grader and 2003 recipient of the Donald L. Tuttle Award for Grading Excellence had this encounter with the technology of his day:

"For Level I [in 1974], we were in . . . a seminar [room] with the big semi-circular tables or desks. And the candidate that sat next to me decided to bring a full-sized adding machine with him to the exam. And as you know, calculations are a big part of Level I, so I got to listen to that crank handle just go kachung, kachung periodically. [To] make matters worse, about every 10 minutes, this guy would just slam his fist down on the table. So, that tended to be a little bit distracting. And then, I was dealing with my own little personal challenges. I remember just sweating profusely because I was nervous."[16]

—DOUGLAS R. HUGHES, CFA
Dallas

David G. Watterson, CFA, class of 1963, served as president of the ICFA for 1968–1969.

. . . from the beginning there has been serious emphasis on the code of ethics and standards of conduct. Disciplinary procedures are elaborate and have teeth. Charters can be and have been revoked.

—C. Reed Parker, CFA, "CFA—What Does It Mean?" Speech to the Men's Club of the North Shore Senior Center, Northfield, Illinois, USA, 31 May 2005

Abbott recommended, the sequence of questions should be rotated, a practice that was adopted in the 1965 examinations. The existence of a formal ICFA Code of Ethics that all could refer and adhere to could only help future candidates.

Adopting the ICFA Code of Ethics was timely in another way. Possible ethics violations were beginning to be seen by the institute. In September 1964, for instance, the Board of Trustees had to rule on the first potential breach of ICFA standards. The case concerned an advertisement made by a Boston bank touting its employees' analytical abilities. The advertisement did not even mention the words "Chartered Financial Analyst," but because one of the bank's senior officers held the charter, the matter was referred to Watterson's committee as a possible example of "flamboyant advertising"—something proscribed by the ICFA Code of Ethics. The committee's consensus was that, although the ad might be objectionable, it did not violate the code and, in any case, was not the work of an individual charterholder. On 12 September 1964, the ICFA Board of Trustees recommended no action in the case and determined that the "conduct of CFA charterholders as individuals" should be the concern, not the conduct of the institutions for which they worked.

THE RISE OF ENFORCEMENT

For the first several years of the CFA Program's existence, ethics investigations tended to be of the "flamboyant advertising" variety; not until 1974 would a sanction be imposed on a charterholder. Yet, by the late 1960s, it had become clear to the trustees and to Stewart Sheppard that the ethical guidelines appended to the Code of Ethics needed updating and that predictable enforcement procedures must be developed. Although insider trading and "inside information" were of considerable concern in the financial industry at that time, the ICFA had not yet conducted any full-scale investigations and had no set procedure for doing so. If, however, the CFA charter was truly to be a "public warranty," in Sheppard's phrase, possession of it had to signify more than the ability to answer ethics questions on exams. It had to also mean that the holder upheld ethical behavior in his or her work life *and* that any charterholder found to be unethical would lose the CFA designation.

Between 1968 and 1970, the ICFA began, in conjunction with the FAF, to reconsider and revise its ethical code. Advised by John G. Gillis, Esq., of the Boston law firm Hill & Barlow, the two organizations formed a joint FAF/ICFA Ethical Standards Committee that was chaired by Carl L.A. Beckers, CFA, who, according to a later ICFA chair, "persistently and with good humor brought vitality to the ethics program."[17]

Impetus for redrafting the Code of Ethics and guidelines for the ICFA arose from forces both internal and external. On the one hand, a founding purpose of the program was to ensure high ethical behavior in those holding the CFA designation; thus, appropriate and current guidelines were essential. On the other hand, the ICFA trustees did not wish to be pushed by outside regulators; rather, they wanted to secure the right of self-regulation.

One conclusion reached by the ICFA members of the joint Ethical Standards Committee was that, like other professional groups—law and accounting among them—the institute would need to separate its legislative and judicial functions in the area of ethics. As committee member Len Barlow, CFA, described it to Stewart Sheppard, this separation would result in clarity. The legislative function would be for creating and periodically revising standards and guidelines, whereas the judicial function would be for investigating and, when appropriate, recommending sanctions on CFA charterholders. By February 1969, John Gillis had proposed revisions to the Code of Ethics and had expanded the guidelines from the 7 adopted in the 1964 to 12. Henceforth, they would be called "Standards of Professional Conduct," as they are today.[18]

Carl L.A. Beckers, CFA (class of 1963), chaired the joint FAF/ICFA Ethical Standards Committee for 1968–1970.

According to Carl Beckers, these changes came about largely because of an "unmitigated desire to self-regulate."[19] Outside the organization, regulators were growing skeptical about self-regulation in the financial industry. To preserve the capacity for analysts to self-regulate and to demonstrate the ability to do so, the ICFA created and publicized its new standards. Beckers' committee also submitted bylaw revisions to the Board of Trustees in an effort to "broaden the powers of the Ethical Standards Committee" (later the Professional Ethics Committee) and to bring into being a "Professional Grievances Committee" to handle the "judicial" element of the ethics and conduct program. Renamed the Professional Conduct Committee in 1976, this committee was charged with the task of formulating enforcement procedures, conducting investigations, and referring any case deemed appropriate to the ICFA Board of Trustees for possible disciplinary action. Using a method similar to case law in the U.S. legal system, the committee would interpret each case in light of the Standards of Professional Conduct and according to "its own facts and circumstances."[20]

Beckers and Gillis also formulated procedures to be followed in the event of an ethics violation and subsequent prosecution. These procedures included a centralized Professional Grievances Committee as well as regional grievances committees, which would "consider professional conduct matters referred to them after an initial review by the Executive Director." The 12 November 1969 issue of the *ICFA Newsletter* published the new Code of Ethics, the Standards of Professional Conduct, and the Rules of Procedure for processing professional conduct matters.

Within a few years, the ICFA enforcement program was fully active, with sanctions and CFA charter revocations beginning. It was not Stewart Sheppard, however, who brought the enforcement process to fruition. On 1 June 1972, he informed the board that he was leaving his position effective 1 September. Sheppard had been named dean of the Colgate Darden Graduate School of Business Administration (at the University of Virginia), succeeding his friend, Charles Abbott, with whose help he had given the CFA Program a home. Sheppard agreed to stay on as an honorary trustee and, for the remainder of his time at the ICFA, worked to effect a smooth transition and to ensure that the CFA Program would maintain the highest standards in regard to the examinations, the body of knowledge, and ethical standards—all of which he had worked so actively to promote. In bidding Sheppard farewell, ICFA Board of Trustees President Edmund A. Mennis, CFA, noted, "The debt we owe him can never be repaid."[21]

Chosen to succeed Sheppard was W. Scott Bauman, CFA, the first ICFA director to be a charterholder. Bauman had worked as an investment analyst at Wells Fargo Bank and as a securities broker with a NYSE member firm. He had also taught at the University of Toledo and Indiana University. And at the time of his ICFA appointment, he was head of Finance and Business Economics at the University of Oregon. Like Sheppard before him, Bauman would split his time between the ICFA and teaching at the University of Virginia, with two-thirds of Bauman's time going to the CFA Program.

During his years as executive director (1972–1978), Bauman faced many challenges, especially in regard to the precarious financial state of the ICFA. His term also covered the first talks about merging the ICFA with the FAF. Reasons for merging—or not merging—the two analyst organizations will be considered later in the book. In the early 1970s, however, one of the most potent motivating forces behind the idea of merging was that of streamlining the effort of these two organizations (which had many common members) to develop and enforce professional standards for all analysts. Both heard the rumblings from U.S. government agencies about the regulation of analysts.[22] By the end of the 1960s, ICFA/FAF counsel John Gillis recalled, the SEC was evincing an "increasing awareness . . . of the importance of analysts and investment advisers in the investment process, and the role of their professional organizations, the FAF and the ICFA."[23] This interest, he continued, "accelerated into the early 1970s."

SEC actions throughout the period manifested this concern—for example, the SEC Special Study of Securities Markets (1963), Amendments to the Investment Company Act relating to advisers (1970), and the SEC Institutional Investor Study (1971). Also telling were speeches given by SEC officials—to and about analysts—advocating further regulation, according to Gillis, and potentially affecting the ability of the ICFA (and FAF) to maintain private self-regulation. In such an atmosphere, communications between SEC representatives and Gillis were frequent.

By 1972, Scott Bauman recalled, members of the SEC had "expressed an interest in licensing financial analysts." In particular, SEC staff were concerned about "alleged inabilities of both the FAF and the ICFA to impose disciplinary sanctions" on their memberships.[24] As noted, in its first decade, the ICFA had investigated mostly cases of "flamboyant advertising." It had neither, as of 1972, imposed censure on any of its members nor revoked a single charter. The SEC indicated to ICFA representatives that the commission was considering a federal regulatory program for analysts that, according to Bauman, might be similar to the model used for the National Association of Securities Dealers (NASD). Clearly, such regulation was not the model that the ICFA members, board, and staff wanted. NASD, although private, was "subject to extensive oversight by the SEC and to legislation by the U.S. Congress that affected its activities," according to John Gillis, and was not a "private self-regulatory organization."[25] ICFA and FAF officials "believed that professional self-regulation would be more consistent with the public interest" and thus felt a "sense of urgency to strengthen their self-regulatory programs."[26]

In response to the pressures, Bauman recalled, the FAF devised a system for regulating the professional "competence and conduct" of individual members. This system met with resistance from NYSSA, however, which in 1973 proposed a separate licensing program with the state of New York. The FAF opposed this move, according to Gillis, and continued to develop its private self-regulation plan. Adopted by FAF delegates on 28 April 1974, it was implemented immediately. (NYSSA continued to seek state regulation until 1976.)

As he waited for this tangle to loosen, Bauman concentrated on moving the enforcement of the ICFA ethical standards forward. When he first came on staff, several professional conduct cases were pending, some of which he recognized as being "legally complicated." Bauman found the existing procedure for investigating and imposing sanctions extremely cumbersome. He asked John Gillis to help him redraft the Rules of Procedure and the institute's bylaws to provide that the executive director and the Professional Conduct Committee (PCC) would have, in Gillis's words, "additional powers and [the] flexibility to process professional conduct matters."[27] Among the powers Bauman sought were "amplified procedures" through the review and investigation processes, "expanded procedures" for hearings conducted by the regional grievances committees, and "the establishment of a procedure to enter into an agreed sanction called a Stipulation." Bauman presented these requests to the ICFA Board of Trustees and received approval on 15 September 1972. He also was permitted to retain a professor from the Law School at UVA as special counsel to assist in processing individual cases of potential professional conduct violations.

As a result of these changes, what Bauman called the "bottleneck of cases" was broken and an "intensified level of investigative work" ensued by both Bauman and the PCC, chaired by M. Harvey Earp, CFA, and his vice chair, George H. Norton, Jr., CFA. The potential imposition of sanctions created "considerable concern," Earp recalled and was an especially sensitive issue for "sell-side" members of the profession:

W. Scott Bauman, CFA, served as ICFA executive director for 1972–1978.

The institutional analyst did not have to worry about the S.E.C., N.A.S.D. and the stock exchanges. The banking and insurance regulations relating to investments offered nothing to fear. On the other hand censure or expulsion constituted a constant threat to the Wall Street analyst.[28]

Earp himself had experience on both sides of the Street—the buy (institutional) side and the sell (brokerage) side of the business—and was thus especially suited to chair the joint committee in the mid- to late 1970s. Because he was working on the sell side at the time, he asked George Norton of Chicago, who "enjoyed wide respect among the 'founding fathers' and members on the buy side," to be his vice chair. Earp felt sure that Norton would provide "extraordinary experience and wisdom"—which, Earp recalled happily, "he did!"

On 28 April 1974, the same day the self-regulation plan was approved, the ICFA stipulated its first disciplinary actions. Two CFA charters were revoked, one public censure and a year's suspension was imposed, and two private admonishments were rendered.[29] It was, as Bauman noted with pride, the first time that a national organization of financial analysts had "imposed sanctions on its members" and signaled that the institute was "willing to enforce high standards of conduct on its membership." Later that same year, the institute conducted its first hearing by a regional panel. Earp and Norton were instrumental in structuring that initial formal hearing, which resulted in the sanction of a charterholder—a recommendation for revocation approved by the ICFA Board of Trustees on 10 January 1975.

As Bauman recalled, prior to this action, regulatory bodies such as Congress and the SEC admired the CFA Program's competency standards and examination program but questioned whether its professional conduct program "had any teeth."[30] By the late 1970s, they did not have to wonder any longer. In 1979, for example, SEC Chairman Harold M. Williams addressed a group of analysts with these encouraging words:

> You are a young profession still, but are well on the way to a self-regulatory system in which high standards of competence and conduct are the rule.[31]

By the end of Bauman's term as ICFA executive director and Earp's term as PCC chair, 111 possible violations of ethical conduct had been reviewed. The steps taken during those years to establish and enforce standards of professional conduct have continued to this day.

Within a few years, the ICFA published the first edition of the *Standards of Practice Handbook* (1982), an interpretive guide to the Code of Ethics and Standards of Practice and, in itself, a form of ethics education. It is now in its 10th edition. Looking back at Bauman's work and the activities of this period, 1977–78 Board of Trustees President Philip "Pres" Brooks, Jr., CFA, credited all this work with "diffusing the SEC threat and converting them from adversary to ally."[32]

C. STEWART SHEPPARD AWARD

This award is presented periodically to individual CFA charterholders in recognition of their outstanding contributions, through dedicated effort and inspiring leadership, in fostering the education of professional investors through advancement of the Body of Knowledge and development of programs and publications to encourage continuing education in our profession. It was established to honor C. Stewart Sheppard, the founding Executive Director of the Institute of Chartered Financial Analysts.

C. Stewart Sheppard served as ICFA executive director for 1961–1972.

1976	C. Stewart Sheppard
	A. Moyer Kulp, CFA
	George M. Hansen, CFA
	M. Dutton Morehouse, CFA
	David G. Watterson, CFA
1977	Gilbert H. Palmer, CFA
1978	Edmund A. Mennis, CFA
1979	Frank E. Block, CFA
1980	Leonard E. Barlow, CFA
1981	Robert D. Milne, CFA
1981	Mary Petrie, CFA
1982	Bion B. Howard, CFA
1982	Marshall D. Ketchum, CFA
1983	William A. Cornish, CFA
1984	Alfred C. Morley, CFA
1984	James R. Vertin, CFA
1985	Richard W. Lambourne, CFA
1986	Charles D. Ellis, CFA
1987	Walter P. Stern, CFA
1989	Paul E. Vawter, Jr., CFA
1990	John L. Maginn, CFA
1990	Donald L. Tuttle, CFA

1991	Frank K. Reilly, CFA
1992	Eugene C. Sit, CFA
1993	Michael L. McCowin, CFA
1994	George W. Noyes, CFA
1995	Gerald I. White, CFA
1996	Frederick L. Muller, CFA
1997	Eliot P. Williams, CFA
1998	Tom S. Sale III, CFA
1999	George H. Troughton, CFA
2000	Brian F. Wruble, CFA
2001	I. Rossa O'Reilly, CFA
2002	Peter B. Mackey, CFA
2003	Thomas B. Welch, CFA
2004	Fred H. Speece, Jr., CFA
2005	Janet T. Miller, CFA
2006	Matthew H. Scanlan, CFA
2007	Frank J. Fabozzi, CFA
2008	James G. Jones, CFA
2009	James W. Bronson, CFA
2010	Gary C. Sanger, CFA
2011	Jean L.P. Brunel, CFA

THE SECOND
CFA EXAM

"In 1964 two of my good friends conversed after they had taken Exam I. They were both several years older than I but had joined the Chicago Society after the magic year 1956 [which would have exempted them from Exam I]. One was Beryl Sprinkel, long-time Chief Economist of the Harris Bank and later Under-Secretary of the Treasury and Chairman of the Council of Economic Advisers under President Reagan . . . . The other was Raymond C.L. Greer, Jr., later to become CEO of Duff and Phelps, but who had begun his career on the financial staff of General Motors. Said Beryl to Ray: 'I may have flunked the exam. I had no idea how to construct a cost accounting plan for a manufacturing plant.' Said Ray to Beryl: 'Oh, that was no problem for me but I was lost on that question about the impact of changing rates of growth in the money supply on securities markets.' They both passed all the exams but, the point is, [CFA] exams cover a lot more than the broader aspects of securities analysis and portfolio management."

—C. REED PARKER, CFA
"CFA—What Does It Mean?" 2005

CREATING RIGOROUS EXAMINATIONS

At their September 1963 meeting, the ICFA trustees reflected on the first CFA examinations given the preceding June and pondered the three exam levels due to be given the following June. They wondered about how to elicit better answers to the Level III ethics question—perhaps by positioning it earlier in the sequence of questions? They also considered the appropriate format and type of questions for Level I and agreed that their purpose was not "to test actual factual knowledge" but to test the candidate's "understanding of factual information."[33] Concerning Level II, whose format had already been through a few iterations (including that brief apparition as a thesis), there was less uniformity of opinion. "The second examination . . . was the subject of considerable debate" between the proponents of essay questions and those of the case analysis method, Stewart Sheppard later recalled.[34] One thing of concern to everyone was how to "clarify the wording of the questions to satisfy those who felt that in some instances the question was not clear."[35] The possibility that a lack of clarity in wording will muddle a question's intent concerns every exam writer to some extent. In 1963, some wondered if such a lack might explain the relatively undistinguished responses to ethics questions, for as Ray Smith put it, ethics was "one of the most difficult areas to construct." Trying to write questions for which "you could grade and say there is a right and wrong to it was difficult."[36]

This peek into an early ICFA Board of Trustees meeting demonstrates how, from the outset, every effort was made to produce a thoughtful, fair, and challenging examination. Then, as now, those preparing CFA examinations sought to ensure that candidates received a balanced but rigorous experience. Those involved in the creation of CFA exams strive to perfect their content and methodology. In 1964, however, their task was simply to write three exams; steady improvements in them would come later.

According to Ray Smith, the exams didn't change much during the first years. At each level, exams were of the essay and short-answer types. In the time before multiple-choice questions and Scantrons, candidates were instructed to "Write legibly, and in ink." Louis H. Whitehead, CFA, counseling nervous candidates in 1967, reminded them that much writing was in store for them and warned, "Don't show up for the exam with a pen that is about to run dry."[37] As Whitehead told his audience, "The nature and scope of the questions will be quite like they have been in previous years." In the days before handheld calculators, Whitehead offered this sage piece of advice: "You may bring a slide rule if you wish and may find it useful."

Changes to the exams in the early years of the CFA Program were incremental: 15 minutes of writing time added in 1966, rotation of the sequence of questions, changes to reflect alterations in accounting standards. With the advent of a thorough curriculum review in the 1967–69 period, however, greater changes occurred. Typically, such modifications reflected developments in the practice of financial analysis that altered what a CFA charterholder needed to know. Regular, periodic reevaluations of the CFA Program continue to this day.

Content of the exams varied as new topics were added and others shifted to different exam levels. The format also gradually changed. From its first administration, for example, Level II had included an actual annual report of a company, about which candidates were required to "write an analysis" that could be used to evaluate the attractiveness of the company as a potential stock purchase. Among the companies used in the first decade of the CFA Level II exam were Consolidated Coal, Glidden, International Harvester, and National Distillers.

By the late 1960s, the practice of including a full company report was becoming difficult to do securely. By then, candidates for Level II numbered more than 400; to obtain such a quantity of annual reports from a given company was fraught with peril, and the situation only got worse by the end of the next decade as candidate numbers continued to grow. In the opinion of a long-time committee member, the CFA Program was reaching a size at which the Council of Examiners was "working away from [the use of real reports] because somebody would say, 'Gee, Caterpillar Tractor just got asked for [hundreds] of reports.'"[38] Keeping a request like that confidential would be all but impossible, so the examiners tried some different approaches. In 1969, no annual report was given at Level II; in 1972, Level II contained a fictional brokerage report on a company rather than an actual annual report.

Two long-time CFA supporters—with decades of grading, board, and committee work between them—were among those to walk into these Level II exams expecting to analyze a company report and come out surprised. One, Michael L. McCowin, CFA, of Chicago, later the 29th chair of the ICFA Board of

---

EXAM STORY: TECHNOLOGY UPS AND DOWNS

Evidently, some things are worse than a loud adding machine:

"I was studying for my third exam [in the early 1970s] and was asked to study with a fellow who had flunked CFA I, then passed it, flunked CFA II, then passed it, and was studying for # III. His wife had insisted that he start to study three months in advance and even dedicate his vacation to cram[ming] for the exam, as she wasn't willing to go through the trauma of another miss. He was dutifully memorizing everything in a frenetic way that seemed to me to be way overboard and pressure packed. The exam was to be taken Saturday morning at the University of Washington campus and entry was restricted to those who had an authorized IBM punch card that was to be given to the proctor.

"I arrived on time, but he was 5 to 10 minutes late, arrived in disarray, barely being admitted to the room. He was totally agitated and proceeded to chain smoke for 5 minutes before he even opened the blue book. It wasn't until the break that I could ask him what had happened. He had driven onto campus, and the small guard station had asked him his business. He said he was there for the CFA exam, and the guard had asked for proof. As he handed the IBM punch card through the partially opened car window, the two fumbled it as only "Murphy" could do, and it slid down the window glass, and months of preparation disappeared into the door! My friend let out a yell and the guard calmly assured him he would write the proctor a note saying what had happened. The frantic test taker convinced him that it wasn't going to work, and the guard told him to pull to the side. Then, the two of them dismantled the door panel and retrieved the punch card and sent him on his way. Despite the trauma, there is a happy ending, as he did pass the CFA III."

—JOHN P. PRIVAT, CFA
Seattle

THERE IS NO GUARANTEE OF PASSING

Ray Smith, who in the early days reviewed each completed examination, remembered one Level II candidate's unfortunate experience with the annual report section. "We had one pretty well known person, a professor of finance, who got the years over the columns mixed up [in the annual report]. So instead of going from 1955 to 1965—or whatever the years might have been—he went the other way. He wrote his whole analysis and answer based on the trends going the wrong way, and had sales declining rather than growing. And he didn't realize it until [it was] too late to do anything about it."[41]

The professor was "unbelieving" that he—who taught these very subjects at university level—had done such a thing. Fortunately, the story has a happy ending, for Smith confirms that the professor in question "came back the next year and passed it with flying colors."

Trustees, remembered it this way: "That year, instead of the annual report, they put in a [fictional] broker . . . I will not say it was an easier exam, [but] it was a different exam." McCowin recalled feeling "a certain bonding with the other people that were taking the exam" because of its unusual elements. One who had a similar experience was Donald L. Tuttle, CFA, who was a long-time chair of curriculum committees, served on the ICFA Board of Trustees, and later became a staff member. His 1969 exam, he recalled, was "the only year in about a dozen years or more when Level II did not have a company analysis as half of the exam."[39] As Tuttle remembered it from later committee work, the omission of an annual report was found to be "unsatisfactory" and from 1970 to 1978, annual reports were once again enclosed with the Level II exams.

By the late 1970s, however, keeping the names of companies used at Level II secure was needed, so instead of ordering and actually enclosing a company's annual report with the exam booklet, data from a particular company's annual—and sometimes quarterly—report were printed within the exam. Charterholders who took their exams during the period when a company's annual report was included seldom forget which company they were asked to analyze. Thirty or even forty years later, a good number of them can readily name the company; others trade Level II stories like fishermen remembering a particularly challenging catch. As one charterholder from that period put it, "The company question at Level II is like other traumatic events that occur in one's life: they become etched in your brain forever."[40]

Other exam changes appeared. Curriculum reviews had dictated the addition of questions on portfolio management at all levels and some questions on quantitative techniques. Some revisions were intended to correct for clarity, for example, putting the command words, such as "state," "describe," "list," "discuss," and "analyze," in boldface type, which was done for the first time in 1973. In 1968, 25 multiple-choice questions had been added at Level I, after considerable controversy, some of it at the board level. In the 1940s and 1950s, one of the initial arguments against establishing a certification program for analysts was the belief that security analysis was an art and, as such, was not subject to testing. The notion that multiple-choice questions should be used to test analytical ability remained anathema to some. Three decades more had to pass before multiple-choice questions appeared at all three levels.

Some changes in the CFA exams arose because of surveys filled out by candidates after they had taken their exams. In them, candidates were asked to comment on the content and format of their tests as well as their effectiveness and suitability. Results were compiled and then reported to the board by Stewart Sheppard. Survey answers varied widely, of course, but the results from 1970 provide a window into what candidates thought about their experiences nearly a decade into the CFA Program. One frequent request was for "greater correspondence" between, on the one hand, the material in the study guides and recommended textbooks and, on the other hand, the actual questions on the examinations. As detailed later in this chapter, eliminating gaps between curricular materials and the examinations formed a large part of CFA Program reviews throughout the 1970s and 1980s, and the issue was not fully resolved until the 1990s. In the interim, various committees and task forces sought to improve and align the exam and curriculum creation processes.

Some of the 1970 candidates requested open book tests or oral examinations, neither of which was added; others wanted to see existing textbooks changed, and most were over time. One request speaks poignantly to how demanding the exams themselves were: Candidates at all three levels—apparently wanting even more time to contemplate and write—asked for a shorter lunch break.

One of the most compelling requests during that time period came from Canadian analysts. In the 1970 survey, several respondents at Level II requested "more recognition of Canadian/American environments," perhaps with some optional questions for Canadians. These questions were added. Not on the survey, but in discussion, was a request from analysts in Quebec to take their examinations in French.

From its earliest days, the CFA Program had included exam takers from the Canadian provinces, with most coming from the Toronto and Montreal areas. When Canada adopted its first Official Languages Act in 1969, the impetus for taking the ICFA exams in French grew stronger. In 1971, a request to allow Canadians to take exams in French was rejected, but a slightly different request was granted. Marion Van Dyke, CFA (now Marion Van Dyke-Cooper), was a board member of the Montreal Society, and later the first woman to chair the FAF. She approached Eugene H. Vaughan, Jr., CFA, at the annual meeting in 1974. Van Dyke wished to ask Vaughan, who was then chair of the FAF, about the possibility of writing the examinations in French. As she remembered it:

> I spoke up, and I explained to the FAF board and to Gene Vaughan that in Montreal, the CFA exam was accepted by the Quebec Securities Commission as a qualification for managing money and for being a securities analyst. [There] were a lot of French-speaking analysts in Montreal, particularly at the Caisse de Dépôt et Placement du Québec, which managed the Quebec Pension Plan . . . who wanted to take the CFA exams but for whom writing in English, under the stress of a time constraint, was overwhelming. I asked, as a *quid pro quo*—I didn't put it quite that blatantly—but I said that I felt that we should be granted that option. So, Gene Vaughan referred it to someone from the ICFA [Scott Bauman, then ICFA executive director] . . . and asked him if the ICFA would be willing to grant that option, and he said they would be willing to do it on a trial basis for one year.[42]

A. Marion Van Dyke, CFA, became the first woman chair of the FAF and lobbied to write the CFA exam in French. Photo courtesy of Wilkinson Studio Ltd.

EDMUND A. MENNIS, CFA

Edmund A. Mennis, CFA, served as ICFA president for 1970–1972.

(b. 12 August 1919, d. 18 March 2009)

Graham and Dodd Award, 1971
Nicholas Molodovsky Award, 1972
C. Stewart Sheppard Award, 1978

PROFILE OF A VOLUNTEER

President of the ICFA Board of Trustees for two one-year terms (1970–1972), Mennis managed to steer the ship with one hand while simultaneously using his other hand to co-author *Quantitative Techniques in Financial Analysis*, to found and edit the *CFA Digest*, to chair the Research and Publications (R&P) Committee, and to serve on the editorial board of the *Financial Analysts Journal* (*FAJ*). Before his two years as ICFA Board of Trustees president, moreover, Mennis spearheaded the first extensive review of the Body of Knowledge; shortly afterward, he investigated the possible merger of the FAF with the ICFA and came up with the first version of what became the Association for Investment Management and Research 17 years later. Remarkably, but not surprisingly, he carried out all of these tasks with aplomb.

Ed Mennis began his career as a financial analyst at Wellington Management Company in Philadelphia, where he worked under ICFA founder A. Moyer "Abe" Kulp, CFA. There, he rose from security analyst to research director. He received his CFA charter in 1964, a member of the second class to do so. "Abe and I often discussed areas with which we thought a well-educated analyst—and later, a CFA charterholder—should be familiar," he recalled many years later.

In 1965, Ed Mennis, as a member of the R&P Committee, began searching the literature for readings to support the emerging CFA Body of Knowledge. By 1966, he was its chair. Mennis served on that committee for 17 years and chaired it for 6. In the early days of the institute, he was practically a one-man R&P Committee, as one who served with him recalls: The committee meetings in Charlottesville often consisted of Mennis's ideas—and a good dinner. Unthinkable now, such single-minded running of an ICFA committee was not common even then and is more indicative of the breadth of Mennis's knowledge and intellectual vitality than of egoism. According to C. Ray Smith, Mennis was "a visionary in many respects," being one of those who "pushed us [to include] the newer areas, like quantitative methods" on the CFA exams.

Economics and finance were the pillars of Ed Mennis's lifework. One of the most remarkable things about him is that throughout his years of exceptional service to the CFA Program, he had a parallel career as a business economist. He was elected a fellow of the National Association of Business Economists (NABE) in 1961, the same year he completed his doctorate. Mennis served on and chaired the NABE board, and also edited its journal, *Business Economics,* for 15 years. "To say he was a prolific writer" would be an understatement, recalled longtime friend M. Harvey Earp, CFA, noting that Mennis "wrote on economics as much as he wrote on finance." As Jack Treynor, former editor of the *FAJ,* said of him, "Every investor who has ever struggled to put his analysis of a public company into the proper macroeconomic context owes Ed Mennis a debt of gratitude." Treynor

Seventh
Board of Trustees
The Institute of Chartered Financial Analysts
1968~1969

Raymond W. Hammell; E. Stewart Sheppard, Executive Director; Edmund A. Mennis,
Leonard E. Barlow, Vice President; David G. Watterson, president; George M.
Hansen, Treasurer; Charles T. Bauer, Secretary; Frank E. Block; R. Austin Hume;
George J. Bissell; not shown, Douglas A. Hayes; M. Dutton Morehouse.

In a photograph of the 1968–69 ICFA Board of Trustees, Ed Mennis (third from left) looks directly at the camera with a smile that conveys enough energy to power the entire meeting. The perception of intelligence and vitality captured by the camera is accurate: In life, Ed Mennis was a dynamo.

continued, "Ed Mennis knew what information was available, who provided it, how they defined and measured it. Even more remarkable, he could explain what he knew in terms most of us investors could understand."

Another longtime professional colleague and friend, Alan Greenspan, former chairman of the U.S. Federal Reserve Board, praised Ed Mennis for his "rare capacity to apply economic principles to security analysis." In 1953, Greenspan recalled, "Ed and the Wellington Fund became my first client as a private economic consultant." Given Mennis's interests, Greenspan was not surprised "in the slightest," that Mennis "became a strong advocate for professionalizing chartered financial analysts."

In his private life, he was a patron of libraries, a supporter of a local hospital foundation, "intellectually active and a positive spirit to the end." Vibrant, opinionated, and keenly intelligent, Mennis was nonetheless lacking in self-importance. As Harvey Earp noted, Mennis's co-author, Jerome Valentine, is listed *first* on their pioneering quant book. "He was an exceptional person," Earp concluded.[43]

Candidates in the Canadian province of Quebec who chose to, were allowed to write their answers in French—although the examinations themselves were always and only printed in English. The practice, which continued until 1999, came to present some considerable challenges, particularly in regard to grading, where translators or French-speaking graders were needed. Eventually, as a result of the impossibility of offering the examinations in dozens of different languages as the candidate pool grew well beyond North America, and for sake of absolute consistency, the practice of allowing answers in French was discontinued.

Throughout the 1970s and 1980s, the Council of Examiners and ICFA staff continued to refine the examinations. In 1970, they considered having the composition of Exams I and II contracted to testing experts outside the institute instead of being written by the Council of Examiners but decided against it. In 1981, they lengthened the exams by 45 minutes at all three levels. In 1982, they included new topics—ERISA (the Employee Retirement Income Security Act of 1974), real estate, and estate planning. Formerly exotic investments such as options, futures, and non-North American securities were incorporated into the exam and study guides in the early 1980s.

"FAIR AND OBJECTIVE": GRADING STANDARDS

In his 1945 debate with Lucien Hooper, Ben Graham had remarked, perhaps ironically, that were a certification program begun and examinations given, one could assume that "the level of competence needed to qualify for the rating" would probably "be set on the low side at first and gradually raised thereafter."[44] In other words, Graham was predicting that the early exams would be "easier" in some fashion—either absolutely or in how they were evaluated—and that, consequently, more candidates would pass. He was a little bit right: More candidates did pass the first two sets of exams than do now. But he was also wrong, as anyone taking those early exams would have been happy to tell him. Despite their years of experience and success, the first CFA candidates were apprehensive and wary; they studied hard, and as a result, they passed. The pass rate for 1963 was 94 percent for Level III; in 1964, it was (at 95 percent) a shade higher for Level III. The *overall* rate, however, for 1964 (the first year all three exams were given) was only 84 percent, with 79 percent of candidates passing Level I, and 94 percent passing Level II.

During its first two decades of existence, the CFA Program experienced a steady decline in the pass rate, even as it experienced an increase in candidates. No doubt, the lower percentage of candidates passing at each level, in contrast to the early high numbers, had to do with having all those senior analysts finish sitting for the CFA examinations and attracting a greater proportion of young candidates with less experience. At the annual meeting in 1966, ICFA Board of

The grading system is as near perfect as it can be made.

—Louis H. Whitehead, CFA, address to New York candidates, 1967

I think the candidate needs to know that these papers are graded properly, and there is a tremendous amount of thought that goes into it.

—Douglas R. Hughes, CFA, interview, 2009

Trustees Chair M. Dutton Morehouse, CFA, cautioned: "As the number taking the examinations under the grandfather clause declines and candidates are less experienced, we probably must expect a higher failure rate on Examination[s] II and III."[45]

Also contributing to the rising failure rates was the establishment of high grading standards. Grading is the capstone of the examination process, the step that completes it and ensures the integrity of the entire program. One can create the perfect exam, based on the most complete and appropriate curriculum possible, but if the grading is compromised or uneven, the whole process is tainted. As one long-time exam grader, Mike McCowin, put it:

> . . . if the grading is not right, it can destroy everything else. You can write the best question in the world. You can have great candidates. [But] if the grading is not done properly, you can undo all of that. . . . I do not know if I would say it is the most important part, but it is certainly a critical part. If you get it wrong, it does not matter what you did everywhere else.[46]

From the CFA Program's inception, therefore, staff and trustees vowed to have a grading process that was equitable and upright. Talking to the *New York Times* shortly after the first exams were administered, Stewart Sheppard noted, "Grading will be done on an anonymous basis."[47] He declared to the ICFA members in 1964, "Every effort is being made to be fair and objective in establishing grading standards."[48]

With the exception of 1963—when there were as yet no CFA charterholders to recruit as exam graders—the bulk of the grading has always been done by charterholders. Some had academic backgrounds, but most were practitioners; some were both. The first year, a group of three local Virginia academicians was asked to grade; after they finished, all the exams were read by Ray Smith and Stewart Sheppard. Beginning in 1964, a trustees' review took place for questionable or failing exams, so that a third (or fourth or fifth) set of eyes evaluated the exams. Ray Smith remembered the grading process for Exam III in 1963 this way:

EXAM STORY: TECHNOLOGY UPS AND DOWNS

Calculators also had their drawbacks:

"Back when I took the exam [Level I] in the early 1980s at a local college lecture hall in Greensboro, North Carolina, one candidate had to sit at the end of the row of desks because he had brought a big plug-in calculator for his use during the exam. Handheld calculators were popular, but this guy was just old-fashioned, I guess.

"During the middle of the morning portion of the exam, one of the other candidates had to go to the bathroom urgently, and, in his haste, didn't see the electric power cord connecting the calculator to the wall outlet draped across the aisle. Trip . . . WHAM! The calculator went flying, the candidate desperate for the bathroom went careening down the aisle and fell onto another candidate, and the test taker, suddenly realizing his bulky calculator, having smashed against the wall, was in useless pieces, started wailing like a soul in hellish torment (no doubt visualizing he would fail).

"Fortunately another candidate had brought an extra handheld calculator and eventually order was restored and quiet again settled over the room."

—CURTIS R. KIMBALL, CFA, Dallas

Nowadays, lending a calculator would be against the exam room rules, however.

The first exam was graded by members of the Council and some other faculty. I reviewed every paper at all levels for several years. I reviewed for consistency in grading and for separating into "piles"—one for clearly fail, one for clearly pass, and one for the mushy middle. The middle stack was carefully reviewed by several ICFA Trustees too and moved to pass or fail. This was a very careful process.[49]

That the ICFA was willing to fail even prominent analysts among the first group of exam takers set the right tone for rigor. That the institute was insistent on putting questionable papers through several reviews set the right tone for fairness and objectivity.

In a talk to prospective CFA candidates in February 1967, Louis Whitehead, himself an early grader, confidently reassured the nervous candidates in his audience that in regard to grading, "There have been, and will be, no flukes, no cases where careless or individual grading resulted in assigning a failing grade to a candidate who deserved to pass."[50] He exhorted them to:

> Get out of your minds any thought that the papers are going to be "ranked" by the grading staff and that passing grades will be assigned in accordance with an S-type curve. Such is not the case. All candidates whose answers are sufficiently comprehensive and responsive will receive passing grades.

Finally, Whitehead told them that candidates would not pass or fail based solely on the "opinion of a single individual" but that "several graders will work on your paper . . . [and] no candidate will be failed until his paper has been studied, graded, reviewed and re-reviewed."

The Board of Trustees' report to ICFA members in 1967 summed up the grading process in a similar way:

> All graders for Exam II and III are selected CFA charterholders (27 in 1966) who spend from a weekend to two weeks in Charlottesville performing the grading function under a carefully planned program. Following completion of the grading, special committees review all Exam II and III papers failed by the grading staff. Finally, the board of trustees itself considers appeal cases where candidates failing examinations request a review by the trustees.[51]

The first order of business for grading was to secure the exams once they had been sent back from various testing centers. Smith recalled that the whole "grading process was very heavily monitored and controlled. And before I left every night, the last thing I did was to check to make sure the exams were secure and everything was accounted for."[52] Then, in late June and early July, the exam grading team, picked by staff from recommendations by trustees and the Council of Examiners, assembled in Charlottesville. According to one early report, CFA exam graders "worked a full eight hour day beginning at 7 each morning for some two weeks."[53] (Although some might start a *little* later nowadays, this description of what happens during grading is still pretty accurate.)

A grader of these early exams, Harold Dulan, CFA, of the University of Arkansas, recalled his experiences with true pride:

Grading of the CFA exams taking place in a Charlottesville classroom in the mid-1960s.

> I had the highest possible respect for the grading teams. They were selected for competence, integrity, fairness and breadth of knowledge in finance . . . . The esprit de corps of the grading team was truly remarkable. It was very common for a grader to call upon one or more of the other graders, to listen to an answer that an individual had given for possible correctness. . . . Another aspect of the work of the grading team was the tendency to stop in the middle of grading a paper and check the library books in finance, which were there and available.[54]

Exams were graded by question, which is to say that one grader graded all of a particular question for a given level. As the number of candidates increased, he or she might not be able to grade all of the exams, so a few graders might split the question. Graders arrived having already studied up on the area they would be grading. Ray Smith recalled that the early practice of having exam graders evaluate an entire question ensured that "we had people with some expertise in whatever area would be [theirs] to grade."[55] As Richard T. Walsh, CFA, an exam grader, put it, grading was and is a wonderful form of "forced continuing education" for the practicing analyst.[56]

Careful, secure, and balanced as the CFA grading process was, not everyone was going to be pleased with the outcome. Ray Smith recalled that he often "dictated as many as 50 letters a night explaining to the candidates why they failed our examination."[57] During his years as executive director, Stewart Sheppard encountered a few unhappy candidates, and he remembered some of them very, very clearly. "A senior partner in charge of the research department of a major Wall Street firm," Sheppard recalled, "directed President Edgar Shannon of the University of Virginia to have me dismissed from the faculty" because the senior partner had failed the exam.[58] Shannon's refusal to do so, Sheppard remarked dryly, cemented their friendship.

The disgruntled executive was not the only one who felt that rank or special circumstance should guarantee a passing grade. "There were other examples of candidate frustration," Sheppard noted. "Analysts in Virginia felt their propin-

CFA Graders in 1965 (left to right): Unknown; Horace C. Buxton, Jr., CFA; Joseph F. Glibert, CFA; Charles H. Wheeler III, CFA; C. Ray Smith; Chenery Salmon, CFA; Lawrence W. Schmidt, CFA; Harold A. Dulan, CFA; Leo D. Stone, CFA; Lyndon O. Adams, CFA; Barney A. Bradshaw, CFA; James A. Close, CFA; Unknown; Leonard E. Barlow, CFA

quity, geographical and academic, to Charlottesville entitled them to professional preference." In addition, "a former German submarine commander felt his honor and high dignity were offended and upon my denial [to change his failing grade] appealed unsuccessfully to [ICFA] President David Watterson of Cleveland."

All these requests were to no avail—not because CFA Program officials were arbitrary or unwilling to reconsider. Rather, those involved in the program's early decades knew that every effort had already been made to ensure a scrupulous grading process. The grading was anonymous and objective; each questionable exam had been thoroughly reviewed before it was given a failing grade. Although grading procedures have changed over the years, and the number of exam graders has ballooned to totals unthinkable in the early decades, the standards set in the early years have lasted.

WHAT DOES AN ANALYST NEED TO KNOW?
DEFINING THE BODY OF KNOWLEDGE

> It is not easy in the case of financial analysis to show that there is a generally accepted body of knowledge.
>
> —Douglas A. Hayes, CFA, "Potential for Professional Status," 1967

One of the most important tasks, perhaps the central task, of the CFA Program has been to articulate an agreed-upon body of knowledge—that is, to delineate what a financial analyst needs to know in order to practice and what all candidates need to master to earn the CFA designation. Stewart Sheppard had seen defining a body of knowledge as his first task upon arriving at the ICFA in 1962:

> The first major order of business was to delineate the current state of the art in the professional practice of investment analysis. This was to provide a rationale for *a common body of knowledge* underlying candidate

testing over a tripartite series of examinations [from] investment principles, through applied security analysis, to the capstone investment management decision-making.[59] [Emphasis added.]

Council of Examiners stalwart Marshall D. Ketchum, CFA, who, together with his University of Chicago colleague Ezra Solomon, had helped set forth the certification program, was even more decided about what came first. "The keystone of a profession is knowledge," he declared, "knowledge and its application to the problems which the profession faces." He continued:

> Some professions have codes of ethics and other marks of professional status, but if an occupation is successfully to claim that it is a profession, it must convince those whom the occupation serves that it possesses knowledge and that this knowledge is useful in serving clients.[60]

What does a financial analyst need to know in order to qualify as a professional? This question underlies the CFA Program to this day. In effect, the early study guides and curricula answered this with the topics listed—accounting, economics, financial analysis, portfolio management, and ethical standards. But, in truth, the Council of Examiners (COE), who wrote the exam questions, and their curricular counterparts in the Research and Publications (R&P) Committee strove to assure themselves: Is the curriculum comprehensive? Are the readings challenging and appropriate? Do the examination questions relate to the readings? Do the readings themselves reflect the daily work of the financial analyst? Throughout its first two decades, the CFA Program staff and committees sought to answer such nagging questions by codifying an agreed-upon body of knowledge from which to draw the curriculum and upon which to base the examinations. In the early years, the committees mainly responsible for this charge were the COE and the R&P Committee, whose work together was sometimes a smooth, tandem-bicycle ride—and sometimes a tug of war.

To the R&P Committee fell the task of combing through extant literature to find readings in all areas that would be covered at each exam level. To the COE fell the task of creating examinations based on what a practicing analyst needed to know in his or her work life and what was contained in the curriculum. For the first exams in 1963, Ray Smith had functioned as a one-man R&P Committee. By the second year, however, an actual R&P Committee, chaired by W. Edward Bell, CFA, of San Francisco, helped out with the literature search, which was needed to create the study guides and the exams.

To a certain extent, the work of these two committees exemplified the old "poultry" conundrum: which came first, the chicken or the egg?—or, in this case, the curriculum or the exam? Ideally, a fully realized curriculum came first, formed the basis of study guides, and based on it, the exams were written. Actual practice, however, was a bit more complicated. Looking back over the first years of

Marshall D. Ketchum, CFA, served on the first Council of Examiners for 1962–1963.

EXAM STORY: AN UNEXPECTED QUESTION

" The first Level I exam was given in 1964, so nobody really had any idea what we were going to be examined on. We had a study outline, very similar to what is still done today, but nobody was quite sure among all that material where the focus of interest was going to be. Interestingly enough, we were assured there would be no detailed accounting questions on the exam. I opened the exam booklet the first day, sitting down at the University of Chicago where the exam was held [with] probably 300 in the room, and the first question was a very complicated sources and uses statement. The room went up in a roar. There was almost anarchy. 'They said we wouldn't have these questions!' "

—JOHN L. MAGINN, CFA[62]

exam and curriculum creation, Ray Smith remembered a hectic sequence for that first exam, when "we were doing everything at the same time."[61] The June 1963 exam needed to be ready by April, but as Smith recalled, "It had to go through a lot of iterations," which was challenging. At exactly the same time, Smith and Sheppard were working on readings. "I spent a lot of time in the summer of 1962, doing library research and reading everything I could get my hands on [about] analysis and portfolio management." Nevertheless, he said, "we didn't have the formal study guides that first year . . . . [In 1964] we got the study guides out in January or February before the exams were to be given in the next June . . . well ahead of the construction of the exams."

In the early years, exam questions did not have the strict correspondence to the curriculum they now have and "Learning Outcome Statements" had not even been dreamed of. Articles and readings were chosen for their general relevance to the work of the analyst, to be sure, and to address an element of the curriculum—accounting or ethics, for instance. If a committee member—or a trustee—thought an article was particularly good or important, however, it might end up in one of the study guides, even though a correlative question might not appear on the exam that year. Similarly, a member of the COE could write a question—sometimes a good question—that did not clearly draw upon any of the readings, even though it might reflect the actual practice of financial analysis.

From its earliest days, those running the CFA Program sought to remedy such situations by coordinating the workings of the COE and the R&P Committee. In 1964, when the makeup of both groups was a mixture of academics and practitioners and all members of each were CFA charterholders, the trustees named Bion B. Howard, CFA, of Northwestern University to act as chair of both groups. Yet, in September 1966, Stewart Sheppard was still acknowledging to the board that "one of the criticisms with respect to the examinations [is] the fact that they may have had a tendency to depart from the study guide materials."[63]

It would take a good while to fully align the curriculum and readings with all examination questions. As late as 1970, for example, post-exam questionnaires from candidates were requesting a closer correspondence between examination questions and the reading materials in the study guides and curriculum. The record of the first 20 years of the CFA Program is littered with attempts to facilitate coordination between the COE and the R&P Committee—and thus between curriculum and exams—with each attempt drawing closer to synchronizing their work.

A problem underlying full coordination between exam and published curriculum was the relative scarcity of appropriate reading materials that could make up the curriculum. Ray Smith recalled that he and Stewart Sheppard were initially optimistic about collecting appropriate readings for the new candidates: "I think we started out sort of assuming . . . there would be books available and articles available . . . ."[64] In reviewing all the published materials ("every investment book that had been written"), however, they discovered that certain areas simply were not covered. Smith and Sheppard compiled what they could as study materials for the first candidates. To fill some gaps, they arranged with publisher Richard D. Irwin to print a section of a book by Baruch College professor Eugene Lerner in the CFA Program materials, prior to the book's actual publication. By 1966, these materials were printed in a separate book—the first edition of *CFA Readings in Financial Analysis*. A second edition came in 1969. Articles from the *Financial Analysts Journal* also helped.

From the first years, however, Ray Smith knew that to cover the expanding body of knowledge in financial analysis, the institute would have to develop its own literature. As early as March 1964, Stewart Sheppard was telling the Board of Trustees, "Eventually the C.F.A should have its own textbook."[65] As Sheppard remembered it some 21 years later, the situation was more dire than the board minutes suggest: "There was little published for our purposes," so to serve the candidates and members, and for the benefit of the analyst community at large, the ICFA had to develop its own publications.

Sheppard proposed the hiring in the near future of "a man with an academic background . . . to work closely with the Research and Publications Committee" in seeking suitable monographs and articles and working on the textbook he thought the ICFA might need to produce. The addition of such a position would free Ray Smith to work exclusively on administrative matters (arranging for nearly 2,000 exams, for example, and working with graders). Sheppard himself could then concentrate on public relations. The proposed position, held originally by Gerald MacFarlane beginning in 1967, was a forerunner to several other administrative positions, including education administrator (established in 1976) and director of candidate programs (1982). Having someone to work closely with the COE and R&P groups was another means of effecting and improving coordination between these two bodies. The expanded staff would prove particularly important in 1968 when Stewart Sheppard accepted the additional position of FAF executive secretary and began dividing his time between Charlottesville and New York City.

Parallel to creating suitable works to augment scarce resources, ICFA staff and trustees were working hard to develop a standard of agreed-upon knowledge necessary for a financial analyst to know and upon which to be tested. Indeed, as Sheppard wrote in his 1992 pamphlet celebrating the 30th anniversary of the ICFA, the Research Foundation was created in part because of "increasing evidence that the examination program required greater specificity and sophistication to reflect the current and emerging state of the art represented in a common body of knowledge."[66]

The first iteration of what would later formally be known as the Body of Knowledge came in 1969, a result of an "intensive review" of the CFA Program undertaken by the R&P Committee over the preceding two years. In 1967, Stewart

EXPANDING ANALYSTS' LIBRARIES:
CFA RESEARCH FOUNDATION

"The organizing phase of the Institute's history being largely over, the encouragement of the writing of articles, monographs, and books useful to CFA candidates and analysts generally is becoming a most important Institute activity."

—C. Stewart Sheppard, 1964

For several years after *CFA Readings in Financial Analysis* was first published, C. Stewart Sheppard had been considering other ways to enhance study materials for CFA candidates. Publishing a textbook was important, of course, but so was sponsoring original monographs, seminars, and papers on topics not well covered in the existing literature. Developing these offerings would also serve to fulfill one of the founding purposes of the ICFA, as stated in its Articles of Incorporation, namely, "To guide and encourage the continuing education of persons engaged in the professional practice of financial analysis." In 1965, Sheppard proposed to the trustees the founding of a formal CFA Research Foundation. It would be charged with creating "original basic research, continuing research on industry and general topics, cooperative research with similar groups, and group seminars," as noted by ICFA Board of Trustees Chair M. Dutton Morehouse, CFA, who served as the Research Foundation's first president. This effort, in turn, would fulfill one of the institute's published objectives: "to stimulate research and disseminate educational materials." Generally favoring the idea, the trustees named an *ad hoc* committee, composed of Morehouse, A. Moyer "Abe" Kulp, CFA, E. Linwood Savage, Jr., CFA, Stewart Sheppard, and C. Ray Smith, to look into its feasibility and search for likely locations. Members of the committee considered several cities but ultimately decided to site the new foundation near the institute in Charlottesville, where a new headquarters for the ICFA staff was being considered.

Although a relatively small number of people, the ICFA staff had fast outgrown its original space within the UVA Business School in Monroe Hall. Sheppard had become aware, however, of a tempting University-owned property on the western edge of Charlottesville, called Faulkner House. Named in honor of recently deceased novelist William Faulkner—who had been the first writer-in-residence and a lecturer at UVA at the end of his life—the antebellum mansion and its outbuildings would provide an excellent, somewhat secluded space for the institute.

While the Research Foundation's work would be associated with continuing education for charterholders—an activity that would occupy the institute in years to come—it had a dual function in also generating and funding much needed curricular materials for CFA candidates. According to Sheppard, the research activities of what was then called the "C.F.A. Research Foundation" were expected to be "helpful in filling in some of the gaps in background material relating to particular aspects of the field of investments."[67]

M. Dutton Morehouse, CFA, believed it was important to put "CFA" on his tombstone.

Sheppard had become convinced that the examination program was in need of revision—not necessarily to increase its difficulty but, rather, to improve its content. In December of that year, having expressed his concerns to the COE, he met with the chair of the R&P Committee, Ed Mennis, about conducting this review. Sheppard thought the review of the CFA Program was necessary because the tandem committees (COE and R&P) were in something of a vicious cycle. As he put it:

> . . . the Council is restricted to published study guides in formulating the
> 1968 series of examinations [which] prevents them in certain cases from
> including questions for which there are no suitable candidate study
> materials . . . . On the other hand, the Research and Publications Committee
> needs clarification on examination objectives if it is to uncover or develop
> materials for new subject areas.[68]

In other words, the Council of Examiners based the exams on the R&P Committee study guides that were, themselves, based on the exams, and so on.

Mennis headed an R&P Committee singularly well qualified to undertake this review. On it were the distinguished academicians and CFA charterholders Henry Latané of the University of North Carolina and Leo Stone of the University of South Florida, seasoned CFA practitioners Dutton Morehouse and Frank Block, and financial luminary Nicholas Molodovsky, CFA, widely considered one of the leading thinkers in financial analysis. Block, Mennis, and Molodovsky were editors of the *Financial Analysts Journal*; Molodovsky, its editor in chief. Like Mennis, he was a proponent of the idea that analysts should familiarize themselves with the newly developing quantitative techniques or risk becoming "illiterate in their own field."[69]

At the May 1968 annual meeting in Boston, Sheppard announced to the assembled charterholders that the ICFA was in the process of an "overall reappraisal of its examination program" with a view to improving coordination (that word again) between the activities of the COE and those of the R&P Committee.[70] For the same annual meeting, the R&P Committee had been readying its report, which defined the Body of Knowledge and suggested the transfer of subject matter from one exam level to another.[71] These changes were recommended largely because the nature of financial analysis itself was shifting. What a Level I candidate needed to know in 1969 was different from what he or she would have been asked in 1964.

Reporting in August 1968, the R&P Committee's intensive review concluded by spelling out for each exam detailed CFA "program prerequisites" and the "specific knowledge" essential for candidates to know at each level in economics, ethical standards, accounting, financial analysis, and portfolio management. This material came to constitute the institute's "Basic Planning Document," on which subsequent examination revisions would be based. Concurrently, Shep-

Mary Petrie, CFA, served as the first woman ICFA president for 1973–1974.

pard wrote out a "General Topic Outline" detailing the subject matter of each exam. This served as the first detailed outline of the Body of Knowledge and replaced the previous, generalized list of topics.

Impressive as the R&P Committee's work was, it was not without hazards. Among its dangers was the potential for packing too much material into what candidates had to review and listing all topics at all three levels. An invaluable achievement, however, was to uncover areas where literature pertinent to the CFA Program was missing. Prime among the missing were portfolio management and quantitative analysis.

To fill one of the documented gaps, the Research Foundation sponsored four seminars on elements of portfolio management: personal trust management (1967), pension fund management (1968), investment company portfolio management (1969), and property and liability insurance investment management (1970). All of the seminars resulted in published proceedings that could be tapped for the curriculum. All were, according to Ray Smith, "areas where there was no written material to speak of out there."[72]

The gap in "quant" literature was remedied in the early days with a textbook, *Quantitative Techniques for Financial Analysts*, written by Jerome L. Valentine (later a chair of the Research Foundation) and Edmund A. Mennis and published in 1971. According to Mennis, the book was directed at CFA candidates, who at the time were still a little bit older (although that demographic was changing, and within 10 years, well over half of the candidates would be under 30). These older analysts were "not inclined to return to the classroom" to learn quantitative methods, Mennis recognized. The book, therefore, "presumed little background"; rather, it dealt primarily with selecting the appropriate techniques and the interpretation of their results.[73]

This flurry of curricular activity, remarkable though it was, was only a precursor to a string of CFA Program reviews and revisions, because refining and redefining the CFA Body of Knowledge is a "never-ending task."[74] In 1973–1974, Mary Petrie, CFA, of Chicago (the first woman president of the ICFA Board of Trustees) requested the "first extensive revision" of the General Topic Outline.[75] Petrie appointed John B. Neff, CFA (who had recently become chair of the R&P Committee), Ed Mennis, ICFA Executive Director Scott Bauman, and UVA professor Robert H. Trent (research director at the Research Foundation). They were to review and reevaluate Sheppard's topical outline. They expanded the 1969 version from five to seven topics, including quantitative techniques as a separate topic for the first time and separating analysis of fixed-income securities from analysis of equity securities. In 1979, ICFA Board of Trustees President William A. Cornish, CFA, commissioned a Portfolio Management Review Committee, whose work is detailed in the next section. In 1983, Alfred C. "Pete" Morley, CFA, who later become the first president and CEO of the ICFA, chaired an Equity Analysis Review Committee. Also examined were fixed-income analysis and economics.

GENERAL TOPIC OUTLINE, 1969

Candidate Level I II III

ACCOUNTING

Principles and Construction of Accounting Statements:

• Balance sheet
• Income statement
• Sources and uses
• Other

Analysis of Accounting Statements:

• Income statement and balance sheet analysis
• Comparative company analysis
• Inventory evaluation
• Depreciation accounting
• Treatment of intangibles
• Stock splits and dividends
• Rights, warrants, convertibles
• Ratio and coverage analysis
• Other

Current Accounting Principles and Practices:

• AICPA opinions
• Controversial areas
• Acquisitions and mergers
• Conglomerates

ECONOMICS

Basic Principles and Source Materials:

• GNP and national income accounts
• The monetary system
• The fiscal system
• The price system
• Flow-of-funds
• Input-output analysis
• Aggregate profit measures
• Indicator series analysis
• Long-term trends in stock and bond prices

Economic Analysis and Forecasting:

• Input-output applications
• Corporate profits forecasting
• Indicator series applications
• Supply and demand of funds in the market
• Economic fluctuations and long-term trends

Economic Policy:

• Monetary policy
• Fiscal policy
• Balance of payments and international policy
• Money supply
• Antitrust legislation
• Employment policy
• Growth of the institutional investor

Candidate Level I II III

FINANCIAL ANALYSIS

Principles of Financial Analysis:

• Sources of information
• Financial instruments
• Financial institutions
• Common stock analysis
• Fixed income security analysis
• Management appraisal
• Quantitative techniques

Applied Financial Analysis:

• Industry appraisal and evaluation
• Dividends and earnings evaluation and projection
• Valuation techniques
• Risk analysis—qualitative and quantitative
• Market and price analysis and areas of speculation
• Capital budgeting

PORTFOLIO MANAGEMENT

Objectives:

• Individuals
• Institutions
  • investment companies
  • foundations and endowment funds
  • pension funds and profit-sharing plans
  • trust funds
  • fire and casualty insurance companies
  • life insurance companies
  • commercial banks
  • hedge funds

Candidate Level I II III

Construction:

• Security selection
• Diversification
• Marketability
• Risk
• Return

Timing and Formula Plans

Bond Portfolio Problems

Performance Measurement

Trading Problems

Tax Planning

Supervision

Quantitative Techniques for Portfolio Management

Computer Applications

Regulation

ETHICAL STANDARDS

C.F.A Responsibilities:

• Public
• Customers and clients
• Employers
• Associates
• Other analysts
• Corporate management
• Other sources of information

Professionalization

Administering Ethical Policy

Security Laws and Regulations

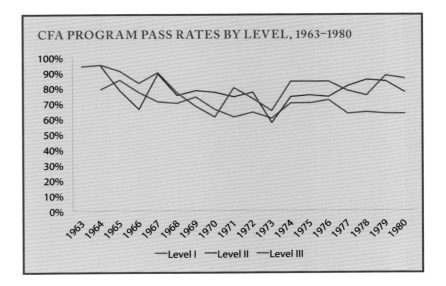

CFA PROGRAM PASS RATES BY LEVEL, 1963–1980

—Level I —Level II —Level III

THE SPECIAL CASE OF PORTFOLIO MANAGEMENT

Of all the areas where curricular materials were wanting, no cupboard was emptier than that of portfolio management. Interestingly, the very idea that portfolio management belonged in the field of security analysis had been repugnant to some of the older analysts when they were faced in the late 1950s with the possibility of a certification program. As Harvey Earp recalled, "There was considerable controversy with respect to the purpose, structure, operation, and independence" of any such chartering program.[76] To understand this concern, he continued:

> One must remember that in the 1950s many [federation] members did not consider portfolio management to be an occupation that merited membership in an "analysts" society. The critical questions concerned whether members who worked for institutions such as banks really did stock and bond analysis or whether they simply used "Street" research and did portfolio management work.

During the CFA Program's first decade, however, the nature of financial analysis was beginning to change and opinions about portfolio management were changing along with it. One longtime member of the Council of Examiners explained it this way:

> In the first 10 years of the Council [of Examiners]'s life, there was beginning to emerge in the academic world a recognition of what later came to be known as modern portfolio theory, the Capital Asset Pricing Model, efficient markets, the relationship between risk and return, and matters of that sort. . . . I remember that Harold Dulan of the University of Arkansas and I were spokesmen in the Council for recognition of these developments and their possible insertion as questions in examinations.[77]

Looking back 20 years later, Ketchum reflected, "Questions on these matters in the early examinations would perhaps have been unwise." Unwise not just because of the relative lack of interest in them in the "world of practitioners" during the early 1960s, but also because the curriculum committees would have been hard pressed to find material for candidates to study. The extensive review of the financial literature and overhaul of the examination program undertaken in the late 1960s and early 1970s found this lack of materials still to be true.

Early in 1979, ICFA Vice President William Cornish of Chicago was commissioned by the board to rectify some of the problems regarding portfolio management by forming a task force "to determine what portfolio management consists of, including its scope and the skills needed to be a practitioner thereof."[78] The group was also to find, or supply, materials that could be used for the CFA Program. The members of this Portfolio Management Review Committee were, like those carrying out curriculum review 10 years previously, an impressive assemblage. Chaired by John Maginn, who worked at Mutual of Omaha and taught part time at Creighton University, the committee included William S. Gray III, CFA, of Harris Trust in Chicago; R&P Committee Chair Robert W. Morrison, CFA, of Canada Life Assurance in Toronto; Harold A. Schwind, CFA, of Investors Diversified Services in Minneapolis; Donald L. Tuttle, CFA, chairman of Indiana University's Finance Department; COE Chair Paul E. "Jay" Vawter, Jr., CFA, of Loomis, Sayles of Washington, DC; and James R. Vertin, CFA, of Wells Fargo Investment Advisers in San Francisco.

If the ICFA building had had a marquee at that time, these names would have been there in lights. All were members of the R&P Committee, and Vawter, Maginn, Tuttle, and Morrison also served on the COE. They represented a deliberately chosen divergence of opinions to reflect, as Vawter described, "the frequent discord within the profession on this topic."[79] Vawter recalled that, despite this philosophical diversity, the group developed "an amazing rapport and camaraderie, first defining portfolio management, then reviewing the literature, deciding that this literature was inadequate and did not well serve our needs...." Vawter remembered an "open and non-contentious environment [in which] the facts could be separated from the fads" that were "so prevalent in the investment business."[80] In its first year, the Portfolio Management Review Committee drafted a definition of portfolio management and redrafted the relevant "tree of knowledge" found in the institute's General Topic Outline to reflect the definition. Other activities included hosting a panel discussion and commissioning a directed literature search by COE member Donald E. Fischer, CFA.

Having conclusively identified the gaps in the literature, the group was then faced with the challenge of filling them. The first result of their efforts was the publication of *CFA Readings in Portfolio Management* in late 1980. It contained what committee members deemed "the most applicable articles currently available in journals and periodical literature."[81] As a group, the committee came to agree that portfolio management was, as Jim Vertin put it, a "process" not a static decision; the committee members were determined to find—if necessary, generate—articles reflecting this view. Vertin advocated for committee members to create their own literature centered on this view of portfolio management, and in 1981, the ICFA published *Determinants of Investment Portfolio Policy*, which consisted of articles by Tuttle, Vawter, Maginn, and Gray. One could argue, only somewhat facetiously, that these two publications doubled the available library of portfolio management books.

Knowing that more was needed, the committee proposed a third publication. They asked the ICFA trustees to consider a book-length project to be edited by Don Tuttle and John Maginn. Tuttle remembered its genesis this way:

> We had spent ... two and a half years meeting around the country as
> members of the Portfolio Management Review Committee in the late

JOHN L. MAGINN, CFA, and DONALD L. TUTTLE, CFA

In 2007, Donald L. Tuttle, CFA (left), and John L. Maginn, CFA (right), joined together to promote the third edition of *Managing Investment Portfolios.*

JOHN L. MAGINN, CFA

C. Stewart Sheppard Award, 1990

Alfred C. Morley Distinguished
    Service Award, 1997

DONALD L. TUTTLE, CFA

C. Stewart Sheppard Award, 1990

Donald L. Tuttle Award for Grading
    Excellence, 2001

Alfred C. Morley Distinguished
    Service Award, 2005

JOINT PROFILE

Ever since the 1983 publication of *Managing Investment Portfolios: A Dynamic Process*, John Maginn and Don Tuttle have been linked in the minds of CFA charterholders and candidates. Yet, there was a time when they did not know each other. In fact, there was a time when neither of them expected to have careers in investment management.

Born in Omaha, Nebraska, John Maginn has lived and worked there most of his life. He thought he would major in economics while at Creighton University. In taking economics courses, however, he began "to get some exposure" to finance. "I was always interested in numbers," he recalled, "so I kind of gravitated to [it]."[82] Maginn furthered his studies at the University of Minnesota, where he received a master's degree in finance in 1962. That same year, he began his investment career, at CNA Financial in Chicago.

In the early 1960s, Don Tuttle, a native of Miami, was completing his master's degree. When Tuttle started college, he expected to major in chemistry or pre-medicine, but in his sophomore year, he "switched over to finance." Tuttle received both a BSBA and MBA from the University of Florida and then earned his PhD at the University of North Carolina. There, Tuttle studied with Henry A. Latané, CFA, an early CFA charterholder and a great proponent of the CFA Program. Latané believed that his students should realize "there is a real world out there on Wall Street and elsewhere, beyond the [academic] position that you might hold," Tuttle recalled. With Latané's encouragement, Tuttle began the CFA study and exam sequence.

John Maginn had attained his charter three years earlier. When he began work in Chicago, Maginn had discovered something new in the air: "I started in the fall of 1962, and all the buzz in Chicago was about this new CFA Program." In fact, his boss, who was preparing to take that first CFA exam, borrowed Maginn's graduate school textbooks to study. Following his example, Maginn recalled, "All of us on the staff signed up to take the CFA exam." Maginn looked upon the CFA Program "as a chance to get a master's degree in investments." In 1968 he took a position with Mutual of Omaha, where he worked for the next 36 years.

Tuttle and Maginn first met at grading in the mid-1970s, at a time when one person graded a single question on all exams—Maginn graded bond analysis, and Tuttle, portfolio management. They formed a friendship at grading that was renewed annually and solidified during their work together on the Portfolio Management Review Committee in the late 1970s. Out of this committee's work came the impulse for producing *Managing Investment Portfolios.* Asked why they were chosen to edit this important work, each responded with characteristic modesty. Maginn believed he was chosen when the other practitioners on the committee "all looked around the table and everybody else blinked." Tuttle thought the committee had no choice but to tap him: "[It] really was by default since I was the only academic involved."

Of course, neither man believed the other got it right: "I think you don't quite state the case, John," Tuttle told him. "You did such a great job as the 'honest broker' that it was an obvious choice for you to represent the other practitioners on the committee." For his part, Maginn recognized Tuttle was by no means the "default" setting but was needed for his considerable knowledge and ability: "Don, having published before as an academic, was a natural. Everybody turned to him and said, 'Well, you have to be the editor.'" Moreover, Maginn continued, "Don had a vision for the book."

As with many great collaborations, Tuttle and Maginn complemented each other well. "We did have a very symbiotic relationship," Tuttle said. The project provided "an opportunity to blend our skills, backgrounds and experience," according to Maginn. Toward the end of the project, when "crunch time" came, they balanced each other in another way. Tuttle recalled with amusement how they got it all done:

> As the work load increased, John would get up earlier and earlier. First at 5:30, then 5:00, then 4:30, then 4:00 a.m. On the other hand, I would go to bed later and later, 10:00 to start, then 10:30, then 11:00, then 11:30, and then 12:00. The net

result was the same—including both our spouses saying we were nuts.

Their sleep deprivation has benefited candidates and charterholders for decades.

In addition to this joint work, each man contributed separately to the CFA Program. Don Tuttle has been involved at every step of the chartering process—bringing order, rigor, and innovation to the CFA curriculum, examinations, and grading. According to Robert R. Johnson, CFA, for years, "There hasn't been a single CFA examination that hasn't had Don Tuttle's fingerprints on it."

John Maginn has served the CFA Program as a grader for 14 years, on the Council of Examiners for more than 10 years, and in his work on portfolio management materials. He was a board member of both the Institute of Chartered Financial Analysts and Association for Investment Management and Research for many years, where he was active in advocacy and governance issues and chaired the ICFA board in 1985–1986 and the AIMR board in 1994–1995.

Asked to characterize both men, those who have known them paint a remarkably consistent picture. Don Tuttle is unfailingly described as a kind mentor, generous with his time and his knowledge. Douglas R. Hughes, CFA, a longtime grader, saw this characteristic in action. Here was "a world-class mind [with] a vast store of investment knowledge," Hughes said,

yet "he always had time for us as inexperienced graders." James R. Vertin, CFA, could "not say enough about Don Tuttle" and what he has meant to the character and quality of the candidate program: "He was there every time [and] would give you whatever kind of hand-holding help you needed."

As Tuttle was a crucial resource for graders, Vertin continued, so John Maginn "was that kind of a resource across the whole scope of the organization." Thomas A. Bowman, CFA, watched Maginn's work over many years: "The commitment of that man over a long period of time has just been amazing to me." Eugene H. Vaughan, Jr., CFA, who served on both boards with Maginn, identified an essential trait: "He always lifted people up. He genuinely saw the best in everyone. [He had] an enormously uplifting influence on our organizations."

Perhaps the greatest testament to the exceptional character of these two men is their enduring friendship. For more than 30 years, even through the trying circumstances of co-editing a book, they have kept their good humor and sense of mutual respect. "Don," John Maginn said, "is like a cousin to me, and we share a common passion for the CFA Program." Thinking about how frequently, and how well, they have merged their talents in the service of the CFA Program, Don Tuttle concluded, "It was a very good marriage, if you will."

1970s, and then, we said, "Okay, what are we going to do with . . . all of this wonderful stuff that we had generated?" And somebody decided we ought to write a book for the CFA Program, so John Maginn and I set upon the chore.[83]

Maginn recalled that the two of them "got together in Bloomington, Indiana, one Saturday and literally in seven hours outlined the entire book." In his opinion, they "forged a very, very good team."[84]

In January 1981, Tuttle reported to the ICFA Board of Trustees about the project and its prospective publisher. He noted that the book would be the "definitive work in portfolio management as it is being practiced by the most astute practitioners, or as it should be and will be practiced within the next three to five years." Rather than a theoretical work, the book would be "thoroughly practical."[85] The volume would be devoted to describing comprehensively the dynamic decision-making process that portfolio management entails.

Published early in 1983 and updated in 1985, *Managing Investment Portfolios: A Dynamic Process* was the culmination of untold hours of volunteer work, which was typical of these individuals who were so devoted to the advancement of their profession. *Managing Investment Portfolios* is now in its third edition (2007). Looking back with characteristic modesty, Tuttle suggests, "It's fair to say it was fairly successful."[86]

Interestingly, a recent demonstration of the widespread influence of the CFA Program concerned the very book that Don Tuttle and John Maginn produced in this fruitful period. On a 2008 trip to Asia, CFA Institute then Senior Managing Director Robert R. Johnson, CFA, had an emblematic experience. "I was in Vietnam," he notes, "and saw the second edition of *Managing Investment Portfolios* in the library at the Hanoi School of Business."[87] Such a sighting, unthinkable only a generation ago, attests not only to the remarkable influence of the book itself but also to the extraordinary growth in numbers, influence, and geographical expanse of the CFA Program—well beyond the wildest imaginings of its dedicated founders.

Looking forward from our vantage point here in 1986, the Institute can be described as an organization that is really beginning to hit its stride, like the long distance runner or the developing corporate enterprise. There is a sense of accomplishment, but more importantly a sense of anticipation regarding what the future holds. The Institute has been and must continue to be willing and able to meet these challenges.

—John L. Maginn, CFA, "Afterword,"
The Institute of Chartered Financial Analysts, 1986

part two

Rigorous, Comprehensive, Consistent— Development of the CFA Program: 1983–1999

chapter three

Setting the Pace: 1983–1989

*I*n the mid-1980s, near the start of its second quarter-century, the CFA Program was indeed like a long-distance runner "really beginning to hit its stride," in John Maginn's words. Candidate enrollments were taking off after a lengthy plateau, and the CFA curriculum and examination program had undergone scrutiny, revision, and expansion to meet new realities facing financial analysts. In addition, strategic planning for the Institute of Chartered Financial Analysts was beginning, revenues were up, and a new program of continuing education for charterholders was under way. Like the financial world in which CFA charterholders worked, the ICFA was at the beginning of a "giddy bull market," as one Wall Street historian called the upcoming decade.[1] In the ensuing years, the CFA Program would show itself to be a good distance runner, but in the 1980s, those managing the program needed first to sprint hard, then clear some high hurdles before finally settling into a steady pace of growth and expansion.

Four major hurdles faced the ICFA during the second half of the 1980s, each requiring deep and creative thinking if they were to be overcome. First, those responsible for the CFA Program would have to develop an administrative structure capable of managing the exponential growth in candidate enrollments and provide organizational stability even as the voluntary leadership of the board and committees changed from year to year. Then, they needed to increase the professional services provided to the ever-growing number of charterholders. Before the end of the decade, moreover, ICFA leaders would need to face the increasing globalization of financial markets, and—most challenging of all—they would have to redefine the relationship of the ICFA to its parent organization, the Financial Analysts Federation. Each of these tasks was daunting. All had to be accomplished while the individuals never lost sight of the *raison d'être* of the entire enterprise: preserving the value of the CFA charter by making steady improvements in the CFA Program itself.

As it turned out, according to the consultant that we used . . . we were setting the pace. The CFA Program exams and processes for developing the exams were the gold standard. And these consultants were taking what we did and recommending it to other of their clients.

—Donald L. Tuttle, CFA, interview with the author, 23 September 2009

Very few businesses are able to manage exponential growth.

—James R. Vertin, CFA, interview with Derik Rice, 26 May 2000

The CFA Program had experienced unexpectedly large candidate numbers in its first few years, but enrollments began to level off in 1967. Between 1968 and 1981, the program showed modest net growth and averaged 1,500 candidates per year. Alfred C. "Pete" Morley, CFA, board president in 1980–1981, speculated that the "relatively slow rate of increase in the number of candidates during the 1970s" might be attributed to several factors.[2] There may have been, he suggested, some "complacency" at the ICFA after the "surprisingly positive initial years." In addition, the nature of the investment management business itself in the 1970s was, he noted, "quite hectic in both equity and fixed-income markets." "Hectic" was a bit of an understatement because the crisis of 1974 was the "culmination of the worst bear market since the Great Crash of 1929," according to financial historian Peter Bernstein.[3] Yet, it did not send frightened analysts scurrying into the CFA Program. Only 44 more candidates sat for the CFA exam in 1975 than did in 1974. Moreover, the enactment of the Securities Acts Amendments of 1975 put some firms out of business and resulted in others being acquired, which, in effect, diminished the pool of CFA candidates. In the world of investment management, the 1970s were a difficult decade by any measure, with the market going down and oil prices going up. The result was a tenacious economic malaise that proved so persistent a new word had to be coined to describe it: *stagflation*.

Beginning in 1981–1982, however, lower inflation and much higher trading volume gave both the stock and bond markets a "considerable new breath of life," as Morley noted. In the United States, the Reagan era was under way and with it came a new emphasis on markets, business, and capitalism. In Britain, the Tory government of Margaret Thatcher brought extensive privatization and, later, the deregulation of financial markets (the "Big Bang" of October 1986). In Japan, the Nikkei 225 Index was at the beginning of a spectacular rise, and Hong Kong and Singapore were developing into world financial centers. As one of Morley's successors put it, the 1980s were "a very lucrative time to be involved in the financial world and attracted a growing number of young people coming out of school who, in turn, furnished a growing bounty of CFA candidates."[4] Until the mid-1980s, nearly all of those candidates came from North America, but by the middle of the decade, that would begin to change.

James R. Vertin, CFA, who followed Morley as board president, saw the beginning of the upward curve in CFA candidates as illustrating something predictable. Recalling a discussion he had had many years before with Charles D. Ellis, CFA (ICFA president in 1983–1984), Vertin noted that growth of the CFA Program from the early 1960s to the late 1980s traced a familiar statistical curve:

> Charley [Ellis] and I had lunch one day and he started talking about the number of acres planted to hybrid seed corn, the number of prescriptions written for penicillin, the dollar value of installed IBM equipment, and

things like that. What he was trying to get me to understand was that if something represents a true technological revolution there is an adoption pattern found in its growth curve—a long left-hand tail, an observable inflection point and … suddenly there it goes!

… [I]f you look at the candidate base and the growth of memberships, there was a long period after the beginning in 1963 when it did not look like much was happening. But if you think about the CFA Program and its rate of acceptance in the marketplace as a technological innovation with revolutionary characteristics, you could see in its record that its growth would become exponential. And indeed it has.[5]

Thomas A. Bowman, CFA, who was president and CEO of the combined ICFA and FAF from 1994 through 2004, had a similar understanding. He noted that it took a while for the CFA credential to become accepted but then "as more people got the charter and others saw it as advantageous, it became almost self-perpetuating."[6] Sometimes, of course, external factors contributed. Longtime CFA examination administrator Nancy Dudley remembers one notable effect of a market disruption:

When the stock market crashed in 1987, we were moving toward the end of the registration period, and the crash occurred in what was typically our slow time. All of a sudden, it became our busy time, and we had this blossoming of candidate registrations. If you were to go back and look at the 1988 program year, you would probably see that there was a significant increase in candidates at that point.[7]

Dudley was correct: In 1988 the program experienced an increase of 1,389 candidates over 1987, the largest single increase (in numbers and in percentage) up to that time. In the next decade, yearly increases would dwarf those of the 1980s, but this initial sharp uptick seemed to illustrate that those working in financial analysis had come to see the advantage that earning a CFA charter would give them. As Bowman observed, however, *after* the mid-1980s, the CFA candidate enrollment was essentially acyclic: In a bull market, enrollment was fueled by enthusiasm, and in a weak market, by fear and defensiveness. As the decade wore on, moreover, candidates would come to the CFA Program from parts of the world it had not reached before.[8]

For all these reasons, the CFA Program was in the midst of a steep increase in candidate registrations by the late 1980s. Between 1980 and 1985, candidate enrollments doubled, and then doubled again by the end of the decade. The number of candidates sitting for the 1989 examinations reflected a total increase of 306 percent over the start of the decade. As might be expected, the number of CFA charterholders also grew during the decade. The number of charterholders increased 53 percent—from 6,449 members in 1980 to 12,405 in 1989. No mat-

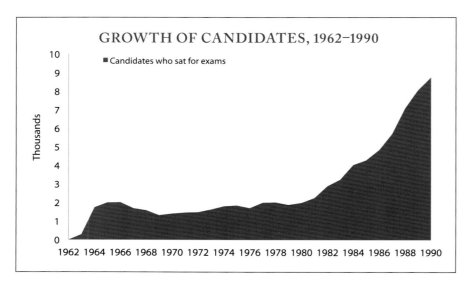

GROWTH OF CANDIDATES, 1962–1990

■ Candidates who sat for exams

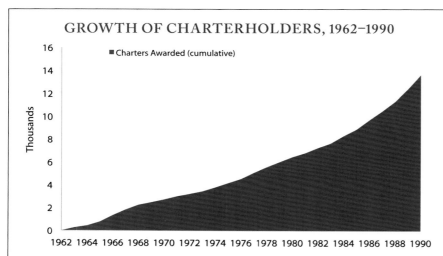

GROWTH OF CHARTERHOLDERS, 1962–1990

■ Charters Awarded (cumulative)

ter how measured, what started out as a mere handful of charterholders in 1963 had grown to the size of a substantial crowd by 1989.

As detailed in Chapter 2, the CFA Program curriculum and examinations had undergone considerable internal scrutiny and experienced many improvements during the 1970s and early 1980s. In the same period, the ICFA had also instituted an expanded program of professional conduct enforcement. By the early to mid-1980s, however, other aspects of the ICFA needed attention, not least of which was its administrative structure. The steep upward incline in CFA candidates created a need for more staff in Charlottesville to manage the examination program; the growing number of charterholders resulting from these examinations created a need to offer more educational programs to members. To accommodate the growth in members and candidates—and to serve both well—the institute needed to begin planning strategically. Those leading the ICFA in the 1980s recognized that one danger of success is complacency. They saw that their inherent challenge was to avoid calcification, as it were, and keep the CFA Program alive and adaptive, not stagnating. Perhaps no one saw this more clearly than two ICFA Board of Trustees presidents from the early 1980s, Pete Morley and Charley Ellis.

Writing to his fellow board members and the institute's administration shortly before taking office, Morley noted:

> There is absolutely no doubt that further considerable progress can and will be achieved. However, it seems to me that a more detailed map and compass now are needed to help assure achievement of that progress.[9]

To create this detailed map, Morley proposed the formation of a Long-Range Planning Committee, the first in the history of the ICFA. The committee was charged with answering the question, what is our long-term goal? They examined five areas—organization and finance, external relations, headquarters, the candidate program, and the member program (i.e., continuing education). ICFA Board of Trustees Vice President Jim Vertin agreed to head the project. From the outset, Vertin and the subcommittee heads resolved that no institute policy, program, or procedure was "too sacred to question"—not the bylaws, not the professional conduct program, not the grading process, not the location of the institute, not even the examination sequence. (Members

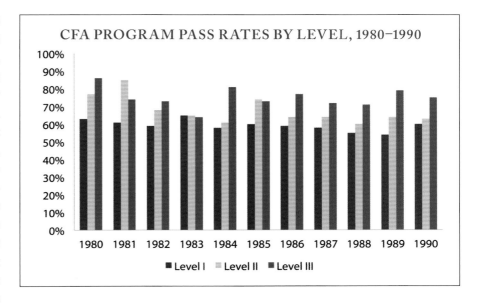

CFA PROGRAM PASS RATES BY LEVEL, 1980–1990

of the subcommittee on candidate programs, for example, asked themselves whether there should be a Level IV examination.)[10]

In their preliminary reports (January 1981), the various subcommittees found the state of the institute to be basically sound, but they did suggest some changes to contemplate. Among them were the need for larger quarters, which they anticipated would be required in about five years; decoupling from the University of Virginia because the cachet of a university affiliation was no longer needed; improved coordination between the ICFA and the FAF; continued professionalization of the administration, including the possibility of hiring a full-time director; and perhaps the most urgent change, a recommendation that the institute make a major commitment to a continuing education program. As will be discussed later, the primacy of the CFA exams never waned, but in the early long-range plans, other areas necessarily received much attention.

One position needing immediate consideration was that of executive director. Since the earliest days of the institute, the executive director's position had been part time. C. Stewart Sheppard, for all he accomplished, was technically giving the ICFA only 50 percent of his time; a similar structure existed for his successor, W. Scott Bauman, CFA, although for him, the percentage was closer to 70 percent. When Bauman left to return to teaching full time in 1978, O. Whitfield Broome, Jr., who had served as examinations administrator since 1973, was named the third executive director of the ICFA. Like his predecessors, Broome was a faculty member at the University of Virginia—in this case, teaching in the Commerce School and, later, adding an appointment to the Law School faculty. However, the crucial executive director position remained part time. Were it to become full time, Broome would not be able to fill it without giving up tenure at UVA.

O. Whitfield Broome, Jr., served as ICFA executive director for 1978–1984.

Whit Broome recognized the need for a full-time director and saw that it would lead to a fully professional ICFA administration. In 1980, he hired Darwin M. Bayston, CFA, of Chicago, as programs director, a position that merged the exam administrator's responsibilities with operational duties. Then, in 1982, on the heels of the first long-range planning recommendations, Bayston moved into the newly created, full-time position of director of Continuing Education, which focused on the programs needed for existing members. A parallel position, director of Candidate Programs, was created at the same time to oversee curriculum content and exam creation in liaison with the Council of Examiners (COE) and the Candidate Curriculum Committee (CCC). The remaining piece of the administrative puzzle was put into place in May 1983 when Broome took a leave of absence from UVA and agreed to serve as a full-time executive director for one year.

With a more complete staff to manage day-to-day business, the trustees were able to focus again on broad policy issues and strategic planning, which was given new life in 1983 by Board of Trustees President Charley Ellis of Greenwich Associates in Connecticut. At the beginning of his term as president, Ellis asked all the trustees and senior staff to send him ideas concerning the long-term needs of the organization. He wanted them to look as far into the future as "1990 or even 2000."[11] What areas of the program needed upgrading or expanding? Did the organizational structure itself need changing? The answers Ellis received were both thoughtful and contradictory. To meld them into a coherent plan, Ellis appointed a new Strategic Planning Committee composed of three trustees—James N. von Germeten, CFA, of Boston; Kathleen A. Condon, CFA, of New York; and Daniel J. Forrestal III, CFA, of Dallas. Their task was to define the ICFA mission, this time in four areas: the candidate program, the member program, the organization's relationships with FAF, and the internal administrative organization and financial structure.

In their preliminary report (September 1983), the committee noted one crucial advantage that having a strategic plan would give to an organization heavily reliant on volunteers:

> The continuity that a strategic plan provides to the constantly changing leadership of a professional organization insures its well-defined, well-understood long-term existence.[12]

With the board focusing on long-range strategic planning and broad policy issues, the need for professional staff to handle everything operational was essential. Throughout its first few decades, much of the CFA Program work had been board driven—and performed by committee volunteers. "You have to remember that this [current] organization is not the organization that it was back then," Jim Vertin noted in 2000. "That little group [of board members] sitting around the table *was* the management."[13] The thousands of volunteer hours donated by prominent analysts had made the creation of the CFA Program possible. In the following 20 years, thousands more volunteer hours led to the expansion of the CFA Program and its eventual prosperity.

The salient point about board and committee work, however, is that it is *voluntary*. The CFA Program has an extraordinary record of attracting volunteers of the highest caliber who display amazing dedication. Devoted to the furtherance of their profession, these men and women, all with demanding jobs and many who are highly prominent in their fields, have served on CFA committees from the organization's earliest days. The first leaders of the ICFA (A. Moyer "Abe" Kulp, CFA; M. Dutton Morehouse, CFA; William C. Norby, CFA; et al.) were determined that "major policy decisions would be placed in the hands of those chartered members voluntarily committed to the betterment of the Institute and the profession."[14] Committee members did a tremendous amount of work and also provided a "seedbed for future Institute leaders." Yet, although such volunteerism continues to be essential to the CFA Program, and although the Board of Trustees (now Board of Governors) still provides significant leadership, the CFA Program in the early 1980s was at a pivotal point. It was turning toward becoming the organization it is today, balanced between volunteer leadership and staff management.

Key to this change was the role of the executive director. As he neared the end of his year as full-time executive director, Whit Broome recognized that he was not willing to leave academia behind and continue in the position. He notified the board that he would return to teaching at UVA (where he continued until his retirement in 2010). Taking this impending change as an opportunity for strategic redefinition, Charley Ellis appointed Board of Trustees Vice President Paul E. "Jay" Vawter, Jr., CFA, of New York to head a search committee for a new director—and to rethink what that position should become in light of the strategic planning of recent years. Vawter saw the assignment as a chance to revamp "the whole style and approach to top leadership" at the institute.[15] The trustees, echoing one of Abe Kulp's main criteria for the first executive director in 1961, generally agreed that the new director had "best be a well-known leader from the profession." In 1983, however, the corresponding prominence in the academic world was no longer deemed necessary. Vawter recalled a "number of good names" surfacing during the search but acknowledged that he had one person in mind from the outset: Pete Morley, who had been board president in 1980–1981. As Vawter put it: "The only candidate I wanted and actively pursued was Pete Morley." A longtime volunteer for the CFA Program, Morley was well known to board and staff alike, in addition to being well regarded within the profession. For the bulk of his professional life (1952–1978), Morley had worked at Wainwright Securities, a research firm where he rose from security analyst to research director and, ultimately, managing partner. Wainwright researchers were renowned throughout the industry for their "extremely well done company research reports," and Morley's experience there made him an ideal candidate.[16] In

EXAM STORY: A MULTITASKING CANDIDATE

"I sat for Level I in 1999 at a time when I was eight months pregnant! I vividly remember carrying a cushion into the exam centre, which caused consternation and a flat refusal by the invigilators, as I doubt they had anticipated a request of the kind. It was only an hour into the test that they allowed me to use it. I passed with very good grades and perhaps I had an unfair advantage over other candidates as two brains were at work taking that test. When I sat for Level III in 2001, my second baby was one month old and needed to be nursed in the break we were given, halfway into the test. You can't imagine the raised eyebrows all around me. So many years later, remembering those three years when I was either expecting or delivering or nursing or reading for the exams while working full time as a portfolio manager in a high-stress job makes me realize nothing is impossible. Today I am the CEO of a merchant bank in Pakistan and very glad to be one of the earliest members of the CFA community in our part of the world."

—AYESHA AZIZ, CFA, Pakistan

EXAM STORIES: CHALLENGES AND DIFFICULTIES

A candidate who later became chair of the CFA Institute Board of Governors had her concentration challenged on the Level I exam as few other candidates have:

"My exams were held at McGill University. Everybody is nervous, especially the first year, as you do not know what to expect. It is a pretty daunting experience, and it has been a lot of work, and everybody is exhausted. We are about an hour into the first exam in the morning—so focused and working so hard. Unfortunately, a fellow in the front row collapsed. Normally that would be a traumatic thing for everybody around, and everybody would participate and go and try to help him. But just to show you how focused we all were, everybody in the room just looked up, and then went right back to the exam. And I can remember looking at the invigilator's face: he was horrified. It is a timed event, so you are on your own. The poor invigilator was on his own with this poor fellow. The rest of us just went back to work."

—MONIQUE E.M. GRAVEL, CFA, Montreal

Another candidate ran into a serious difficulty with the Level II exam but gained inspiration from the experience:

"Although I still work every day, I am an old-timer in terms of the CFA charter. My charter number is 3171. In the years just before my taking the exam, a number of senior investment professionals were 'grandfathered' in by taking just one or two exams. I was in my 20s and wanted to prove to some of those seniors at my employer (Mellon Bank at that time) that I was just as good. I began the three-year exam series as soon as I was eligible. Unfortunately, after easily passing exam one [Level I], I ran into a problem with exam two [Level II]. Ten days before the exam, I had major back surgery to repair an injured disk. Knowing it was given just once a year, I attempted to take the exam. The morning went fine, but the pain was too great in the afternoon. As I got up to leave, dejected in not finishing, the other exam-takers gave me a spontaneous round of applause. That gracious act in the midst of their own important tasks gave me encouragement that lasted throughout my investment career. I went on to complete the exam series, to serve as the President of my local analyst society, and to serve as a delegate at several national conventions. I proudly display my CFA designation on my business card to this day."

—DON J. CASTURO, CFA, Pittsburgh

his capacity as a volunteer, moreover, he was well respected. Additionally, of course, Morley was appreciated for his work as a board member and recent ICFA Board of Trustees president.

Although Morley would often declare his professional relationship with the ICFA to be a labor of love, he did not immediately jump at the offer to become the next director. He was amenable to the idea, Vawter recalled, and had a desire to serve but also had some reluctance. Tom Bowman, who was working with Morley at Frank Russell Investment Company in Tacoma, Washington, when the offer first came, said:

> I got called into Pete's office one day in 1984. He had a letter from Charley Ellis, who at the time was president of the ICFA board, which was searching for a CEO. . . . In effect, the letter said, as Pete read it to me, "We believe we have reached a stage where we no longer can function with a part-time executive director, and we want to adopt a corporate model and have a president and chief executive officer full time to run this organization the way it ought to be run."[17]

According to Vawter, negotiations went on for several months and included many hours on the phone. Although we do not have Morley's own words as to why he was reluctant to take the position despite his obvious love for the CFA Program, his hesitation probably arose from two sources: first, his actual contentment with the work he was doing for Frank Russell Investment Company in Washington state, as suggested by Bowman, and, second, his unwillingness to assume a directorship in the model that then existed. Except for a one-year period with a full-time executive director, the institute had only had part-time people, and all of those had been as much academicians as practitioners. Morley was decidedly a practitioner. As such, he was used to the organizational model of a business rather than that of a university.

Those looking for a new director had a personal appreciation of the corporate model themselves, however, and considered how the executive director position might be modified to a more traditional business form—not simply to suit Morley but to meet the needs of the organization as it was in the early 1980s, not as it had been the early 1960s. After what Vawter described as a "long meeting" between Morley and several trustees in Washington, the job was defined as that of president and CEO and would be structured in such a way that Morley, should he accept it, would "truly run the institute's day-to-day activities," leaving the board free to direct "its energies and skills to broad policy matters."[18] Shortly after this restructuring, Morley did accept the position, and he was unanimously elected by the board on 5 July 1984, effective 1 September. Placing Morley in this role, Bowman noted, brought to the organization "real investment world leadership and CFA experience."[19]

"It took six months," Vawter noted proudly, "but I was able to convince Pete to come on board."[20] Vawter, and those who worked with him in seeking a new executive director, had realized a new model of governance was needed. Given "his stature in the profession," Morley deserved the title of "President rather than [Executive] Director," as Vawter put it, but more importantly, the institute deserved a new mode of operating, especially one that would fully professionalize the staff and leave the executive free to actively promote the CFA Program within the profession, still largely centered in North America. Eventually, Pete Morley took the CFA charter around the world.

A CONTINUING EDUCATION

Over the next several years, the CFA Program expanded not only in numbers but also in offerings. Primary among these expanded services was a formalized program of continuing education for members. There was an important reason to turn attention toward charterholders: By the 1980s, some existing members had held their charters for 10, 15, even close to 20 years. For those still practicing financial analysis, what did a charter earned in the 1960s mean in the 1980s?

The profession had undergone tremendous changes in that interval from an explosion in knowledge and theory, including portfolio theory, as well as the "incredible progress made in computing" and consequent revolution in techniques—all of which accompanied dramatic increases in the number of individual investors and the growth of institutional investing.[21] The pace and enormity of change in the profession led William A. Cornish, CFA, board president in

I am an advocate of continuing education and have been a participant in that aspect of being a CFA for nearly 25 years. In fact, I still keep a CE diary.

—Charles C. Walden, CFA, correspondence with Wendi Ruschmann, 24 August 2010

ALFRED C. "PETE" MORLEY, CFA

Pete Morley, CFA, served as president and CEO of ICFA/FAF/AIMR for 1984–1990.

(b. 16 January 1927, d. 25 October 2002)

C. Stewart Sheppard Award, 1984
Nicholas Molodovsky Award, 1990
Distinguished Service Award, 2000

PROFILE OF A VOLUNTEER

The campus of Texas Tech University boasts more than 30,000 students, hundreds of academic programs, and an oak tree planted in honor of Alfred C. "Pete" Morley, the first president and CEO of the Institute of Chartered Financial Analysts. Donated by TTU alumnus Anthony S.W. Yeung, CFA, to honor Morley—his mentor and friend—the oak stands in a grove near the International Cultural Center, a fitting location for a memorial to "the man who brought the CFA Program to the world."[22]

Born in Geneva, Ohio, Pete Morley was educated at West Virginia University, where he also held his first full-time job as a statistics instructor. While writing his master's thesis on the financing of the railroad industry in the 1920s, he discovered that "the world of investments greatly appealed to me" and found his calling.

In 1950, National City Bank of Cleveland hired him as a security analyst in its trust department. Also located in Cleveland was the firm of H.C. Wainwright, the premier institutional research firm at the time. Sent to the firm on a one-year "lend-lease" agreement, Morley stayed with Wainwright for more than 25 years. He served as director of research and later became a managing partner. When Morley headed research at Wainwright, recalled Thomas A. Bowman, CFA, the firm's published reports were "models of how good research reports should be written."

Pete Morley earned his CFA charter in 1965, one of the first class to take both Levels II and III, and he began volunteering for the ICFA in 1967 on the Public and Industry Relations Committee, a good choice for a top-notch industry analyst. After a stint on the Professional Ethics Committee, Morley began serving on the Council of Examiners in 1974. For the next 10 years, he wrote the always-memorable Level II "annual report" question. Charterholders who remember questions about Walt Disney Company, Ford Motors, or Corning Glass Works probably experienced Morley's handiwork. In 1976, he was tapped to become an ICFA trustee; four years later (1980–1981), he became ICFA Board of Trustees president. According to John L. Maginn, CFA, Morley was a "superstar analyst" at the height of his career as president of Frank Russell Investment Company. In the mid-1980s, when the ICFA board decided to reorganize the administration and hire a full-time executive, Pete Morley—the "practitioner's practitioner"—was the person they sought.

Morley could be enigmatic. James R. Vertin, CFA, a longtime friend and close colleague, saw Morley as "a very private person in some ways," but he noted that he was "gregarious in public, friendly as a coworker, and effectively cooperative." He did, indeed, "hold his cards close to the vest," Vertin acknowledged but added, "he never held back any necessary detail or facts, nor did he hesitate to state preferences, conclusions or the action steps he envisioned." To Tom Bowman, who worked with him at Frank Russell and the ICFA, Morley was indeed complex:

> Pete was probably one of the most kind-hearted gentlemen that I have

ever met. But you might not know that, [for he] had a gruff side, a very professional side, and a very formal side to him that really belied what was underneath. Underneath was a teddy bear.

His employees remember him as an avuncular figure who hosted holiday parties at his house (when the ICFA, Financial Analysts Federation, and Association for Investment Management and Research staffs were small enough to fit), where his wife, Kathy, played the piano, and as the person who instituted the 25¢ soda machine at the Charlottesville headquarters and the monthly birthday parties—*and* as someone unfailingly kind. One young staff member recalled being introduced to him during her first week on the job and saying, "It's so nice to meet you, Mr. Morley." To which he replied graciously, "Mr. Morley was my father. Please just call me Pete." When the Christmas party came that year she, by chance, drew Pete Morley's name and gave him a T-shirt on the back of which was printed "Call me Pete." All remember him as "considerate," "kind," "caring and attentive to everyone"— someone who helped his young staff "grow professionally."

The same man who made sure staff birthdays were celebrated was also a strong and effective leader at the institutional and international levels. According to Jim Vertin, Morley challenged everyone to work at a high level:

> Working closely with [Morley] often meant a need to move quickly yourself, lest the next matter to be dealt with arrive before the last one was fully put to bed. [Morley] pushed those he had confidence in

and did so in a way that made one bring one's own useful qualities to the table in support of the plan. I don't think I would describe Pete as being a "visionary" so much as I would call him an extraordinary manager of people and ideas.

Tom Bowman found him to be "extremely effective with senior board members, senior volunteers, and international relationships, especially senior people [whom] he would meet around the world. He really was the one who opened the doors for us in many of these places."

One who received Morley's overseas overtures appreciatively was Gentaro Yura, Morley's counterpart at the Security Analysts Association of Japan in Tokyo. As Yura recalled:

> I learnt a great deal from his rich practical experiences and professional expertise. I felt a particular sympathy for his firm sense of mission to bring about international development of the investment profession. His sense of mission went a long way in supporting me.

Also memorable to him was Morley's belief that "the international relationship among all national bodies should be cooperation and communication" rather than "unilateral action."

When Morley announced his retirement in 1990, the Board of Governors of the Association for Investment Management and Research paid an immediate tribute by presenting him with the Nicholas Molodovsky Award, an occasional honor given to someone who has "made outstanding contributions of such significance as to change the direction of the profession and raise it to a higher standard of

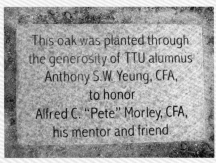

This tree was planted at Texas Tech University International Center in Lubbock, Texas, USA. Photos courtesy of the International Culture Center at Texas Tech University

accountability." After his death in 2002, the governors renamed the Distinguished Service Award in his honor. It is now given annually as the Alfred C. Morley Distinguished Service Award.

A forceful, effective leader, a kind, compassionate boss, a complex man— Pete Morley was perhaps most of all a dedicated professional. He cared "very, very deeply about the profession," John L. Maginn, CFA, noted, "as deeply as anybody I have ever known."

1979–1980, to point out to members, "Anyone who received a charter in the 1960s would find little remaining in the Study Program that can be used now."[23] Even more amazing, Cornish continued, the same statement could be made "about a person who received his charter in 1975." This state of affairs left the trustees resolved to "strengthen our Continuing Education activities"—lest a "Rip Van Winkle, C.F.A., of the class of 1963" awaken and find himself unable to "pass any examination in 1980."

Did the CFA Program have any obligation to verify or remedy this potential gap in knowledge? Was the charter, as some saw it, a permanent, discrete achievement, like a university degree, or was it, as others saw it, "a symbol of professional competence" that must be demonstrated continuously through further study?[24] If the latter, how would—or should—such ongoing competence be demonstrated? Throughout the early 1980s, the trustees, contemplating this question, considered whether a formal program of continuing education for charterholders should exist and, if so, whether it should evolve into some form of post–CFA charter accreditation, perhaps even a mandatory one.

The idea of providing ongoing educational services to members was, in a sense, nothing new. As early as 1964, ICFA trustees had discussed whether to establish some kind of ongoing program for members, and at the institute's first annual meeting, Abe Kulp had declared, "The Institute must develop a dynamic program to maintain the continuing interest of those who have received the C.F.A. charter."[25] In 1967, the Research Foundation began sponsoring seminars on aspects of portfolio management, the published proceedings of which filled gaps in the CFA curriculum *and* provided members with ongoing professional education. The *CFA Digest* was first distributed to members in 1971, and its stated purpose was to "help those members of the profession who have already received their C.F.A. charters."[26] In addition, members received a volume containing the collected papers of Nicholas Molodovsky, CFA, and the Darden School of Business at UVA, where former ICFA Executive Director C. Stewart Sheppard was dean, sponsored seminars for CFA charterholders only.

Thus, the idea of providing education to members was not new. What was new in the early 1980s was the prospect that this service might become a formal program, a menu of options, perhaps even an accreditation requirement for keeping the knowledge represented by one's charter up to date. If attaining a CFA charter could be looked upon as similar to earning a university degree, then an accreditation program might be its graduate school analog. Jim Vertin, an advocate for continuing education during this period (and long after), put it this way:

> A long time ago, I said the ICFA is like a university. . . . The graduates are
> our charterholders. [But] if we think our job stops when we graduate, it
> does not, because this business evolves, and we have to be an important

resource to every graduate in exactly the same way that we are an important resource to every candidate. [That] is where the continuing education program came from.[27]

By 1981, a confluence of factors enabled the ICFA Board of Trustees to make a strong commitment to providing continuing education for its ever more numerous members. (In 1981, for example, whereas slightly more than 2,000 candidates were enrolled to take the CFA examinations, charterholders numbered more than 6,000.) Significantly, institute leaders in the early 1980s were also leaders on this issue: Board presidents Jim Vertin, who had long advocated establishing a continuing education program, and Charley Ellis, who had chaired the Continuing Education Committee for several years, recognized the need. Moreover, a survey of other professions and their ongoing educational efforts by the Members Program Task Force, chaired by Ellis, produced the

VOICES OF CONTINUING EDUCATION VETERANS

Among those participating in annual continuing education (CE) activities are several who have participated every year since its beginning. Here are two of their stories:

"I received my charter in 1967 and tried to stay active . . . in the CFA Program, including grading for 15 years. I began participating in the continuing education program in 1985, continuing on an annual basis. I admit pride in keeping up with that program for 25 years, even though there were years when the requirements were vague and uncertain . . . I believe a strong Continuing Education program is absolutely essential to maintaining the status and the prestige of the overall examination process."

—ROBERT H. SHAW, CFA, 25-consecutive-year participant in the CE Program

"Since the beginning, I have diligently participated to further expand my knowledge, but there were certainly some challenges in the formative years of the program. In 1987–1988, my family and I were living in Tokyo where I set up and managed the Wertheim Schroder office. Our primary communication, besides the telephone, was fax and telex. There was not a Tokyo CFA Society, so I remained a member of the San Francisco Society. The ease of use the Internet and local Society CE presentations provide today is light years beyond the days when we were mainly reading various books and periodicals for credit!

For me, the Continuing Education Program is a 'labor of love,' but also one that is crucial in helping meet the challenges that CFA charterholders face every day."

—DONALD L. GHER, CFA, 25-consecutive-year participant in the CE Program

following observation: "Relative to its peer groups the Institute has very low dues and a low level of continuing education."[28] In addition, in 1981, the Task Force compiled the results of a set of questionnaires sent to charterholders; they found members eager for opportunities to learn and improve their skills. Also contributing to the decision to go forward with a continuing education program was the fact that the ICFA was in a strong enough financial position to expand its offerings to members.

The trustees took up the matter of funding such a program in September 1981. Jim Vertin remembers it this way:

I was president in 1981–1982 and was more or less just sitting in that chair when the money came down. I had asked for a commitment of three years and $40,000 a year to get a continuing education program going, to do half of what the board had approved of . . . and before I could get out of the

In early 1983, the third ICFA conference focused on "microcomputers and automating the analyst."

room, they had given me $150,000 a year for three years and said, "Go do it!"[29]

The board knew it was time, Vertin remembered. Some of the money allocated first went toward assembling a staff, and some, toward preparing programs. Also formed at this time was a volunteer Council on Continuing Education (CCE), which began meeting in June 1982. Its initiating members included Vertin, Ellis, Bayston, Dean LeBaron, and von Germeten (all charterholders), as well as academicians Roger Murray (Columbia University), Jay Light (Harvard Business School), Larry Selden (Columbia Business School), and Stephen Ross (Yale University). The mission of the CCE was to identify "areas of developing knowledge" in the field of financial analysis and to organize these identified areas into programs and publications that charterholders, candidates, and others could use to "maintain and enhance their professional expertise and effectiveness."[30]

Darwin Bayston, the director of continuing education, approached the establishment of a continuing education program "like a true entrepreneur," according to Charley Ellis, by developing an increasingly compelling series of educational programs for CFA charterholders and candidates and enriching considerably the substantive strength of the institute's programs.[31] In October 1982, the institute conducted its first continuing education seminar. Although previous seminars held by the ICFA, the Research Foundation, and the FAF could be said to have benefited charterholders and candidates alike, this 1982 seminar was the first program targeted specifically for continuing education of charterholders. Called Management Skills for the Investment Manager and held in Washington, DC, in October, the seminar drew more than 100 participants; its proceedings were published and distributed to members early in 1983. That same year, the ICFA cosponsored with the FAF two days of seminars titled Microcomputers: Automating the Analyst and Portfolio Manager, which took place in Houston in February 1983. From the perspective of 40 years later, it is striking to realize that the use of microcomputers was almost a novelty in 1983 and that even the most seasoned professional needed schooling in how to use them in his or her work.

By far the most successful of the early continuing education seminars was one titled The Revolution in Techniques for Managing Bond Portfolios, which was held in New York City on 3–4 February 1983 and attended by more than 200 people. The seminar was so highly rated by those in attendance that it was repeated in San Francisco in late March. Its proceedings, edited by Donald L. Tuttle, CFA, were sent to all charterholders two months later. Some of the seminar proceedings were also adopted for the CFA curriculum to "fill a void," according to Tuttle, thus helping candidates as well as members.[32] Reducing the turnaround time, from seminar to publication, to two months was a feat but worth it, according to Jim Vertin, because it enabled everyone to benefit from the seminars almost simultaneously:

Before two years were out, we had done seven seminars, six proceedings, [the] Maginn and Tuttle book [*Managing Investment Portfolios*], a couple of Research Foundation papers, [and] some things called occasional papers, all of which flowed to members as a part of their involvement as ICFA members. [33]

By July 1985, the ICFA had announced a formal—although voluntary—program of member accreditation whereby participating charterholders could choose from a menu of activities, including seminars, workshops, and independent study. To be included on this menu, an activity had to be deemed rigorous and helpful for the participant's understanding of investment theory and its practical application. ICFA Board of Trustees Chair Jay Vawter reminded charterholders of the "new instruments arising almost daily" that they would have to master and continued: "Many of us received our Charters 10 or more years ago when duration, interest rate swaps, options, and futures were not on the scene."[34] Vawter called for a "grass roots movement" to enhance the value of the charter.

Eugene H. Vaughan, Jr., CFA (left), presenting C. Stewart Sheppard Award to Paul E. "Jay" Vawter, Jr., CFA (right), in 1989.

In essence, that grass roots movement was already happening. In three surveys, charterholders had voiced their support—and desire—for such a program. Seventy-five percent of those responding expressed support for a "voluntary" and practical program in which members could choose areas and subjects of their own professional interest. Charterholders also felt it would be appropriate to recognize publicly those who participated in such a program.

By 1 August 1986, at the end of the first full reporting year for the new Accreditation Program, more than 1,000 charterholders had participated, with nearly 85 percent of those earning the requisite 50 accreditation units needed to receive a Certificate of Professional Achievement. Beginning in the 1986–87 accreditation year (which ran from 1 August to 31 July), the names of those completing continuing education activities were listed in the *CFA Newsletter*. Although board members might have wondered sometimes whether charterholders understood and appreciated the array of services offered to them by the institute, those choosing to participate in the accreditation process certainly did.

Interestingly, one of the first books sent to all charterholding members as part of the continuing education program was *The CFA Candidate Study and Examination: A Review*. Beginning in 1983, the arrival of the new edition of this book each year gave members a chance to learn (or relearn), right along with each year's class of candidates, what an analyst needed to know according to the current Body of Knowledge. These volumes also allowed charterholders to see the previous year's CFA examinations. With this book in hand, even Rip van Winkle awakening from a 10-year slumber would have a fighting chance to pass the most recent CFA exam.

"CURRENCY AND RELEVANCY": EVALUATING
THE CANDIDATE PROGRAM

The examinations and curriculum represent the very foundation of the institute.

—Thomas A. Bowman, CFA, memo to ICFA Board of Trustees, 2 December 1987

To say that institutional issues dominated the agenda for the ICFA in the 1980s is both true and misleading. Certainly, those running the CFA Program were preoccupied with the weighty tasks that did not directly affect the kinds of questions appearing on exams or the kinds of materials chosen for study guides. In fact, by the end of 1989, more than one board member would express concern over the amount of time institutional issues were taking. Reorganizing the administration of the ICFA, creating a Continuing Education (CE) Program, and especially, debating a possible merger with the FAF—these issues dominated board agendas so much that Pete Morley worried at the May 1989 board meeting that "progress on the ICFA's strategic plan was [being] limited due to merger matters."[35]

Nevertheless, the CFA examination, curriculum, and grading process—the "heart" of the institute —maintained its place as the primary focus of the ICFA. The structural reorganization and strategic planning done by successive boards actually helped guarantee that it would. With the change toward a corporate administrative structure, the ICFA Board of Trustees had created the position of vice president for Candidate Programs, parallel to that of vice president for Continuing Education. Both positions reported directly to the president and CEO—at the time, Pete Morley—and all three individuals were responsible for implementing the board's strategic plans. By making Candidate Programs a separate department, the board, in effect, protected its work. Thus, even as the possibility of merging with the FAF was receiving enormous attention, the CFA Program itself was able both to undergo close scrutiny and to look ahead toward a whole new phase—globalization.

The directorship of Candidate Programs changed hands frequently in the first years following the department's establishment. Douglas Van D. Leathem, CFA, served from 1982 to 1983, and his successor David J. McLaughlin, CFA, from 1984 to 1985. In 1986, Pete Morley hired Tom Bowman, CFA, to lead the candidate area as vice president for Candidate Programs. Originally from Washington, DC, Bowman had worked as a portfolio manager in Baltimore and Washington before taking a position in 1982 with Frank Russell Investment Company, where Morley was president, in Tacoma, Washington. When it came Morley's turn to fill the vacancy in Candidate Programs, he immediately thought of Bowman.

Although he was to focus on the CFA Program, with its emphasis on exam construction, curriculum content, and grading, Bowman did not have academic experience. Like Leathem and McLaughlin before him, he was a practitioner from his earliest days in the industry. Bowman remembers the challenge of his first assignment from Morley:

> I had spent 16, 17 years as a practitioner, not an academic. My association with the ICFA had really begun and ended during my candidate years; I was

not active. [The] first thing Pete said was, "We would really like you to come on board" . . . . Then he picked up this study guide that was probably the thickness of a major metropolitan phone book . . . threw it on the table in front of me, and [said] "I want you to do something with this!"[36]

At least momentarily, Bowman admits, he wondered what he had gotten himself into. It was "intimidating," he recalls, to have a CFA study guide cast down like a gauntlet. In addition to being asked to revamp the study guides, Bowman was also charged with ensuring the "currency and relevancy" of the CFA Program. From the time he assumed the position of vice president for Candidate Programs in January 1986, moreover, Bowman worked to ensure that institutional and organizational matters never interfered with or distracted from the work of the CFA Program—to "shield it," in his words.

Just prior to Tom Bowman's arrival as vice president for Candidate Programs, and fast on the heels of the Portfolio Management Review Committee's work in helping to fill holes in the available literature for the CFA curriculum, the ICFA Board of Trustees had commissioned a significant review of the examinations— their format, content, and methodology. Jay Vawter, then chair of the board, recognized that "the methodology of conducting these exams had not changed greatly over the history of the institute."[37] Therefore, he appointed an exam review committee, chaired by Don Tuttle, whose charge was:

> to look into all aspects of the exam program, including further use of multiple choice questions, offering the exam more often, the structure of the Council of Examiners and the Candidate Curriculum Committee, and any other matters relating to the educational and examination process.

Formed in 1985 and called the Select Committee to Review and Evaluate the CFA Candidate Program, this organization tapped another distinguished group of dedicated volunteers. Several members of the Portfolio Management Review Committee reunited to work on the new project: Don Tuttle, who acted as chair, John Maginn, Jay Vawter, Jim Vertin, and Robert W. Morrison, CFA. ICFA President Pete Morley joined them. Rounding out the committee were Donald Fischer, CFA, of the University of Connecticut; James LaFleur, CFA, of Old Kent Bank and Trust in Michigan; and Leonard Patenaude, CFA, of Nichols and Pratt in Boston.

In a sense, the work of this committee was like nothing the ICFA had ever undertaken. The level of specificity in Jay Vawter's initial charge determined that its work would be different and directed toward methodology. According to Tuttle, who reported to the board in August 1984, the committee's initial focus was on "short term tactical issues related to the candidates' study and examination program."[38] One month later, the committee issued a more extensive review of their discussions and preliminary recommendations. First among them was a recommendation that the COE be expanded in number "up to 20 members."[39] Despite

EXAM STORY:
A SANGUINE SURPRISE

"I was sitting in the afternoon session of the Level II exam, when all of a sudden a drop of blood splattered on my paper. Oh no! I had a nosebleed. I do NOT have time for this, I thought. I rushed to the proctor to be excused, ran to the bathroom to grab a supply of tissue, and returned to my desk. How embarrassing! How distracting! Well, I passed anyway, thankfully. Since I'm not prone to spontaneous nosebleeds (it's happened neither before nor since), I can only attribute this event to the extreme stress I was under at the time. I literally bled to attain my CFA charter."

—RANDALL BAUM, CFA
Denver

HISTORICAL SPOTLIGHT

Fourteen members have participated in CE activities for 25 consecutive years. They are as follows: John H. Conley, CFA; Joseph T. Dabney III, CFA; David G. Diercks, CFA; Richard B. Dole, CFA; Donald L. Gher, CFA; Clayton L. Liscom, CFA; John G. Mebane, Jr., CFA; George W. Noyes, CFA; John D. Richardson, CFA; Robert H. Shaw, CFA; Robert W. Templeton, CFA; C. Thomas Tull, CFA; Charles C. Walden, CFA; and Ralph C. Walter III, CFA.

some concern that larger numbers might "erode the team spirit so important to the Council's effective functioning," the committee recommended the increase because the COE's role was expanding. Its work would now include the writing of "guideline answers" to examination questions and "outlining a procedure" to involve "exam graders, ICFA staff members, and professional editors" in the process. The COE would also be responsible for composing "backup essay and problem questions." To keep things tightly focused, the Select Committee also recommended increased training for new COE members and fixed terms for COE membership (although the latter recommendation was later rejected).

The next area the Select Committee examined was how to standardize the "recruiting, training and evaluating" of those volunteers critical to the CFA Program's annual cycle: exam graders, members of the COE and of the CCC (which had replaced the Research and Publications Committee in 1982). The Select Committee also wished to set up a process for pre-testing CFA exam questions, a key component of which would be "having subcommittee [i.e., topic] chairmen answer proposed questions from their topic area on an open-book basis." Although the report does not state so explicitly, having CCC members take a sample exam would indeed serve to coordinate directly between its work and that of the COE, as had long been sought. The Select Committee also considered whether the institute should take a larger role in candidate preparation but decided to first poll FAF societies to see how this issue might be received because the societies were mostly responsible for study programs.

The Select Committee's most intense level of scrutiny was directed at the use of multiple-choice questions on the CFA examinations. In the September 1984 report, Select Committee Chair Don Tuttle informed the ICFA Board of Trustees that, although the committee was "assuming no change in the role of multiple choice questions," it did recommend they be used to test three areas of Level I —accounting, economics, and ethics. The committee also requested that the institute seek "expert advice from testing specialists and opinions from a sample of CFA charterholders." In January 1985, Tuttle issued a report on the Select Committee's meeting with just such a testing specialist, a "psychometric consultant," LeAnn Gamache, who was the assistant director of the American College Testing (ACT) Program in Ames, Iowa.[40] Gamache was asked to discuss multiple-choice questions as an effective means for testing, to evaluate the quality of the most recent Level I multiple-choice questions (from the 1984 exams), and to comment on which areas of the curriculum would best lend themselves to multiple-choice testing at each exam level. Gamache also commented on procedures used in "building and maintaining a first class testing program."

One important tool used by psychometricians in test construction is "Bloom's Taxonomy," and Gamache drew parallels between it and the CFA examination sequence. Developed in the 1950s by Benjamin Bloom, PhD, an educational psychologist from the University of Chicago, Bloom's Taxonomy is a way to classify the cognitive complexity of certain intellectual tasks. It is arranged in six levels of increasing complexity: knowledge, comprehension, application, analysis, synthesis, and evaluation. Gamache maintained that the CFA Program's testing scheme ran parallel to these levels of knowing. As she demonstrated to the Select Committee, knowledge and comprehension were tested at Level I; application and analysis, at Level II; and synthesis and evaluation, at Level III. In shorthand terminology soon to be commonplace among those leading the CFA Program, Level I was about tools, Level II was about analysis, and Level III was about judgment.

Gamache made specific suggestions for the CFA Program's testing. Her first suggestion would come as no surprise to those who had been striving to coordinate the functions of the COE and CCC. It was urgent, Gamache told the Select Committee, that "the content of the curriculum . . . be tightly outlined for purposes of item (question) development."[41] She also suggested that questions be written with sufficient specificity that they would target even "sub-subheadings in the outline."

John D. Richardson, CFA, participated in CE activities for 25 consecutive years and served as a long-term grader.

On 30 May 1985, the Select Committee issued its full-year report. It accepted some of LeAnn Gamache's recommendations but rejected others as either not feasible or inapplicable given the particular nature of financial analysis. Remarkably, most of the changes, listed below, had already been implemented by the time the report was issued:

- the validity of multiple-choice testing had been researched and confirmed;
- ACT had been retained as a consultant on multiple-choice testing to "edit multiple choice questions written for the 1985 exam" and was being considered "for more involvement in the preparation of multiple-choice questions" for later exam cycles;
- the COE membership had expanded to 20, and its responsibilities increased; its orientation and training had also been enhanced;
- much work had been done on the grading program:
  - a formal procedure for recruiting graders had been updated;
  - arrangements had been made for greater coordination between veteran graders and new graders, all of whom would be invited to participate by January, rather than by March; and
  - more Canadian graders had been recruited.

Robert H. Shaw, CFA, participated in CE activities for 25 consecutive years and served as a long-term grader.

In addition, the report noted—almost in passing—"for the first time we will have a grader from London and one from the Middle East."

Some of the consultant's recommendations were found to be unworkable. For example, finding 50 individuals to pretest the examination was not possible because of the amount of review time needed and the extreme importance of security and confidentiality. Instead, the committee agreed that pretesting of exam questions was essentially met by having the ICFA staff member in charge of Candidate Programs and President Pete Morley review all final drafts of the exams. They agreed that the review group might include CCC topic subcommittee chairs in the future.

A detailed report of the Select Committee's unusually concentrated and productive work was presented to the general membership at the ICFA Annual Meeting in Washington, DC, on 11 June 1985. It was dense with detail but clear in its thinking. Although the institute had hardly been idle for the previous 20 years in regard to updating and improving all aspects of the CFA Program, so great a number of specific recommendations for exam and curriculum changes had not come together so quickly before.

The timing was excellent. Within a few years, the ICFA would experience an exponential increase in the number of candidates it served and an extraordinary geographical expansion. Reporting to the ICFA Board of Trustees two days before the 1985 annual meeting, Don Tuttle had noted that future work by the Select Committee would focus on "global and longer-term issues." No doubt in using the word "global," the committee's hard-working chair was referring to concentrating on issues of wide significance. Yet, he might as well have been talking about the CFA Program's next 25 years, in which it would extend to 133 countries. No longer would it be news that CFA exam graders were being recruited from beyond North America. In 2011, they came from more than 50 countries.

Approximately one year after the Select Committee finished its work and instituted its reforms to the examination program, Tom Bowman took the reins as the head of Candidate Programs. He was coming into a program that was already well formed and had been closely scrutinized in recent years by two stellar committees: the Portfolio Management Review Committee and the Select Committee to Review and Evaluate the CFA Candidate Program. From the outset, Bowman was given directives from the board based on its strategic planning to examine the CFA Program for "currency and relevancy"—to ensure that the CFA Program reflected "the changing dynamics of the investment management industry."[42] He was also to see that the administration created a plan to pursue the board's "greater interest in international exposure." Candidate Programs, they noted, should similarly examine the "greater trend" in the industry toward "specialization by existing and prospective CFA candidates."

For the remainder of the decade, work on the CFA Program would focus on these strategic goals and their subsequent restatements. As Bowman noted, the board's strategic planning initiatives represented one of the two ways in which the CFA Program was continually scrutinized and updated. Board directives formed a kind of top-down approach of looking at what the curriculum and examinations might be or how they might broaden as the profession itself did.[43] The second approach, which will be detailed in the next chapters, was

EXAM STORY: AN INTERNATIONAL PIONEER

One of the earliest non-North American candidates was Akio Mikuni, CFA, the first CFA charterholder in Japan.[44] Mikuni, who had been a high school exchange student in Massachusetts, remembers being amazed to hear his U.S. friends "talking about stock markets." In Japan at the time, that was unheard of because saving rather than investing money was the common practice. His interest in the "securities markets" was piqued, and after graduating from Tokyo University with a law degree, Mikuni went to work for Nomura Securities. In the mid-1960s, his company sent him to New York, where he became acquainted with the CFA Program. Attending night school at New York University, Mikuni had a friend who kept telling him that the CFA examination "was starting to take place" (in 1964), and that it would be "worth our efforts to try to get a CFA designation." Recognizing that the program would give him "all-around knowledge of the securities market, portfolio investments, and security

analysis," Mikuni decided it "would be the best way to study," applied for the CFA exam, and joined a study group.

Mikuni sat for the Level I exam at NYU in 1966 and for Level II the following year, but because the CFA Program had age requirements at that time and he was not yet the required 30 years old, he returned to Tokyo without completing Level III. Wanting to finish the program, but aware of how difficult it would be to travel back for one day's exam, Mikuni recalls, "I wrote a letter" to the staff at the ICFA asking whether "it was possible to take the examination in Tokyo." C. Stewart Sheppard and C. Ray Smith agreed to make an exception and have the examination itself delivered to Japan by Carl L.A. Beckers, CFA, chair of the joint FAF/ICFA Professional Ethics Committee at the time. According to one well acquainted with him, Beckers was "a true friend of Japan."[45]

Reflecting back on his experience 40 years later, Akio Mikuni recalled that studying for the CFA designation had

given him "good direction," a "good perspective," and a "good opportunity to study comprehensively." Within a few years of his receiving the first CFA charter in Japan, he said, "There was quite good interest" in Japan for the CFA Program, and today, many in Japan hold a CFA charter.

Still, he notes, "it is always fun to be the first."

Akio Mikuni, CFA, class of 1969, charterholder from Japan.

from the bottom up: Bowman, staff, and key volunteers—the COE, the CCC, the graders—worked to provide a structural framework (a "discipline" in Bowman's words) within which to write and evaluate the CFA exams and to modify and expand the Body of Knowledge.

Also affecting the CFA Program in the late 1980s was the outreach to candidates and programs beyond North America. A mere trickle at the beginning of the decade, candidate enrollments from countries outside of North America would "explode," in Pete Morley's words, as the decade was ending. Any further reevaluation of the exam and study program, therefore, would need to consider the question of "how we test an increasing number of non-North American candidates on such topics as accounting, economics, and ethics when their respective practices may differ."[46]

(left) Peter van de Paverd, CFA, class of
1967, charterholder from the Netherlands.

(right) Roland H. Schwab, CFA, class of
1973, charterholder from Switzerland.

WHO CAN BECOME A CHARTERHOLDER?

From its earliest days, the CFA Program had established admissions criteria. In
other professions, those eligible to sit for a qualifying examination might be easy
to determine, but the eligible practitioner in financial analysis was not so simple
to define. In the early 1960s, when the issue of grandfathering for experienced
analysts still had importance, "eligibility requirements were almost sacred," C. Ray
Smith recalled.[47] A successful applicant had to be of a certain age and to have
demonstrated that he or she had worked for a designated numbers of years in a
position deemed to be in the field of financial analysis. As Smith noted, those formulating the original CFA Program were particularly concerned about the experience requirement: "People had to actually have experience in security analysis."
Eligibility requirements, he continued:

> were looked at very carefully, recommenders were called, sample[s] of work
> were asked for . . . . [It] was strict. [We] had a lot of potential candidates—
> people who applied—who weren't accepted.

The CFA Program, established mostly by those on the buy side of the financial industry, did not recognize sales positions as necessarily meeting the criteria
for candidate admissions. At the outset, moreover, positions that would not give
anyone pause today were considered for exclusion. At the time the program was
founded, some looked askance at those who worked in portfolio management,
for instance, or those in fixed-income securities. As noted previously, M. Harvey

Earp, CFA, recalled that many FAF members did not think that portfolio managers "merited membership in an 'analysts' society."[48] This possible exclusion was no small thing for a portfolio manager wishing to attain a CFA charter. Ultimately, both portfolio management and work with fixed-income securities were regarded as acceptable; in fact, questions about each of these areas appeared on the early exams.

Although admissions criteria altered over time, discussion about what those criteria *should* be did not wane. As the grandfathered generation worked its way through the program in the 1960s, the age requirement was dropped. The number of years of work experience decreased from a high in 1963 of six years for Level III to the more moderate experience requirements of one year for Level I, two years for Level II, and three years for Level III by 1977.

In 1979, the Admissions Committee, headed by William R. Johnson, CFA, of Milwaukee, proposed more sweeping changes, including the possibility of eliminating all experience requirements.[49] The examination of these possibilities continued until, in February 1982, the board announced revised admissions criteria in the *CFA Newsletter*, with a headline that read: "Significant Change in Requirements for Charter." The trustees, reasoning that the CFA examinations were sufficiently rigorous and the CFA curriculum so comprehensive that anyone passing the three exams should be considered qualified, had decided to remove the requirements of specific education and occupational experience. As the newsletter reported, experience requirements were removed "in recognition of the institute's success in developing a comprehensive written body of professional knowledge and an effective series of examinations with which to test the knowledge of candidates."[50] Effective immediately, the successful completion of the three CFA exams and compliance with the Code of Ethics and Standards of Professional Conduct would be sufficient for one to earn a CFA charter. The article concluded by soliciting comments from current charterholders.

Comment they did. Addressing charterholders at the annual meeting in Boston in May 1982, ICFA Board of Trustees President Jim Vertin called their response "extraordinary." More than 50 percent of the membership responded. Based on their thoughtful comments, he continued, it was evident that the board's decision, although "sound and appropriate," was perhaps "ahead of its time." As a result, the trustees reconsidered and, at their May meeting, voted to reinstate the educational and experience requirements listed in the FAF bylaws, namely, "a bachelor's degree and three years' experience"—requirements that were to be met prior to the award of the CFA designation (although not before beginning

M. Harvey Earp, CFA, served on the ICFA Board of Trustees for 1974–1977.

The ICFA Management Committee members in 1988 were (left to right) Pete Morley, CFA; Darwin Bayston, CFA; and Tom Bowman, CFA. All three men would serve as president and CEO of the ICFA as it evolved.

the exam sequence).[51] The trustees themselves took an object lesson from this experience: "In the future, members would be surveyed" about such changes.[52]

Although the ICFA Board of Trustees reconsidered its decision on eligibility requirements, the discussion and debate about these requirements did not disappear. In part, the continuing debate reflected the changing nature of the profession as its numbers expanded and as investment vehicles multiplied. When the CFA Program began in the early 1960s, few firms on Wall Street, or in other financial centers, had sizable research departments. By the 1980s, that condition was changing and analysts were beginning "their rise to stardom."[53] Yet, in light of changes in the investment industry, the question remained: Who should be considered as engaged in the "investment decision-making process" when the nature of investing itself was changing?

Throughout the 1980s, the ICFA trustees wondered whether the definition of who was involved in the investment decision-making process was being written too narrowly. If so, the CFA Program might not be reaching all who would legitimately qualify. When, at the close of the decade, trustees for the ICFA and the FAF turned their attention to a possible combining of the two organizations into one, membership requirements became all the more important. If the organizations merged, would all members need to hold a CFA charter? What would happen at the local society level for those who did not?

In 1986, just as the concept of an ICFA/FAF combination was beginning to poke its head above the horizon, the ICFA Board of Trustees once again took up the topic of whether admissions standards for the CFA Program should be liberalized. The trustees appointed an Ad Hoc Committee on Admissions as part of its overall reevaluation of the CFA Program. In addition, the three senior staff members—ICFA President Pete Morley and the vice presidents, Darwin Bayston and Tom Bowman—were to review the program, then share their findings with the Ad Hoc group, whose goal was to expand the pool of candidates while maintaining the rigors of the examination program or, in other words, to expand the CFA Program in breadth without shrinking its depth. The Ad Hoc Committee on Admissions and the staff also considered the question of "whether there should be different tests designed for each specialty." Finally, they were adamant that the emphasis on "ethical standards not change in any way."[54]

At the September 1986 board meeting, Tom Bowman reported on the senior staff's conclusions. Focusing on the "experience clause," they found that the problem lay in "interpreting the already written standards."[55] Some trustees appreciated the committee's approach of concentrating on job *content*, not job title, but others were mindful of the board's recent experience in acting before consulting the membership. "If we don't communicate to members there will be an uprising," Lea B. Hansen, CFA, of Toronto reminded her fellow board members. She noted that in grappling with admission standards, the trustees also had to recognize the "broad market" out there and "keep in mind that the exam is the great discriminator."

The board did approve a "more liberalized interpretation of the institute's experience requirements."[56] As Bowman reported, the board's action did not establish new criteria but, rather, was an "interpretation of already existing criteria."[57] The 1986 ICFA Annual Report, which coincided with the CFA Program's 25th anniversary year, noted that the definition of "investment decision-making process" had necessarily "changed and expanded over the years" as new investment vehicles—including "real estate, tangible assets, precious metals, and derivative securities"—had become "widely accepted alternative asset classes."[58] In such a dynamic environment, the ICFA Board of Trustees had thus:

Lea B. Hansen, CFA, served on the ICFA Board of Trustees for 1985–1988.

> [e]ndorsed a policy stating that candidates could be eligible for eventual award of the CFA Charter if they are involved in the analysis, evaluation, or implementation process as it relates to investments, and if a better grasp of the ICFA body of knowledge could enable the candidate to do his or her job more professionally.

Job content—actual work performed—was to be given precedence over job title. Current CFA charterholders would be given a chance to express their views on the changes through a member survey. No "uprising" greeted the change, but members expressed concern that admissions standards remain high.

The reevaluation of eligible work experience continued throughout the remainder of the decade, into the 1990s, and well beyond. As Tom Bowman noted recently, "Membership standards have changed over the years, but it is still a very, very contentious issue."[59] The broadening of admissions requirements, together with an extended outreach program, did result in increased candidate enrollments. One thing that Bowman and his staff noted immediately was that "the number of new candidates being notified that they are not meeting the experience requirement has declined dramatically from recent years."[60]

The "contentiousness" surrounding eligibility to participate in the CFA Program would next be felt strongly when the ICFA and FAF began to consider seriously a merger of their two organizations (detailed in Chapter 4). As the decision on a merger neared, the ICFA Board of Trustees once again heard member complaints that they were "lowering standards."[61] At the ICFA Annual Meeting in May 1989:

HISTORICAL SPOTLIGHT

The FAF's professional regulation program, which was a joint effort with the ICFA, received a presidential citation that year from Ronald Reagan as "one of nine outstanding programs in the United States."

Several attendees at the meeting asked questions about the rationale of admittance standards to the CFA Candidate Program being changed whereby those not closely allied to the investment profession, and/or those in the investment business and financial planners compensated entirely by commissions, could become CFA charterholders."[62]

Outgoing board chair Eugene C. Sit, CFA, responded, stating, "Admittance standards have been broadened, but not knowingly lowered." Sit reassured members that:

> based on the concern expressed, the Trustees have asked the staff to evaluate the entire admittance procedure, including the guidelines, and to communicate this to the Board and to the members.

The issue of admissions criteria would be taken up thoroughly again in the 1990s. The prevailing recognition was that the definition of "investment process" itself was broadening within the financial industry; this recognition was matched by the wish of CFA Program leaders to fulfill the organization's "obligation to help educate and professionalize a wider array" of those involved in the investment process.[63] In light of this educational mission, the expansion of admissions standards stood.

REBALANCING THE PORTFOLIO

Enumerating the tasks set for his department by the ICFA trustees' strategic plan in an April 1987 report to the board's Ad Hoc Committee on the CFA Program, Tom Bowman listed three related aspects of the candidate curriculum and examination programs that were to be scrutinized:

1. eligibility criteria for admissions to the examination program,
2. purpose, scope, and testing frequency of Level I, and
3. purpose, scope, and testing frequency of Levels II and III.

The third aspect, he noted, would include a review of the possibility of "substituting or adding examinations for specialty investment functions."[64]

Deciding who would be allowed to take the CFA exam was an important topic in the late 1980s but not more so than deciding what those admitted should *study* and what they should *be tested on* once they arrived at examination centers. Scrutiny of what was then called the "Tree of Knowledge" and of the examination sequence began immediately after admissions criteria were reconsidered and lasted, in a very focused fashion, well into the 1990s.

As with the admission issue, the three senior staff members consulted among themselves and also talked with the chairs of the COE (Michael L. McCowin, CFA)

> My own feeling is that the curriculum, and the exposure to the curriculum through the Study Guide, is far more important than the exam itself. The exam is just kind of the frosting on the cake.
>
> —John L. Maginn, CFA, interview, 1 July 2010

> It was from the mid-seventies and, especially, the eighties, that innovation really became an integral part of financial activity.
>
> —Youssef Cassis, *Capitals of Capital*, 2009

and the CCC (Gary G. Schlarbaum, CFA). A report with their recommendations was presented to the full board at its May 1987 meeting. Although everything had been "on the table" for possible change—and change was certainly in the air at the ICFA in the late 1980s—the group concluded that the CFA examination and study program was doing what it needed to and did not recommend substantial alteration:

> We recommend that the underlying philosophy of the Institute should be to concentrate its program on ethical standards and those asset classes [with] which the program has traditionally been associated, and not to attempt to dilute its scope by trying to be all things to all people. Thus, common stocks and bonds, their derivatives, real estate and the management of these assets within a portfolio (both personal and institutional) should represent the heart of the program.[65]

In essence, the program was sound, although the Body of Knowledge should always be dynamic and should reflect changes in the industry. By keeping the Body of Knowledge current, the CFA Program staff and the board could feel confident that they were keeping exam content current as well.

Nevertheless, the staff identified some modifications that could improve the program. They saw the CFA curriculum as "progressive" in nature—that is, paralleling the progression of an analyst's career—and agreed that the curriculum and examinations should do the same. Yet, the review noted, for some time, both the COE and the CCC had "struggled with the progressivity concept of the Study and Examination Program," and concluded that the "primary reason for this has not been the Body of Knowledge itself, but rather the subject matter covered at each exam level."[66] That is, the content was correct (and ever changing), but the arrangement of topics was not.

The group of staff members and committee heads, therefore, recommended some changes in the allocation of the curriculum, which, if adopted by the board, should be phased into the examination program over the course of three years. The suggested changes would bring both the curriculum and examination topics into closer correspondence with the levels of cognitive complexity listed in Bloom's Taxonomy and allow for the further development of appropriate command words in each exam. Level I, it was suggested, should focus on the "tools of the trade"—accounting, economics, quantitative analysis, the "attributes of asset classes," and similar topics. Level II should concentrate on the analysis of asset classes. Level III should be concerned with the application of this analysis in judgments about the investment process in the context of portfolio management. Woven throughout all three levels would be readings and questions on the "ICFA Code of Ethics and Standards of Professional Conduct."[67]

These changes followed from the use of Bloom's Taxonomy, which had been

EXAM STORY: TESTING ETHICAL BEHAVIOR

A candidate who later served as CFA Institute chair in 2009–2010 faced a most unusual situation when he arrived for his Level III exam:

"In 1988, I took Level III on the campus of Memphis State University. Like many diligent candidates, I went to the campus early to make sure I had the right location. I arrived much too early and decided to pass the time by strolling to the exam site and the exact floor and room where I was to be when the exam started.

"I walked into the building, which was largely empty. So was the room for the exam. Empty, except for me and a big stack of Level III exams! Neatly arranged on the proctor's desk, but no proctor anywhere to be found. Just me, an empty room, a stack of exams, and 90 minutes to go before exam time. What worse temptation could there be for a candidate?

"I don't know which scared me more, the temptation to cheat, or the thought that I would be seen in the room and falsely accused of cheating. I didn't hang around to think about it. I got out of the room as fast as I could, went back to my 1984 Dodge minivan, and tried to cram for one final hour. It was hard to concentrate, knowing that the precious information I needed most, the exam content, was just a few minutes away.

"Later, when at the proper time, I opened the exam book, I almost started laughing. The first question was on the topic I knew best, business cycle theory. Cheating wouldn't have given me an edge at all, only a permanent sense of personal failure.

"I passed Level III that year, but the bigger test was the one I faced before the exam started."

—THOMAS B. WELCH, CFA, Eden Prairie, Minnesota, USA

recommended to the Select Committee a few years earlier. For example, moving all of the tools of investment analysis to Level I would correspond to Bloom's first level of cognition, namely, knowledge of facts and information. Such placement would make for an exam that logically "could become all objective"—that is, Level I could be composed entirely of multiple-choice questions. If it were all multiple choice, then it could be administered "more than once per year."[68]

Another change recommended for board consideration was that the subject mix at Level II be altered, with equity analysis decreasing from 50 percent to 30 percent of the exam, thereby allowing fixed-income analysis to "represent a larger portion of the exam," a change that reflected the growing importance of fixed-income analysis. Including questions that would "address the problem of international differences" was also considered. At Level III, the senior staff recommended that several case-based questions be given and that "alternative cases be presented so as to recognize international differences, client base differences, and other areas of specialization." Finally, rather than having prescribed readings in the Study Guides, committee members suggested that there be a "gradual movement away from specific to suggested readings in each topic area." A later iteration proposed that a "bibliography or reading list" might be offered to candidates at Levels II and III in lieu of a study guide.

At the May 1987 ICFA Board of Trustees meeting, and at many meetings throughout the next two years, the ICFA trustees considered these recommendations and their subsequent revisions. A current charterholder, or a current candidate, would find little that is controversial in most of these recommendations because many have been part of the CFA Program for years. An all-multiple-choice examination at Level I given more than once a year looks mighty familiar nowadays. Yet, it was a radical departure in 1987 when it was first recommended, and it met with resistance. Members of the Ad Hoc Committee on the CFA Program and ICFA trustees were reluctant then to depart from the tradition of CFA exams that contained "rigorous essay questions at all levels." They were also reluctant to break the "common bond" that "all 10,500 CFA charterholders have in terms of preparing for and passing three similar examinations."[69]

As it turned out, opinion among board members and volunteers from the COE and the CCC was divided on *every* recommended point in the 1987–89 study of the CFA Program except this one: moving to 100 percent multiple choice at Level I was *unanimously and strongly* rejected. By early 1989, the percentage of the Level I exam proposed for multiple-choice questions had been pared down from the originally suggested increase to 100 percent to a recommendation of 70–75 percent, and the change was to occur over a three-year period. Program reviewers thought that the ICFA needed more experience and training in developing consistently "rigorous" multiple-choice questions capable of discriminating fully between acceptable answers before Level I could become all multiple choice.[70] The idea of administering the test more than once a year, first proposed to the Ad Hoc Committee on the CFA Program in April 1987, had fallen away completely. In the meantime, the institute would begin "to develop a bank of multiple-choice questions internally" and planned to consult with "appropriate psychometricians to ensure proper difficulty and construction." As the 1990s unfolded, the methodology used by staff and volunteers for exam construction, especially for creating multiple-choice questions and assessing their effectiveness, would sharpen considerably.[71] In 1989, however, no one was willing to throw all their Level I questions in the multiple-choice basket quite yet.

Some issues from the CFA Program reviews undertaken by the ICFA volunteers and staff in the late 1980s attracted board support; others repelled it. A

EXAM STORIES: RAIN OR SHINE

"It was raining the morning of my exam, so I had to wear a rain jacket over the layers of clothing I was wearing in anticipation of any exam room conditions, hot or cold. I took the exam in a large Armory on the upper west side of Manhattan that had been converted into a track and field venue. There was ample natural light coming through the large windows located beneath the canopy covering the facility.

I didn't think I did as well as I would have liked on the first session and figured I didn't have much room for error during the second. Nonetheless, I enjoyed a nice lunch at a cafe nearby. By that point, the sun was out and it was beautiful day. Revived and in a positive state of mind, I sat for the second session with the intent of nailing it. Halfway through, I started to get a headache and I felt my head was going to explode. I sat up, stretched my muscles, and rubbed my neck—only to discover I was sunburned on one side of my face and neck. I got a drink of water, a long drink of water, which alleviated my headache somewhat, and put my rain jacket on with the hood over my head. I'm sure I looked ridiculous but I persevered, thanks to the rain in the morning. I earned my charter in 2009, and the other exams, while I wouldn't say they were pleasant experiences, went off without a hitch."

—STEPHEN J. BURNETT, CFA, New York City

"The year was 1981. Thankfully, it rained that June day in New York City or perhaps I would not have gotten my CFA charter. In the morning session of my first exam, I finished only a little more than half the questions as I badly allocated my time. I was depressed at lunch and seriously contemplated quitting. I love golf and tennis, but with the rain I figured why not prepare for next time by taking the afternoon session. Afterwards, I knew I had aced the afternoon but still expected to fail. Obviously, others must have had problems as well, as I was thrilled to find out in August that I had in fact passed. I got through the next two years without problems and I have proudly held the CFA designation for over 27 years. And for some reason, I never mind if it rains on that first Saturday in June!"

—JOHN M. MCMILLIN III, CFA, Jersey City, New Jersey, USA

few board members, for example, favored the idea of giving candidates bibliographies; others felt the candidates would be at sea without the guidance of "carefully planned-out programs of study."[72] Ultimately, giving a bibliography to candidates was neither supported by the review group nor recommended by the trustees. Yet, all agreed that in publishing its own study guides and books, the institute needed to be careful not to create in its readings "a 'Bible' of how to conduct investment analysis"—nor should it seem to be advocating "singular approaches to the concepts addressed in the curriculum."[73]

Most areas of the study and examination program were reviewed: exam length, grading criteria, and exam format. One proposal made in late 1987 was to reconsider the criteria for passing the exams, altering it from attaining a total passing score on the exam as a whole to a system that required each candidate to attain a passing score on *all* topics individually evaluated. That idea was rejected, and a total passing score at each level remained the standard for attaining a charter.

Because of the sheer number of topics that had been added to the Body of Knowledge in recent years, the trustees considered lengthening the exams. A list appended to an April 1988 report on the study program noted that between 1984 and 1988, 70 discrete additions had been made to the CFA Tree of Knowledge, as it was then called. This aspect is not surprising because, as one financial historian has noted, "The almost constant arrival of new financial products since the mid-seventies has been an unprecedented phenomenon in financial history."[74] While they recognized that the profession was expanding in scope, the reviewers were concerned that expanding the length of each exam might result in "question creep"—that is, "a natural tendency to cram [in] more questions since there was more time, instead of offering the same number but with more time for each."[75] The examinations stayed at six hours per level at that time and have ever since.

Interestingly, one change proposed in the late 1980s was a throwback to an idea considered—and rejected—at the start of the CFA Program, namely, having candidates write long papers instead of an exam. At the outset of planning the CFA exam program, the early trustees discussed having Level II be a thesis instead of a test (see Chapter 1). The acknowledged difficulty of assembling "thesis committees" to grade such a Level II project had eliminated it from consideration in 1963. The CFA Program review of the late 1980s, however, did not propose anything as lengthy as a thesis, but what it did consider was perhaps a more radical challenge. In its April 1988 report to the board, the review committee suggested a series of alternatives to the currently existing exam structure, the first of which was to "change the exam structure from three progressive levels [of tests] to a series of six, three-hour papers." The proposed six papers would be sequenced thus: The first would be on the fundamentals (accounting, economics, and quantitative techniques); the second on ethics and professional standards; the third on equity analysis; the fourth on fixed-income analysis; and the fifth on portfolio

EXAM STORY: AN EPIC EXAM TALE

"Coming from a middle-class background in a third-world country like Bangladesh, I find some of my professional achievements are near miracles, especially my attaining a CFA charter. In 1987, I was lucky to get a managerial job in a remittance company in Kuwait, managed by the bank I worked for in Bangladesh. This was the opportunity to work my way through to find a job in a good international bank or investment company. But to get a good job, my MBA from Dhaka University was not good enough. (A bank in Kuwait called me for an interview but refused to conduct my interview when they learned that my MBA was not from the USA.) I could not afford to pay for an MBA degree in the United States, as I needed to earn for my family. I am the eldest son of a family of nine brothers and sisters—so I needed a way around the problem.

"When I came to know about the CFA Program, I was in my fifth year of service, about 30 years old, and could see this was the program I had been looking for. So I started, and in 1989, I was the only one who qualified at Level I from Kuwait and the only one who did not work in an investment company. . . . I was well respected and promised a job at the earliest opening available. After [I had taken] the Level II exams, however, Kuwait was invaded by Iraq on 2nd August of 1990. I fled away by road through Iraq, Turkey,

Iran, Pakistan, and India to arrive in Bangladesh in December 1990.

"I [did] not even know my results of the CFA Level II exams, so I asked them to send me my results in Bangladesh. I was depressed, as the possibility of having a good career abroad was very slim again and with low salaries here I could not even continue with the CFA Program, so I wished I had failed Level II. But to my surprise, I did qualify. It made me more depressed as I felt that it would be utter stupidity to stop now after qualifying at two levels consecutively. Yet, I was unable to finance Level III, so I wrote to CFA Institute for a withdrawal explaining the reasons.

"I was not expecting any help from them, neither did I know about any scholarships or financial support programs. I was very sad and hopeless. Much to my surprise, the Institute again came to my rescue by offering a free-of-cost exam and a set of books. It was already March 1991, a little late for appearing for the exam in early June. Nevertheless, I knew I had to do it now or never. I agreed. Then I needed to register formally. Communications through letters were not very quick. I guess the Institute understood that, and I received a letter by DHL on 28 April 1991 asking me to confirm registration by 15 April if I was to sit for that year's exam. Now I really needed a time machine.

"To make things even more challenging, on 29 April, a hurricane devastated Bangladesh, destroying the only satellite link of the country [and] severing all international links. My intention to make a phone call or send a fax became impossible. I knew I had to do something—but what? I went around places to find a solution. I learnt that somehow the old telex links were working but the Institute did not have a telex. I had to think hard to find a solution again.

"I had a friend working in Dubai, so I sent a message to the AIG office in the UAE [United Arab Emirates] requesting them to send the message to my friend. My friend then confirmed my candidacy on my behalf to CFA Institute. This is how I completed my CFA exams. Following my appearance for the CFA Level III exams in 1991, Dhaka is now a regular CFA exam center. Dozens of candidates appear each year.

"Often, when I sit back and think what the inspiration was, and who ever helped me to achieve my goals, [I recognize that] my ambition was my inspiration and [that] help and encouragement from CFA Institute changed the course of my career. And this was the greatest help and inspiration I ever received from anyone, anywhere in my entire life. Thanks to CFA Institute!"

—MAHBUBUL ALAM, CFA, Bangladesh

Allan W.B. Gray, CFA, class of 1969, charterholder from South Africa.

management. The sixth and final paper would be an elective, or specialized, paper. A candidate could choose to write further on one of the five previous topics *or* choose something from a new topic area: derivative securities, real estate, or corporate finance, to cite a few. This proposal came in the context of attempting to weave more specialty material into the CFA Program, but it also was rejected. The process of grading CFA exams will be discussed later in the book, but at this point, one cannot help but wonder, if such a change had gone through, how many graders it would take to read papers at the fiscal 2011 level of enrollment (209,885 per year), and whether candidates would get their results back within the same decade the papers were submitted. Even more significant, as then Senior Managing Director Robert R. Johnson, CFA, pointed out, is the effect this proposal might have had on the meaning of the charter itself: "How would one value a CFA charter with a concentration in equity versus one with a concentration in fixed income? The strength of the program is that the letters mean the same thing" for everyone.[76]

The idea of specialization within the CFA Program is the topic that generated the most conversation among all these groups in the late 1980s—and one that would surface again in the 1990s. Should the program offer specialized or alternative questions at Levels II and III? Should there perhaps be a Level IV exam? Tom Bowman remembers the discourse on the topic of specialty exams this way:

> There was a debate going on in the late 1980s about specialization in the CFA Program. At the time, more and more niche positions were being created. You had hedge fund people, you had options and futures people, you had "quants," you had this, you had that . . . . There was a big push to have at least a portion of the exams [become] specialized. A person, for example, could elect, as part of the Level III exam, whether he or she wanted to take an equity analysis module or an options and futures [or] a derivatives module . . . to really hone in on their area of expertise or specialty.[77]

As in other areas under debate in the late 1980s, this topic provoked strong reactions on both sides of the issue. With the advent of "niche positions" and specialization within the profession, some board members believed the CFA Program must also specialize and the exam offer a means of testing specialized knowledge, at least electively. Others held strongly to the opinion that the CFA Program always had been and should always remain a generalist's program. Some argued that the ICFA could better address the specialization issue through the CE Program—perhaps via a Level IV examination, the passing of which would earn the charterholder a special, advanced designation. As with other proposed changes to the CFA Program that came about during the late 1980s review process, however, the concept of specialty exams did not take hold. A further, more intense look at the issue would take place in the 1990s, but at the January 1989 ICFA Board of Trustees meeting, where the Report of the Candidate Program

Review was debated and ultimately endorsed, the creation of a specialty examination was not recommended.

Given the dynamic nature of the profession, the CFA Program always needs reevaluating and updating. In the late 1980s, the senior staff, volunteers, committee members, and trustees—all spent many hours reviewing the program. When the review was completed, little was changed and the CFA Program was judged to be sound. Despite the lack of change at the time, however, Bowman maintained that it was "healthy for us to have evaluated our Program from a 'zero-base' standpoint, and to have gradually worked our way back close to our current structure" in the late 1980s review process. The zero-base approach had dictated that nothing should be held sacred in evaluating the program. Yet, even starting from that point, everything held:

> [T]he consensus at the time was that the CFA is the CFA. It is *a broad-based educational program*, and even if you happened to be an options and futures person, you really should understand other aspects of the body of knowledge. So, it was decided that the CFA exams would remain the same, from top to bottom. [Emphasis added.]

The next 10 years would bring so much change in the candidate base and in candidate numbers, not to mention upheaval and change within the profession of financial analysis itself, that those endorsing the CFA Program's soundness in 1989 would have to question it again, and review it from top to bottom once more. Interestingly, in the next decade, many of the reforms considered but rejected in the late 1980s would be adopted by those leading the CFA Program. By the end of the 1990s, moreover, few would recognize the institute (which would not even be called "the institute" by then). Yet, new and old charterholders alike would still be participating in a rigorous, generalist, "broad-based educational program"—even if the majority of those participating came from places and in numbers unimaginable in 1989.

THE FIRST GLIMMER OF GLOBALIZATION

The history of the CFA Program's expansion beyond North America will be taken up in the rest of this book, but it is important to note here that the second half of the 1980s marked the beginning of this worldwide momentum. In one sense, the CFA Program had always been international. Investment professionals in both the United States and Canada brought it into being. (Of the first 284 sitting for the 1963 exam, for instance, 7.5 percent were Canadian.) As early as April 1964, Abe Kulp was telling the first CFA charterholders that "analysts in a number of foreign countries have expressed interest in pursuing the C.F.A."[78] Yet, although technically "international," the CFA Program was for most of its first 25 years a decidedly North American enterprise. In the second half of the 1980s, that characteristic changed.

We have a duty to promote worldwide investing as a force for understanding and cooperation between peoples and nations. Through this effort, we can and do help all people worldwide to enjoy more prosperity, peace, and brotherhood.

—Sir John M. Templeton, CFA, dedication of the ICFA building, 5 April 1986

The path that led the CFA Program around the world began with a small enough step. In October 1984, ICFA Board of Trustees Chair Jay Vawter attended and participated in the Congress of the European Federation of Financial Analysts Societies (EFFAS) in Madrid. It proved to be a propitious step:

> In October of 1984 I was invited to the Madrid Conference of the European financial analysts, both to be a speaker, representing the Institute, and to get myself more acquainted with the foreign analyst community. I was greatly impressed by the interest in the Institute [among] officials of various European societies and decided it was time for the Institute to take a formal step into the international arena.[79]

At the 1985 FAF Annual Conference in Washington, DC, the ICFA formally joined the International Coordinating Committee, which at that time was composed of EFFAS, the Security Analysts Association of Japan, and analyst organizations from Brazil, South Africa, Australia, South Korea, New Zealand, Malaysia, and Hong Kong.

The trail blazed by Jay Vawter was soon well trodden. In August 1985, ICFA President Pete Morley traveled to England, India, Singapore, and Japan. In the next two years, ICFA staff and trustees undertook one overseas itinerary after another: October 1985, a dinner in London; January 1986, another trip to England, India, Singapore, Australia, and New Zealand; May 1986, attendance at a seminar cosponsored by the ICFA and the Society of Investment Analysts (SIA) in London. In October 1986, Vawter and Morley participated in the EFFAS congress in Florence, Italy, and journeyed again to India and England. In March 1987, a groundbreaking seminar on "global investment opportunities in the Pacific region" was held in Singapore and cosponsored by the ICFA and a number of "government/investment groups from the host nation."[80]

The Singapore Society of Financial Analysts, the first federation society outside North America, had come into being, under the visionary leadership of George E.K. Teo. Teo recalls being introduced to the CFA Program "around 1986 by Mr. Koh Beng Seng," who was then the deputy managing director of the Monetary Authority of Singapore.[81] Koh also introduced him to Pete Morley. According to Teo, Koh "saw the CFA Program as a way of raising the standards of financial analy-

Sir John M. Templeton, CFA (at the podium), commemorating the opening of the new ICFA headquarters in 1986. Seated (left to right): Pete Morley, CFA; Ted Muller, CFA; and John Maginn, CFA.

sis of market participants in Singapore's fund management industry and capital markets." Although he was "on the sell side of the securities industry," Teo "undertook the challenge to promote the CFA Program in Singapore." Within a year, the first CFA examinations were conducted there.

Pete Morley wrote about his extensive second trip abroad in the April 1987 *CFA Newsletter* in an article titled "Around the World in Eighteen Days." Morley, informing members of his work on two continents, noted that he had "literally circled the world," stopping in Tokyo, Hyderabad (India), Hong Kong, Singapore, London, and Paris. He was traveling toward the stated ICFA goal of taking a "leading position in enhancing professionalism and the body of knowledge in line with the increasing globalization of the capital markets."[82] Already, things were beginning to happen. Morley reported that a publisher in Japan was in the process of translating the early edition of *Managing Investment Portfolios* into Japanese at the request of the Asian Security Analysts Council. According to Gentaro Yura, executive managing director of the Security Analysts Association of Japan (SAAJ) at the time, Maginn and Tuttle's text was considered to be the "best book to learn the basic theory and practice of portfolio management" and was thus "worthy of translation into Japanese."[83] Yura credited Pete Morley with the idea of having the book translated, a work that was carried out by "a team of 18 experts selected from all departments of the then Nikko Securities Group." The translators were supervised by Mamoru Aoyama of Yokohama National University—who would later perform another important translation function for the CFA Program (see Chapter 5). In a gesture of reciprocity predictive of international things to come, John Maginn suggested to the ICFA Board of Trustees one year later that "texts from Japan and London should be seriously considered for the CFA curriculum."[84]

During this period, the ICFA was engaging in discussions with SIA (London) and SAAJ concerning the possibility of reciprocal examination programs. Pete Morley and Tom Bowman worked with Gentaro Yura of SAAJ and Anthony H. Newman of SIA, both of whose organizations had testing programs of their own. SAAJ, which dated from 1962, was almost as old as the ICFA and had offered an Executive/Examination Program for the CMA Charter since 1977. The SIA had been offering examinations since 1979.

At around the same time, Morley met Beat Gerber of Schweizerische Bankgesellschaft (SBG), known also as Union Bank of Switzerland, or UBS. Gerber, who noted that there were no formal or systematic education programs for analysts in Switzerland at the time, was visiting New York in 1987 looking for a program UBS employees might use. Gerber continued:

George E.K. Teo was the first president (1987–2001) of the first member society in Asia, located in Singapore.

The five Chartered Financial Analysts being congratulated by Mr. Stephan Haeringer, Executive Vice President (left), and Mr. Alfred Morley, Senior Adviser to the Institute of Chartered Financial Analysts (right).

"An important step in your professional career"

First Graduates of UBS-CFA Program Honored

On November 21, Mr. Alfred Morley, CFA, Senior Advisor to the Institute of Chartered Financial Analysts (ICFA), presented five UBS employees with their CFA charters in Zurich. They are the first graduates of the three year sequential study and examination program which UBS has supported since 1987.

Mr. Morley congratulated the successful participants on their formidable achievement which attests to their competence, perseverance and willingness to make an extraordinary effort. Becoming a CFA is an important step in your professional career, but your training as an investment professional can never stop, since the industry is always evolving. CFAs automatically become members of the Association for Investment Management and Research (AIMR) which will keep them informed of new developments. Mr. Morley encouraged the new CFAs to keep up-to-date.

Mr. Morley also praised UBS for its exemplary support of candidates in the CFA program. He expressed particular thanks to Dr. Beat Gerber as father of the CFA program at UBS and presented him with a Certificate of Appreciation by the Board of Directors of ICFA.

The presentation took place at a special luncheon for the new CFAs hosted by Mr. Stephan Haeringer, Executive Vice President in charge of the Financial Division. Mr. Haeringer congratulated the newly chartered CFAs for being the first to realize a vision, namely to improve the professional skills of UBS employees in the financial departements through the successful completion of the UBS-CFA program. By becoming CFAs they have identified themselves as having high standards. They must realize that expectations on them are equally high. He also expressed special thanks for the support of the candidates' wives or girl friends which is critical to success. As a token of appreciation of the Bank he handed each CFA a well-deserved bonus.

Dr. Gerber presented a brief review of the history of the CFA program at UBS. It all started back in 1987 when he met Mr. Morley by chance in an elevator in New York! Since then, there have been excellent relations and close cooperation between ICFA and UBS. The experience with the joint program has been very encouraging and the interest among UBS staff is still growing. Indeed, for the 1990/91 CFA courses the following number of participants have registered to date: 53 Level I, 24 Level II and 11 Level III. We have now reached a well-balanced program with all three levels running in parallel. It includes an orientation meeting in July for UBS employees interested in joining the program (the next one is already scheduled for July 26, 1991!), and two training seminars in finance sponsored by the Bank (in January and May). These are led by a faculty of highly qualified and experienced university professors from the United States (see box), headed by Prof. Richard McEnally, Professor of Investment Banking at the University of North Carolina.

Dr. Gerber then read a letter from Prof. McEnally addressed to the new CFAs, in which he expressed his pride in their accomplishment and assured them that he would be watching their career progress at Union Bank of Switzerland with the greatest interest.

Dr. Gerber also expressed his deep appreciation to Mr. Bernhard Huber, Head of Training in the Financial Division, for his invaluable support in the organization and infrastructure of the courses and seminars. He thanked Dr. Hermann Attinger, AIPA, for his administrative support and his role as liaison person with the seminar faculty.

With the UBS-CFA program entering its fourth year, Dr. Gerber considers it the appropriate educational answer to the ongoing globalization of the financial markets and the heightened competition within the international financial industry. To stay in the forefront of the investment community we need a sound, modern and continuously updated financial education program. The effort and money put in by both the candidates and the Bank are well invested toward facing the challenges of the future.

Hermann Attinger, Ph. D., AIPM/AIPA

Erfolgreiche SBG-CFA-Absolventen

Am 21. November konnten die ersten fünf SBG-Absolventen des Hauptsitzes sowie ein Mitarbeiter der UBS Securities Inc., New York, nach dreijähriger Ausbildung das begehrte CFA (Chartered Financial Analyst)-Diplom entgegennehmen.

Die Übergabe erfolgte in kleinem Kreis und in Anwesenheit von Mr. Alfred Morley, Senior Adviser im Institute of Chartered Financial Analysts (ICFA), und GD Stephan Haeringer. Beide unterstrichen in ihrer Gratulationsadresse die Bedeutung des CFA-Diploms, das als Auszeichnung darauf hinweist, dass der Diplominhaber zum Kreis der «Investment Professionals» gehört. Zur Unterstützung ihrer Kandidaten führt die SBG jährlich zwei CFA-Seminarien durch, die von anerkannten amerikanischen Finanzprofessoren bestritten werden. Studium und Examen erfolgen ausnahmslos auf englisch.

Das Diplom erhielten:

| Wilfried Ospelt, AFWE/AFON | Jürg Schiller, AIPM/AIPA | Christoph Schweizer, AIPM/AIPE | Patrick Senn, ANI2/ANZ7 | Dr. Thomas Vock, AIPM/AIPF | Dr. Joachim Rudolf, UBS Securities Inc., New York |

CFA Seminar Faculty

Topic covered at UBS Seminar

● Richard W. McEnally, "Dean" CFA	Professor of Investment Banking University of North Carolina, Chapel Hill	Ethics, Quantitative Analysis, Derivatives, Fixed Income Analysis
● William E. Avera CFA	Principal in FINCAP, Inc. Financial Consulting, Austin, Texas	Ethics
● O. Whitfield Broome, Jr., CPA	Professor of Commerce University of Virginia	Accounting
● Randall S. Billingsley CFA	Assoc. Professor of Finance Virginia Polytechnic Institute and State University	Equity Analysis
● Keith C. Brown CFA	Assist. Professor of Finance University of Texas, Austin	Economics, Quantitative Analysis
● Don M. Chance CFA	Professor of Finance Virginia Polytechnic Institute and State University	Fixed Income Analysis, Derivatives
● Ronald E. Copeley CFA	Assoc. Professor of Finance University of North Carolina, Wilmington	Equity Analysis, Portfolio Management
● Richard F. DeMong CFA	Professor of Commerce McIntire School of Commerce, University of Virginia	Portfolio Management, Equity Analysis
● Donald E. Fischer CFA	Professor of Finance The University of Texas, Tyler	Economics, Portfolio Management
● Aki G. Pampush CFA, CPA	Vice President, Trustco Capital Management Atlanta, Georgia	Fixed Income Analysis
● Kathrin F. Staley CFA	Principal of Staley & Co. Investment Management Atlanta, Georgia	Equity Analysis
● Rebecca B. Todd CFA	Assist. Professor of Accounting New York University	Accounting

UBS publication recognizing new charterholders. Photo courtesy of Group Long-Term Archives, UBS

I realized that we (i.e., SBG, the Swiss bank) had to [make] a special effort in training the bank's employees in economics, financial accounting and ethical matters. I was [wondering] about the best program for that very purpose. Clearly, the CFA Program was in my mind. When I took the lift to go out for lunch in the spring of 1987 I happened to observe a gentleman with CFA papers fixed under his left arm. I briefly introduced myself to the gentleman, who turned out to be Alfred Morley, [of] the Institute of Chartered Financial Analysts. We were both in a hurry, quickly exchanged business cards and promised to keep in touch, which indeed was the case....[85]

Their contacts continued, and soon, Union Bank of Switzerland started its own internal CFA review course, with Richard W. McEnally, CFA, acting as its head. By 1990, the first UBS employees to take the CFA Program had received their charters. Tom Bowman attended an early ceremony:

I remember being asked to either the first or second luncheon to award CFA charters [at UBS]. There were probably eight people at the lunch from UBS who had gotten their charters. Now, of course, it is in the hundreds, maybe more. But it was that first elevator meeting with Pete and Beat that really planted the CFA flag in Europe.[86]

By the end of the 1980s, Pete Morley, an "ambassador" for the ICFA, in John Maginn's words,[87] was reporting to the ICFA Board of Trustees that "the number of candidates outside the U.S. and Canada has exploded."[88] Indeed it had. As recently as 1984, candidates taking the CFA exams outside North America numbered only "79 persons at 13 locations."[89] By 1988, that number had increased

(left to right)

Chu Ching Ming, CFA, class of 1984, charterholder from Hong Kong.

E.M. Burrows Poitier, CFA, class of 1981, charterholder from the Bahamas.

Location	Expected Number of Candidates
New York, New York, USA	1,450
Toronto, Ontario, Canada	700
Boston, Massachusetts, USA	500
Chicago, Illinois, USA	470
Los Angeles, California, USA	330
San Francisco, California, USA	310
Singapore	260
Washington, DC, USA	250
Montreal, Quebec, Canada	240
Hartford, Connecticut, USA	230

Of the 90 exam centers worldwide, the exam centers that were experiencing the most rapid growth of candidates outside North America were Singapore (260), Tokyo (150), Zurich (90), London (75), and Hong Kong (70).

to nearly 600, with more than 40 UBS employees alone sitting for the exam in Zurich. Although these numbers would soon be overshadowed by those from the 1990s and although much about globalizing remained to be settled—including languages to be used, ethical standards, even the timing of the examinations once the international dateline was crossed —the work done by the early leaders on globalization in the late 1980s set the institute on a course from which it has never wavered.

Most remarkably, this global work—as well as that of establishing the CE Program and scrutinizing the CFA Program itself—was taken up at a time when the institute was undergoing one of its most difficult periods. As detailed in the next chapter, the years from 1987 to 1989 were characterized by a lengthy, complicated, and often exhausting debate over the possibility of combining the ICFA with the FAF. In light of this situation, it may be a wonder anything else got done. Those entrusted with the CFA Program, however, held firm, shielded it from distraction, and much was accomplished.

chapter four

The Merger Years: 1987–1989

*L*ingering behind all the program scrutiny, expanded offerings, and global outreach undertaken by the Institute of Chartered Financial Analysts in the 1980s was a crucial question: What was the right relationship between the ICFA and its parent organization, the Financial Analysts Federation? As detailed in Chapter 1, the ICFA owed its very existence to the FAF. The debate about professionalizing financial analysts arose within the National Federation of Financial Analysts Societies, as the FAF was called in the 1940s and 1950s. Federation directors were the ones who decided to go forward with a CFA Program in 1959 and provided seed money for it. Those designing a certification program were federation members, as were all who took the first CFA examinations. In every sense, the CFA Program emerged from the FAF. The ICFA was a "de facto educational creation of the FAF," as Robert B. Hardaway, Jr., CFA, former president of the Los Angeles Society and a longtime CFA exam grader, put it.[1]

When it came time to set up a CFA examination program, however, FAF leaders deliberately did *not* make it part of the federation. As a confederation of societies, the FAF lacked the centralization needed to administer a national examination program. Moreover, the founders of the CFA Program wanted a formal university affiliation for the program, realizing that would give the program cachet as well as access to people comfortable working with graduate-level finance curricula and those with knowledge about constructing examinations. A university location, moreover, would have the salutary effect of removing the CFA Program from the tumult of Wall Street, assuring its independence. Thus, they set the CFA Program up within a freestanding institute, the ICFA.

Talk of joining the ICFA and FAF into one organization began less than a decade after the first CFA exams were given in 1963. In 1972, FAF President Robert T. Morgan, CFA, and ICFA President Frank E. Block, CFA, met to discuss the desirability of a merger. Soon afterward, Block asked Edmund A. Mennis, CFA, immediate past president of the ICFA, to envision what a single professional organization for analysts might look like.[2] Mennis proposed a centralized institution

The matter of overriding importance was to have faith in an "over the horizon" vision of what the profession could become if we united our talent, energy and resolve.

—Eugene H. Vaughan, Jr., CFA, first chair of AIMR, notes for a keynote address and conversations with John G. Gillis, 2010

ICFA/FAF/AIMR headquarters from 1986 to 1999 in Charlottesville.

with direct, individual membership, uniting the work of the institute, federation, and even the Research Foundation into one multifaceted entity. Although the ICFA trustees approved the idea in principle, as long as it did not "diminish the significance of the CFA charter," CFA charterholders rejected the idea at their 1973 annual meeting.[3] Institute members were unwilling to sacrifice purity for the power of large numbers.

In the meantime, the FAF was taking steps to support the CFA Program, led by FAF President (later, ICFA Chair) Eugene H. "Gene" Vaughan, CFA, and based on work by Walter P. "Wally" Stern, CFA, and the Committee on Qualifications in the 1970s. On 28 April 1974, the delegates of the FAF member societies approved the new "FAF Private Self Regulation Program" and amended the FAF bylaws. These amendments, among other things, established a class of individual membership in the FAF for persons who were also regular members of a member society. As of 31 December 1976, all new regular members of member societies (who were thereby also FAF individual members) had to pass the CFA Level I examination. Voting rights remained with the member society delegates.

For the next 15 years, merger discussions continued to percolate, sometimes breaking through to the surface, sometimes quietly bubbling just beneath. As part of a 1983 strategic planning process, for example, ICFA Board of Trustees President Charles D. Ellis, CFA, examining the relationship of the two organizations, questioned "how [best] to work with the FAF."[4] In 1984, a "first step" was taken, Ellis noted, when the ICFA agreed to "find ways to work jointly with the FAF where cost savings would make sense and cooperatively with the FAF when we can define separate spheres of responsibility, and, in the process, avoid duplication or conflict." Two years later, in April 1986, merger ideas were nudged forward when Frederick L. "Ted" Muller, CFA, then incoming FAF president, raised the issue at the celebration of the 25th anniversary of the ICFA: "At the dedication of the new ICFA headquarters building in Charlottesville, I stuck my neck out . . . to address the assembled celebrants, by making a public plea to engage in a serious effort to bring about a merger."[5] Muller urged both boards to "move forward" in an "enlightened direction."

Certainly, these two organizations had overlapping interests and many shared members. Sometimes, this meant that the ICFA and FAF worked together: establishing a joint committee on professional standards, adopting substantially similar codes of ethics and standards of professional conduct, and having standards enforcement programs. At other times, however, there was duplicated effort, even a sense of rivalry. According to Bernadette B. Murphy, 1988–89 FAF chair, the two groups were "falling into a competitive mode" by the mid-1980s. Had it continued, it would have been "damaging to both organizations."[6] One way to avoid duplication of effort and eliminate rivalry, of course, was to join the two organizations into one—a family reunion of large proportions, with significant implications for the profession.

Between 1987 and 1989, just such a reunion was planned.

THE FIRST GREAT DEBATE

In the first great debate concerning financial analysts, which took place in 1945, Benjamin Graham and Lucien O. Hooper, CFA, sparred over whether security analysts should have a professional rating. The second great debate came 40 years later. This time, the issue was not whether financial analysis was a profession and thus deserving of some kind of program for professional designation. Instead, the debate of the late 1980s centered on whether the profession of financial analysis would be better served by having only one professional organization. Within the ICFA, a further debate ensued over whether the CFA Program, by then in existence for more than 25 years, could stay as single-minded within a large, diverse, multi-focused organization as it had been within the clearly focused Institute of Chartered Financial Analysts.

Both organizations occupied the world of financial analysis and investment management and, in fact, had many members in common. As FAF Chair Murphy noted in 1989, almost 67 percent of all CFA charterholders were society members and for years, charterholders had made up 80 percent of the FAF board.[7] Yet, the ICFA and the FAF were *very* different. In form, function, and culture, they were worlds apart. The FAF had begun in 1947 as a creation of four large local societies and added scores of new societies over the decades. It continued to be controlled by member societies' representatives. Even though a class of individual FAF members (who were also regular members of member societies) was established in 1974 and passing the CFA Level I exam was required of new members beginning in 1977, all voting rights remained with the societies. Through its national officers and board, the FAF had established a strong presence with U.S. federal regulators and Congress beginning in the early 1970s and was the "voice" of the profession for improved flow and quality of corporate information, regulation of the profession, and other national issues. However, as noted by Hardaway, the FAF was "profoundly federative in nature" with autonomous societies—each of which had a unique leadership structure.[8] The ICFA was entirely different. An "autonomous educational enterprise of near academic standing and substance," Hardaway continued, the ICFA was a "credentialing agency." As such, it was best kept "aloof from the hurly-burly of the day-to-day activities of the FAF and local constituent societies." It had to be "single minded in its mission," whereas the FAF could not be.

Others also saw this telling distinction. As Charley Ellis put it, the FAF had "specific complexities" built into its very nature and often had "political difficulties" in its functioning.[9] The ICFA, in contrast, "was a simple, unified organization reporting directly to its members and focused on one inspiring mission that was increasingly successful in adding value." Those distinctions would be expressed in various ways throughout the merger debate: purity versus politics, elitists versus egalitarians, exclusivists versus inclusivists, or even Athenian democrats (one charterholder, one vote) versus American federalists (only society representatives vote at the national level).

There was another important contrast. Like a healthy child, the CFA Program was beginning to outstrip its parent. The ICFA had overcome the financial problems it faced in the 1970s and grown very prosperous by 1987—able to fund expanded opportunities for its members and add professional staff to manage its burgeoning growth. Although the FAF had not remained static—growing from five founding societies in 1947 to 59 societies 40 years later[10]—it was, nonetheless, experiencing serious financial difficulties.

As the debate over combining with the FAF took shape among the ICFA Board of Trustees in 1987, three main issues emerged for those entrusted with the CFA Program. Trustee Daniel J. Forrestal III, CFA, who became the designated ICFA negotiator that same year (Wallace B. Millner III, CFA, was the designated negotiator for the FAF), summarized the issues: First, there was a financial risk, given the federation's deficit; second, there was a risk to the "identity" of the CFA charter, depending on how membership in the new organization was defined; and, third, there was a risk to the ability of the ICFA (board and staff) "to control the destiny of the Institute."[11] In considering a merger, the ICFA board was willing to look hard at what was best for the entire profession, as the outgoing chair, James N. von Germeten, CFA, encouraged. But first, they were concerned about what was best for the institute and the CFA Program. How would membership be determined in a blended organization? As Eugene C. Sit, CFA, put it, the difficulty was that, although 8,000 FAF members were charterholders, there were "another 8,000 who choose not to be accredited."[12] "How," he wondered, "do we come to terms with that if there is one organization?" Sit was putting his finger on what would determine whether a healthy combination could be made. What would it mean to be a member of the blended organization? Who would belong when only half of current FAF members had elected to go through the rigors of the CFA Program?

As noted in Chapter 3, eligibility issues had concerned ICFA leaders from the CFA Program's inception. During the merger discussions, the significance of eligibility grew. Unlike the law or medicine, where eligibility requirements were well delineated, one trustee noted, "In our business, it's not so clear," because "almost anybody can offer financial advice."[13] For a merger to work, trustees would "have to be tough on membership requirements." Another trustee, expressing similar doubts, declared, "Talking about membership requirements confirms my worst anxieties."[14] He wondered whether membership issues would result in "dual classes of citizenship" and how any organization could cope with that.

Also of serious concern was the financial state of the FAF and what that might mean for the CFA Program. By the late 1980s, the ICFA had accumulated a substantial reserve fund and seen its revenues grow. Because of this, it had been able to hire more staff to meet the needs of an increasing—and geographically expanding—population of candidates as well as to fund a continuing education program for members that offered seminars, published proceedings, and some books. The ICFA Board of Trustees could afford to hire the staff to run a member program. At the same time, the FAF was in serious financial difficulties, despite cost-cutting measures instituted by Alfred C. "Pete" Morley, CFA, in his capacity as its president and CEO. Merging with the ICFA would help right this listing ship.

Several ICFA trustees cast a wary eye at such a prospect. One trustee not feeling sanguine at all was James R. Vertin, CFA, who stated flatly, "I am implacably opposed to the merger."[15] Vertin's opposition lay in his deep concern for protecting the CFA Program, but he also expressed disquiet about FAF finances and asked—using a metaphor that would be picked up by other board members and revised by one—"If you are in the water with someone who is drowning, do you want to put yourself in that position or not?" Trustee George W. Noyes, CFA, also expressed doubts about "the prospect of rescuing a drowning organization."[16] Did the ICFA want to effect a rescue at the risk of being pulled under?

The most compelling issue for the ICFA trustees, however, was maintaining the integrity of the CFA charter and retaining their ability to do so. The ICFA was single-mindedly focused on the CFA Program. It was responsible for maintaining

HISTORICAL SPOTLIGHT

Tom Bowman, CFA, remembers that at the September 1987 dinner meeting, each ICFA trustee found at his or her place a copy of *Getting to Yes* (a book on successful negotiation by Roger Fisher, William Ury, and Bruce Patton)—all provided by Charley Ellis, CFA. It was, Bowman recalls, a disarming gesture that helped "relieve the tension."[19]

and upgrading the curriculum and Body of Knowledge; for creating, administering, and grading all CFA exams; and for awarding all charters. In its program for CFA charterholders, it was responsible for continuing education, for enforcing procedures against ethics violations, and if necessary, revoking charters. If the CFA Program became part of a larger organization that focused on many things, would the charter's luster be maintained? Vertin, for one, did not want to see the ICFA become a "white knight" nor to create "an organization that doesn't contain only CFA charterholders." Other trustees asked whether blending the ICFA and FAF together would "dilute" the value of the CFA charter.[17] How would that sit with "the 10,000 individuals who have worked hard for the charter, revere it highly and who want no lessening of standards?" Dan Forrestal asked.[18] ICFA leaders and ordinary charterholders alike were keenly aware that having attained the CFA designation was an *achievement*. They had studied for three difficult examinations, mastered a body of ever-expanding knowledge, and shown the tenacity to take exams over if not successful the first time. To them, the CFA charter was what C. Stewart Sheppard had called a "public warranty" of professionalism. If the ICFA combined with the FAF, what would membership in the new organization mean?

Membership. Integrity. Rescue—These were at issue.

THE PROCESS BEGINS: 1987

In August and September 1987, the ICFA Board of Trustees met with Charley Ellis, who had been asked to study how the two organizations might combine and "come up with a solution that makes sense to the industry."[20] Ellis had already presented his findings to the FAF Board of Directors in September 1987, which expressed interest in pursuing some combination of the two analyst groups, and he acknowledged that he expected to recommend to the FAF directors that they "re-constitute themselves" into a national organization. "Other than that," Ellis noted, "I have no final conclusions."

Reaction from the trustees ranged widely, but Ellis saw the ICFA debate as between "optimists and realists." The optimists, he said, "focused on the overall profession and its needs as we saw them—in the abstract."[21] The realists looked at the actual, contrasting organizations and found many reasons why they might not fit together well. Among all the ICFA trustees, however—whether optimist or realist—reservations centered on the three main issues: membership qualifications (that is, who would belong to a reconstituted organization?); maintaining high professional standards (would the CFA charter retain its identity and value?); and the troubled finances of the FAF (would the ICFA be pulled under?). Of these, Pete Morley concluded, the most important problem was: "Who belongs?"[22]

No trustee wished to see the CFA Program sink under the weight of the FAF's current difficulties or to tarnish in any way the significance of the CFA charter, and no one wished to turn over the future of the program to anyone who had not earned the CFA designation. Yet, because virtually all saw that true benefits might accrue from combining the two organizations, they knew that these issues would have to be faced. To Gene Vaughan, who had lived with the merger idea since he was FAF president in 1973–1974, there was no turning away. "I'm concerned about the drowning man analogy," he had said at the close of the ICFA Board of Trustees meeting in May 1987. In the "broad professional sense," he reminded his fellow trustees, the two organizations were not drowning parent and rescuing child. Rather, he concluded, they were "Siamese twins."[23]

In the "considerable discussion" that took place during 1987, no clear consensus emerged. Rather, trustees voiced "repeated concerns" that there be no "loss or dilution of identity of the Institute in general, and [the CFA] charter in particular."[24] As fiduciaries, the trustees needed to be confident that they were protecting the integrity of the CFA charter.

Each organization brought different concerns to the table, of course. The work of the two negotiators, Forrestal and Millner, was to represent their respective sides while moving the process forward. According to Ted Muller, the two men charged with this delicate task "did not disappoint, with their unselfish and enlightened efforts to move the two organizations to the final stages of voting on the merger."[25] Because of "the integrity and soundness of their efforts as negotiators," he continued, "the profession owes Dan and B. its full gratitude for a job superbly done."

For the ICFA, protecting the value of the CFA charter was paramount. ICFA trustees insisted that leaders of the new organization would have to be char-

HISTORY REPEATS ITSELF?

While the merger process moved slowly forward during 1987, practicing analysts had enough other things on their minds to let it rest. "Black Monday," 19 October 1987, sent markets crashing in every time zone in the world and showed the largest one-day drop by percentage in the history of stock markets. Those who had been party to the first serious merger discussions in 1973–1974 must have wondered if the mere mention of the word "merger" was enough to send markets into a tailspin, because 1973 and 1974 had seen a bear market collapse of nearly 50 percent, one characterized by steep ups and downs, although nothing as spectacular as the one-day drop in 1987.

(left) Daniel J. Forrestal III, CFA, served as ICFA negotiator.

(right) Wallace B. Millner III, CFA, served as FAF negotiator. Photo courtesy of Dementi Foster Studios

Bernadette B. Murphy served as FAF chair for 1988–1989. Walter R. Wiese Photography

terholders (at least after a certain brief period of settling in). Grandfathering was not desired. Moreover, membership standards would have to be kept high—if not as high as requiring that *all* members be charterholders, then at least that all pass the Level I CFA exam (as the FAF had required for all new regular members since 1977) and that, perhaps over time, all would hold charters. In addition, membership in any combined organization would have to be individual, not through local societies. Equally important, the finances of the CFA Program would have to be shielded in some way.

On the FAF side, some of the societies, especially the larger societies, feared losing autonomy and individual society control and feared that all members would be required to become charterholders.[26] Bernadette Murphy recalled that from the FAF point of view, it was essential that becoming a CFA charterholder be optional, not required, for membership in the combined entity.[27] Both sides, of course, wanted high ethical standards safeguarded.

THE PROCESS CONTINUES: 1988

By September 1988, FAF Chair Murphy was reporting to the ICFA that federation finances were looking better and the concept of one-share, one-vote was advancing among FAF delegates, which would greatly improve the chances for a merger because the ICFA trustees had insisted that any new organization have individual (not society) members. ICFA Chair Gene Sit indicated that a draft proposal for a merged organization would be ready "in about three weeks."[28]

Once framed, any draft proposal would have to be approved by many different bodies, in sequence. The executive committees and full boards of both organizations would have to approve. Should the FAF formally move to having individual voting members (not just delegates voting on behalf of societies plus nonvoting individual members), the "new" individual FAF members would also have to approve the proposal, by a two-thirds majority, at its annual conference scheduled for Montreal in May. If individual FAF members approved, then FAF society delegates would have to approve the proposal in June. In August, the ICFA trustees would also have to approve it or reject modifications of the original agreement. Finally, in October, the CFA charterholders would have to approve it, by a simple majority.

This complex system of voting set up some interesting possibilities. CFA charterholders who were members of societies (and most were) and individual FAF members who were also charterholders might vote twice. CFA charterholders who were delegates from societies might vote three times—or four (or five!)—if they were also board members of either or both organizations. This long and cumbersome process, in one sense, epitomized the duplication of effort the merger was meant to eradicate. It was also a true attestation of the radical shift that any such combination would represent within the profession: Everything needed consequential consideration at every level.

Throughout 1988, representatives of both organizations communicated weekly, and often met personally, to build the mutual understanding and confidence that would be necessary to effect the combination. Moreover, the process was advanced because of the trust among many individuals who bridged both organizations, including Gene Vaughan, Wally Stern (who had been chair of both the ICFA and FAF), negotiators B. Millner and Dan Forrestal, and several members of the current and past ICFA and FAF boards.

A draft proposal called an "Operating Plan of Combination" was being considered by the boards of the ICFA and FAF. It called for the establishment of an overarching entity, a holding company tentatively called the Investment Professionals Association (IPA), within which the FAF and the ICFA would continue to exist and retain their own boards and some of their own committees. The IPA would also have a separate board of governors composed of nine members each from the ICFA and FAF. Pete Morley and FAF Chair Bernadette Murphy crisscrossed the country visiting societies to answer questions, explain the proposal, and drum up support for the new organization, much as Stewart Sheppard had traveled from coast to coast promoting the CFA Program nearly 30 years before. At one point, both Morley and Murphy ended up in Chicago, along with ICFA negotiator, Dan Forrestal, for what must have been a highly informative session.

Walter P. Stern, CFA, served as president of the ICFA board for 1976–1977 and the FAF board for 1971–1972. Elson Alexandre Photography

SECOND GREAT DEBATE AND RESOLUTION: 1989

As 1989 dawned, the final round of the second great debate was near. In January, the New York Society of Security Analysts (NYSSA) voted against the merger; the Boston Society did the same in February. These intrasociety votes were not binding but did give a good indication of how delegates from large societies felt about the issue at that time. In March, the negative society trend continued as an initial vote in Chicago went against the merger. One problem manifesting among some society members in Chicago was that members had "come to the conclusion that the merger was really a disguised hostile takeover of the FAF by the ICFA and had persuaded others to take a position in opposition," as Michael L. McCowin, CFA, past president of the Investment Analysts Society of Chicago, put it.[29] In 1989, the words "hostile takeover" resonated loudly to analysts and investment managers

SOME UNWELCOME PUBLICITY

Just two weeks before the ICFA and FAF annual meetings were to take place, *Barron's* magazine published an article that must have set many members' teeth on edge.[30] Written by Diana Henriques, now a senior financial writer for the *New York Times*, the article was entitled "Analysts, Unite!" and reported largely from the side of those opposed to the merger, who were not shy about expressing their antagonism. Henriques noted, for instance, that a leader of the "Boston Security Analysts Society reportedly plans to tote symbolic teabags to Montreal to illustrate his conviction that the dues provisions of the merger plan constituted 'taxation without representation'"—an act of political theater 20 years ahead of its time. The article also reported that members of NYSSA, which had voted down the merger in January, had ordered campaign buttons with a "Ghostbusters" motif. Others, the article added, "had disparaged the merger" as one that would make non-charterholders into second-class citizens and typified "creeping credentialism."

Although the views of the ICFA on the merger received some attention, the article indicated that the major hurdle to a merger was concern among some FAF member societies over the one-member, one-vote rule (direct elections on main issues). It gave scant mention to what most concerned members and leaders of the ICFA: the criteria for membership and leadership (the CFA charter), control of the CFA Program, and the issue that had started the entire conversation in the first place: *Who speaks for analysts?* Near the article's close, Pete Morley, CFA, was quoted, and he cited a telling example, "A few months ago, we had the opportunity to have one hour with the chief counsel of the Securities and Exchange Commission to talk about the language of the proposed insider-trading legislation, and we spent fully half of that time answering his questions about the difference between the FAF and the ICFA." For Morley, the bottom line was "to have one voice that speaks for the profession."

who were coping in their daily work lives with all too many hostile takeovers. This was the era of junk bonds and of corporate raiders, Carl Icahn, Ivan Boesky, and Michael Milken.

On 3 March, the FAF Board of Directors voted to approve the "Operating Plan of Combination" but with some crucial modifications—including a new provision that the officers of the new organization need *not* be CFA charterholders. When the revision was presented to the ICFA Board of Trustees three days later, they viewed it as a rejection of the previously agreed upon version of the Operating Plan and, in turn, rejected the modifications. On 10 March, the FAF board reconvened and, in a split vote, approved the originally agreed Operating Plan of Combination. Three days later, the ICFA reaffirmed its approval of the plan but added two conditions: (1) They required vote approval percentages for FAF societies and individual members and for ICFA members, and (2) they wanted evidence of broad support within the largest FAF societies. On 4 April 1989, ICFA Chair Gene Sit and FAF Chair Bernadette Murphy signed a Memorandum of Understanding containing the Operating Plan of Combination. After 15 years of consideration and two years of intense negotiation, agreement for a combination of the ICFA and the FAF had finally been reached.

The remaining obstacles to a merger were faced in the middle of 1989. In May, individual FAF members voted directly for the first time at a formal meeting that FAF Chair Bernadette Murphy opened by noting the passing of Lucien Hooper, CFA, Ben Graham's antagonist in the 1945 debate on whether "security analysts" should have a professional rating. The individual FAF members favored the proposal by a margin of 61.6 percent to 38.4 percent. Ironically, the ICFA Board of Trustees, wishing to see widespread support within the federation, had required a two-thirds majority of individual FAF members for passage, with the same percentage (67) needed also from the eventual delegate vote. The ICFA trustees had particularly wanted to see demonstrably "strong support" from within the six largest societies—New York, Boston, Chicago, Toronto, San Francisco, and Los Angeles—whose members made up the overall majority of individual FAF members, but it did not come. A telephone conference was convened, and after a lengthy, contentious debate, the ICFA trustees agreed to accept 61.6 percent as sufficient and let the proposal move forward.

On 30 June 1989, delegates from the FAF societies voted to approve the merger proposal, with 75 percent favoring the combination. NYSSA, the largest FAF society, remained opposed but did not, as had been feared, secede from the federation. CFA charterholders were scheduled to vote in October; prior to that, the ICFA board was to send the members its recommendation for approval or disapproval. Two years into the merger discussions, what exactly would the ICFA trustees recommend?

Eugene C. Sit, CFA (left), chair of the International Committee for 1990–1993, and A. Michael Lipper, CFA (right), of Lipper Analytical Services.

The great debate about combining analyst organizations was effectively concluded at the 3 August 1989 meeting of the ICFA Board of Trustees in Charlottesville. No photo exists of the trustees entering that meeting at 3:30 on the afternoon of 3 August or of them leaving at 12:30 on the morning of 4 August. Yet, one may assume each entered somberly and left exhausted. No official record exists to capture the debate among the ICFA trustees, but the feelings it generated are not lost to the mists of time. Even 20 years later, none who were present have forgotten what transpired, and they describe it as "contentious," "enervating," "frank," "eloquent," "fierce," "well articulated," "tense," and "serious." *Profoundly* serious, one might say, and, as Ted Muller noted, admirably focused "entirely on the issues and not at all on trustees as individuals."[31]

ICFA Vice Chair Gene Vaughan recalled the main points made by each side. For combination proponents, he stated, it was crucial "to redirect the divisiveness, cacophony, and wasted energy toward [a] powerful, unified effort and passion to elevate the entire profession."[32] In addition, proponents thought it essential to have one voice speaking for the profession. "This is too small a profession," Vaughan said, "to have two groups speaking for it."[33] At the time, the total of those involved in the profession of financial analysis was around 30,000, according to Vaughan. Having two organizations speaking for them was cumbersome, at best, confusing or contradictory, at worst.

The 1989 ICFA Board of Trustees—front row left to right: Daniel J. Forrestal III, CFA, ICFA negotiator; Eugene C. Sit, CFA; Greta E. Marshall, CFA; Eugene H. Vaughan, CFA; back row left to right: George W. Noyes, CFA; Gary P. Brinson, CFA; Alfred C. Morley, CFA; James R. Vertin, CFA; William J. Gillard, CFA; I. Rossa O'Reilly, CFA; not shown: James K. Dunton, CFA; Frederick L. Muller, CFA; Eliot P. Williams, CFA.

For those opposing the merger, there were financial fears—expressed in the drowning man analogy—and apprehension that autonomy for the CFA Program would be lost. For those on both sides, of course, there was a genuine concern that the "hard won charter would be, in some way, diminished" by the merger. Vaughan summed up the discussion this way: "These were people who devoutly believed in what they were saying. In effect, some of the ICFA trustees were saying, why take the risk? [The] answer back from Ted Muller and myself . . . was 'it's for the profession,' and for how much better [it would be] if we put aside the issues between the two organizations."

The discussion continued for about four or five hours, at which point the merger was finally put to a vote. Pete Morley and FAF Chair James K. Dunton, CFA, abstained from voting because of their relationship to the federation. That left 10 trustees to vote. Tom Bowman, present only as an observer, recalled the whole panorama:

I was front row center that night and remember it as if it were yesterday. . . . There were 11 ICFA trustees in the room for the first vote . . . (The 11th Trustee was Pete [Morley], who had decided ahead of time that he would abstain.) . . . At the beginning of the meeting, Gary [Brinson] asked each trustee to spend a few minutes talking about why he or she either was going to vote in favor of or against the merger. [Each] spoke very frankly, and very eloquently in many cases. . . .[34]

After a dinner break, the meeting reconvened and the chair, Gary P. Brinson, CFA, asked for a vote. By prior agreement, Bowman noted, there "had to be a majority in favor. It could not be a tie." Months earlier, Dan Forrestal had reminded all the trustees that, customarily, "on anything of major magnitude the [ICFA board] vote was either unanimous or very close to unanimous."[35] He expressed his hope that "this spirit would apply as the merger issue is addressed," and certainly when it was voted on. Yet, at the 3 August vote, things were far from unanimous. As Bowman recalled:

When the vote was taken, Gary Brinson went around the table asking each Trustee to say "aye" or "nay." The vote was 5–5 with two abstentions, meaning that the merger proposal was defeated. I even made a note: "Merger is dead."[36]

After two full years of discussion, it had come down to this: a tie. The room was silent, until finally someone asked for a break. The moment has stayed with Vaughan: "I will never forget that hush when the votes were being counted, " he recalled. "Five-to-five. Utter defeat. A tie."[37] To him, the merger was dead. "After all these years, and two years of tremendously hard work by the FAF, the societies, the ICFA—all to naught. We were exhausted. We took a short break, and it was so quiet . . . there was no exultation of the winners."

Vaughan remembers feeling "not only exhausted but despairing." Then, trustee Gene Sit came over to him and said, "I'll switch my vote if you'll agree to be chairman for the first year and a half."[38] Before he answered, Vaughan recalled, he could not help but think "my family, my firm!" and wondered what it would take out of him to give a year and a half to the formation of the new organization. Yet, "this fantastic reversal" was impossible to turn down, and Vaughan assented. FAF Chair Jim Dunton agreed to be the new organization's vice chair.

The meeting was called back to order and a new vote taken: six-to-four in favor of merging and of sending a positive recommendation to the ICFA membership. "By that slim a margin!" Vaughan recalled with awe. Not with unanimity, as Dan Forrestal had hoped, but by one vote, "this all moved forward." Vaughan concluded: "I have never in my 50-year career been in a meeting as intense or as dramatic as that."

On 3 October 1989, a special meeting of ICFA members was held to vote on

Wendi E. Ruschmann (left) has been with the organization since 1987 and is the current historian/archivist. James K. Dunton, CFA (right), was AIMR chair for 1991–1992. Elsa Ruiz Photography

the merger. Of the total votes cast, 83 percent were in favor, 15 percent against, and 2 percent abstained. "This was overwhelming affirmation of the belief of CFA charterholders in the good sense of combination, and their faith in the future of a unified professional organization," said Vaughan.[39] "The wisdom of the charterholders somehow knew this was an historic opportunity for advancing our entire profession."

That same month, the *CFA Newsletter* announced the merger as official. It detailed how the new organization would be structured and that its name would be the Association for Investment Management and Research (AIMR), not IPA. As Pete Morley had informed ICFA trustees in September, there was an entity in Washington, DC, that already used the acronym IPA, namely, the Investment Partnership Association. "Their legal counsel requested we select another name to avoid confusion," Morley told the trustees, and then added jokingly, "the International Polka Association also might object!"[40]

Although they had been preoccupied with the merger decision during 1989, once the combination was authorized, the ICFA board again picked up its steady, long-distance pace. Strategically and individually, board members needed to look ahead. "Healing the rifts within the ICFA, and with the NYSSA, had to be the first priority after the merger," Gene Vaughan remembered.[41] The combination of the ICFA and the FAF was effective on 1 January 1990. Both organizations became entities within the newly established AIMR.

Time does heal wounds, and the passage of time can change one's perspective. George Noyes, who opposed the merger, noted that he was:

> pleased to have represented the side of the argument that was concerned with financial prudence and charter integrity, but, that said, I was a loyal and committed participant in the post merger entity for virtually all of the years from 1990 [until] I retired through 2008.[42]

When asked in 2010 about how he believed the merger turned out, Jim Vertin, one of its staunchest opponents, replied: "I have to say circa 2010 that I was mistaken [and] my fears were overdone."[43] Vertin cited Pete Morley "as a catalyst at the management side" and Ted Muller and Wally Stern, "who were CFA charterholders but had been very active in the FAF management hierarchy," for helping make things work: "Lo and behold, we have a very successful, single-minded, focused organization with worldwide influence on our hands in 2010—far differ-

ent from what we were looking at in 1989." At the 20th Anniversary Celebration in New York City on 13 January 2010, Chair Vaughan saluted Vertin:

> A major reason for the enormous success of AIMR, and then CFA Institute, is Jim Vertin and other admirable stalwarts who intelligently and relentlessly probed every possible defect in advance. Would that all mergers were so brilliantly conceived, vetted, launched, and nurtured.[44]

Given the extraordinary growth, the global acceptance, and the worldwide success the CFA Program has seen since in the 1990s, it seems fair to say that the affirmative carried the second great analysts' debate in the long run—as it had the first.

In January 2010, members of the inaugural AIMR Board of Governors reunited in New York City to celebrate their 20-year anniversary. Pictured are members of the first board, the 2009–2010 CFA Institute Board of Governors, and other past board members and guests. Elsa Ruiz Photography

chapter five

Facing New Realities: 1990–1994

*T*he newly created Board of Governors of the Association for Investment Management and Research met for the first time on the morning of 11 January 1990 in a chandeliered meeting room of the Biltmore Hotel in Los Angeles. Wendi Ruschmann, a staff member who was present, remembers "electricity in the air . . . camaraderie . . . almost giddiness."[1] Presiding was Association for Investment Management and Research Chair Eugene H. Vaughan, CFA, whose willingness to serve for 18 months had propelled the merger forward. According to Ruschmann, Vaughan "did a great job of bringing everyone together and making everyone feel a part of something special that was created out of all their efforts."

At the beginning of the meeting, Vaughan noted the historic times in which the merger had taken place. Just two months earlier, on 9 November 1989, the Berlin Wall had fallen, taking with it shards of the Cold War and prefiguring a new Europe whose unification later in the 1990s would have consequences for financial markets worldwide. The Wall, Vaughan noted, had gone up in 1961, just as the Institute of Chartered Financial Analysts was coming into being as an entity separate from the Financial Analysts Federation.

The ICFA and FAF now existed under the aegis of AIMR, but the significant fact was that they both still *existed*. The merger that created AIMR was "a fragile combination in the early days," as one who reflected about it recently noted.[2] Not only had AIMR been structured to ensure equal representation from both groups (its board consisted of nine governors each from the FAF and the ICFA), but separate boards for each were also retained. If you were a member of the senior staff, or on the AIMR board, the chances were excellent that you would also be attending meetings of the other boards. Thomas A. Bowman, CFA, AIMR senior vice president for Candidate Programs at the time, remembered the early years of AIMR as a time of migrating from board meeting to board meeting and making sure to put on the proper "hat" before entering each gathering. By the end of the decade, the organizational structure of AIMR would look very differ-

I suppose there are professions that one could find where everything is written down and already known. Such is not the case in the world of the financial analysts.

—C. Roderick O'Neil, CFA, 1978–79 president of ICFA, letter to Charles D. Ellis, CFA, 1978

Inaugural Association for Investment Management and Research Board of Governors and Officers 1990 - 1991

Seated (L-R): Walter P. Stern, CFA; Wallace B. Millner, CFA, FAF Chair; Alfred C. Morley, CFA, President and CEO; Eugene H. Vaughan, Jr., CFA, AIMR Chair; James K. Dunton, CFA, AIMR Vice Chair; Darwin M. Bayston, CFA, AIMR Exec. VP and COO; Frederick L. Muller, CFA, ICFA Chair. Standing (L-R): Thomas A. Bowman, CFA, AIMR Sr. VP; I. Rossa O'Reilly, CFA; Donald M. Keller, CFA; John J. McCabe; Eugene C. Sit, CFA; George W. Noyes, CFA; Nancy C. Smith, CFA; Greta E. Marshall, CFA; A. William Bodine; Bernadette B. Murphy; Eliot P. Williams, CFA; Daniel J. Forrestal, CFA; Peter B. Reid, CFA; Michael L. McCowin, CFA; Arnold S. Wood.

ent, but as the 1990s dawned, the leaders of AIMR were striving to preserve and enhance what was most important in each of its two components and determine how the unimportant elements could be made to vanish gracefully.

The new realities facing those responsible for the CFA Program were, in a sense, epitomized in Gene Vaughan's allusion to the fall of the Berlin Wall. The world was changing—and changing fast. Within a few years of the founding of AIMR, the Warsaw Pact was dissolved and the Soviet Union divided into 15 states (1991), China began incorporating some elements of capitalism into its economy, the European Union was created (1993), and the North American Free Trade Agreement was signed (1994). Each of these events alone signaled enormous shifts in political and economic realities, but just beyond their arrival lurked an even more pervasive change: the information technology revolution typified by

REALIZED LOSSES

Not long after its inaugural meeting, the fledgling AIMR board was dealt an unexpected blow. Alfred C. "Pete" Morley, CFA, informed Eugene H. Vaughan, Jr., CFA, of his intention to resign as president and CEO, effective 30 June 1990. Although Morley had previously indicated that he anticipated winding down his work at AIMR within a few years, the earliest date the board expected that to happen was June 1991. However, Morley's years of devoted service to the ICFA and the rigors of the merger years had taken their toll. Spending time with his family, which now included grandchildren, beckoned, and he decided to resign a year earlier than planned. The AIMR board was quickly notified of what Vaughan later referred to as "Pete's surprise." Morley agreed to stay on in an advisory capacity to work particularly on international relationships, and in March, the AIMR Board of Governors accepted his resignation "with deep regret." Darwin M. Bayston,

CFA, then executive vice president of AIMR, was named Morley's successor, with Thomas A. Bowman, CFA, moving into Bayston's role as executive vice president. At the May 1990 meetings of the AIMR and ICFA boards—the last in which Pete Morley reported as president and CEO—he reflected back on his career as a security analyst, a charterholder, an ICFA volunteer, and finally, an official of all three professional organizations serving analysts.

Morley joked that he had had "a lot of bosses in a short period of time . . . Mr. Vawter, Mr. Forrestal, Mr. Maginn, Mr. von Germeten, Mr. Sit, Mr. Brinson, Mr. Vaughan. And now Mr. Muller . . . and all were great."[3] Then, consummate professional that he was, Morley, "in the interest of going ahead with the agenda," ended his report and his career as president and CEO.

To remain vital, every organization needs to see young people replace older leaders, of course, but AIMR itself was so young, its leaders could not

have been looking for such a change so early. An even more shocking blow came just two months later when Daniel J. Forrestal III, CFA, an ICFA trustee, founding governor of AIMR, and "one of the architects of the merger," died suddenly on 22 July 1990. He was 49 years old. Few would disagree that Dan Forrestal had been at the heart of things for nearly a decade. Coming so close on the heels of the merger, in which he was so instrumental, this blow was difficult to absorb.

Forrestal was particularly admired for his strong ethical sense, and when the AIMR board made a decision to honor him, it did so by creating the Daniel J. Forrestal III Leadership Award for Professional Ethics and Standards of Investment Practice. The list of its recipients is a hall of fame of those who have helped keep ethical behavior in the professional lives of analysts at the center of the CFA Program.

the advent of the internet. The first webpages went live in December 1990; by the middle of the decade, web browsers came installed on most computers.

CFA Program leaders looking around in the early 1990s saw new realities everywhere they turned. Not only did a new organizational structure surround them, but the world beyond was shifting, and so were financial markets. "In their own way, the 1990s proved to be as volatile as the preceding years," one historian of Wall Street declared.[4] Considering that the "preceding years" had included the heyday of junk bonds, hostile takeovers, London's "Big Bang," Black Monday, and the Thrift Crisis, to call the 1990s "volatile" was really saying something. According to another financial historian, "The almost constant arrival of new financial products since the mid-seventies [constituted an] unprecedented phenomenon in financial history."[5] CFA Program leaders did not need a crystal ball to recognize

HISTORICAL SPOTLIGHT

Sometimes service to the investment profession is multi-generational. Samuel B. Jones, Jr., CFA, 2002 winner of the Daniel J. Forrestal III Leadership Award and a CFA Institute board member for 2004–2010, is the son of Samuel B. Jones, Sr., who was president of the original professional organization for analysts, NFFAS, for 1953–1954.

Recipients of the Daniel J. Forrestal III Award for Professional Ethics and Standards of Investment Practice: Richard P. Halverson, CFA (1994), left, and Samuel B. Jones, Jr., CFA (2002), right.

that their profession faced new realities. What they had to decide in the first half of the volatile 1990s was whether the CFA curriculum was adequately adapted to this new world, whether the program for members ensured that charterholders were keeping up with the financial whirlwind, and whether the CFA Program adequately addressed the needs of candidates from all over the world.

Candidate Education. Continuing Education. Globalization. These three areas would occupy the ICFA board and staff for the rest of the decade and beyond.

UPDATING AND EXPANDING THE CANDIDATE PROGRAM

The CFA Program is on top of the world right now and needs to maintain a standard of excellence.

—Eliot P. Williams, CFA, Minutes of AIMR Board of Governors, 19 May 1991

For the ICFA trustees, who prior to January 1990 had been sole proprietors of the CFA Program, maintaining the program's integrity and preserving the value of the charter remained the first priority. Yet, as the minutes of the first postmerger board meeting reveal, ICFA trustees (all but two of whom had served in the years prior to the merger) were unsure about where their authority lay. For the first time in that organization's history, responsibility for the program was not exclusively theirs. Key CFA Program committees, such as the Council of Examiners and the Candidate Curriculum Committee, were tucked under the wing of AIMR. What would this new reality mean to the ICFA board and the CFA Program? In the larger organization, jurisdiction was crucial and would affect everything.

The first postmerger ICFA board meeting was loaded with questions: Who sets the fees for the examination program? Which organization should decide whether to have specialty exams, and should they be for candidates or for charterholders? Underlying all these questions was one that Michael L. McCowin, CFA, who was ICFA vice chair in 1990–1991, articulated: Was the CFA Program

William H. Donaldson, CFA, chair of the U.S. Securities and Exchange Commission for 2003–2005, received the Daniel J. Forrestal III Award for Professional Ethics and Standards of Investment Practice in 2010. Bachrach Photography

Michael L. McCowin, CFA, served as chair of the ICFA for 1991–1992. Austen Field Photography

"going to become a little piece on the side, with other issues becoming more important?" Was everyone "still going to focus on the examination program the way they used to?"[6]

Despite the genuine structural and jurisdictional issues that surfaced once these two very different organizations came together under one name, the simple answer to McCowin's second question was yes. The ICFA board and the candidate program staff continued to hold the CFA Program at the center of their vision. It was not pushed to the side. Perhaps because the ICFA perceived a threat to its primacy (or, more likely, because the profession itself was changing so rapidly), those entrusted with the CFA Program put it under a sharply focused lens in the early 1990s. Much of what had been taken up in the late 1980s but left unchanged was scrutinized again. This time, however, many changes that did not pass in the late 1980s were adopted. It is not an exaggeration to say that in the decade following the merger, the CFA examinations, curriculum, and grading process underwent greater revision and expansion than in any other decade of the program's history. In effect, the work of the 1990s created the rigorous, comprehensive, and consistent program known to candidates all over the world today.

"The first substantive task" confronting the ICFA board in 1990, according to ICFA Chair Frederick L. "Ted" Muller, CFA, was to form a task force to create "a new 'taxonomy' for the Body of Knowledge."[7] Muller saw two pressing reasons for this. First, technology had changed the investment decision-making process through the introduction of new instruments and tools, which necessitated bringing the Body of Knowledge (BOK) up to date. Second, and equally important, the ICFA needed to "demonstrate in a tangible way to the full AIMR constituencies that the quality of the CFA Program would continue to be improved post merger."[8]

Having been both an FAF chair and an ICFA trustee, Muller was in a unique position to help the ICFA board face the new realities of being part of a larger organization while keeping the CFA Program in sharp focus. Two keenly interested observers of the immediate postmerger period, James R. Vertin, CFA, and Gene Vaughan, acknowledged the importance of Muller to the eventual success of the merger. Vaughan cited Muller as "a leader on the ICFA side, on the FAF, and an immense leader for the combined organization."[9] And Vertin noted that Ted Muller could "see things and suggest things and do it in a way that was diplomatic, [that] didn't hurt anybody's feelings, and yet drove the stake right through the heart of the problem."[10] Many have remarked that it was a stroke of good fortune to have Muller as ICFA chair during the crucial postmerger year.

Muller assumed chairmanship of the Task Force on the Body of Knowledge and recruited its members. "One of the brightest memories in my years of participation in the leadership," he recalled, "was to select . . . [and] chair this very talented and dedicated group from the starting point in 1990 to the transmittal of the final report in January 1991."[11] Few would argue with Muller's choices, who were unusually able people. Serving on the task force were fellow ICFA board member I. Rossa O'Reilly, CFA; Candidate Curriculum Committee Chair Fred H. Speece, Jr., CFA; Guy G. Rutherfurd, Jr., CFA; Arthur Zeikel; and W. Van Harlow III, CFA. Rounding out the group was financial economist William F. Sharpe, an originator of the capital asset pricing model, who had just received the Nobel Prize for Economics. In selecting these people, Muller said he:

> tried to achieve a balance between those who have had experience in working directly with the CFA Study and Examination Program (CFA Program) and those who have had none, including non-CFA charterholders, so as to access new ideas and constructive criticisms.[12]

The task force was to consult with the Candidate Curriculum Committee (CCC) and the Council of Examiners (COE) and included senior staff members Tom Bowman and Darwin M. Bayston, CFA. It was scheduled to hold its first face-to-face meeting on 22 May 1990.

In April 1990, as the BOK Task Force was forming, Tom Bowman presented its chair, Ted Muller, with a 143-page binder of information and analysis titled "ICFA Study and Examination Review." A compilation of documents relevant to the whole CFA Program (not only the "Tree of Knowledge," as it was then called), the binder laid out areas the task force would ultimately need to consider: candidate admissions, what the BOK was and should be, whether the examinations themselves were structured correctly or needed alternative formats or specialty exams, and how to "meet the challenge of a growing international constituency."[13] Bowman's hefty report must have been both daunting in size and familiar in content. The ancient Greek philosopher Heraclitus counsels us that no man steps in the same river twice, but those shepherding the CFA Program in 1990 may have questioned his wisdom: These topics certainly had floated past before.

Despite all the attention given to merger issues during the late 1980s, it was a matter of pride to Tom Bowman to have maintained focus on the program:

> Our number one priority was that the process of the CFA Program be shielded from all activity surrounding the merger discussions. It is a credit to the volunteers at the time that the Program went forward *as if we had earplugs against all the noise.*[14]

EXAM STORY: SOGGY IN MONTREAL

As one candidate in Montreal learned, technology affects not only the investment industry but also the taking of CFA exams:

" I was utterly prepared to write the Level I exam in 1994. In addition to having intensively studied, I had two calculators. I had energy bars, grapes, and water to last me the whole day.

"At the end of the morning session, I packed everything in my bag and went to meet colleagues (also writing the exam) for lunch. On my way there, I felt something strange against my leg. I opened the bag and I saw that the water bottle had spilled at the bottom. Water was covering both calculators.

"To my relief, the calculators worked. To be on the safe side, over lunch, I removed the batteries and dried the calculators. I used a hair dryer to dry off any possible moisture and practiced discounted cash flow calculations. I was ready to head back to the second part of the exam.

"Fifteen minutes into the afternoon session, numbers on the first calculator disappeared. Turning off and on the calculator did nothing. Fear was settling in. I removed and reinserted the batteries. Still blank. By then, the invigilators had a watchful eye on me. I took the second calculator. It worked. Great! A few minutes later, numbers disappeared. Turn it on. Turn it off. Nothing. Remove/reinsert batteries. Blank. The invigilator kept watching me. Finally, I asked him for a spare calculator. He had none. Someone lent me his extra calculator. Much like a new car, a new calculator [needs] getting used to. I scrambled to finish the exam. So many precious minutes wasted. Needless to say, the following year, I made sure the water bottle was well closed and kept it separate from the calculators."

—ANNE LANDRY, CFA, Montreal

Soon after her experience, tighter security rules prevented the exchange of calculators and bringing water bottles into the testing room.

That these elements needed further scrutiny just a few years later resulted from the nature of the profession. As former CCC Chair Donald L. Tuttle, CFA, pointed out, how frequently one reexamines the body of knowledge of any profession depends on how dynamic the profession is. If the discipline is ancient history, you may need a reassessment only "every 20 years," he noted. But for a "Body of Knowledge like ours, where it is just changing all the time, you really do need to recalibrate things frequently. It's just in your best interest and in the interest, of course, of the candidates and our members."[15]

That the CFA Program was basically sound, as concluded in the late 1980s,

EXAM STORY: HOT AND NOISY IN DC

For this candidate, new technology wasn't the challenge; the problem was old equipment.

"Washington, DC, in early June can be blazingly hot and humid, and in 1991, it was particularly so. In those days, everyone in the area took CFA exams on the American University campus. The room was full to capacity and fairly stuffy but had some overhead fans. As the day wore on, the room got hotter and more humid, and we were poring and pouring over our exam books. The proctor turned up the speed on the ceiling fans, which moved the air around more quickly, but the motors also made a loud humming noise and the fan blades made a loud whooshing sound. Suddenly, one of the test takers piped up, 'I don't know if I can hold her steady any longer, Chuck!' as if flying a Douglas DC-3 prop plane in an old airplane disaster movie. The classroom full of test takers broke out in laughter, and neither the weather nor the tension of the exam seemed to matter any longer. I hope everyone in the room did OK on the test; at least everyone in my study group passed."

—MATTHEW D. GELFAND, CFA
Washington, DC

was still true in 1990, but that conclusion could not go unchallenged in the face of the dynamic new realities in the investment profession. A technological revolution was under way. The number and kinds of investment vehicles, especially derivatives and securitized debt, were growing fast. The number of investors had grown considerably since 1980, together with a "dramatic increase in trading volume" on various exchanges.[16] Moreover, financial markets had become truly global. In the face of all this innovation and the spread of trading worldwide, the time had surely come to take another look at the CFA Program for currency and relevancy. And this scrutiny had to start with the BOK from which the curriculum and exams were derived.

When C. Stewart Sheppard first published a BOK for financial analysts in 1969, it was called the "General Topic Outline" (GTO) and consisted of five topics arranged in a list, with dark, vertical bands delineating which topics would be tested at which levels (see Chapter 2). The GTO (later called the "Tree of Knowledge") had undergone revision in the 1970s and 1980s. Over time, the number of topics had increased from five to seven, and the number of subtopics and subheadings had multiplied dramatically. During its most recent scrutiny (1987), Bowman and others had proposed a rearrangement of topics in the Tree of Knowledge and a redrawing, as it were, of its graphic depiction. All in all, however, by the beginning of the task force's work in 1990, much had been added to content, but little had changed in format.

BOK Task Force members recalled the work as intellectually heady. Chair Ted Muller remembered being "overwhelmed in a positive way by how cerebral, focused, and relevant the conversation remained throughout the process."[17] Their breakthrough, as Fred Speece put it, was in "awakening" to the fact that any progression in the BOK should be structured around the "three functions in the business: the tools you use, the valuation, and the portfolio."[18] Level III was not necessarily going to be more difficult in content than Level I or II, but it was going to reflect a certain stage in the progression of an analyst's career that might be more difficult than the previous stage. All levels would now reflect a stage in one's career—from learning to use the basic tools and concepts of the profession to the valuation of investments and, eventually, to managing portfolios.

This recognition was, as Tom Bowman saw it, a matter of returning to the original intent of the ICFA founders, whose program closely paralleled the analyst's typical career progression.[19] Correcting the BOK was not, however, a matter of merely reshuffling the deck and dealing the topic cards onto new piles. Rather, the task force needed to reconceptualize the format and organization of the BOK. By the time the task force completed its work in February 1991, the Body of Knowledge was organized and presented in a substantially different way from its previous incarnation. It was now organized functionally rather than topically. In its new form, which was reported to the ICFA board in February 1991, the progression went through three functional phases:

- Tools and Inputs for Investment Valuation
- Investment Valuation
- Portfolio Management

The fourth element, Ethical and Professional Standards, was necessary at all stages of one's career and thus included at all three levels.

This new representation of the BOK was expected to appear in the Level I Study Guide in 1993 and in those for Levels II and III in 1994. The new BOK was expected to be fully integrated into the Level II and III curricula by 1995. Task force members were convinced that by organizing functionally, they were greatly improving the overall design of the CFA Program. Although some reservations were expressed about the impact of the new form on candidates, the proposal to reorganize the BOK met with a positive response from the ICFA trustees and the AIMR governors.

Certain moments in every organization's history stand out as times of harmonious activity. The time when this BOK Task Force was working was one such moment, and members of the group speak warmly of the experience. Bill Sharpe, the Nobel laureate, indicated that the group's work was "the most remarkable and effective set of committee meetings" he had ever attended.[20] Reflecting back on the experience nearly 20 years later, Fred Speece remembered the work as both stimulating and significant for the CFA Program.[21] Perhaps Muller summed it up best: "We all enjoyed the considerable intellectual challenge of creating an outcome of practical value to the profession that would be relevant into future years. From my viewpoint, working closely with this group was a personally satisfying experience of the first magnitude."[22]

William F. Sharpe, a Nobel laureate, served on the Body of Knowledge Task Force for 1990–1991.

LINKING THE CFA CURRICULUM TO THE BODY OF KNOWLEDGE

From 1991 to 1993, the BOK reorganization needed to be metabolized by those who chose the curriculum for the study guides (the CCC) and those who created the CFA exams (the COE). To ease the transition to a curriculum based on the new BOK, Tom Bowman hired George H. Troughton, CFA, as a consultant to make a formal review of the curriculum and its relation to the BOK. A professor of finance at California State University at Chico, Troughton, having been a grader since 1982 and a member of the CCC since 1987, was experienced in both the CFA curriculum and the exam processes.

Starting in May 1992, Troughton worked on editing and formatting the study guides to coordinate with the revised BOK. He also began formulating what would later be called the "Gaps and Overlaps" (G&O) report—a thorough review of all the curricular materials to find in them any "redundancies, duplication, and contradictions."[23] As Troughton recalled, the G&O report started "as a means to insure that the assigned readings in the curriculum were covering the Candidate Body of Knowledge." In 1993, he and two other staff members who were also

(top) George H. Troughton, CFA, served as a curriculum consultant and longtime grader. In 1999, he received the C. Stewart Sheppard Award from Janet T. Miller, CFA, AIMR governor for 1998–2004.

(bottom) Tom S. Sale III, CFA, served as chair of the Council of Examiners for 1989–1992 and as a longtime grader.

working as curriculum chairs for each level, Don Tuttle and Tom S. Sale III, CFA, conducted an audit to compare the curriculum content at all three levels with the respective BOK topics. If they found that a topic was not covered, and thus constituted "a gap" in the curriculum, they gave it priority when new readings were chosen. If a topic was covered in more than one place, and was thus "an Overlap," one of the redundancies was slated for elimination. The G&O report became even more useful later in the decade with the introduction into the curriculum of Learning Outcome Statements (discussed later in this chapter and in Chapter 6). Even in the early 1990s, however, the process was beginning to serve candidates better than the old approach. It was also helping accomplish a goal sought since the founding of the CFA Program: reliable coordination between curriculum readings and the exams. According to Jan R. Squires, CFA, a managing director for CFA Institute and a longtime volunteer on the CCC and the COE, the G&O report was "one of the first attempts to be completely systematic."[24]

The introduction of systematic discipline into exam creation and curriculum development represented one of the most important changes in the CFA Program after 1992. This discipline was necessary pedagogically; administratively, it was essential. Between 1990 and 1994, the number of candidates sitting for the CFA exam increased 75 percent, rising from 8,760 to 15,413 in those few years. Notably, this increase came on the heels of a doubling of candidate enrollments during the 1980s. In the 14 years between 1980 and 1994, candidates sitting had increased by more than 600 percent. If staff members looked a little bleary eyed in the first half of the 1990s, it was understandable.

During the same period, candidates from outside North America also skyrocketed, from 79 persons in 13 locations taking exams in 1984, for example, to nearly 4,000 persons taking CFA exams in locations outside North America in 1994. Even more remarkable, as the next chapter details, is that by the end of the 1990s, candidates from outside North America composed fully 36 percent of all candidate registrations.

Despite this upward trend, the ICFA (and later AIMR) trustees and staff continued to budget conservatively lest the market become saturated and registration numbers begin to decline. The continually anticipated decrease did not come, however—not in the first half of the 1990s, not in the second half, and certainly not in the 2000s. By 2009, more than 140,000 candidates were sitting for the CFA exams each year.

Because *estimates* of candidate numbers were so conservative, actual enrollment totals regularly exceeded projected numbers for the CFA Program, which was the financial engine supporting AIMR. This revenue stream was helping to fund the necessary expansion of staff, the continuing education programs, and the global outreach needed to serve members and candidates. The explosion of candidate growth, manifested most prominently abroad, necessitated a tight "rein on the process," as Tom Bowman put it; otherwise, such an extraordinary jump in numbers—from 8,760 CFA candidates in 1990 to 53,345 in 2000—could never have been managed well.[25]

Although many of the new systems that grew out of this increasing discipline were developed fully only after 1995, hints were visible before then. Tom Bowman recalled a question and answer session he conducted with CFA candidates in San Francisco in 1989. One candidate asked him about the current curriculum and indicated that he had read the AIMR proceedings on derivatives in the candidate readings (in fact, he told Bowman, he had read it twice), but he was still confused: "I don't know what you wanted me to get out of it." Bowman remembers this dialog as a "light bulb moment" that has stayed with him to this day. How were candidates to best use all the new material set before them? How should they use it in terms of their upcoming exams, and ultimately, how should they use it in their work? CFA candidates, like practitioners, had an enormous amount of material to digest. What professional nourishment, as it were, were candidates expected to derive from it?

Although that candidate's puzzlement about what to derive from a reading resonated strongly in 1989, it took half a dozen years and the right confluence of factors before this moment resulted in what CFA candidates now know as Learning Outcome Statements. As early as February 1992, however, Bowman was reporting to the ICFA board that one of the first steps in implementation of the new BOK would be "to develop a set of candidate requirement statements that would help link the efforts of the CCC and COE to the Body of Knowledge."[27] By July 1993, he and COE Chair J. Clay Singleton, CFA, were telling the ICFA board about an initiative to develop Learning Outcome Statements as a blueprint for both curriculum and examination development.[28] Within a few years, all candidates would benefit from this initiative.

ETHICS AND STANDARDS

Any discussion of the history of the CFA Program needs to consider the refinement of its ethical code and the enforcement of it, both so crucial to the integrity of the profession and its ability to self-regulate. Ethics and professional standards are core topics of the CFA Program—and were the first topics covered at all three levels of the program and examinations. Most developments in this important area occur "offstage," however. Incremental modifications to the Code of Ethics are made; new professional standards are added to reflect the changing nature of the investment profession; charterholders and candidates who may have vio-

HISTORICAL SPOTLIGHT

In 1991, AIMR staff consisted of only 57 people, 3 of whom were in New York and the rest in Charlottesville. This small staff was responsible for the needs of nearly 10,000 CFA candidates, 22,581 AIMR members (of whom more than 14,000 were CFA charterholders), 66 societies, 130+ graders, 3 governing boards, and hundreds of volunteers. In looking at the performance of this staff in 1991, Pete Morley, CFA, compared them with "the Royal Air Force at the Battle of Britain in World War II —so few who gave so much."[26]

There is no more important project that we as members, that we as a profession, that we as the Institute can devote our time and effort to than further improving the ethical conduct of all people who participate in our business.

—John L. Maginn, CFA

CFA candidates are not the only ones who remember vividly the anxieties of test day:

"The first Saturday in June 1991, I was working as the Omaha Exam Coordinator. It started off as a beautiful early summer day, but during the afternoon session, the sky darkened and at about 3:15 p.m., the civil defense sirens sounded for a tornado warning. A tornado had been reported south of the city but was still a long ways away from the exam site. While most people in the plains states take tornados very seriously, the CFA exam appeared to trump the weather, and the candidates continued to write. Our exam coordinator and proctor directions had detailed instructions on how to administer the exam, handle exam materials, seat candidates, etc., but contained no tornado procedures.

"While the candidates continued to feverishly write, I went outside to peer at the sky and listen to a portable radio for tornado location updates. The other proctors [there were two per room] continued to monitor the exam. A few minutes later, it began to hail and the radio reported another tornado, closer than the first.

"I had heard enough. The exam was stopped, the timing stopwatch was stopped, the candidates were directed to cease writing immediately and all were reminded that the CFA Standards of Practice required them to not discuss the exam or refer to any materials. I started another stopwatch to time the delay. The other proctors herded all of the candidates into the designated tornado shelter in the basement of the business administration building while I secured the exam rooms. A few minutes later a campus police officer arrived and chased me to the basement as well. After about an hour's delay, the tornado moved by without damaging anything, the rain let up, the sky brightened, and the all-clear siren sounded. Candidates were allowed to return to the exam rooms. Once everybody was settled in, the candidates were allowed to resume taking the exam, the stopwatch was restarted and the rest of the exam went off without a hitch, ending at 5:45 p.m. instead of 4:30 p.m.

"Exam proctor instructions now include procedures for extraordinary events such as tornado evacuations, but [to my knowledge] such a dramatic weather event has never occurred again during a CFA exam."

—W. BRUCE REMINGTON, CFA, Lincoln, Nebraska, USA

lated the Code or Standards are investigated. Those found to be in violation are reminded or sanctioned. In serious situations, charters are revoked and candidates dismissed. What lies mostly out of sight is the considerable and sometimes intense activity that goes into changes and enforcement.

By the early 1990s, the Code of Ethics had been in existence for nearly 27 years and the Standards of Professional Conduct had been functional for 17 years. *The Standards of Practice Handbook* (its fifth edition) included "new sections on international ethical considerations and [on] calculating and presenting performance standards."[29] Between 1974 and 1991, the Professional Conduct Program had reviewed 1,475 cases of potential unethical behavior by AIMR members. Of those, 791 cases had been processed. The result was 125 reminder letters issued and 49 sanctions imposed—including the revocation of 14 charters.[30] At the time, moreover, the investment community was just coming out of one of the worst decades in history for insider-trading scandals, personified by arbitrageur Ivan Boesky. Those investment professionals belonging to AIMR and its antecedent organizations, however, had much to be proud of because only two members were involved in these scandals. As Gene Vaughan put it, the investment industry had been "tarred by the 'Boesky brush'" but not CFA charterholders or AIMR members in general.[31] Vaughan regretted that this ethical achievement had not been noticed: "The fact was lost that only two of our over 20,000 AIMR members were implicated in insider information cases."

Of course, most professionally ethical behavior by analysts and investment managers did not make it into the newspapers. It consisted of small, daily deci-

sions to act in an upright manner and in ac-
cordance with the published Code of Ethics
and Standards of Professional Conduct. CFA
charterholders, and also CFA candidates, have
always been required to file a yearly Professional Conduct Questionnaire and disclose
any professional conduct–related complaints.
In the early 1990s, fully 85 percent of ethical
violations processed each year by the Professional Conduct Program arose from these self-
administered questionnaires. The remaining
15 percent came through such other sources
as "complaints from individuals, notification
of action by the [U.S.] Securities and Exchange
Commission, the National Association of Securities Dealers, and/or securities exchanges;
and information in the press."[33] As John L.
Maginn, CFA, once put it, analysts were responsible for a great deal of invested wealth,
and all of them—especially charterholders and those who wished to earn the CFA
designation—needed to be mindful of this
fiduciary responsibility and be exceedingly
careful in all their ethical dealings.

A CASE OF ETHICAL INDEPENDENCE

In 1990, one member was at the center of an ethical storm that
received widespread coverage in the business media around the
world. It was not, however, a case of misusing insider information.
The member in question, Marvin Roffman, epitomized ethical
behavior and analytical independence. Roffman issued a report
containing negative comments about the financial prospects of
Donald Trump's Taj Mahal Casino in Atlantic City, New Jersey, USA.
Although his firm acceded to pressure from its famous client to retract Roffman's findings and the analyst initially agreed to retract his
report, Roffman quickly changed his mind and refused to disavow
his analysis of the company in question.

This stand caused a tempest in the press, to which Pete Morley,
CFA, and the Public Awareness Committee devoted much time. In
an article in the *New York Times* on 27 March 1990, Morley acknowledged to a *Times* reporter, "We have had a number of calls from
analysts around the country, who are very concerned about this."[32]
What was of concern to them, he continued, was that an analyst's
responsibility (to make fair and honest assessment of companies)
must not be "in jeopardy because of an outside influence." Analysts
must be able to remain independent, as well as ethical and honest.
The analyst later sued his former employer and won a substantial
judgment, rendered by a New York Stock Exchange arbitration
panel, against the firm.[34]

In light of the ethical challenges facing the profession in the early 1990s, it is
fitting that the first award created by the newly formed AIMR went to someone
who cared deeply about ethical behavior in analysts. In 1991, the AIMR governors
awarded this new honor, the Award for Professional Excellence, to Sir John M.
Templeton, CFA, a renowned international investor and fund manager, a one-
time student of Benjamin Graham, and a noted philanthropist. Upon receiving this award, Templeton, given his phenomenal success as an investor, might
well have chosen to speak about strategies and hedging. Instead, he spoke
about responsibility, professional conduct, and establishing "a bill of rights for
shareholders."[35]

After acknowledging the generous introduction Gene Vaughan had given
him ("My own mother couldn't have done better"), Templeton presented his
unique view of what analysts were called to do: "A career as a security analyst,
in my opinion, is a ministry." An analyst, he continued, should "work diligently to
provide superior and honest results" for those being served, the clients. Templeton believed deeply in the value of investing and wished to increase greatly the
number of those who owned part of their economies by means of capital investment. Always a globalist, he invested worldwide himself and urged others to

PERFORMANCE PRESENTATION STANDARDS

Originating in the FAF in the mid-1980s, the AIMR Performance Presentation Standards (AIMR-PPS) were intended to codify and standardize how analysts, and the firms employing them, represented to prospective clients the firms' actual performance and how that measurement was achieved. Frederick L. "Ted" Muller, CFA (the 1986–87 FAF chair), his professional colleague Claude N. Rosenberg, Jr., and others had come to the conclusion that "some kind of standard reporting [of performance] was necessary because there was . . . skullduggery going on in the way firms presented their investment performance."[36] Muller asked Rosenberg to chair a "blue ribbon committee" (consisting of Dean LeBaron, CFA; John J.F. "Jay" Sherrerd, CFA; Robert G. Kirby; and Robert H. Jeffrey) to develop presentation standards.

The committee published its proposed AIMR-PPS report in the September/October 1987 *Financial Analysts Journal* and invited comment from investment professionals, the industry, charterholders, and FAF members. After revising the standards, they presented the refined AIMR-PPS standards to practitioners and other interested parties, including an SEC staff member. The AIMR Board of Governors endorsed them in August 1990 and established an implementation committee composed of experts in equities, fixed income, institutional consulting, international investing, and quantitative measurement. Muller chaired this committee with staff support from AIMR Vice President Katrina F. "Katy" Sherrerd, CFA, whom he credited with making "a huge contribution" in shaping the AIMR-PPS standards into a form embraced by

practitioners.[37] CFA charterholders, other members of AIMR, and their firms were requested to be in compliance with the standards by 1 January 1993.

Although voluntary, the AIMR-PPS standards were strongly encouraged. Neither CFA charterholders nor other AIMR members could be held responsible for the behavior of their firms, but charterholders' influence within their organizations was crucial in spreading compliance. Through contact with the SEC and with leaders in corporations and investment management companies (several of whom were active members of the Implementation Committee), AIMR sought to exert influence throughout the industry. Firms that claimed they were in compliance but were not might be subject to criticism in an SEC examination. In addition, it was understood that peer pressure to conform—especially from CFA charterholders—would help spread adherence to the AIMR-PPS standards among firms and individuals.

By creating performance

presentation standards and the guidelines for interpreting them, AIMR was taking an "important step in reassuring the public of the credibility and trustworthiness of investment practitioners."[38] Just as the CFA Program had pioneered professional education for analysts and the Code of Ethics and the Professional Conduct Program had pioneered self-regulation for analysts, the AIMR-PPS standards (now called Global Investment Performance Standards, or GIPS) were also pioneering. All of these actions contributed to public trust.

In the coming years, AIMR would be challenged to promote the CFA Program not only among candidates and charterholders but also, through its increasing presence outside North America, in many locations with different standards of reporting and of acceptable professional behavior. One of the greatest challenges for the global expansion of the CFA Program, in fact, was to promulgate an international code of ethics, and with it a high standard of performance reporting, among investment professionals worldwide.

Frederick L. Muller, CFA (right), presents the Daniel J. Forrestal III Leadership Award for Professional Ethics and Standards of Practice to Claude N. Rosenberg, Jr. (left), in 1992.

do so. Templeton also encouraged individuals in countries around the world to invest in capital markets—at a time when that practice was not as common as now. Helping others to attain prosperity was a personal goal that he encouraged in his fellow analysts and investors:

> It is well known that the rich invest in entrepreneurship whereas the poor save and conserve. You are the ones entrusted with guiding people out of an attitude of fear of the poor and into the confidence and security of the truly rich in mind and heart.

To help others create and maintain prosperity in this way, he stressed, was a goal worthy of a great profession. "There is no professional title more honorable," he concluded, "than the title of Chartered Financial Analyst." In the decade that followed Templeton's speech, that honorable title would be earned all over the globe as the CFA Program expanded worldwide.

CONTINUING EDUCATION FOR MEMBERS

If any topic taken up by CFA Program leaders could be called a hardy perennial—coming back year after year no matter how long the winter—it would be the question of a continuing education program for members. Throughout the early 1990s, successive board members, staff members, task forces, and committees looked carefully at the question; charterholders were surveyed about it. All this attention arose from a basic conundrum: Why was participation in the Continuing Education Program so comparatively low when members seemed to enjoy and find valuable the continuing education offerings of the institution? Was the CE Program in the right form? Should it become mandatory?

Like everything else after the 1990 merger, the Accreditation Program, as continuing education for members was then called, needed to find its proper home and, if necessary, assume a new shape. It was already a bit of a chameleon. Sometimes it comprised a loose program of continuing education options—ranging from reading articles in the *Financial Analysts Journal* (*FAJ*) to attending seminars or workshops. Sometimes it was formulated as a structured program of accreditation, the completion of which would earn the charterholder some recognition. Designed to help charterholders keep their skills current and to offer opportunities for improving skills, the CE Program had shown a steady but disappointing level of participation since its founding in 1985. In most years, it averaged around 10 percent, but it climbed closer to 20 percent occasionally. As noted in Chapter 3, the program was self-reporting, with recommended ranges of participation options.

In 1992, 29 years after the first candidates received their charters, the ICFA took another approach to the matter of continuing education for the 14,270 individuals who had attained a charter since 1963 and were still active in the pro-

On 12 January 1993, the Caisse de dépôt et placement du Québec honored Robert Auger, CFA (second from left), for earning a "Five-Year Certificate of Achievement" by participating in the Accreditation Program for each of the previous five years.

gram.[39] Don Tuttle, known to virtually all charterholders from his work with John Maginn on *Managing Investment Portfolios*, was hired to work on the candidate programs and to give thought to a continuing education curriculum. As part of his work, Tuttle was also to provide coordination between the CCC and the Continuing Education Steering Committee. He was singularly suited to provide this coordination because he had served on each, been CCC chair, and been a Level III curriculum coordinator. He also served on the Educational Technology subcommittee, which was examining how to apply the new electronic media for the benefit of both candidates and members, an area of growing importance.

Tuttle's assignment was to develop a prototype for a specialization program for members. In the 1980s, there was much talk on the ICFA board concerning the need for specialty exams. The profession had developed many niche specialties since the CFA Program was first founded, and some board members thought there might be a need for a "fourth exam." As recently as the start of the BOK Task Force work in 1990, Tom Bowman was asking its chair, Ted Muller, "Should there be specialty exams?"[40] Ultimately, the board decided that any program of specialization belonged within the continuing education (accreditation) program, and Don Tuttle was engaged to move it forward.

Tuttle's work on this prototype program stretched over several years, as discussed in the next chapter. In the meantime, new approaches to member programs were being developed. In 1992, Tuttle and Jim Vertin, chair of the Council on Education and Research, created a CFA Refresher Course. Offered from 1992 to 1994, the refresher courses were residential five-day programs for charterholders conducted in Charlottesville in June and in Los Angeles in October. Participants took classes on such topics as international accounting and ethics, options and futures, convertible securities, and asset allocation.

Like all continuing education options, the refresher course remained voluntary. Whether this was the right approach troubled many board members and staff throughout the 1990s. At issue was whether the CFA charter was compromised by not requiring its holders to show evidence of their continuing education and upgraded skills. Given the "growing array of asset classes" and the emergence of "new and more sophisticated investment technology," was it sufficient for a practitioner to receive the CFA charter and be done?[42]

At a February 1992 ICFA board discussion, trustees acknowledged that investment management was one of the few professions that did not have "some sort of mandatory continuing education requirement."[44] As AIMR Counsel John G. Gillis noted, in the United States, such requirements were usually mandated for state-licensed professions, such as law, public accounting, or medicine. The CFA charter did not, of course, confer a license; rather, it certified a certain level of knowledge and adherence to a code of ethics. Yet, by 1993, the Milwaukee Society had begun to require participation in accreditation activities, and other societies were considering it. Moreover, other areas of the investment business were examining such options. The National Association of Securities Dealers (NASD), Gillis pointed out, was developing a policy to require broker/dealers to "participate annually either in employer-sponsored or NASD-approved continuing education programs." As the CFA Program expanded abroad, moreover, it would have to consider what was customary or required of analysts in other countries.

In the mid-1990s, participation in the continuing education offerings was again affirmed as remaining voluntary. The Accreditation Committee, chaired by Eliot P. Williams, CFA, recognized that the membership did not "seem ready to accept mandatory accreditation."[45] Nevertheless, any program was to be

IS THERE AN APP FOR HONESTY?

At a time when "there's an app" for everything, concerns about data-storage calculators may seem quaint. In the early 1990s, however, finding a way to let candidates do necessary calculations during their exams without allowing anyone unfair advantage was a real concern. Gone were the days of the slide rule and the adding machine. Although simple, four-function calculators had been in use since the 1980s, calculators with data-storage capacity presented a new challenge. Recognizing a potential security problem, CFA Program staff decided to purchase and issue identical calculators to all candidates taking the 1992 exam because, as exam administration staff member Betty Crutchfield recalled, "it was possible that candidates were storing notes in the calculators."[41]

"We ordered thousands of custom-made four-function calculators with the CFA logo on them," Tom Bowman, CFA, noted, "and sent them to all candidates as part of their exam package with study guides, etc."[43] The practice of sending candidates calculators with the CFA logo didn't last long, however, according to Bowman: "Over the course of several months, we got so much grief from candidates that we finally relented and let them use their own calculators with the proviso that if they were programmable, the memory had to be cleared." When the practice ended, Crutchfield recalled, "We had a large supply left in the warehouse." Happily, some continue to be used, at least by a few CFA Institute staff members, including Crutchfield, who noted, "I still have mine in my drawer and use it when I need a calculator!"

Mike Bailey Photography

Eliot P. Williams, CFA (left), was chair of the ICFA for 1993–1994. George W. Noyes, CFA (right), served as board member of ICFA for 1985–1989, AIMR for 1990–1991, and CFA Institute for 2002–2008.

conducted "with the rigor, quality, and consistency that a mandatory program should have." The CE Program's format would change, however. According to Tuttle, "We decided to [stay] with the voluntary route and develop a specialization program where CFA charterholders could take courses in various specialized forms of investment."[46] Once specialization was developed, participating charterholders would be able to take an examination and, if they passed, would be awarded recognition in that specialization. The area of fixed-income securities was to be the first curriculum created; equities, the second.

By creating a program equal in rigor to the candidate program, the Accreditation Committee intended to cultivate in charterholders a sense of ongoing responsibility for keeping their knowledge and skills up to date.

REACHING THE GLOBAL MARKET

You cannot reach out if you stay in your own backyard.

—Amaury Jordan, CFA, founder of Swiss CFA Society, *Society Leader* interview, 2000

When the CFA Program ventured outside North America in the mid-1980s, it was both self-propelled and pulled forward by invitations from analyst communities abroad. Even as Pete Morley, the program's Magellan, set sail for distant shores, those in other parts of the world, having become aware of the excellence of the CFA Program, began requesting programs and workshops from the ICFA. Moreover, representatives from two groups that had established their own testing programs requested the creation of reciprocal affiliations between the CFA Program and their certification systems.

These requests may have delighted the leaders of the ICFA (and later AIMR), but they also posed some interesting dilemmas. Globalization was surely important. One could hardly be perched on any branch of the investment industry tree from the 1980s on without noticing how radically different the view was becoming. One no longer looked only to Wall Street or the City of London for investment activity. Asia was especially prominent; in 1981, the Tokyo Stock Exchange became the second largest in the world in terms of capitalization.[47] Increased capital market activity was also beginning in Australia and Africa. "Most of the world," Ted Muller noted, was "moving toward market-driven systems," and the CFA Program had the "tools and educational ability to help in that process."[48] Yet, to take the CFA designation outside North America in a substantial way required caution. CFA Program leaders had to be scrupulous about maintaining the value of the CFA charter and careful about not taking on more than they could manage in terms of staff and volunteers.

In February 1991, AIMR President Darwin Bayston presented to the ICFA board his analysis of how international expansion might proceed. He identified three approaches that might be taken:

1. Continue to pursue candidates on a worldwide basis, as in the United States.
2. Pursue reciprocal arrangements with other certification entities.
3. Respond to requests from foreign entities for consulting and training that will provide education consistent with our Body of Knowledge and lead to participation in the CFA Program.

The last approach, Bayston concluded, posed a real difficulty in maintaining "the integrity of the Charter as it exists for current charterholders" while making the CFA Program available to investment professionals around the globe.[49] Ultimately the first approach—whereby overseas candidates would register directly in the CFA Program—came to dominate. It was, as Pete Morley remarked back in 1991, "the cleanest, best approach."[50] Yet, before the CFA charter came to be adopted as "a global standard, a portable standard," alternate arrangements between the CFA Program and others were tried.[51]

In 1989, for example, the ICFA reached an agreement with Swiss Bank to develop and provide a workshop on portfolio management for its investment personnel in Basel. Swiss Bank officials asked the ICFA to develop a three-week seminar based on the CFA curriculum, a program that was educational but not specifically candidate preparation. According to Tom Bowman, this venture would be "a departure from the Institute's policy of sponsoring education programs which are either candidate or member driven" but would provide the ICFA "with a foundation for sponsoring similar seminars for members."[52] Bowman assembled a faculty for this program composed of CCC and COE volunteers who had worked on the topic. For the series of three sessions, two instructors and one ICFA staff person went to the bank's offices in Basel for a week at a time. At the end of the full instruction period, an exam was given. Bowman, who participated together with staff members Katrina F. Sherrerd, CFA, and Darwin Bayston, recalled that in the final analysis, the experience of delivering such a course was deemed to be outside the mission of the CFA Program. "We didn't like the idea of cutting the CFA into pieces," he recalled and, therefore "never did a similar thing again."[53]

Two years later, early in 1991, AIMR received a proposal from an analyst group in Indonesia requesting a "series of training and educational programs." Unlike the Swiss Bank program, which isolated a single topic for study, the proposed Indonesian program had a different purpose. It would contain two elements— the training of Indonesian instructors and the eventual establishment of a certification program in that country. For the former, the ICFA "would send over instructors to train Indonesian [investment] professionals," who would be able to "conduct their own training sessions."[54] Don Tuttle, who recruited the trainers, recalled that "all of the instructors in the Indonesian program were U.S. university professors with CFA charters."[55] They taught the Level I curriculum.

In the second element of the proposal, the Indonesians wished the ICFA to "assist them in development of their own certification examinations."[56] Also in the proposal was a request that, should the Indonesian group create a certification program, it would have reciprocal value and give those who attained the Indonesian credential "partial or total credit toward the CFA designation." This last request was rejected out of hand because the policy of the ICFA was to consider establishing a reciprocity arrangement only with a "mature, developed program."

The ICFA trustees agreed to the training proposal, however, which was put in place in early 1991 on an experimental basis. At the October 1991 board meeting, Darwin Bayston reported that the ICFA had administered the equivalent of a Level I exam (prepared by the COE) to those candidates who had been jointly instructed by "two U.S. and two Indonesian instructors." The results of this hybrid program were sufficiently disappointing that it was decided individuals in Indonesia seeking certification would be better served by applying directly to the CFA Program, and the experiment was discontinued.

In the late 1980s and early 1990s, the ICFA developed two reciprocal agreements with programs abroad and considered several others. If adopted, the agreements were to provide certified members of each group partial exemption from the requirements of the other group's program. Reciprocity agreements can be fraught with problems as each side seeks to reassure itself that the integrity of its own program will be preserved. Yet, at a time when the CFA Program was just beginning to reach out globally in a substantial way, the ICFA and AIMR boards recognized that building such relationships was important. Nonetheless, CFA Program leaders were adamant about protecting the charter. They reminded each other over and over that in agreeing to accept the credentials of others as sufficient to exempt individuals from part of the CFA Program, they must not weaken the substance of the charter or diminish its value to charterholders. Thus, they built into each reciprocal agreement a provision for its review and rescission. CFA Program leaders insisted that candidates from other countries whose certifications might entitle them to a waiver of some of the requirements of the CFA Program had to possess "the same exposure and the same depth of exposure" to a rigorous curriculum and testing series as anyone going through the CFA Program would have had.[57] For this reason, only two contacts from mature programs resulted in formal reciprocal agreements. In 1988, a reciprocal agreement was put in place with the Society of Investment Analysts (SIA) in London, and in 1991, with the Security Analysts Association of Japan (SAAJ), which was effective in 1992.

The London connection began in earnest in 1986, when "the Institute was approached by SIA concerning the feasibility of granting certain exemptions to the members of one organization who wish to become members of the other."[58] At issue was whether the two programs were compatible in terms of what they demanded of their candidates. SIA gave CFA Program staff its syllabus (the curriculum for its Associate Program), which Tom Bowman examined "side by side" with the CFA Program. He was pleased with what he saw:

> [The] SIA program was a quality program. It really did cover a lot of the same things the CFA did, and, frankly, it covered a lot of the same things a bit better.[59]

"Had it looked deficient," Bowman confirmed, the ICFA would not have agreed to a reciprocity agreement. Although substantial and comprehensive, the SIA program did not cover some topics the CFA Program deemed important, including U.S. financial accounting and CFA questions on ethics. In the areas where SIA lacked elements essential to the CFA Program, Bowman proposed to his counterpart at SIA, Anthony H. Newman, that the ICFA "cut and paste" missing elements into the SIA exam: that is, the questions from that year's CFA exams that addressed areas where the SIA program had gaps would be inserted into their examinations. SIA Associate candidates would be required to pass those CFA questions over the course of two years and, having passed both exams, could receive the CFA charter without taking all three CFA exams.

The original reciprocity arrangement continued for two years, at which time SIA changed its program and requested that the ICFA staff take a new look at it to see if they had closed any of the identified gaps. As Bowman recalled, "In our opinion, they had." As a result, the ICFA "instituted the next tier of the reciprocity agreement where people coming in under that new SIA program only had to take our Level III." The reciprocity relationship continued for many years with the London SIA (which became the Institute of Investment Management and Research in 1992). As detailed in the next chapter, a growing demand for CFA affiliations abroad, as well as considerations of consistency, made reciprocity agreements no longer feasible.

In the 1990 AIMR Annual Report, Pete Morley reported that a similar arrange-

PROCTOR STORY: NOISY—BUT TASTY—IN LONDON

A longtime proctor in London remembers an unexpected bonus:

"For the past two years, a large Christmas food exhibition has shared the ExCeL London with us in December. Last year [2009], in the middle of the afternoon session, one of our halls was interrupted when the commentary from one of the cooking demonstrations started coming through on our PA system. Candidates were urged to raise their hand if they would like to learn how to make the perfect Béarnaise sauce, a woman in a white T-shirt was invited to join them on stage, and the chat went on for about five minutes before we could get them to stop. It turned out one of the exhibitors had used an unauthorized microphone frequency and it came straight into our hall. It made for some good comments on the Candidate Forum! Luckily, the organizers felt so bad that they came over with free passes to the evening show for all proctors who wanted to attend.

—EILEEN PENMAN, exam proctor, London, 2010

HISTORICAL SPOTLIGHT

In April 1992, an article in *The Darden Report*, an internal publication of the University of Virginia's Graduate School of Business began: "Name a U.S. export that is surging in popularity, particularly in Japan and Singapore." Readers were offered a small hint: The commodity in question "was created at the Darden School 30 years ago." As readers of *this* book have probably guessed, the answer to the brainteaser was "the Chartered Financial Analyst designation."

ment was being discussed with SAAJ. Morley also informed members that the European Federation of Financial Analysts Societies (EFFAS) was "evaluating the feasibility of a common study and examination program" and "looking to AIMR" for technical assistance, "with the hope of an eventual cross-recognition of designations."[60]

LANGUAGE QUESTIONS EMERGE

Although the work at EFFAS would not be ready for several years, discussions with SAAJ were well under way by the time the 1990 Annual Report was issued. According to Gentaro Yura, senior adviser of SAAJ in the early 1990s, he and Pete Morley met first in 1985 during one of Morley's first trips abroad. Yura was aware that, at the time, "the number of [CFA] candidates outside North America was paltry" and that the ICFA was looking to Asia, where "there was a growing need for advanced educational program[s]."[61] India or Singapore, where English was spoken, were a readier fit for the CFA Program, but Japan was attractive because SAAJ had its own examination program for analysts and investment managers leading to the designation Chartered Member of the Association (CMA). In 1988, SAAJ "approached the ICFA about the possibility of reciprocal recognition of their successful candidates."[62] A reciprocal arrangement might mean that attainment of the CMA designation would exempt its holders from certain provisions of the CFA Program, while having received a CFA charter would exempt charterholders from certain provisions of the CMA program. As trade and financial activity between Asia and North America increased, holding both designations seemed to have clear advantages.

As with the London program, the ICFA scrutinized the SAAJ curriculum and testing methods to see how closely they matched the standards of the CFA Program. SAAJ, organized in 1962 as the Tokyo Securities Analysts Association, had offered its first certification examinations in 1978. The first CMA designation was awarded in 1981.[63] By the early 1990s, the program consisted of two examinations with a total duration of 12 hours. Because the topics differed significantly from those in the CFA curriculum, CFA Program officials proposed that the differences be made up through further ICFA-developed examinations. In this way, CMA candidates could reach an equivalency and become exempt from some CFA Program provisions. Proposed were an additional "three-hour exam on Level I and Level II questions and a six-hour exam to be taken the following year on Level II and Level III questions."[64] An agreement for this program was signed in February 1991, and the first modified examinations were administered in Japan in 1992.

The results of the initial administration of the modified examination in Japan disappointed CFA Program staff but did not truly surprise Gentaro Yura, who believed that the "language handicap" had been a formidable factor.[65] Yura also cited "the Japanese way of studying and preparing for exams" as a contributing

Gentaro Yura (front left), executive managing director of SAAJ, and Darwin M. Bayston, CFA (front right), AIMR president and CEO, sign a reciprocity agreement in 1991.

factor because it was "quite different" from the way North American CFA candidates prepared. The latter, he considered to be "more used to being involved in debating" and to discussing various points, whereas in Japan, "we are quite good at remembering theories."

Yet, as Tom Bowman recalled, despite these acknowledged difficulties, the Japanese did not think that taking the examination in Japanese was a good idea, in part because of the nuances in translating from English to Japanese but also because they recognized that English proficiency was needed to engage in business and commerce worldwide. English had become "the world's lingua franca" for business.[66] As Ted Muller remembered it, during the initial discussions about whether the CFA exam should be offered in Japanese or English, "Mr. Yura insisted that the exam be in English since English is the international language of investment management."[67]

Bowman cited a telling example of the nuances easily missed. The AIMR staff conducted a translation experiment:

> We took a past Level III exam question and had three people [in the United States] who wrote financial reports in Japanese translate it. We just did not go to the Japanese department here at the University of Virginia. We had people who worked for financial firms and who wrote in Japanese. We had three different people translate these questions, which we then sent over to the SAAJ for them to "grade" the quality of the translation.
>
> Every one of the three failed—in terms of getting across the question that was really being asked. Exam questions are so specific and every word is so important. It is not like translating a novel or a magazine article where

HISTORICAL SPOTLIGHT

Professor Mamoru Aoyama also supervised "a team of 18 experts" in translating *Managing Investment Portfolios: A Dynamic Process* into Japanese in the late 1980s and checked the translation in detail. The resulting translation was published in Japan, in two volumes, in 1989.[70]

if you get the gist of it, you are okay. In an exam or in a question, every word can be very, very important. If there is a certain nuance to the word that is missed, the whole question is thrown off.[68]

In a recent interview, Yura recounted a salient example of the perils of translation. A Japanese scholar, Mamoru Aoyama of Yokohama National University, who was on hand to "grade" the sample translations sent from Charlottesville to SAAJ, pointed out that the name of Jack Treynor (editor of the *FAJ*) had been mistranslated as "trainer"—i.e., "someone who trains trainees," as Yura put it.[69] Clearly, for the translations to be precise, exam translators would need to understand not only concepts and technical jargon but even proper names that happen to be homonyms for common words.

Soliciting the help of bilingual Japanese professionals to translate the questions was considered, according to Tom Bowman, but decided against: "Having the translation done by bilingual Japanese analysts would have meant that questions would have to be furnished to the translators prior to the exam administration. This presented the ICFA with significant security risks that we were unwilling to take."[71]

George Troughton, curriculum consultant at the time of this experiment, recalled another example of the difficulty posed by rendering ideas back and forth between these two particular languages:

> One of the most famous propositions in finance theory is contained in an article published by Modigliani and Miller (M&M), some 50 years ago. [We had it] translated into Japanese; then professional business translators outside of AIMR translated it back into an English exam question.[72]

The M&M hypothesis followed an English-to-Japanese-to-English path—and with the same unsatisfactory results as the earlier experiment. "If you want to see how things change from the original," Troughton said, "have an English [hypothesis] translated into Japanese and then have the Japanese translate that hypothesis back into English!"[73]

The modified exams given in Japan remained in English. The reciprocity agreement itself was modified in May 1994 in such a way that CMA holders would be exempt from taking CFA Level I examinations.[74]

As the CFA Program candidate pool increased in numbers outside North America, questions about language use increased. Ironically, the only language exception ever granted occurred *within* North America (see Chapter 2). That arrangement was made with French-speaking Canadians and presented many problems over time, not least of which was fairness. Throughout its history, the CFA Program has striven for absolute consistency: consistent rigor in questions, consistent comprehensiveness in curriculum, and especially, consistent fairness in grading. Extraordinary pains have been taken over the years to refine the grading process and to build in checks and balances—all to ensure that each candidate is judged equitably. As illustrated in the discussion of reciprocity, the act of translating contains inherent problems. Quality safeguards were needed and various methods tried for dealing with exams written in French in answer to English questions. As Nancy Dudley, exam administrator at the time, remembered, the process was complicated even for the comparatively few exams answered in French:

> If [candidates] were going to answer in French, we'd put them all in a room by themselves so that when their exams came back, the exams were all together. We then brought translators in from Montreal to transcribe the exams for us. [They] worked with the Dictaphone, and we would then type up the responses and bind the exams and send them through to be graded.[75]

Nancy Dudley served as exam administrator for 1983–2006. She is now head of Key Stakeholder Services.

Later, she noted, "it got to the point where there were too many people responding in French for us to translate the exams in time for grading because we had [only] two to three weeks to get ready for grading." Instead, graders who were fluent in French had to be found. According to Don Tuttle, "All or almost all of these graders were French Canadians with CFA charters."[76] As will be discussed in the next chapter, this process was ultimately ended, but not before the possibility of giving CFA exams in languages other than English had been analyzed again and again.

If the journeys taken by Pete Morley seem to have gone in one direction only—outward from North America—that was not the case. Certainly, Morley and others worked to spread the word about the excellence of the CFA Program outside North America. But explorers not only venture out; they also return—laden with new experiences and new knowledge and, sometimes, souvenirs. What Pete Morley and the others brought back were intellectual souvenirs: new ideas for what the program needed to contain in order to be truly international, new methods of education seen elsewhere, and the fresh perspectives provided by new friends.

As early as 1990, International Committee Chair Eugene C. Sit, CFA, had reminded trustees that the CFA curriculum and examination "should be undergoing review in order to assure appropriate international content, not only to the benefit of global but also North American candidates."[77] Benefits for both did ensue. In studying the SIA program in preparation for making a reciprocity agreement, for example, Tom Bowman noticed that its curriculum contained some "description of why things were in the 'syllabus' and 'what was expected of the candidate'."[78] This glimpse of a different way of doing things—after the idea had percolated for a while and, as noted earlier, been personalized in a CFA candidate's questions—led Bowman to propose in February 1992 that the CFA

Program "develop a set of candidate requirement statements that would help link the efforts of the CCC and COE to the Body of Knowledge."[79] Ultimately, this idea became the Learning Outcome Statements so integral to the study program today. In addition, George Troughton recalled that corporate finance, "which is now a mainstay of our curriculum," was added because "to a certain extent, we saw that was a vital link in the British SIA curriculum."[80]

Within months of the initial reciprocity agreement with SIA, Michael Theobald, FSIP, of the University of Birmingham in England was working as a consultant with CFA Program staff; within a few years, non-North American COE and CCC members and graders were commonplace. By the end of the decade, a Swiss national, Philippe A. Sarasin, CFA, was the ICFA board chair. Those running the CFA Program knew that globalization was a two-way street. According to Tom Bowman, CFA leaders had to "reach out and get some volunteers who were CFA charterholders from other countries and other cultures [to help] make this examination more globally generic."[81] The goal was that any CFA exam question "would be just as relevant if you were sitting in New Delhi as if you were sitting in New York City." At its finest, the move to internationalize the CFA Program embodied reciprocity in the highest sense.

LEADERSHIP TRANSITIONS

The first five years of the 1990s brought a dazzling amount of change to the CFA Program. It went from being administered by a single-purpose, stand-alone institute to being part of a much larger organization with many moving parts. Candidates taking the CFA exams rose from 8,760 in 1990 to 15,413 in 1994. The CFA

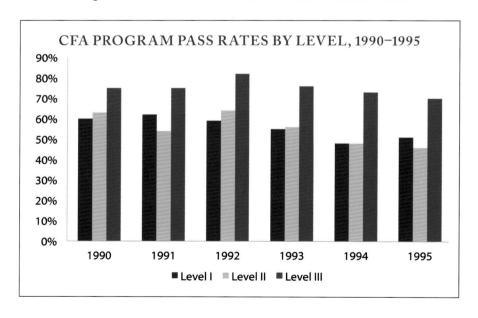

CFA PROGRAM PASS RATES BY LEVEL, 1990–1995

Program staff increased by 60 percent. But even more significant was that its top leadership changed three times in five years.

The year 1990 began with Pete Morley firmly in charge. Shortly into that year, however, he retired and Darwin Bayston took over. Bayston guided AIMR through the tensions involved in creating new structures. In 1993, Bayston returned to private work as an investment manager, after a career at the ICFA and AIMR that spanned 13 years. Executive Vice President Tom Bowman, content in

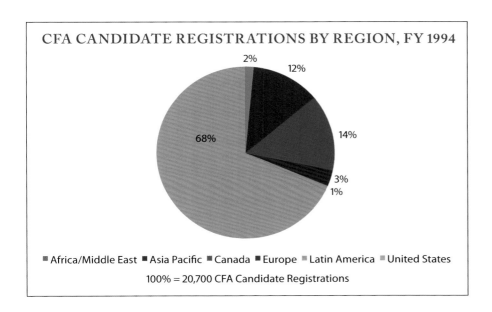

CFA CANDIDATE REGISTRATIONS BY REGION, FY 1994

- Africa/Middle East ■ Asia Pacific ■ Canada ■ Europe ■ Latin America ■ United States
100% = 20,700 CFA Candidate Registrations

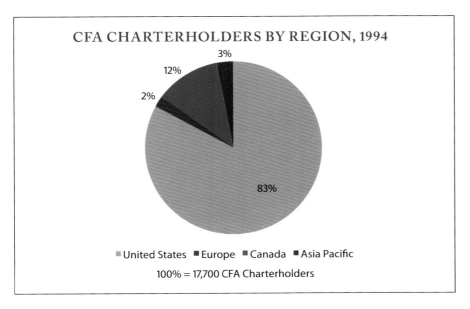

CFA CHARTERHOLDERS BY REGION, 1994

■ United States ■ Europe ■ Canada ■ Asia Pacific
100% = 17,700 CFA Charterholders

CHARLES D. ELLIS, CFA

Recipient:

Graham and Dodd Award, 1975

C. Stewart Sheppard Award, 1986

Award for Professional Excellence, 2003

PROFILE OF A VOLUNTEER

Asked about his friend Charley Ellis, Dean LeBaron, CFA, constructed an image: "[Picture] Charley standing in the bow of a river craft navigating the Colorado rapids in the Grand Canyon and telling river rat, 'Smedley,' which way to go to avoid the turbulence around the rocks."[82] On such a risky journey—as in the investment business—LeBaron explains, "Charley [sees] the goal as safe passage" —while others, like "Smedley," just want to "give the customers a thrill."

One means of ensuring safe passage in the perilous waters of the investment industry, Ellis realized, was, in LeBaron's words, to "push for professionalism"— and he did, by supporting the CFA Program. Katrina F. "Katy" Sherrerd, CFA, saw Ellis as a "leader in our industry [with] a strong commitment to the mission of the ICFA/AIMR/CFA Institute, [and] an advisor to most if not all leaders of the organizations." He really worked hard, she added, "to make sure that a lot of [industry leaders] were aware of CFA Institute."

Charley Ellis, a native of Boston, received his undergraduate degree from Yale University, an MBA from Harvard Business School, and a PhD from New York University. Ellis earned his CFA charter in 1969. Expecting to take the Level III exam a few years earlier, he had begun preparing for it when he received a letter expressing regret but informing him that he would not be permitted to proceed that year because he was "too young." Under the age requirements then in place, he needed to wait another two years to qualify. Ellis was surprised about this— particularly when he discovered that the exam for Level III contained a question instructing candidates to "comment" on an article that *he* had written. Charley Ellis may be the only person in the history of the CFA Program to appear *on* the Level III exam before he could appear *in* a room taking it.

Luckily for the investment management profession, Ellis continued to publish. He has authored 14 books and more than 100 articles. Many have appeared in the *Financial Analysts Journal*; some were used in the CFA curriculum. Ellis served as an Institute of Chartered Financial Analysts trustee for 10 years and was chair of the ICFA Board of Trustees in 1983–1984. Also a governor of the Association for Investment Management and Research, Ellis served as chair of the AIMR Board of Governors in 1993–1994.

Ellis began his long career in the investment profession with a stint in the not-for-profit world by working in management at a public radio station in Boston and, later, for the Rockefeller Foundation. He subsequently worked at Donaldson, Lufkin and Jenrette until, in 1972, he founded Greenwich Associates, an international research, strategy, and consulting firm characterized not only by the quality of its research but also for its advice to clients on how to implement the research findings.

Among those benefiting from Ellis's skills were the Financial Analysts Federation and the ICFA when they were contemplating becoming one organization. Ellis was asked to study how the two organizations might combine and come up with a solution that made sense for the industry. Ellis's friend James R. Vertin, CFA, appreciated the significance of this assignment:

> While many, perhaps most, institute leaders [focused] on the differences between the ICFA and FAF, Charley was looking at the many similarities in their memberships and in their goals. He envisioned a future for them as a unified whole, in which the best features of each organization would meld to create a level of success and effectiveness that neither might reach on its own.

In 2003, Charles D. Ellis, CFA (right), received the Award for Professional Excellence from Abby Joseph Cohen, CFA (left), AIMR chair for 1997–1998.

The man who brought strategic planning to the ICFA "saw farther ahead than the rest of us," Jim Vertin noted, and Ellis's longer-term perspective was used to good effect by the CFA Program and the institutions that have nurtured it. During his service in the early 1980s, the CFA Program began to undergo the systematic review that still characterizes it. "Every organization needs a visionary," Vertin continued, and Charley Ellis has been an "excellent corporate ICFA visionary." By helping trustees to look ahead, he transformed an organization whose primary motion had always been "here to here to here—this year's exam, this year's curriculum, this year's grading, next year's study guide, next year's exam, next year's grading" into one that saw a much bigger picture. Under his counsel, the organization began to ask itself: "What about five years from now? What about 10 years from now? What do we need? How do we do it?"

People who have met him or heard him speak remember Ellis for his intelligence and wit. One who saw another side of Ellis—a deep thoughtfulness—was Thomas A. Bowman, CFA. Bowman recalled the day on which he became CEO of AIMR. His selection was to be announced at the annual conference in Washington, DC, Bowman said, and Ellis found out that Bowman's parents lived in suburban DC. "Charley sent out a limousine" to pick them up and bring them to the conference, as a surprise to Bowman, so that they could be at the luncheon when he was introduced. "I will never forget that," Bowman said. "Charley made that a special time."

A person capable of great attention to such detail, Ellis has also been a visionary looking far into the future and a tireless supporter of the CFA Program. As his longtime friend Jim Vertin put it, "If Charley Ellis hadn't existed, the ICFA would have had to invent him."

Location	Tested Candidates
New York, New York, USA	1,614
Toronto, Ontario, Canada	1,449
Boston, Massachusetts, USA	921
Chicago, Illinois, USA	889
San Francisco, California, USA	568
Los Angeles, California, USA	498
Montreal, Quebec, Canada	471
Upper Montclair, New Jersey, USA	443
Hong Kong (SAR)	416
Singapore	404

Thomas A. Bowman, CFA, served as AIMR/CFA Institute president and CEO from 1994 to 2004.

his work with the CFA candidate programs, indicated he was not interested in the president's job but agreed to serve as interim head while the board mounted a national search for a new chief executive officer.

During the months that followed this agreement, one significant thing happened: Bowman changed his mind. He called and let the chair of the AIMR Board of Governors, Charley Ellis, know of this change. Aware that the search had uncovered several good candidates, Bowman had no expectation of being chosen. Then, he recalled, one day in 1994 as "we were getting ready for the annual meeting in May, I got a call from Charley Ellis late one afternoon."[83] Ellis asked him what he was doing, to which Bowman replied that he had Board of Governors books scattered all over the floor and was getting them assembled and "trying to get ready for these meetings." To Bowman's puzzlement, Ellis suggested that Bowman and his wife take a vacation and "relax." With an annual meeting looming, Bowman thought this request was particularly weird and said as much. Then, Ellis explained to him why a rest might be in order: "I want to tell you that you are going to be the next president of AIMR." A few days later, on 16 May 1994, the board officially elected him and Bowman began his term as the third president of AIMR.

Charley Ellis also remembered that time. His perspective highlights the good fortune that came to AIMR from Bowman's change of heart:

Fortunately for all CFA charterholders, Tom Bowman reversed his first inclination not to be a candidate for President because he was not interested in extensive travel and knew many tough—often painfully political—"people" decisions must lie ahead for whoever took the job. Tom changed his focus to the extraordinary importance of the CFA Program and community and agreed to take up the role as our leader. Of course, he went on to excel and his gentle, cheerful, steady hand contributed immeasurably to our eventual success.[84]

chapter six

Expanding the Infrastructure: 1994–1999

*S*hortly before Thomas A. Bowman, CFA, was elected president and CEO of the Association for Investment Management and Research in May 1994, Dwight D. Churchill, CFA, incoming chair of the Candidate Curriculum Committee, wrote to John L. Maginn, CFA, who was about to become chair of AIMR. Churchill set out his plans for the committee for the coming year and expressed his conviction that the CCC would need restructuring "to meet the evolving demands of the candidate program."[1] Among Churchill's concerns was the growing burden on volunteer time because of the expansion of available literature to survey. Churchill praised the "high level of commitment by the volunteer[s] and staff" but also stated his belief that the relatively loose structure of the CCC as it then existed was "no longer suited" to the needs of the program.

The increasing complexity of financial instruments and industry changes made for ever-greater amounts of reading matter that CCC members needed to review to find suitable curricular materials. Moreover, the CCC was also being asked to find materials for an accreditation program—part of continuing education for charterholders—then under consideration. Unfortunately, these increasing obligations came at a period when most CCC members had little time to dedicate to the work. If left unchecked, Churchill suggested, this tendency of trying to pack more work into fewer volunteer hours could mean that the effectiveness of the committee would "gradually decline." Such a decline would be unacceptable at any time in the history of the CFA Program, but at this particular moment, the program was reaching new countries every year, which opened the door to greater scrutiny and "reduced tolerance for error."

Having discussed his concerns with AIMR senior staff—including Tom Bowman, Robert M. Luck, Jr., CFA (then vice president for Curriculum and Examinations), and curriculum consultant George H. Troughton, CFA—Churchill urged Maginn and the AIMR Board of Governors to develop an infrastructure in Charlottesville that would allow for continued use of volunteers but have sufficient staff to shift the organization and administration for managing the curriculum to

We looked at the infrastructure of the organization [and] how fast we had grown. We'd underestimated . . . [but] we wanted to make sure that we had the infrastructure in place—not only that we had enough people but we had the right people in various positions throughout the organization in staff positions [and on] the volunteer side of it as well.

—John L. Maginn, CFA,
1994–1995 AIMR chair, July 2010

John L. Maginn, CFA, served as ICFA chair (1985–1986) and AIMR chair (1994–1995).

Dwight D. Churchill, CFA, served as CCC chair (1994–1997) and AIMR chair (2002–2003).

Marilyn R. Irvin, CFA, COE chair 1999–2002.

the central office. Churchill concluded his letter with the often-heard wish that progress would be made toward greater coordination between the CCC and the Council of Examiners.

Methods and approaches were also being reconsidered on the COE side of the table. At the 15 May 1994 meeting of the ICFA (Institute of Chartered Financial Analysts) Board of Trustees, J. Clay Singleton, CFA, incoming COE chair, expressed concerns about the demands on volunteer time incurred by his fellow council members. Like the CCC, the COE was in the process of developing an action plan to deal with its growing workload. Singleton reiterated the need for "further Charlottesville administrative support" (that is, an increase in AIMR staff members dealing with the CFA Program) because of the "dwindling availability of volunteers."[2] The amount of time volunteers had available to devote to the program seemed inversely proportional to the expanding amount of work asked of them. Interestingly, exactly 50 years earlier, Lucien O. Hooper, CFA, had argued against the establishment of a professional rating for analysts because he believed that the volunteer work needed for such a program would "naturally demand much of the time of many of our most competent and busiest members."[3] No doubt, some volunteer leaders in the mid-1990s felt as though they were living that reality.

As discussed in Chapter 3, the ICFA had reached a pivotal point in the early 1980s where a turn from volunteer-managed programs to staff-managed programs was necessary. By the mid-1990s, however, the load again needed rebalancing. When Alfred C. "Pete" Morley, CFA, was hired as CEO in 1984, the CFA Program was serving approximately 4,000 candidates and had awarded 8,000 charters. Ten years later, the candidate load had grown to more than 15,000 (and would soon increase further) and the number of CFA charters awarded was in excess of 20,000. Moreover, candidates and members were now from countries all over the globe—a trend that would continue in the coming years—and the curriculum, examinations, and member programs needed to reflect that globalization. The two key committees of the CFA Program (the COE and CCC) needed help to accomplish all that was asked of them; in fact, all aspects of the program would benefit from an increase in administrative staff members, a deepening of their roles, and a streamlining of the process.

Several proposed changes to the *modus operandi* of the volunteer committees for the CFA Program were in evidence at the May 1994 ICFA Board of Trustees meeting. The COE, for example, had instituted a multiple-choice question-writing project under the direction of H. Kent Baker, CFA, of American University. To be completed by the end of 1994, the project was developing a bank of multiple-choice questions that could be drawn upon in creating Level I exams. The COE was also contemplating whether to outsource the writing of essay questions for Level I. If adopted, this approach would put the COE in the "policy role of editors."[4] Their broad experience made them particularly suited

EDUCATION ADVISORY COMMITTEE AND COE CHAIRS

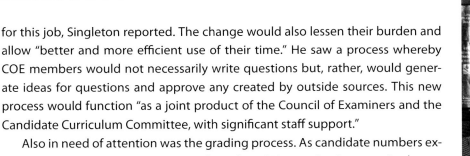

EAC (formerly CCC) Chairs
Donald L. Tuttle, CFA: 1982–1985
George H. Wood, Jr., CFA: 1985–1987
Gary G. Schlarbaum, CFA: 1987–1990
Fred H. Speece, Jr., CFA: 1990–1993
John W. Peavy III, CFA: 1993–1994
Dwight D. Churchill, CFA: 1994–1997
Scott L. Lummer, CFA: 1997–1999
Brian D. Singer, CFA: 1999–2000
Peter B. Mackey, CFA: 2000–2004
James W. Bronson, CFA: 2004–2005
Matthew H. Scanlan, CFA: 2005–2006
Alan M. Meder, CFA: 2006–2008
Matthew H. Scanlan, CFA: 2008–2010

COE Chairs
1962–1967 no appointed chair
Gilbert H. Palmer, CFA: 1968–1975
Brierly W. Anderson, CFA: 1975–1977
Paul E. "Jay" Vawter, Jr., CFA: 1977–1982
Robert G. Puchniak, CFA: 1982–1984
James M. LaFleur, CFA: 1984–1987
Michael L. McCowin, CFA: 1987–1989
Tom S. Sale III, CFA: 1989–1992
Jeffrey L. Winter, CFA: 1992–1994
J. Clay Singleton, CFA: 1994–1996
Terry L. Arndt, CFA: 1996–1999
Marilyn R. Irvin, CFA: 1999–2002
Thomas B. Welch, CFA: 2002–2005
James G. Jones, CFA: 2005–2008
Susan A. Borrelli, CFA: 2008–2010

Scott L. Lummer, CFA, CCC chair 1997–1999.

Susan A. Borrelli, CFA, COE chair 2008–2010.

for this job, Singleton reported. The change would also lessen their burden and allow "better and more efficient use of their time." He saw a process whereby COE members would not necessarily write questions but, rather, would generate ideas for questions and approve any created by outside sources. This new process would function "as a joint product of the Council of Examiners and the Candidate Curriculum Committee, with significant staff support."

Also in need of attention was the grading process. As candidate numbers exploded and essay questions remained, grading CFA examinations required more and more people. Bob Luck, reporting on preparations for grading the 1994 exams, expected the task would require 260 graders. He also projected that if candidate enrollments continued to increase at the same pace as just experienced, 560 exam graders would be required by 1998. In fact, the rise in candidates sitting for the CFA exams was even steeper than projected, and in 1998, 651 exam graders were needed. Like Churchill and Singleton, Luck expressed concern about preserving the quality of the program; in particular, he stressed the need to do everything possible to ensure quality in the grading process and maintain its integrity in the face of truly exponential growth.

To accommodate increasing numbers of candidates and a growing Body of Knowledge, the structures supporting the CFA Program were renewed in the second half of the 1990s, which proved to be an unusually challenging but remarkably fertile period. Many innovations that now define the program were put into place. Changes to the CCC and COE in composition and in responsibility occurred during this time. Also in this half-decade, the first Job Analysis was conducted, the first Learning Outcome Statements were written, the first all-multiple-choice CFA exam was given, the fixed-income curriculum was strengthened, and the CFA Program staff expanded considerably. In every sense, something new was forming.

IDENTIFYING BEST PRACTICES

We went to the experts to ask, "What is the right way to do this?"

—Robert M. Luck, Jr., CFA, 1994

Robert M. Luck, Jr., CFA, vice president, Curriculum and Examinations, 1987–1999.

A few months before Dwight Churchill and Clay Singleton expressed their wishes for a restructuring of the CCC and COE, Tom Bowman had convened an Education Summit in Charlottesville. Senior staff members working on the candidate and accreditation programs attended, as did volunteers on the COE, CCC, and Accreditation Committee and members of the various boards within AIMR. At the time, AIMR maintained a tripartite board structure. The ICFA, the Financial Analysts Federation (FAF), and AIMR itself—each held separate board meetings, with individual but often overlapping agendas, and certainly with many shared members.

Given the unwieldiness of this institutional structure, it is no wonder that the purpose of Bowman's Education Summit was to get a handle on all the sponsored educational activities within the purview of AIMR—from the society level to the CFA Program and beyond. (Society activities are beyond the scope of this book, but throughout the organization's history, local analyst societies have sponsored educational activities ranging from luncheons with industry speakers to CFA review courses and conferences.) Bowman was aware of the increasing complexity of overseeing the myriad educational activities within AIMR, so he in-

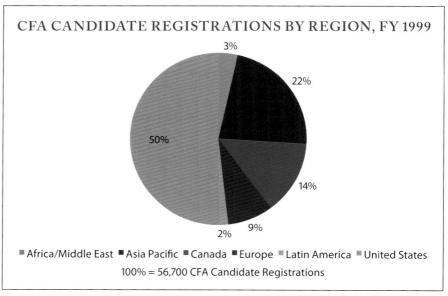

CFA CANDIDATE REGISTRATIONS BY REGION, FY 1999

3%
22%
14%
9%
2%
50%

■ Africa/Middle East ■ Asia Pacific ■ Canada ■ Europe ■ Latin America ■ United States
100% = 56,700 CFA Candidate Registrations

tended the Education Summit to facilitate communication among all the groups responsible for the activities. Without integration, the various groups were in danger of becoming pigeonholed into their respective functions.

The need for integration grew pressing as the numbers of candidate registrations and charterholders continued to increase. In 1994, for example, the 15,413 candidates who sat for CFA exams contrasted substantially with the 8,064 exam takers in 1989 and the 4,030 candidates who sat in 1984. In 1999, 45,143 people took the CFA exams—in 70 different countries. Charterholder numbers had increased also, although not quite as dramatically: By 1994, 20,150 charters

HISTORICAL SPOTLIGHT

Prior to 1994, a single receptionist handled all calls and inquiries coming into AIMR. Raymond J. De-Angelo, who became AIMR marketing director in 1994, was surprised to find a system this primitive serving a population of approximately 35,000 members and CFA candidates: "The receptionist was doing it *all*," he recalled, "and as call traffic increased, her/his job was getting too full and calls were being routed every which way"—because there was no precise system for getting calls to the right person. Under DeAngelo's direction, AIMR Information Central was established to remedy this situation.[5]

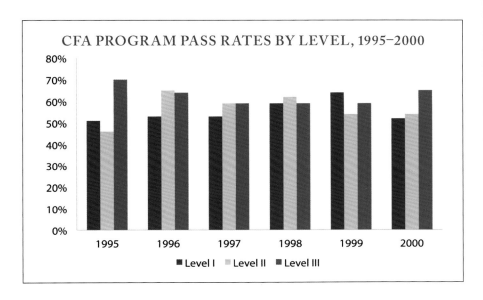

CFA PROGRAM PASS RATES BY LEVEL, 1995–2000

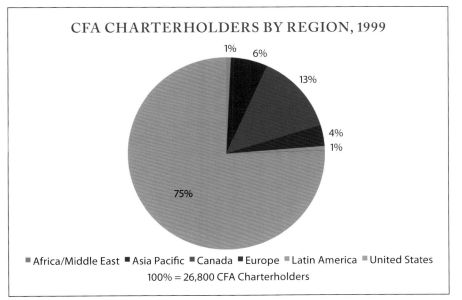

CFA CHARTERHOLDERS BY REGION, 1999

100% = 26,800 CFA Charterholders

HISTORICAL SPOTLIGHT:
TEN LARGEST EXAM CENTERS, 1999

Location	Tested Candidates
New York, New York, USA	4,378
Toronto, Ontario, Canada	3,829
Hong Kong (SAR)	3,414
Singapore	2,394
Boston, Massachusetts, USA	2,191
Chicago, Illinois, USA	1,538
London, UK	1,402
San Francisco, California, USA	1,276
Los Angeles, California, USA	1,261
Tokyo, Japan	1,007

had been awarded, up from 12,405 in 1989 and 8,306 in 1984. In 1999, CFA charterholders numbered 35,071.

An even greater explosion in growth was coming in the 21st century. Participants in the 1994 Education Summit may not have guessed just how extraordinary this growth would be, but they had certainly noticed the trend. The large increase in numbers was accompanied by geographical expansion, especially into the Asia Pacific region. True coordination had to be attained—and quickly—otherwise the CFA Program was at risk of smothering under the weight of its own success.

An important tangible result of the summit was the creation of an AIMR Education Board (later, the Education Committee) whose *raison d'être* was coordination. Comprising senior education staff and the volunteer leaders from all the education committees, the Education Board was chaired by AIMR Governor Eliot P. Williams, CFA. Abby Joseph Cohen, CFA, of Goldman Sachs and Frank K. Reilly, CFA, of the University of Notre Dame, who were AIMR governors and ICFA trustees, served as vice chairs.

Perhaps the most significant result of the summit was the open recognition, seen in the reports from Clay Singleton and Dwight Churchill cited previously, of the need to add staff members who could assume part of what had historically been committee work. The hope was that "greater efficiencies" would result from a substantial increase in AIMR staff to tend to all aspects to the CFA Program.[6] Soon after the summit, the staff in Charlottesville was restructured into three areas: (1) member and candidate curriculum, (2) examination and standards, and (3) educational products. AIMR then–Senior Vice President Katrina F. "Katy" Sherrerd, CFA, and Senior Vice President Donald L. Tuttle, CFA, were to co-head the educational efforts; Sherrerd was to focus on continuing education products, and Tuttle, on curriculum and examinations. Also formed at the time was an AIMR Management Committee, a precursor to the CFA Institute Leadership Team that manages the organization today.

Some key components of the CFA Program traditionally dependent on volunteers now resided with the Charlottesville staff and its consultants. As Churchill and others acknowledged, the crucial issue was that the staff work in conjunction with the volunteers in a way that ensured that "the creativity and imagination of the volunteers [are] not stifled but promoted."[7]

WHAT DOES A CANDIDATE NEED TO KNOW?

Leaders of the CFA Program seldom had an idle moment in the first 30 years of the program's history. Staff and volunteers continuously scrutinized the program's key components—the curriculum, the examinations, and the grading process. Year by year, they adjusted and modified incrementally. This constant tweaking is so commonplace in CFA Program history that it hardly sounds like news to say that it continued in the middle to late 1990s, but the period is noteworthy for the particularly active and fruitful way in which the educational mission of the program was modified and defined. The changes were characterized by a turn toward pedagogical theory, best practices in educational testing, a new methodology for determining the Body of Knowledge (BOK) on which the CFA Program is based, a realistic focus on changes in the fixed-income field, and the introduction of Learning Outcome Statements. The innovations and modifications made in the second half of the 1990s tremendously increased the sophistication of the entire CFA Program. It is almost impossible to overstate how greatly refined its methodology and pedagogy became during the decade.

The Third Generation Body of Knowledge

An early manifestation of the shifts in the program was the formation of a task force to refine the GBOK (Global Body of Knowledge). Headed by Don Tuttle, the task force included several non–North American representatives and did its work in 1994 and 1995. In response to the globalization of financial markets and growing interest in the CFA Program from analysts around the world, the task force was charged with systematically weaving international aspects into what became the GBOK.[8] Although the CFA Program had not focused exclusively on security analysis as practiced in the United States and Canada for many years, Tom Bowman remembered a time in the 1980s and early 1990s when "we used to have a section of the curriculum entitled 'international,' where readings pertaining to issues outside the U.S. [and Canada] would go."[9] That approach gradually changed, but in the mid-1990s the growing internationalism in capital markets was still not reflected fully in the curriculum. Everyone realized, however, that international issues "were relevant to us all and should be blended with the rest of the curriculum."

The evidence of international links was everywhere: The Channel Tunnel (Chunnel) between England and France opened in 1994, and at the end of the decade, the euro was introduced. The joining of countries and economies was not merely symbolic. Financial behavior in one part of the world rapidly affected other parts. In 1997, for example, a financial market crisis in Southeast Asia was precipitated by an "excessive inflow of foreign funds" into domestic investments in the countries of the region and at "foreign exchange rates that were hard to sustain."[10] Too much foreign investment flowing in was quickly followed by too much foreign investment racing out as "many American mutual funds that had holdings in [South Asian] stock markets began selling."[11] The withdrawal of foreign capital helped to speed the spread of currency deflation and stock market collapses in the region. The world of the 1990s might not have been quite as

EXAM STORY:
AN UNEXPECTED
CHALLENGE AT
A TEST CENTER

"When I sat for CFA Level I in 1993, the exam program was held in the classrooms of the John Marshall Law School in the South Loop area of Chicago. The morning session proceeded uneventfully, but no sooner had we started the afternoon session when the sounds of a very large, very loud, and very long parade wafted to our classrooms from the street below. To my recollection, it was the Puerto Rican Day Parade. Regardless, it was an unwelcome distraction to those of us trying to concentrate on an exam we had spent months preparing for. Looking back on that day, it seems to me that the parade is an allegory for all of the distractions in the markets today—we investment professionals have to stay laser-focused on the task at hand and tune out all of the noise!"

—KAREN SCOTT WILSON, CFA
Winnetka, Illinois, USA

BALANCED ON THE CUTTING EDGE:
THE RESEARCH FOUNDATION OF CFA INSTITUTE

The Research Foundation was founded in 1965 to create material that would fill voids and expand knowledge for investment professionals. Initially focused on creating works for the CFA Program curriculum, for which reliable materials were sadly lacking, the foundation also sponsored original research useful to the practicing financial analyst or investment manager. Even its earliest seminars on portfolio management, held between 1966 and 1970, filled a significant gap in the candidate curriculum while expanding the libraries of practicing analysts and portfolio managers. By 1972, the foundation had formally broadened its mission to include the conduct of "basic and applied research of a disinterested nature" that would have potential value not simply to the practitioner or CFA candidate "but also to regulatory agencies and the academic community."[12] To some extent, that mission continues to this day.

According to longtime Research Foundation board member James R. Vertin, CFA, the Research Foundation —composed of "academic, industry, and practitioner talent"—sponsors a type of research that is "not available from the Street, in subject areas where knowledge and factual relevance could be used with confidence by our members and by the profession broadly."[13] Over the years, the foundation has published monographs on diverse topics, including insurance swaps (1995), asset allocation (1987),

and Islamic finance (2009). In the 1970s, it sponsored the first of the highly regarded Roger Ibbotson and Rex Sinquefield studies of historical market data (since that time, available in the annually updated *Stocks, Bonds, Bills and Inflation* series).

Throughout the Research Foundation's history, the various antecedents of CFA Institute have given it financial support. In 1986, the ICFA contributed $500,000 toward building a significant endowment for the foundation; in 1992, AIMR provided $100,000. Yet, the foundation is also partially self-supporting; it conducted its first fund-raising campaign in the 1970s and since then, has raised and maintained an endowment. According to Katrina F. "Katy" Sherrerd, CFA, formerly executive director of the foundation, "Pete Morley, Gene Sit, George Noyes, and Fred Speece, in particular, worked tirelessly to raise an endowment."[14] By 1993, the foundation's endowment totaled $2 million; by 2010, close to $9 million.

CFA charterholders have also been a dependable source of support. Some authors who are charterholders have donated royalties from their books, and graders have often given all or part of their stipends to the foundation. Over the years, "these contributions were significant," Sherrerd noted.

In 1997, the Research Foundation received its largest gift ever, when a former chair of the ICFA Board of Trustees, Gary P. Brinson, CFA, donated $1.5 million dollars. Noting that research

had been important "in shaping my thinking and in challenging my ideas and concepts," Brinson's wish was to give something back to the profession in a way that would help others and "over time would provide increasing expansion of the Body of Knowledge."[15] Katy Sherrerd recalled Brinson's fostering of the Research Foundation: "Gary focused on . . . the importance of research in our industry" and saw the value of differences of opinion, "so that people would be challenged to keep thinking and to be innovative."[16] One result of this generous gift has been the establishment of the Brinson Endowment Challenge Fund.

The Foundation's main mission, "to promote the development and dissemination of relevant research for investment practitioners worldwide," has resulted in cutting-edge research beneficial to those in the profession.[17] This research also continues to help CFA candidates because Research Foundation publications appear in the CFA Program curriculum today as they did at its beginning.

According to Jim Vertin—one of the Research Foundation's staunchest supporters—although its publications may not have "always hit the bullseye," nevertheless, the "basic aims and benefits served the Institute and its members very well indeed over the many years the foundation has [been] an objective source of relevant knowledge."

1998–1999 Research Foundation Board of Trustees

(Seated left to right) Deborah H. Miller, CFA, chair; Gary P. Brinson, CFA; Keith C. Brown, CFA; James R. Vertin, CFA; Katrina F. Sherrerd, CFA, executive director.

(Standing left to right) Thomas A. Bowman, CFA; George W. Noyes, CFA; James L. Farrell, Jr., CFA; Fred H. Speece, Jr., CFA; Frank K. Reilly, CFA; Eliot P. Williams, CFA; R. Charles Tschampion, CFA; Robert H. Jeffrey; H. Gifford Fong.

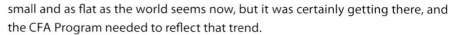

EXAM STORY: A SHORTER TRIP TO THE TEST CENTER THAN EXPECTED

"Before I sat for the Level I test in 1997, there was no exam center in Beirut. I was antsy—planning for travel to Amman, Jordan, the closest test center. Then, I was happily informed that since there were going to be five of us sitting for the Level I exam out of Beirut, CFA Institute (AIMR at the time) had decided to organize a test center at the American University of Beirut. What a relief! My house was a seven-minute walk to the exam center, and from then on, Beirut was put on the CFA Institute global map of test centers worldwide."

—FADI N. KHATIB, CFA
Dubai, UAE

Carl S. Bang, CFA, 1987 charterholder from Norway.

small and as flat as the world seems now, but it was certainly getting there, and the CFA Program needed to reflect that trend.

The new GBOK constituted the "third generation of the Body of Knowledge," as Don Tuttle put it.[18] First came the General Topic Outline, written by C. Stewart Sheppard in 1969, modified in the following years, and often referred to as the "Tree of Knowledge." Then, in 1990, the Task Force chaired by Frederick L. "Ted" Muller, CFA, reorganized the BOK to reflect the stages of an analyst's career: Level I focused on tools; Level II, on valuation and analysis; and Level III, on portfolio management. When that BOK was implemented, the intent "was to eventually make it international . . . ." The document Tuttle presented in 1995 was exactly that: "truly global in scope in its coverage of the investment management body of knowledge."

One reason the expansion was finally happening was that the number of non–North American members invited to grade had increased. "The change came with the graders first," Tuttle remarked;[19] that is, the international perspective that graders from outside North America provided helped spur the process. Then, "the curriculum became much more international, and we would have articles [and] chapters in books" that were internationally oriented. Through these means, and their manifestation in the GBOK, the CFA Program became truly global in nature. As the 1995 AIMR Annual Report announced, the new "comprehensive outline of topics critical to the current practice of investment analysis and portfolio management" was notable for covering "new instruments and markets" and for integrating "international content into each of the main topics."[20]

The First Generation Job Analysis

Work on the first GBOK paralleled another important innovation, namely, a professional survey of practitioners about their work. During his time as chair of the GBOK Task Force, Don Tuttle raised the issue of obtaining data about their professional needs from practitioners themselves by performing what was then called a "Job Analysis Study."[21] Known now as "Practice Analysis" and undertaken on an ongoing basis, the 1995 Job Analysis Study was, at that time, an entirely new means of taking the pulse of the profession in order to verify the relevance of the GBOK. To develop a truly global, practitioner-oriented curriculum, Tuttle reasoned, the CFA Program had to "relate back to the profession"—that is, it had to hear firsthand from practitioners about what work they engaged in daily.

In one sense, the CFA Program had always been in touch with practitioners for it was created and run by them. Even following the transition to a staff-managed organization in the 1980s and 1990s, practitioners are still in charge because the great majority of those in senior staff and decision-making positions have earned CFA charters. But the profession changes rapidly and constantly. In 1994, analysts and investment managers were working with new investment vehicles, in new places, and at new positions in comparison with even 10 years previously. The time was right for a formal check-in that included a sampling of a large number of members, a growing number of whom were now located in financial centers around the globe.

When Don Tuttle first proposed the Job Analysis Survey, he reminded the trustees that other professional associations had begun conducting such analyses. Tuttle had attended a session on the use and value of job analyses at a conference of U.S. certifying organizations and came away convinced that the CFA Program needed and would greatly benefit from conducting one. ICFA Trustee Frank K. Reilly, CFA, echoing Tuttle's sentiments, remarked that an organization of financial planners was producing a similar study. As Tuttle noted, the GBOK Task Force, which he chaired, was already trying to define what analysts worldwide needed to know. But to do this thoroughly, they had to hear back from the profession. A job analysis would put the CFA Program in direct contact with practitioners. At the request of ICFA Board of Trustees Chair Brian F. Wruble, CFA, Tuttle agreed to bring a formal proposal to the September board meeting for discussion and action.

Gerald J. Brady, CFA, 1989 charterholder from Ireland.

Submitted to the trustees in September 1994, Tuttle's proposal recommended that the ICFA engage the Educational Testing Service (ETS) of Princeton, New Jersey, to conduct a systematic six- to nine-month study whose results would tie together "the Body of Knowledge, the [CFA] exam and the positions held by CFA charterholders."

Job analyses identify the performance domain of a job (that is, its actual dimensions and tasks) as well as its knowledge domain (namely, what an individual would need to know in order to perform the job). By determining both, a job analysis would provide the CFA Program leaders with assurances that they were measuring what they should measure, that test results would be reliable in determining who was qualified to receive a CFA charter, and that the CFA examinations would remain fair to all candidates. The expectation was that CFA exams would be objectively verified as having appropriate content and being related to jobs.

Approved unanimously at the September ICFA board meeting, the Job Analysis proceeded in several phases. First, current program materials, such as study guides and the BOK, were reviewed. Next, experts in topic areas were identified and asked to review a draft survey. An AIMR advisory committee also reviewed it, and then a pilot survey was to be given to a small number of CFA charterholders. The pilot survey would then be followed by a survey of a large number (initially 2,500 but raised to 3,500) of charterholders across industries, geographical locations, levels of experience, gender, and ethnicities.

In January 1995, Tuttle reported to the ICFA board that "good progress"

JAMES R. VERTIN, CFA

James R. Vertin, CFA

Recipient:

C. Stewart Sheppard Award, 1984

Nicholas Molodovsky Award, 1992

Donald L. Tuttle Award for CFA
    Grading Excellence, 2001

PROFILE OF A VOLUNTEER

Not everyone can be called a "Father of the Index Fund" and "Most Valuable Player" for the Institute of Chartered Financial Analysts, but Jim Vertin can. The first accolade stems from his work at Wells Fargo Investment Advisors, where, together with James McQuown and William Fouse, he set up the first functioning index fund in July 1971. Vertin's second title was a tribute paid by Frederick L. "Ted" Muller, CFA, chair of the ICFA Board of Trustees when Vertin retired from it in May 1991. Citing Vertin as a "devout advocate [for] the ideals of the CFA Program," Muller declared "he can never be replaced."[22] Luckily, Jim Vertin did not have to be; he continued helping. After he "retired," he served on 11 committees and the Research Foundation Board of Directors for more than another decade.

This prodigious volunteer grew up in Silicon Valley—when it was still called Santa Clara Valley and fields and orchards stretched out in every direction. Vertin recalled an "idyllic childhood" in the small town of Los Gatos, California, USA, "roaming the mountains [and] fishing the creeks." He joined the U.S. Navy right after high school, served in World War II, then studied economics at San Jose State University. The course that intrigued him most was "Security Analysis," he recalled: "I ate it up." Encouraged to attend graduate school by the course's professor, Vertin received an MBA from Stanford University in 1951.

Hired by Wells Fargo Bank as a junior analyst in 1952, he had become manager and chief investment officer of Wells Fargo Investment Advisors by the mid-1960s. There, he teamed with Fouse and McQuown, and the index fund was born. Initially, Peter Bernstein has noted, it "met with a cool reception." But Vertin was persuasive:

> We took it to the board, the trust committee, and I remember quoting Abraham Lincoln—something to the effect that ideas of the past are no longer suitable for the turbulent future. And they bought it!

According to his longtime friend Charles D. Ellis, CFA, "Jim initiated what became one of the world's largest investment units—investing time, energy, drive, and understanding—with very little help and lots of resistance."

"Vertin exudes fervor," Peter Bernstein said, and others concur. To Fred H. Speece, Jr., CFA, a longtime colleague on the Research Foundation board, Vertin "did everything he did with passion and intensity."

Katrina F. "Katy" Sherrerd, CFA, saw someone whose passion and energy always served the purpose "of getting to excellence." Nothing so evoked Vertin's passion for excellence as the CFA Program. During his long service to the ICFA, Vertin was as adamant about high standards as those who created the program in the 1960s. Long a proponent of "Education with a capital E," Vertin wanted those high standards applied to the examination program and especially to continuing education.

Vertin did not declaim from above. He worked at ground level, purposely—writing questions on portfolio management for the Council of Examiners for 10 years and grading CFA exams for more than 20 years. He did not believe one could function satisfactorily at an executive level without knowing how things looked at the candidate level:

> I did not see how a board member . . . could think well about the exam or plan for its future if he was not there in the trenches when the results of those exams came in.

Vertin wanted to see firsthand "what candidates did in response to the exam that we all thought was the greatest thing since sliced bread when we put it together." So, he "insisted on being that close."

In a profession as ever changing as investment management, Vertin also insisted that practitioners must keep up with new ideas, and he devoted his considerable energies to helping charterholders do so. The Continuing Education Program was begun when he was president of the ICFA board. He founded and served on the Council on Education and Research for 12 years and on the Research Foundation board for 25 years, including as Trustee Emeritus. Vertin's driving goal in this work was to bring charterholders up to date on developments in their profession—from new academic theories to the latest investment instruments. Practitioners were welcome to "reject" any theory, as long as they took the time to comprehend it: "If they understand it, they will figure out if they like it [and] how to make it useful to the client, which is the be all and end all of our business." In 1996, when the Research Foundation established an award recognizing the contributions of those who had "produced a body of research notable for its relevance and enduring value to investment professionals," they named it for Jim Vertin.

Vertin has always been clear-eyed about the needs of candidates and members for education and about the need to sponsor original research for the profession. Moreover, this characteristic extends to his private life. Charley Ellis, for one, noticed it: "Jim is a crack shot as a duck hunter with super eyesight. [He] could tell the age of individual ducks in a flock, always picked his targets by their age—and never missed." Vertin was "modest" and never mentioned his keenness, but "those who saw it couldn't *not* tell."

Morally as well as visually acute, Vertin has been a staunch defender of everything he believed in, especially the CFA Program. Faced with difficult choices, whether about a candidate's score, an exam question, or continuing education, Jim Vertin made the decision and took a stand. He did it, as Charley Ellis put it, "like everything he ever did—because it was the right thing to do."

EXAM STORY: A VETERAN OF MANY DIFFERENT TEST CENTERS

"There is no other professional designation in the investment industry that gets as much attention, respect, and recognition as the CFA charter. When I joined Goldman Sachs Japan Ltd. in 2000, our CEO at the time, Henry "Hank" Paulson, recognized the value of the CFA charter and encouraged everyone, regardless of position, to take the exam. All the employees who signed up for the exam were given support by our human resources staff, who organized evening and weekend exam review classes in the office as well as providing calculators and study materials to all the employees who had registered for the exam.

"When I returned to the U.S. two years later and joined Franklin Templeton, my manager, Bill Deakyne, Jr., CFA, was also taking the CFA exam and encouraged our team to take the exam. Thanks to the global presence of the CFA exam, I was able to take the Level I exam in Tokyo and then complete the next two levels in the U.S. after I had returned home.

"I enjoy the people whom I have met through the many CFA Institute events and volunteer opportunities in which I have participated. I have learned so much by listening to their fascinating experiences and stories. Moreover, I now have friends around the world, thanks to the many opportunities/events offered by CFA Institute that have brought us together. Our local CFA society also offers many educational and social networking events to bring members together. It is definitely one of the most enriching lifelong learning experiences that I have by being a CFA charterholder."

—ANNIE LO, CFA, San Francisco

had been made on the Job Analysis, which he described as a "systematic, fact-finding process to identify the important job dimensions and tasks performed by CFA charterholders, and the knowledge required to perform them."[23] The final questionnaire was ready and would be sent to a group of 3,500 charterholders from the United States, Canada, and places outside North America. The allocation, Tuttle noted, was to approximate the "expected near-term" geographical breakdown of charterholders.

The Job Analysis Survey was sent in February 1995, and its results were tabulated and analyzed in March and April 1995. Although survey results were expected to "verify the validity and soundness of the CFA exam process" —which had so frequently been reviewed and updated—the assumption was that some "fleshing out of underemphasized knowledge areas" and some "shifts in the weighting of subject areas treated on the exams" would occur. Most significantly, the survey would provide a "distinct *linkage* between tasks performed" by charterholders and "knowledge expected of candidates." This link would demonstrate job relatedness and be helpful "in providing documentation for exemption [of CFA charterholders] from securities licensing exams by state regulatory authorities"—in North America and beyond.

The Job Analysis survey was completed by 42 percent of the 3,500-member sample, with the lowest response rates from the United States and the highest from Switzerland and Japan. Inherent biases (age, experience, and the like) among those sampled were noted. The ICFA Board of Trustees conducted a lively discussion and analysis of the survey results at the May 1995 meeting, with the general consensus being that the Job Analysis gave the program's leaders, as John Maginn put it, "the ability to focus on the topics that are viewed by charterholders as important" to the practice of the profession.[24] Happily, Tuttle noted, "no real conflicts were found" between the Job Analysis Survey results and the GBOK. He concluded the discussion with a recommendation that "a survey of this nature be conducted every four to five years." In fact, the second survey (by that time titled "Practice Analysis") was conducted in 2000, and the third, in 2004–2006. Continuous surveying began in 2007.[25]

A New Approach to Fixed Income

Even as the Job Analysis was being completed, the ICFA Board of Trustees and CFA Program staff set out to improve other aspects of the program. An important focus of the CCC in the mid-1990s was strengthening the fixed-income curriculum. According to Dwight Churchill, the goal was to "balance the exam and get away from the traditional, more classic education of fixed income."[27] As he saw it, "real-world fixed income was evolving rapidly, and classic texts (and the CFA Program) were falling behind." He believed the inclusion of new material that was more quantitative in nature than old fixed-income material was important. This idea was, he recalled, "not without significant controversy" because the CFA exam had been viewed by many as an "equity exam." Adding more fixed-income, particularly quantitative fixed-income, material did not seem to some people "consistent with the 'fundamental' nature of the program historically." Churchill wished, however, "to help educate our candidates on the developments within fixed income so that they could sort through the financial engineering that was occurring on the Street." He saw the need as a turning "away from an equity exam with the occasional convertible bond and credit research question to a more balanced exam" that included a focus on a variety of instruments and markets beyond U.S. equities.

Learning Outcome Statements

Other significant changes were coming to the program. As mentioned briefly in Chapter 5, one of the great innovations of the 1990s was the advent of Learning Outcome Statements (LOS). In 1994, curriculum consultant George Troughton was asked to begin drafting an early version of an LOS. In 1995, he was joined in the work by Robert R. Johnson, CFA, who was then a professor at Creighton University in Nebraska and an instructor in the Financial Analysts Review course. Johnson, who had received his charter in 1991, was invited to grade exams in 1995 and remembered a fateful encounter that occurred upon his arrival in Charlottesville: "[On] the very first day of grading, there was a note at the desk of the Cavalier Inn that Don Tuttle wanted to talk to me. I thought: I just showed up! What could I have done wrong that Don Tuttle needed to talk to me?"[28]

Of course, Tuttle simply wanted Johnson to participate in developing the first LOS, then known as "learning objectives" or "learning expectations." As Johnson recalled, "Don and some other people who worked on the CFA Program had this

HISTORICAL SPOTLIGHT

In 1996, AIMR established its first scholarship program for those wishing to take the CFA examinations but unable to do so because of cost. Scholarships were distributed by AIMR societies and by universities with CFA charterholders on their faculties.[26]

Poh Fun Lai, CFA, 1991 charterholder from Malaysia.

HISTORICAL SPOTLIGHT

Bob Johnson, CFA, was one of the candidates taking the CFA examination in Omaha, Nebraska, when the tornado described in Chapter 5 came through. He returned home after the exam to find his own house intact but his neighbor's house destroyed.

idea that we would direct candidates more about what they needed to know [and] study . . . instead of just giving them a reading list."[29] Together with George Troughton, Johnson, working specifically on material for Level III derivatives, drafted the first LOS.

The idea for Learning Outcome Statements had been in the air for a while, but the need for them crystallized in the mid-1990s. After a July 1995 meeting of ICFA trustees, senior staff, and key volunteers to discuss several areas of the CFA Program needing immediate attention, Tom Bowman noted the particular concern among those assembled that the curriculum and examinations had become "so broad in terms of topics covered that candidates are having difficulty focusing their exam preparation efforts."[30] The sheer volume of material was the problem: "thousands of pages," from which a candidate was expected to sort out the salient points. Bowman believed the ICFA board should "approve a Learning Outcome Statement of Objectives"—that is, a statement of what a candidate was expected to know, what she or he should derive from a particular reading.

Although some people considered providing guidance to be spoon-feeding the candidates, few could deny that the volume of material to wade through had grown enormously. The parameters of learning also needed to be delimited. Were candidates expected to have a *mastery* of the BOK, or were they expected to have a *"fundamental understanding* of its concepts?" Referring to Bloom's Taxonomy (see Chapter 3), Bowman noted that the system could serve as a model for "exactly how we might determine expected learning outcomes" at each exam level. Learning expectations would specify the extent of cognitive complexity a candidate needed to demonstrate in regard to each topic and at each exam level. Bowman proposed the creation of sample LOS following the Bloom model—that is, ranging from familiarity (knowledge) to mastery (evaluation)—and that the samples be submitted to the ICFA Board of Trustees for review at its September meeting.

At the 7 September 1995 ICFA board meeting, ICFA Chair Abby Joseph Cohen (1995–1996) noted that the general consensus of the trustees was that the CFA exams should not attempt to test candidates in depth on every single subject. Additionally, to reduce the amount of material the candidates needed to review, the board and staff should consider what properly constituted prerequisite knowledge and need not appear in the study materials. They should also identify which subjects were advanced beyond the scope of the exam and might appear instead in the specialization program that was being prepared.

Clay Singleton, by then a senior staff member of AIMR, reported on the status of the LOS project at the meeting. He cited a memo from George Troughton, who had been working with Bob Johnson on LOS creation for several months. Troughton, using examples of LOS for five topics from the Level III curriculum, aligned each LOS precisely to readings from the curriculum, specified to board members the GBOK item to which each corresponded, provided test specifications (at which level to test each topic and how frequently), and pointed out the portion of Bloom's Taxonomy to which each related. It was a wholly disciplined approach detailing what a candidate needed to know.

Although the publication schedule for the 1996 study guides precluded the inclusion of Learning Outcome Statements in them, a supplement was published that contained LOS for all topics at Level III. The 1996 supplement noted that LOS were "designed to help candidates master the Body of Knowledge" and to "show how the readings support each topic area." The *Supplemental Study Guide* also included a graphic representation of command words and the corresponding levels of cognitive complexity (from Bloom's Taxonomy) that each evoked. Those reading Troughton's memo or seeing the published LOS surely must have thought: This is it! The 1997 study guides included LOS at all three exam levels.

As Bob Johnson noted some years later, the advent of Learning Outcome Statements and the necessary correspondence between the curriculum and exams they engendered "brought a lot more process into the whole CFA Program system."[31] With these first LOS samples, the goal of coordinating between the COE and CCC was finally attainable. As a report to candidates on the CFA Program put it, "The COE views the LOS as a contract with the candidates: If candidates can do what LOS indicate, they should be well prepared for the examinations."[32]

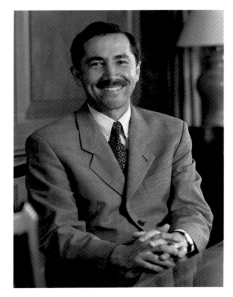

Manuel Gomez Rubio, CFA, 1993 charterholder from Mexico.

MEANS OF TESTING

Paralleling the tightened structure that the LOS epitomized was a growing sophistication in the writing of the CFA examinations. In 1994, Clay Singleton noted that the CFA exam "should challenge the candidates and discriminate adequately"; that is, it must be sufficiently rigorous to ensure that the CFA charter is awarded only to those who merit it by discriminating fairly between those who know the material and those who do not. In the mid- to late 1990s, CFA Program staff and volunteers considered how best to ensure that the exams would fulfill the discrimination criterion, given the changing and growing population of candidates.

As noted previously, the ICFA Board of Trustees had authorized the creation of a question-writing project to develop a bank of multiple-choice questions. It also had discussed the *expanded* use of multiple-choice questions at Level I. In particular, considerable thought was given to how the use of multiple-choice questions would affect those candidates whose first language was not English. In September 1995, Bob Luck informed the ICFA trustees that research into the question had concluded that a 100 percent multiple-choice exam "will neither impede non–North American candidates nor disadvantage non-native-English-speaking candidates." Luck enumerated the advantages of moving to all multiple choice: greater efficiency without loss of quality, great increase in the potential to administer Level I more than once per year, and assurance of "greater

ICFA trustees (left) Brian F. Wruble, CFA, and (right) Frank K. Reilly, CFA, review CFA exams in the final phase of the 1994 CFA grading process.

consistency from year to year."[33] After years of carefully considering but rejecting this option, and after recent thorough investigation of the potential consequences of such a change, the ICFA board voted to change Level I to all multiple choice. According to Brian Wruble, 1994–95 chair of the ICFA Board of Trustees:

This was not an easy decision. . . . Given the pressures of the explosion in candidates (the program was growing extremely rapidly), and given the "bottleneck" that the grading process presented, we adopted a multiple-choice format for Level I . . . . Trustees' intuition was uniformly the same—"multiple choice is too easy." That notion was disputed successfully by experts we brought in from ETS.[34]

Moreover, Wruble noted, explosive growth "was overwhelming a highly 'people intensive' grading process"—a process, consequently, that "was ripe for redesign." Adoption of a multiple-choice exam at least for Level I would facilitate that redesign.

At the request of Chair Abby Joseph Cohen, incoming CFA candidates were informed of the change, and the first all-multiple-choice Level I exam was administered in June 1996.

An all-multiple-choice exam was going to be effective, consistent, and fair only if the questions were well designed. Throughout the mid- and late 1990s, therefore, the ICFA Board of Trustees, volunteer committees, and staff sought to increase the sophistication of these questions. For example, they looked for ways to improve the quality of "distractors" (plausible but incorrect answers) and eliminate "all of the above" answers. The wish was to create a truly rigorous multiple-choice exam equal in difficulty to the essay format in use from the beginning but eliminating any disadvantage non-native-English-speaking candidates might feel in writing essay answers.

When he joined the CFA Program staff in August 1996, Bob Johnson recalled, one of his first tasks was to "take a look at the Level I exam after it had been given" to evaluate not the candidates' answers but, rather, the questions themselves.[35] Johnson was not entirely satisfied with what he saw, although he knew it met industry standards for the time. The CFA Program could exceed those standards, Johnson believed, by introducing an enhanced review process throughout the exam creation system. "My mantra is 'review, review, review,'" Johnson said. Throughout their history, the CFA exams had always had sound financial content because, he noted, from 1963 on, those putting them together "knew finance." By the mid-1990s, however, more was needed: The creators also had to "know testing."

In addition to ensuring the excellence of the exams themselves, managing the steady (then, exponential) growth in candidate registrations was a motivating force in professionalizing the exam process. As Bob Luck remembered, growth in the number of candidates was "a motivating factor, a driving factor."[36] Analogizing the growth in exam administration to a university setting, he remarked, "It's one thing for a faculty member to be able to judge 30 essays, [but] when you start talking about dozens of people trying to judge 3,000 or 30,000 essays, it becomes much more difficult." Luck credits Clay Singleton for being a driving force behind the consistent use of consultants and in making fully professional testing a priority.

The advent of LOS during the exam creation cycles for 1996 (Level III) and 1997 (all three levels) meant that each question not only had to be well written and clear but also had to correspond to a designated learning outcome or outcomes and a recognizable element of the Candidate Body of Knowledge (CBOK). Clay Singleton, who also served as COE chair from 1994 to 1996, reiterated an often-stated intention: "The goal is to have the Council of Examiners and the Candidate Curriculum Committee work in tandem, rather than sequentially, with a focus on the CBOK."[38] A new means for achieving this goal was devised when, starting in 1995, the COE and the CCC began exchanging members, with a volunteer serving on the CCC for several years, for example, then moving over to serve on the COE. Such a systematic exchange, Singleton reasoned, would "enhance both the curriculum and examination."

For several years, the COE had been using "level coordinators" to oversee the writing of each of the three CFA exams. By 1995, their duties had increased and

EXAM STORY: AN UNEXPECTED PROBLEM WITH PENCILS

Although machine scoring of Level I greatly simplified grading, it did not escape the call to "review, review, review"—as this story illustrates:

"I took the Level I exam in 1995. The exam site was in Istanbul, and there were only a handful of candidates. I thought that I did quite well in the exam, but when the results came, I was shocked. I failed the exam.

"I had worked hard for the exam and was so disappointed that I even thought of dropping from the program. Towards December, I received a phone call from Charlottesville with the news that I had actually passed the exam. Somehow the computer could not read my markings on the answer sheet of the multiple-choice exam. Another candidate (obviously a person with greater self-confidence than I) objected to his exam result. His exam was checked manually and he passed. So, the CFA Institute [staff] went over all the multiple-choice exams manually to find out that, globally, some people failed the Level I exam because of 'incompatible' pencils.[37] CFA Institute did not charge us for the Level II exam and the exam material that year. I gained my confidence back and passed Level II and Level III exams in the following years to become one of the first charterholders in Turkey."

—ATTILA KOKSAL, CFA, Istanbul, Turkey

Left to right: Lawrence Speidell, CFA; Attila Koksal, CFA; Artunc Kocabalkan, host of Turkish CNBC "Market Screen."

EXAM STORY:
CONCENTRATION
TRIUMPHS OVER
DISTRACTION

"In Seattle in 1999 (I was taking Level II), the exam was held at a hotel near the airport. Unfortunately, there turned out to be a Teamsters' rally going on in the ballroom next door! For much of the exam, we would periodically hear loud applause, hooting, and feet stomping, which was highly distracting to say the least. However, that was not all. About half of the way through the afternoon session, the fire alarm went off! Everyone looked up but not a person moved from their seats."

—M. AIMÉE HUFF, CFA
Seattle

Phillip Yang Wu, CFA, 1993 charterholder from China.

they were expected to write for their teams "General Marching Orders" (GMOs), which were to "describe the general thrust of the examination."[39] Coordinators were also to draft question specifications, including the LOS on which the questions should be based. Exam creation was growing ever more sophisticated— and to good effect. Singleton reported that "having the Job Analysis and the GBOK direct both the examination and curriculum means candidates will learn more and the examinations will better identify candidates who have mastered what it takes to be a CFA charterholder."

Bringing the World into the Exams

As the drive toward perfecting coordination between curriculum and exam continued in the late 1990s, another challenge faced exam writers, the ever-growing need for questions that reflected global investing realities. Writing the CFA exams became, as Don Tuttle noted, "a bit of a challenge" because COE members had to create questions that featured situations in non–North American countries.[40] To do so, they needed to be able to work in other currencies and be knowledgeable about non–North American securities, investment products, and practices. To meet the challenge, he continued, "We brought members from other countries onto the Council of Examiners, [who] wrote questions themselves and were helpful in counseling others so we had a truly global exam." By the end of the 1990s, members on these key committees came from Europe, Asia, and the Middle East.

GLOBALIZATION, ONE CHARTER AT A TIME

The changes in the CFA Program detailed thus far in this chapter all took place in the foothills of the Blue Ridge Mountains, about 120 miles southwest of Washington, DC—at AIMR headquarters in Charlottesville, Virginia. If viewed by itself, this concentrated work would make one think that everything about the CFA Program in the mid- and late 1990s happened there. In fact, much of the action surrounding the CFA Program was happening far, far away. From the mid-1990s on, an almost volcanic eruption of interest in the CFA Program emerged outside North America, and program leaders looked abroad as much as they looked within.

The groundwork for this interest had been laid in the 1980s with the many travels of Pete Morley, Jay Vawter, Ted Muller, and others. Their goal was not only to make the CFA Program known internationally but also to work toward international cooperation among analysts. Gentaro Yura of the Security Analysts Association of Japan (SAAJ), who knew Morley during the period, noted of Morley that his "leadership went a long way in not only helping us but also helping Asian emerging markets to move forward."[41] Moreover, the result was to establish "universally recognized educational standards [and] examination programs." Yura

THE SPECIAL CASE OF SPECIALIZATION

Since the 1980s, the ICFA had looked into the possibility of offering specialty examinations. Because charterholders concentrated on particular areas during their careers, the idea for some kind of specialty program—even a set of specialized tests—took hold. Frank K. Reilly, CFA, who chaired both the ICFA and AIMR boards in the late 1990s, saw the need for such a program: "We all recognized that once you got your CFA [charter] and went to work, you really became a specialist in stocks, bonds, derivatives, etc."[42] Because the CFA Program is for generalists, he noted, the way to help charterholders was through specializations. Considered for nearly a decade without resolution, the possibility of a CFA specialization program lingered.

In 1995, the ICFA Specialization Committee began its work by acknowledging, "Members need help and support to effectively compete and thrive in this specialized environment."[43] AIMR Senior Vice President Donald L. Tuttle, CFA, was put in charge of formulating the fledgling program. From 1995 to 1997, Tuttle investigated and fleshed out a possible specialization program. By May 1996, he reported that two specialty curricula were being developed; a fixed-income curriculum was nearly ready, and an equity securities curriculum would be ready by January 1997.

In February 1997, focus groups were held to good effect in New York, Boston, Chicago, and Los Angeles, and the specialization staff was already writing LOS for specialty material. A target date of June 1999 was set for the first specialty exams, which would be voluntary. As Tuttle reported to the ICFA board in February 1997, "If the material is timely, relevant, and applications oriented, the Program will succeed [with members]."[44]

Three months later (May 1997), the program was under way; final exam drafts were reviewed in September. The pilot program had 50 participants, with approximately 15 percent coming from outside North America. The program's rollout had a sample two-hour exam scheduled for October 1997, a seminar for participants ready for February 1998, and a full program launch scheduled for June 1999. A potentially thorny problem was resolved at the September 1997 ICFA board meeting: Current Continuing Education participants would *not* be grandfathered; they would have to take the CFA Specialization Exam to earn the advanced designation.[45]

Then, in January 1998, the Specialization Program took a turn so sharp, it was effectively upended. The AIMR Education Committee decided that the program should not be a separate entity at all but should become "part of a continuum" of professional development options.[46] Committee members'

concerns about administrative costs, sufficient charterholder participation, and whether the "certification feature" of the Specialization Program might detract from the effort to position the CFA charter as the ultimate designation for investment professionals—all derailed the program. If it proceeded at all, the committee decided, specialization would neither offer an exam nor award an advanced CFA designation.

The report engendered considerable discussion at the 6 February 1998 ICFA board meeting, which took place right after the first phase of the pilot program was completed. Trustees debated the recommendation from the committee to not have a specialization exam. Some reasoned that without an endpoint, the program would attract little interest. Others thought any exam, even though voluntary, might "diminish the value of the current CFA charter."[47] The "lengthy discussions" continued until the board reached agreement that the advanced curricula being developed—in fixed income and equity securities—should be placed on the AIMR internet site and that work on other related materials, such as a workbook series, be continued. No separate Specialization Program, per se, was offered, and no specialty examination was ever given.

Sonia Julia Sulzbeck Villalobos, CFA, 1994 charterholder from Brazil.

believed that "his accomplishments left an important mark in the history of the development of the investment profession worldwide."

An early means for achieving the goals of CFA Program recognition and international cooperation was the establishment of reciprocity agreements. These agreements specified that participants in sanctioned programs would be exempt from one or more of the CFA examinations, and the same was true for charterholders seeking certification via other programs. The two reciprocity agreements were with the London-based Society of Investment Analysts (later, the Institute of Investment Management and Research) in 1988 and with SAAJ in 1991. Centered in strong financial markets themselves, analysts in those two organizations had developed examination programs of their own. Although neither program corresponded completely with the CFA Program, both were deemed similar enough to warrant exemptions for their qualified members from one or more parts of the CFA Program.

By the mid-1990s, many more requests for reciprocity agreements were forthcoming. Analyzing carefully the consequences of broadening this policy, the ICFA board approved a modification in the reciprocity policy in 1995 so that exemptions would be granted only to the Level I CFA exams and only to holders of recognized designations from organizations having agreements with AIMR. Everyone would have to take and pass Levels II and III to earn a CFA charter.[48]

Few new reciprocity agreements were considered. In May 1996, the ICFA board did reach an agreement with Deutsche Vereingung für Finanzanalyse und Anlageberatung e.V. that its certificate holders be exempt from taking the CFA Level I exam. Toward the end of the decade, the ICFA was still investigating possible agreements with a small number of other groups in Europe and in Asia.

For some time, however, serious consideration had been given to whether or not reciprocity agreements should continue at all. Few programs were considered sufficiently comparable, and the onus of determining comparability fell on an already busy staff. Moreover, as Katy Sherrerd noted, with more international organizations approaching AIMR to seek reciprocity, "the burden of evaluating their educational programs [became] increasingly complex."[49] Even if a program was deemed equivalent upon initial investigation, subsequent monitoring would be needed. To give this attention to numerous other programs around the world would put a considerable strain on staff. Expansion of these efforts might also eventually lead to serious issues of quality control and consistency. Tom Bowman remembered, "If you think about where that would have led us, it would have been chaos, having a different program [to monitor] for each country."[50] Such reciprocity programs not only caused what Bowman called "administrative complexities," but also resulted in a concern that "true equality" in the exam program could not be achieved this way.[51]

Questions of language use persisted. As noted several times in this book, CFA exams have been printed only in English, which provides utter consistency in what candidates in each year's administration see. Yet, for many years Canadians living in and taking the exam in Quebec could write their answers in French as the result of an exception granted in the mid-1970s. By the late 1990s, other countries were seeking language exceptions. AIMR could not easily assent to these requests. The costs and personnel needs for managing any program exceptions were great, as was assuring quality control over the translations. Even more important was that allowing for even one exception flew in the face of the standard of absolute equality sought by those leading the program. As the CFA Program became more and more the worldwide standard of education and certification for analysts, AIMR believed that to assert *absolute* consistency by permitting only English to be used in writing answers was essential. Thus, in 1999, AIMR Board of Governors Chair R. Charles Tschampion, CFA, informed those in Montreal and Quebec City that after a grace period to be determined, all CFA exams had to be written in English. By that stage in the development of the program—and of the profession—English was the language of finance. Also, allowing for multilanguage CFA exams would, in Tschampion's words, "disrupt and 'ineffectualize' the entire Program."[52]

Underlying both the decision about an English-only policy for examination answers and the issue of reciprocity agreements was an ethical question: How could the CFA Program maintain a standard of absolute fairness in the absence of absolute sameness? As Tom Bowman remembered it, these two decisions were among the most difficult of his tenure as president and CEO of AIMR because both involved canceling agreements made in good faith with good friends. In both cases, however, what was evident and most fair was that either the CFA Program must offer reciprocity for any and all who qualified or it must offer none at all. Likewise, it must offer the exams in any and all languages requested or only in English.

Simplicity and consistency won out. Clearly, the proper way to administer the CFA Program was uniformly: the same examination in the same language, during one span of time, everywhere in the world. As John Maginn once noted, becoming certified as a Chartered Financial Analyst is a unique experience: "I don't know of another professional organization that provides the same examination . . . all over the world."[53]

Globalization meant more, of course, than simply an increase in candidates from outside North America. It also meant a conscious reaching out abroad by the CFA Program. For many years, graders, for example, had come from outside

AN UNEXPECTED VISITOR

One day in 1998, Information Central, the AIMR call center, began experiencing call difficulties. Staff members investigating the problem traced it to a closet that housed pipes and call center wires. A contemporary magazine reported what they found:

A SNAKE IN THE OFFICE: SLIPPERY SUSPECT ELUDES AIMR STAFF

"While members of the Association for Investment Management and Research were tackling investments trends at AIMR's 1998 conference in Phoenix, staffers back in Charlottesville, Va., were bedeviled with a more slippery subject: a snake.

"It seems heavy rains in the area drove serpents and other wild creatures to higher ground; in this case, one of AIMR's three office buildings. The snake didn't disrupt workers, although some employees felt more comfortable working on their desks rather than at them.

"The snake hasn't been seen for weeks. However, one staffer noted that at one point the snake was headed for the offices housing AIMR's lawyers. No word on whether the snake was looking for food or companionship."

—PAUL G. BARR
Pensions & Investments, 15 June 1998
Reprinted with permission,
Pensions & Investments.
Copyright Crain Communications, Inc

HISTORICAL SPOTLIGHT

AIMR opened its first office outside North America, in Hong Kong, in 1997. Astonishingly, more than 6,000 people stopped by to get information during its first year of operation.[54]

The CFA Institute Hong Kong office opened in 1997. Hector Emanuel, photographer

North America. This practice greatly increased in the late 1990s and early 2000s—and continues today. Non–North American members were also recruited to the GBOK Task Force, and charterholders all over the globe were interviewed during the first Job Analysis Survey. In addition, in 1995, the Thomas L. Hansberger Leadership in Global Investing Award was created. The first award was given to George E.K. Teo, of Singapore, who was highly instrumental in promoting the CFA Program there. That same year, the first Asian conference was held, in Singapore. The first international Education Summit was conducted by AIMR in London in November 1997. It was hosted by Philippe A. Sarasin, CFA, of Switzerland, who had become the first non–North American ICFA and AIMR board member in 1996. The topic under discussion was truly international: the pros and cons of adopting International Accounting Standards. Two other summits on the topic were held within the year, in Hong Kong in February 1998 and New York in May 1998.

In 1998, Sarasin became the first ICFA chair from outside North America, and three years later, he was elected AIMR chair. More non–North American board members were also recruited. Before the end of the 1990s, the AIMR board included George W. Long, CFA, of Hong Kong, Khalid Ghayur, CFA, of the United Kingdom, and Ong Seow-Beng, CFA, of Singapore. At the end of this decade of change and outreach, the Performance Presentation Standards, whose origin is described in Chapter 5, were internationalized, becoming Global Investment Performance Standards, and were promoted worldwide.

Not every venture out in the wider world was serene. In the 1990s, for example, a dispute arose with an organization in India over the use of the CFA designation, and legal issues ensued that have not yet been fully resolved. In addition, the administration of CFA exams at more than 200 centers worldwide by 1999 meant ever-increasing security measures. So did crossing the international dateline, as it made for an extremely long span of exam administration time and increased security risks. The day for administration was changed, beginning in 1998, to a Sunday offering in countries east of the 60th meridian (from Pakistan to New Zealand). Those putting together a testing program for analysts in the 1960s could hardly have dreamed of such security issues. Today, however, the CFA Program serves a worldwide investment management community. As Bob Johnson noted:

> The investment management profession is globally more integrated now than it ever was before, and I think that we have played at least a small role in that and have helped facilitate that. The fact that we have a program that the letters behind somebody's name mean the same thing in Tokyo as they do in Tampa, Florida, is, in my mind, quite remarkable.[55]

Philippe A. Sarasin, CFA, served as ICFA chair for 1998–1999 and AIMR chair for 2001–2002.

TRUE MERGER: 1999

What is commonly referred as "the merger" of the FAF and ICFA in the late 1980s was, in fact, a combination of organizations, *not* a true merger. The move created a tripartite structure containing three separate boards—for AIMR, the FAF, and the ICFA—with the FAF and ICFA under the overall jurisdiction of AIMR. An additional board served the international constituency, the International Society of Financial Analysts. Philippe Sarasin remembered his first encounters with this Byzantine structure:

> When I first looked at the AIMR structure as a candidate, I knew I wanted the CFA charter, but I really did not understand what these four boards were all about. And when I got the call [to be a board member], I had a hard time understanding where I would sit at first and what my role would actually be.[56]

Nearly as soon as the legal documents forming AIMR were signed, talk began about effecting a true merger. Successive AIMR governance committees looked at ways the organization might truly become one, but time and again, they did not agree or postponed the question. Although the tone for healing and melding was set early on, the cultures of the two organizations were too different to slip together easily.

Tom Bowman, who headed AIMR during the postcombination years, recalled, "Just because we signed an agreement, that was not the end of it [because] there was so much distrust."[57] People involved at the time often compared the "merger" to a marriage, sometimes calling it a "shotgun wedding," sometimes a "marriage of convenience." But even marriages that begin with some difficulty can end well, and thankfully this one did. Fred H. Speece, Jr., CFA, who chaired the ICFA and then AIMR in the late 1990s, remembered using the example "it's like marriage with a mortgage and a station wagon and a bunch of rug-rats. You figure out a way to work it out."[58]

That "way" was finally recognized at a February 1998 AIMR board retreat in

Illustration: Robert Meganck. Image appeared on the front of the July/August 1999 *AIMR Exchange*.

New York City. Philippe Sarasin, then ICFA vice chair, recalled a breakout session during the retreat in which members of his group "came back with the suggestion that maybe the structure, for governance reasons and clarity of the message sent to a global constituency, was too fuzzy with four boards."[59] The group asked, "Why cannot we just have a single governance structure that would lead the organization? That will make it save a lot of time [and] a lot of paper, and bring clarity of vision and of leadership direction." When some of the attendees seemed shocked at this question, Sarasin started to explain that "if you look at it from an international perspective . . ." Before he could finish, however, AIMR Chair Abby Joseph Cohen interrupted him with an exclamation: "Bingo!" As Sarasin quickly realized, "She got it." Soon others did as well, and discussion of a true merger moved forward. What Fred Speece described as the years of "meetings, where you'd go and you'd repeat, and you'd repeat, and all this did was perpetuate the we/they" were finally coming to an end. In 1999, the three boards approved a true merger and sent their recommendation to the members for a final vote.

Change often comes with difficulty, and this change—which seemed so self-evident to volunteer leaders and AIMR staff and so much the desired outcome of the ICFA/FAF combination created a decade before—came at a cost. Although the merger passed overwhelmingly among AIMR members, it was not before some had staged an acrimonious and unsuccessful proxy fight. Fortunately,

This Charlottesville building became the headquarters for AIMR in September 1999. Gitchell Studios, photographer

AIMR members ultimately agreed that true union (the "one voice" sought years before) was needed more than ever.

In the late 1990s, CFA Program leaders had fully recognized that the program must speak with one voice in order to reach across the world and succeed in the coming decades. Despite the difficulty of ending reciprocity agreements and altering language arrangements reached with good friends, the curriculum and examinations had to become utterly uniform: one series of examinations, in one language, given during one span of time. So, too, did the leaders of AIMR, the organization responsible for the CFA Program, face the necessity of becoming one. A few years would elapse before the last piece of the merger dropped away (the name AIMR), but by the end of the 1990s, the organization had assumed a long desired, unified form, and a true merger had at last occurred.

The infrastructure rebuilding and the global expansion that took place during the 1990s were capped off in September 1999 when this now fully unified organization moved into new headquarters in Charlottesville. What had begun in 1961 with one employee and one office on the mezzanine of the University of Virginia's Monroe Hall now occupied three full floors of an office building and housed more than 130 staff members. With a satellite office in Hong Kong and a unified organizational structure, AIMR and its "jewel," the CFA Program, were ready to greet the new century with confidence.

It's true teamwork—the teamwork between the academics and the practitioners, the teamwork between the staff and the volunteers, the teamwork now that's transcending borders all over the world.

—John L. Maginn, CFA,
1994–1995 AIMR chair, July 2010

chapter seven

Best Practices:

2000–2004

*A*t the Association for Investment Management and Research, as elsewhere around the world, 1 January 2000 rolled around uneventfully. The dreaded Y2K bang was not heard, just the steady hum of computers processing without pause.

Although the year began placidly enough, tranquility in the financial world was quickly swept away by turmoil. In March 2000, the dot-com bubble burst, shattering the trust of investors. By the end of 2001, Enron Corporation was bankrupt, the premier accounting firm Arthur Anderson had dissolved in disgrace, and New York's twin towers had fallen. Fraud and scandal continued in 2002, which featured the collapse of WorldCom. Then, in 2003, a different kind of calamity struck as a previously unknown viral illness called Sudden Acute Respiratory Syndrome (SARS) spread rapidly worldwide. This epidemic coincided with the CFA exam administration, and test centers had to be closed in Beijing and Shanghai during a year of record enrollments in those cities. More than 4,000 candidates were displaced in China alone. The test center closings caused a drop in the number of candidates sitting for the exam, even though 2003 was the same year in which registrations for CFA exams surpassed 100,000.

The astounding growth of the CFA Program, a challenge as well as a blessing, had been fueled by developments in financial markets. Industry trends toward globalization and the relaxation of banking regulations, together with strong employment in financial services, helped drive this growth, according to John Rogers, CFA, current president and CEO of CFA Institute.[1] John C. Stannard, CFA, FSIP, 2005–2006 chair of the Board of Governors, described the trend this way: "Many investment professionals wanted a global career, wanted global opportunity. And so, the CFA [designation] was becoming increasingly popular."[2] As a result, the graph of candidate enrollments grew steeper every year; it was heading upward at a sharp incline by the year 2003. The number of members needing services and continuing professional education was also growing.

As the investment industry has become more global, the CFA Program is seen as a beacon . . . in terms of best practice: establishing rules for market transparency, ensuring good education, ensuring a focus on ethics.

—John C. Stannard, CFA, FSIP, interview, 2010

注册金融分析师考试在全球开始

本报讯 世界规模最大的考试注册金融分析师 (CFA) 考试今年的考生数量再创新高，达到 86421 人。注册金融分析师考试每年举行一次，被认为是世界上规模最大的同时进行的职业考试。CFA 认证是世界上增长最迅速的证书之一。AIMR 是全球性的专业人士协会，负责管理 CFA 项目和主办 CFA 考试。

The paragraph below summarizes the article above, which was printed in the *International Business Daily* (China), on 5 June 2001.

CFA Exam Held Globally

The Chartered Financial Analyst exam gets even bigger this year, with a record 86,421 CFA candidates registered worldwide. The exam is conducted annually and is believed to be the largest simultaneously administered professional examination. The global expansion of the CFA credential has led to it being the fastest growing among other comparable qualifications. AIMR is the global association of investment professionals responsible for administering the CFA Program.

In the years 2000–2010, the CFA Program would adapt to change—technological and otherwise—at a furious pace. The proliferation of computing in all areas of life, which had generated fear of the "millennium bug" and Y2K fever, had a great effect on the investment profession. To the CFA Program, technology brought benefits in the form of instant contact with candidates and members but also difficulties: Security issues increased.

Many questions needed answers. How do we keep pace with staggering growth? How do we defend and ensure analyst independence and restore trust in the face of burst stock bubbles, accounting fraud, and corporate collapses? How do we deal with the tragedy of terrorism on Wall Street, and perhaps most urgent for the integrity of the CFA charter, how do we adapt the program to a brave new technological world? All these questions occupied CFA Program leaders in the first years of the 21st century. As with every other change it faced, the CFA Program proved resilient and highly adaptable. By seeking the best practices in all elements of its mission—in testing, in security measures, in assimilating a now global constituency, and in fostering analyst independence and professional development—it would not only adapt; it would lead.

FROM SLIDE RULES TO SPREADSHEETS TO SECURITY WALLS

When the first CFA exam was given in 1963, the integrated circuit had recently been invented (1958) and computers were just beginning to shrink in size from the punch-card guzzling UNIVAC of the 1950s. At the stock exchanges, stock price information was still transmitted on ticker tape as it had been for a century. CFA candidates headed into their calculation-heavy exams armed with slide rules, pens, and the occasional adding machine. And at the headquarters of the Institute of Chartered Financial Analysts, C. Ray Smith was having difficulty convincing the trustees to spend money on data storage:

> From the very beginning, I insisted that we had to capture data in punch cards [and] requested an O26 Printing Card Punch and $50 a month to lease it. I had a hard time getting the $50 approved to rent that keypunch.[3]

However, the days of looking askance at the need for data capture soon vanished. By 1966— the same year that the first CFA candidates who were not grandfathered received their charters—an electronic ticker had replaced telegraphic tape at the New York Stock Exchange (NYSE). Within 10 years of the first CFA examinations, handheld calculators, floppy disks, microprocessors, and VCRs had all been invented; not many years later, two of these advances would be obsolete. The incredible pace of development in the electronics industry affected the daily conduct of business in the financial industry, with electronic trading and banking and a 24-hour business day.

Things are going a lot faster.

—Peter L. Bernstein,
CFA Institute Conference,
February 2005

From the late 1860s until the early 1960s, stock prices were transmitted via telegraph onto ticker tape, shown here being studied by brokers and analysts in the 1930s.
C.P. Cushing / Classicstock.com

By the turn of the 21st century, the Association for Investment Management and Research staff had integrated many technological advances into candidate and member programs, and they upgraded these programs constantly. These advances included the first computerized call center (1994), the first live video-conference (featuring John C. Bogle in 1997), and the first AIMR educational webcast (conducted in 1998 by Dean LeBaron, CFA, whose topic, appropriately enough, was "Using the Web for Investment Research"). In 2000, aimrpubs.org was launched, which gave members access to a searchable database of publications, beginning with the *CFA Digest*. In 2001, an "e-commerce" initiative began for CFA candidates that allowed the electronic distribution of exam tickets and on-line availability of exam results in July and August. Candidates for the 2002 exam were able to register online for the first time.

Keeping pace with electronic advances was absolutely necessary as the first decade of the new century unfolded—if for no other reason than to communicate with younger candidates, who were living life online. Within a few years, candidate study material was also on the AIMR website, which solidified the CFA Program as the accessible, distance-learning program it has become. As described by Thomas B. Welch, CFA, 2009–2010 chair of the CFA Institute Board of Governors, "Shaking off past practices that technology has made obsolete" was part of the governing mission.[4]

Dean LeBaron, CFA, appeared in the first AIMR educational webcast in 1998.

In June 2009, CFA Institute Board of Governors Chair Thomas B. Welch, CFA (center), met with (right) Professor G. Sethu of the National Institute of Securities Markets and (left) Sunil B. Singhania, CFA, president of the Indian Association of Investment Professionals, a member society of CFA Institute. An agreement was signed to jointly organize education, training, and research for the investment industry in India.

A SENSE OF SECURITY

The technological improvements that made candidate study materials available at the touch of a keyboard also presented challenges to those in charge of exam security. Often, it seemed, no sooner had the CFA Program added technological capabilities to benefit members and candidates than it had to defend against their potential misuse. In the early 1990s, for example, handheld calculators, which had been allowed in test centers since the 1980s, became capable of storing data and needed restriction. Even as the new decade opened in 2000, discussions continued among staff and the board over how best to determine which calculators would be acceptable and how to communicate that information clearly to candidates. The security of data was becoming a constant concern.

Adding to the challenge of keeping up with technological change was the growth in candidate numbers and the expansion of their geographical locations. When the 1990s began, the CFA Program was seating 8,760 candidates for the CFA exams, roughly 10 percent of whom were living outside North America.[5] When the next decade began, the total number of candidates had more than quintupled—53,345 candidates were taking CFA exams at 165 test centers in 69 countries. Within a few years that challenge would seem easy: In 2004, 81,000 candidates sat for exams, and in 2007, more than 100,000 sat. By 2004, more than 50 percent of exam registrations came from outside North America.

To meet the demands of growth, technology, and geographical expansion, AIMR undertook a proactive review of the CFA Program with the goal of ensuring that policies and procedures not only conformed to U.S. law (regarding, for

HISTORICAL SPOTLIGHT

From 1963 until 2004, all CFA charters, which are larger than a standard size, were printed on a single printing press located in Red Wing, Minnesota, USA. A unique machine (the only other one like it was at the Smithsonian Institution in Washington, DC), the printing press was 100 years old by 2001—and the demands on it were ever increasing. Because it required a laborious two-step process, in which the oversized charters were hand fed, one by one, delivering charters expeditiously was becoming impossible. In 2004, CFA Institute contracted with a different printer that used a newer, more efficient machine that, fortunately, can accommodate the large size of the CFA charter.

CFA CANDIDATE REGISTRATIONS BY REGION, FY 2004

4%
38%
32%
2%
14%
10%

■ Africa/Middle East ■ Asia Pacific ■ Canada ■ Europe ■ Latin America ■ United States
100% = 118,000 CFA Candidate Registrations

PRACTISE YOUR SPOKEN ENGLISH FOR YOUR FUTURE JOB INTERVIEWS.

The following ITEMS ARE NOT ALLOWED in the testing room.

Signs posted at all CFA Institute test centers.

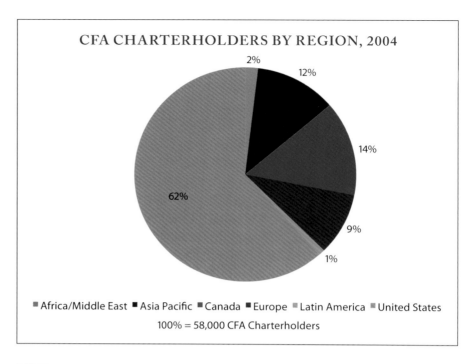

CFA CHARTERHOLDERS BY REGION, 2004

2%
12%
14%
62%
9%
1%

■ Africa/Middle East ■ Asia Pacific ■ Canada ■ Europe ■ Latin America ■ United States

100% = 58,000 CFA Charterholders

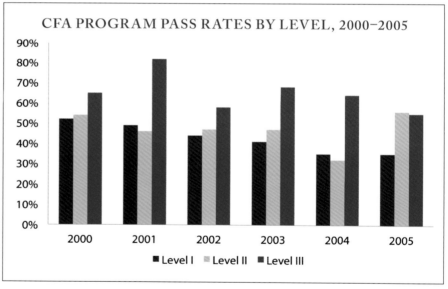

CFA PROGRAM PASS RATES BY LEVEL, 2000–2005

■ Level I   ■ Level II   ■ Level III

example, accessibility statutes and fair trade practices) but also had sufficient safeguards in place to protect the security—hence, the integrity—of CFA exam construction, administration, and grading.

The review was not undertaken because of known problems but rather to forestall them. The hope was that conducting an intensive review would serve as a preventative measure—taking into account rapid growth of the CFA Program and guaranteeing that processes and procedures protected its integrity.[6] Program leaders were aware that since the mid-1990s, the CFA exam had become "a high-stakes exam," as Peter B. Mackey, CFA, now head of CFA Program and Exam Development, phrased it.[7] More and more employers recognized the charter's significance; many required it for employment or favored those who possessed a CFA charter. By the early 2000s, regulators in many countries accepted the completion of at least Level I in place of other testing or licensing requirements. By the late 1990s and early 2000s, moreover, pass rates had begun to drop sharply. As a result, according to Mackey, "People started to recognize how difficult it was" to earn the CFA charter. When stakes get this high, he noted, some people will "risk cheating or stealing to get the letters after their name." Needless to say, Mackey noted, "These threats were extremely distressing to staff and members, given that the cornerstone of the CFA Program is to foster ethical professional practices."[8]

HISTORICAL SPOTLIGHT: TEN LARGEST JUNE EXAM CENTERS, 2004

Location	Tested Candidates
New York, New York, USA	5,178
London, UK	3,540
Hong Kong (SAR)	3,491
Toronto, Ontario, Canada	3,453
Singapore	2,049
Seoul, South Korea	2,019
Boston, Massachusetts, USA	1,808
Chicago, Illinois, USA	1,779
Taipei, Taiwan	1,471
Shanghai, China	1,458

Conducted over several months, the review was completed early in 1999, and its recommendations were enacted over the next year. The reviewers found the CFA Program to be in compliance legally but noted that the dramatic growth in the previous decade had left the program vulnerable in terms of security. Under the weight of "such staggering growth," as the AIMR 2000 Annual Report put it, a system devised for a much smaller pool of candidates and many fewer locations could be at risk.[9] In their opening remarks in the 2000 Annual Report, CEO Thomas A. Bowman, CFA, and Chair of the Board of Governors Fred H. Speece, Jr., CFA, acknowledged the extent and expanse of this growth but also noted an important shift in demographics. In 1990, only 3 percent of AIMR members were from outside North America. By 2000, AIMR members from outside North America had grown to 10 percent; 45 percent of CFA exam registrations were outside North America, with CFA exams administered in 69 different countries. Neither staff increases nor the infrastructure expansion that occurred in the late 1990s had prepared the program sufficiently for growth of this kind.

Happily, some findings of this intense review could be acted on immediately. As noted in Chapter 6, the practice of allowing candidates from Quebec City and Montreal to write their answers in French was discontinued in 1999, in part, as a result of the review and, in part, for fairness. In addition, the CFA Program increased the use of the larger test centers, thus concentrating the personnel needed to administer exams. This practice coincided with the huge explosion in registrations, which was already making sufficient college classroom space for the exams difficult to locate. Nancy Dudley, former head of Exam Administration and Security, recalled that by 1999, for example, at the University of Toronto,

Janko Trenkoski, CFA, 2003 charterholder from Macedonia.

"We had every building on campus and every room that was available, and we still couldn't accommodate all the candidates."[10]

The tightening of on-site security measures, and most other changes to procedures stemming from the review, were implemented early in the 2000s. In general, the analysis resulted in targeted training for exam administration supervisors, proctors, and graders and in formal employment agreements with the graders. The AIMR governors made clear that they took these precautions seriously as part of the ongoing review of practices that CFA Program staff conducted each year to ensure exam security.

One element of heightened training was the creation of examination administration specialists (EAS), who acted as observers at test sites. EAS were staff members who had received rigorous and specific training. Ultimately, they monitored for operational consistency and helped institute changes at test centers where 70–80 percent of the candidates sat.

In many cases, tightening of security was driven as much by changes in technology as by the explosion in numbers and testing centers. As Robert R. Johnson, CFA, put it, "We are always concerned about people cheating [and

The Toronto CFA Institute test center above is one of the largest CFA exam test centers. Donna Crossan (left) was the exam supervisor for this 2005 administration. Here she is pictured with Tim McLaughlin, CFA (center), chief administrative officer and chief financial officer of CFA Institute, and Jeffrey J. Diermeier, CFA (right), president and CEO of CFA Institute (2005–2008), using scooters to traverse the almost one-mile-long testing venue. B.J. Morris, photographer

about] electronic methods of stealing examinations."[11] Cheating wasn't invented in the year 2000, of course. W. Bruce Remington II, CFA, a longtime proctor in Omaha, Nebraska, recalled a moment during a 1987 exam when he noticed that a candidate seemed to be taking an unusual interest in his calculator's instruction manual. After a game of "cat and mouse" with the candidate, during which Remington observed the candidate peeking into his instruction manual while answering an accounting question, the proctor's suspicions were confirmed. At the end of the exam, Remington confiscated the manual and found it loaded with

On-site testing personnel enter the Kathmandu, Nepal, test center to receive their assignments for that day's CFA exam.

crib notes. "He was toast!" Remington said of the candidate, whose exam was not even graded.[12] Crib notes in an instruction manual would seem quaint once cell phones appeared in virtually everyone's hands—cell phones with camera, data storage, and internet capabilities. Soon all electronics were banned from testing rooms.

Personal items are left outside the Seoul, South Korea, test center as CFA candidates sit for the CFA exam.

Instances of cheating were handled administratively prior to 1998, but after that time, they were referred to and investigated by the Professional Conduct Program. Candidates found in serious violation of policies could be barred from the program.

As the decade progressed, additional security strictures were placed on testing centers and on candidates—restrictions on what could be brought into test centers, what could be brought into the exam room itself, what kind of calculators were acceptable (now limited to two specific models), and, equally importantly, what kind of identification was needed. Beginning in 2011, only a valid international travel passport was accepted as identification for enrollment and on exam day.

Other factors governing the general evaluation of risk included the likelihood of physical danger, which became especially relevant in light of the rise of ter-

EXAM STORY: FUNKY IN ATLANTA, 2003

One of the first EAS was Donald L. Tuttle, CFA, who remembered an experience in Atlanta that did not affect the security of the exam but may have affected the sanity of the candidates. Everything started off well, he recalled, until about half an hour into the exam, when the large testing room filled up with exceptionally loud music, coming, it seemed, through the walls and the floor. Any CFA candidate in the room who was a fan of Rhythm & Blues must have recognized the sound: One floor below the room, the distinctive pop band Earth, Wind & Fire was in full rehearsal for its evening performance. The shocked Tuttle left the proctors in charge and went in search of the manager to rectify the situation. He was told that the band had contracted for a rehearsal at this time. As Tuttle pointed out, the CFA Program had contracted for "silence" at this time.

Eventually, the band took a break and quiet was restored—but not long enough for the CFA candidates to finish in peace. When practice started up again, Tuttle noted, "I was screaming at the management" to put a stop to it. Remarkably, the CFA candidates, renowned for their ability to concentrate, completed their exams despite the funky "soundtrack."[13]

EXAM STORY: THE CASE OF THE MISSING IDENTITY

"For the Level I exam in 2002, I showed up at the test center punctually, stood in line with my ID, my TI BAII+, and my #2 pencils. Anxiously awaiting my seat assignment, I was eyeing other candidates hoping to find those looking nervous and unprepared. Unfortunately, I never got to take my seat [because] the most unprepared person in the room turned out to be myself. I had forgotten to check one important item: the expiration date on my driver's license. It was expired! It had been expired for nine months, in fact. I guess I was too busy studying to concern myself with those trivial state laws. Whenever I get the opportunity to share my story with other candidates, I frequently get the response, 'Oh, I heard about you . . . .'"

—EDWARD S. FORRESTER, CFA, Atlanta, USA

rorist activity. Security measures grew even tighter in the wake of the World Trade Center attacks of 9/11. "Though the safety measures place severe restrictions on the materials allowed within testing centers," the 2002 AIMR Annual Report noted, candidates appeared "to recognize the changes as only a minor inconvenience" and find them more than justified in ensuring "a more secure testing environment."[14] To CFA Program leaders, then as now, protecting the safety of CFA candidates and the integrity of the examination process was essential.

INNOVATIONS CONTINUE

Changes in the CFA Program did not stop with increased security and expanded training for exam administration. The early 2000s also saw the introduction of item sets, a second administration per year of the Level I exam, the institutionalization of Practice Analysis, and the production of proprietary literature.[15]

Item Sets

Item sets are a kind of multiple-choice on steroids.

—Joseph T. Dabney III, CFA, July 2009

By 2000, not only were CFA candidates facing tight security measures on test day, but those taking Levels II and III were also looking at a new kind of exam. After years of debate and investigation, multiple-choice questions, in the form of item sets, were added for the ethics portions of CFA exams at all levels for the June 2000 administration. Multiple-choice questions were increased to 50 percent of the Level II and III exams in 2001, and in 2005, the Level II exam became entirely multiple-choice—or, more precisely, item set—questions.

As Donald L. Tuttle, CFA, recalled, "As a matter of desirability and a matter of practicality, we decided to explore other kinds of testing than essay."[16] This was done, in part, because creating sufficiently rigorous essay examinations was becoming more and more difficult and, in part, because managing the consistent grading of the essays was unwieldy. In addition, research in the field of educational testing indicated that multiple-choice questions could more accurately and equitably test all candidates compared with essay questions and that multiple-choice questions constituted best practice for testing.

The kind of multiple-choice questions that appeared at Levels II and III in 2000 were called "item sets" and were completely new to CFA exams. For the CFA

Program, the creation of item sets began late in 1998 with the organization of the Higher Order Knowledge Team (HOKT). According to one of its members, Thomas R. Robinson, CFA, the HOKT initially included 11 university professors who were also CFA charterholders and four members of the AIMR staff. Later, practitioners joined the team and the group became part of the Council of Examiners (COE). Jan R. Squires, CFA, who joined the CFA Program staff in 1999 as head of Examination Development, coordinated this work. Higher-order thinking (or knowledge) lies at the upper end of the spectrum classified in Bloom's Taxonomy and includes such cognitive skills as analysis, synthesis, and evaluation (see Chapter 3). The CFA Program intended to develop a vehicle similar to multiple-choice questions but one that tested a higher level of cognition.

Item sets are rigorously constructed vignettes or short stories, similar to a brief case study, and are typically no longer than two pages. Each vignette depicts a complex professional situation that invites analysis, calculation, and judgment. Six multiple-choice questions are asked about each vignette—all requiring the candidate to think critically and solve problems. In other words, item sets are designed to effectively test higher-order thinking. "The item sets," Tuttle recalled, were considered very innovative by the consultants, who had never seen "any organization of our size and our testing situation try this before."[17]

The HOKT first met in February 1999 and for approximately two years, worked on a program that ultimately resulted in the addition of item sets to the CFA examinations. The group sessions were led by a renowned expert in the field of higher-knowledge testing, Thomas Haladyna, a professor of educational psychology at Arizona State University.[18]

EXAM STORY: PREPARED FOR ANYTHING IN CANADA

This Canadian charterholder "still laughs" when he thinks of his experience with heightened security during his first CFA exam:

" Being from small towns in Newfoundland and Labrador, where my high school graduation class consisted of eight students, my first experience at a CFA Examination center [in 2001], where a crowd of eager students crammed into the lecture hall to take CFA Level I, was interesting to say the very least.

"I quietly took my seat and placed my CFA-approved calculator, two sharpened pencils, sharpener, and eraser (without the cardboard wrapper) neatly on my desk. One fellow sitting two rows down in front of me almost made me laugh out loud: he thought it was necessary to bring three calculators, a stack of pencils that I'm sure he needed two hands to carry, and several erasers. I couldn't help but think: I could break one pencil and not waste any time sharpening it, but if a handful of pencils break, and three calculators stop working, and I need to erase enough little shaded circles to wear out a full eraser, well . . . it just wasn't meant to be and I should get up, leave, and enjoy the rest of my day.

"As I began the exam, I have to admit, I was a little gentle with the pencil for the first couple of shaded circles, but that caution quickly passed as all of the information stored into my head was being called upon. I was in the zone! Then, an eager exam proctor reached across in front of me and picked up my brand new white vinyl eraser with his thumb and index finger, turned it over to look at the bottom side, then placed it back on the table.

"My initial startle turned to uncontrollable laughter—to the point that I had to leave the exam room. If my passing or failing this exam hinged on forgetting the quantity of information that can be written on the underside of a one-inch by two-inch eraser, then the last months of studying were wasted. My uncontrollable laughter came from a thought about the chap two rows down. He could have covered half the Body of Knowledge on his erasers!

"I did return and pass Level I. But I didn't see the other poor chap the following year."

—BRADLEY N. ROWE, CFA, Halifax, Nova Scotia, Canada

Neither charterholders nor volunteers nor board members instantly rallied around the use of item sets. By 2001 multiple-choice questions had been a successful part of the Level I exam for 33 years, yet adding them substantially at Levels II and III required a whole new series of discussions. "Level III was the toughest nut to crack," Tuttle said, "because we had some very strong opinions in influential groups like the Board of Governors who wanted to see us keep essay questions for all of Level III." Staff and HOKT members had to present a convincing argument for the inclusion of item sets in CFA exams. Jan Squires remembered that the idea that "you can test portfolio management skills in item set or multiple-choice format" really "got people's attention."[19] Many were "convinced that you were reducing the exam [to] a game of probabilities."

As discussed in Chapter 6, whether multiple-choice questions are "easier" than essays had been frequently debated in the past, as had whether multiple-choice questions could truly test judgment, whether they disadvantaged non-native-English speakers, and whether they were sufficient discriminators of those who deserved a CFA charter. According to research in the testing industry, however, multiple-choice questions—especially those evoking higher-order thinking, as item sets are designed to do—are effective and could overcome the objections raised by board members. According to Bob Johnson, who was then head of the CFA Program and an HOKT participant, Don Tuttle was the individual who "did all the research on item sets, put the first item set team together, and reported back to the Board of Governors that this was something that we could do and that this is something that would actually enhance the CFA Program."[20] As Tuttle remembered it, people became convinced by seeing evidence that item set tests could be every bit as rigorous as essay tests and, in fact, were "better than essays in terms of some of the standard criteria that you use for measuring whether an exam is good or bad."[21]

A letter to AIMR members in February 2000 noted that "the science of exam administration has seen substantial evolution, with alternative testing techniques gaining credibility within the professional certification community." Item sets, moreover, combined the best elements of objective multiple-choice questions with the individual analysis needed for essay (constructed) answers. The evidence was persuasive. Michael L. McCowin, CFA, who served on the COE for many years and understood firsthand the difficulty of creating CFA exams that were not "harder or easier from year to year," confessed that, at first, he was reluctant. "I was a little skeptical," he said, "but I became convinced that a properly structured item set question [could] be just as effective, if not more effective," than an essay.[22] Dwight D. Churchill, CFA, an AIMR governor during this time, also recalled the debate over the growing use of item sets:

> We heard from staff and experts regarding the shifting nature of the exam, and we worked to convince ourselves that the integrity of the exam could

be maintained with greater use of item set questions. We did convince ourselves, but it was not an easy task.[23]

When it came time to decide, however, the AIMR Board of Governors voted unanimously to accept the use of item sets. Once item sets were in place, Jan Squires recalled, things changed:

> After we got a couple of years of results in and we could then show that all of the exam performance characteristics were basically unchanged from when we had done the same topics in essay, then it became a nonissue.[24]

Left to right: Khalid Ghayur, CFA, Denise M. Farkas, CFA, and Lee N. Price, CFA, joined their fellow Board of Governors members in voting unanimously for significant changes to the CFA Program.

December Exams

Another unanimous decision was reached on 20 May 2001 when the governors approved a second yearly administration of the Level I exam beginning in December 2003. As far back as the mid-1980s, what was then the ICFA Board of Trustees had considered the possibility of offering a second exam once Level I became entirely multiple choice. This idea had been considered periodically since then, and by the early 2000s, the time was right to implement it. Not only were numbers of new candidates coming into the CFA Program at astonishing rates, but also employers were increasingly looking for people who had earned or were in the process of earning their CFA charters. In such circumstances, having the exam available two times a year made sense. Moreover, as the 2001 AIMR Annual Report noted, "More and more regulators [have] come to rely on Level I of the CFA exam as a substitute for their own licensing exams."[25] This situation was true not only in the United States, where CFA Program officials had pushed for its acceptance since the beginning of the program, but it was also increasingly true outside the United States. The Monetary Authority of Singapore, for example, had accepted Level I for years. The trend toward acceptance of the CFA charter continued throughout the decade. By 2011, 22 countries and territories had accepted the CFA designation for all or part of their licensing requirements.

For the first administration of the December Level I exam, 12 test sites were chosen for their geographical diversity and to serve the largest populations of CFA candidates. By the time the enrollment period was completed, however, 26 sites were needed worldwide. Fortuitously, the December administration meant that Chinese candidates—as well as those in Toronto and Singapore, where some centers had also been closed in June because of the SARS epidemic—could sit for Level I in December of the same year. According to Nancy Dudley, "We had not planned to offer [the December exam] in China, but because of SARS, we then opened Beijing and Shanghai in December to accommodate those candidates."[26] Less than a decade after its first administration, the December exam

REMEMBERING 9/11

Three blocks north and two blocks west of the NYSE, planes flew out of a clear blue sky and into the World Trade Center (WTC) on the morning of 11 September 2001. Few in the financial community will ever forget that day, to which so many had direct connections. The AIMR database alone showed more than 200 candidates and members had WTC mailing addresses. Although other sites in the United States were also attacked, the WTC was not hit simply because it was the tallest target in Manhattan; it was also the eponymous symbol of the global financial markets that the CFA Program serves.

CFA charterholders and candidates were among those who died; in all, AIMR lost at least 60 members. Large numbers of charterholders worked in the twin towers, in other buildings within the WTC complex, or nearby on Wall Street, Broad Street, Trinity Place—storied locations in lower Manhattan where the financial industry in North America began. The offices of the New York Society of Security Analysts—of which Ben Graham was a founding member—were crushed when the north tower collapsed. Fortunately, all the employees had been evacuated, although many records were lost. With a resilience characteristic of the markets in general, NYSSA found other office space in Manhattan and was able to resume its programs for members on 1 October 2001.

In Charlottesville, AIMR employees came together through a staff fund drive, which raised $11,000—a sum that was matched by AIMR—for a gift to the American Red Cross Disaster Relief Fund. Soon after the attacks, the AIMR Board of Governors established an 11 September Memorial Scholarship Fund, launched with an initial $1 million donation from AIMR capital reserves. Its purpose was to "provide annual scholarship grants to those permanently disabled in the attacks, as well as to their family members, domestic partners, or dependents who are pursuing undergraduate degrees in finance, economics, or a related field."[27] In recognition of the fact that victims of the 9/11 attacks came from more than 80 countries, scholarships were not restricted to U.S. citizens and the funds awarded could be used for any qualifying college or university in the world. "This is a global profession," board member Janet T. Miller, CFA, acknowledged.[28]

In reflecting back on that awful day and its aftermath, Thomas A. Bowman, CFA, recalled one particularly poignant incident:

> After 9/11, I received a letter from the sister of a young man who had recently received his charter but was a victim in the Trade Center attacks. She went on to say how proud he was of his charter and had shown it to her and their mother when he had hung it in his WTC office. She wanted to know if it would be possible to produce a replica of his charter so she could give it to her mother.

He responded immediately saying that he would be privileged to provide one and would deliver it himself.[29]

© 2010 Robert Van Beets, iStockPhoto

was administered at 63 locations and the number of candidates sitting for it had more than doubled (from 20,657 in December 2003 to 46,644 in December 2010).

Practice Analysis

In the first half of the 2000s, two other best practices were established in the CFA Program. In 2000, the second job analysis, by then called Practice Analysis, was conducted, this time by the research firm of Knapp and Associates International. As with the 1995 survey, this one established panels of CFA charterholders selected for the diversity of their geographical locations, employment situations, and professional roles. After working with them, the consultants and staff created a survey that was sent to more than 10,000 charterholders. From the data collected, the group established a Candidate Body of Knowledge that reflected the "knowledge, skills, and abilities required of a generalist investment practitioner with four years of experience."[30] In 2004, the third Practice Analysis was conducted, and in 2007, the process of surveying practitioners to determine the appropriate Body of Knowledge was made continuous and online elements were used to reach participants.

Proprietary Literature

EXAM STORY: A TESTING ENGAGEMENT, 2001

"My CFA Level I exam story is a love story. . . By the Friday before the Level I exam, I had done all the studying I could do. If it wasn't in my brain by now, I wasn't going to master it in the next 24 hours. I went to work (and reviewed all day) and came home, looking forward to a night of relaxation. My goal that evening was to get a good night's rest, which seemed impossible given how nervous I was about the next day's test.

"After a nice home-cooked meal with my boyfriend, I proceeded to get ready for bed, putting my pajamas on and washing my face. As I was reading, my boyfriend's pager, which he had lost earlier in the day, started to buzz. Happy that it had been found, I reached down and felt for it. I found it —attached to a wooden box. As I slowly picked up the pager/box, my heart started racing. I instantly understood what was happening —he was going to propose! I was sort of expecting it but thought he might do it the next night. I never once thought he would do it THE NIGHT BEFORE THE CFA EXAM!!!!

"I opened the box, and there was a beautiful engagement ring. My boyfriend then asked me to marry him. 'Yes, of course!' I said, laughing and crying and so happy! I had to call my parents and my girlfriends and tell them, of course. And then I had to go to bed. Ha! I don't think I slept a wink that night.

"On the morning of the exam, I felt prepared, but my mind had already started to wander off into wedding land. All I remember of that exam is that I frequently would sit there and stare at my engagement ring. I had to repeatedly tell myself to focus on the test and not daydream! Fortunately, I passed. To this day, my now-husband is teased by my friends and colleagues about proposing to me on one of the most stressful nights of my life. I guess everything worked out!"

—LIZ DHILLON, CFA, Pomona, California, USA

The development of proprietary literature for the CFA Program illustrates perfectly the adage that the more things change, the more they stay the same. Although the idea met with reluctance when proposed by CFA Program staff in the late 1990s, the development of proprietary literature—educational materials written specifically for the CFA candidate curriculum—was actually nothing new. From the program's earliest days, staff and volunteers had difficulty finding materials that specifically targeted what a practitioner needed to know. The original CFA study guides and readings, compilations of other extant works, were soon supplemented by original, program-specific texts: *Quantitative Techniques for Financial Analysis* in 1971,[31] *Managing Investment Portfolios* in 1983,[32] and throughout the years, numerous ICFA seminar proceedings, the content of which served both practitioners and candidates.

For Candidate Curriculum Committee members seeking curriculum materials, for staff seeking permission to use materials, and certainly among candidates paying for study materials, the cost in both time and money of using external source materials was high. As Bob Johnson saw it, "One of the biggest problems with the curriculum was that candidates were buying stacks of books of which they were reading very little."[33] A recommended book might contain 60 articles, only 6 of which were relevant to the CFA study program. Articles covering all aspects of the curriculum were scattered throughout dozens of textbooks.

Moreover, because the CFA Program identified as its mission serving generalists around the world via distance learning and self-study, ensuring that all study materials were written as plainly and as much in keeping with practitioner knowledge as possible became essential. To achieve this goal, and to provide candidates with materials at a low cost, the CFA Program began to commission and publish curriculum textbooks. The first was *Fixed Income Analysis* by Frank J. Fabozzi, CFA, in 2000. In 2001 a new quantitative methods book was added,[34] and in 2002, one on equity asset valuation.[35]

According to Bob Johnson, the basic reason for commissioning and publishing CFA Program texts was "to provide a comprehensible curriculum for the distance learning candidate, with embedded examples, end of chapter problems, [and] complete solutions."[36] The creation of proprietary literature benefited the CFA Program in other ways. For one thing, it obviated the need for a "Gaps and Overlaps" report (see Chapter 5) because omissions and duplications were corrected by the texts themselves. In addition, ownership of the readings enabled the CCC, as Peter Mackey noted, "to update and improve existing readings every year, rather than waiting several years for an author to revise a text."[37] Having literature written expressly for CFA candidates resulted in what he called "huge improvements in quality and efficiency." Efforts to provide relevant curricular materials to candidates continued to develop and the means of presentation continued to evolve during the first decade of the new century.

MANDATORY CONTINUING EDUCATION:
WHAT DOES A CHARTERHOLDER STILL NEED TO LEARN?

Members should be on the cutting edge of learning . . . ahead of what the marketplace demands. That is what will push the profession forward.

—Harry E. Tutwiler, CFA, *AIMR Exchange*, March/April 1999

The mission of the CFA Program as articulated in the early 2000s was to focus on distance learning for the *generalist*. In a sense, this mission was the obverse of efforts to address specialties within the investment management and analyst profession, perhaps by offering specialty exams at Level III, which would earn a kind of "graduate" designation for charterholders. Such specialization had been thoroughly investigated, and a curriculum and a testing protocol had been developed through the efforts of Don Tuttle, Frank K. Reilly, CFA, and others. But the specialization program was eventually abandoned, primarily because of its testing component (see Chapter 6). The program's curricular materials became part of a continuum of professional development offerings for CFA charterholders and AIMR members. Exactly how CFA charterholders should interact with these materials was the subject of heated debate from 2000 to 2002.

As had been true since its founding in 1985, the Continuing Education (CE) program for charterholders remained voluntary in the early 2000s. Like other issues in the history of the CFA Program, however, whether professional development work should be mandatory was not fully resolved for many people, and the issue returned. John L. Maginn, CFA, tells a story of Edmund A. Mennis, CFA, taking him aside when he first came onto the ICFA Board of Trustees to warn him, "About every 10 years, you'll see an idea cycle through and you'll see people dive into it, spend a lot of time on it—not recognizing that 10 years before, we all did the same thing."[38] Mennis was talking in general terms about life on a volunteer board, of course, but he could easily have been referring to the CE program because consideration of making it a required program has come up time after time.

At the turn of the new decade, a serious effort was mounted to transform the voluntary CE program into mandatory continuing education. Proponents of the measure, who included board members, charterholders, and staff members, believed that such a mandatory program would help maintain the integrity of the CFA charter and that the CFA Program suffered in comparison with other professional designations in not requiring continued professional education of its charterholders. For some people, the fact that their profession did not have mandatory continuing education was an anomaly. By 2000 and 2001, moreover, scandals in the financial industry lent urgency to considering the issue again.

HISTORICAL SPOTLIGHT

On 1 November 2001, AIMR opened its first European office. The need for a European presence had been growing for years, and early in 2001, the choice between Zurich and London was a "dead heat," according to Raymond J. DeAngelo, then AIMR senior vice president for global affairs. When the two existing London analyst groups, the Institute of Investment Management and Research and the London Society of Investment Professionals, merged to form the UK Society of Investment Professionals, which established the CFA charter as its industry's U.K. benchmark, the scales tipped toward London.

The CFA Institute London office opened in November 2001.
© 2010 David Joyner, iStockPhoto

WHAT'S IN A NAME?

A lot, apparently. The name "Association for Investment Management and Research" or "AIMR" was chosen as a compromise in 1990 to avoid the ill feelings that using either "CFA" or "Federation" in the name might have caused. But the name AIMR was confusing to some, loathed by others, and mispronounced by many in its 14-year life. Given the chance in May 2004 to vote on changing the name, 86 percent of the members voted to do so, and with the approval of the board in July 2004, "CFA Institute" was born.

Our true identity *revealed.*
{ AIMR changes name to CFA Institute. }

CFA Institute launches its new identity with this headline and image.

A Continuing Education Task Force, formed in 1999, worked toward establishing a CE program that would be, according to Katrina F. "Katy" Sherrerd, CFA, "credible, flexible, and low in cost"[39]—and possibly mandatory.

For three years, by means of surveys, focus groups, research into other professions, and frequent communication with members via e-mail and letter, the CE Task Force sought to construct a prototype mandatory CE program that would be acceptable to and approved by charterholders. Katy Sherrerd noted that open debate was extremely important to the functioning of the Task Force:

> We put together a committee that was, by design, very, very diverse. We had very vocal opponents from Boston, . . . we had members from the Philadelphia Society, we had an international representative . . . . We tried to cover the whole spectrum—[from] people who wanted specialization to the people who wanted nothing.[40]

The Task Force "surveyed the landscape of all the other professions" to determine how continuing education was handled by each: how many hours were required, whether or not it had to be attested to, whether self-study was allowed, "what you're allowed to read, whether you're forced to go to conferences"—all sorts of aspects were studied.

In mid-2000, a survey of 40,000 members (a 28 percent response rate) showed that most did not participate in CE activities because they did not "have time" but fully 95 percent thought continuing education was necessary and stressed that it was important "to maintain knowledge." Regulators who were surveyed endorsed the idea for mandatory CE by a wide margin: 83 percent favored it. Employers surveyed were open to the idea. By late 2000, an article in the *AIMR Exchange* reported that 62.3 percent of charterholders responding to the survey would vote in favor of a 25-hour mandatory program, whereas 15 percent would not favor mandatory CE in any form. Two-thirds of voting CFA charterholders would need to approve the mandatory program for it to take effect.[41]

As they had since C. Stewart Sheppard first crisscrossed the country to promote the early CFA exams, staff and board members visited societies and held town hall–style meetings to inform charterholders about a mandatory CE program and answer questions. The scene was not always pretty, according to Fred Speece, who, as chair of AIMR in 2000–2001, made a lot of those visits. In fact, he recalled, some meetings were "brutal" and featured "700 people yelling at me."[42]

Despite a six-month public comment period, which included distribution of materials related to mandatory CE to members, Speece realized that a lot of confusion and disagreement remained. He was clear, however, about his own task: As chair, his duty was to "bring this before the members in an objective way and to lay out continuing education programs that seemed to make sense." The point was not, in Speece's view, to "sell" the program to members but "to deliver a cogent program that we thought was acceptable and have [the members] vote."

In May 2002, they voted. Board members expected the decision to be close, but it was not. CFA charterholders defeated the proposed mandatory CE program by a vote of 57 percent to 41 percent, with 2 percent abstaining. Fred Speece, who had as near a view as anyone of what was brewing, thought the measure was likely to fail, but even he did not expect the magnitude of the rejection. "It was an eye-opener," as incoming AIMR board member Monique E.M. Gravel, CFA, put it.[43]

Although many still held that the best practice for a profession is to require mandatory continuing education, the reality of charterholder reluctance was recognized. Within two months, the board had approved the formation of a CE committee to oversee a voluntary program. By 2003, a diary for CE (by then, known as CFA Professional Development) was online at the AIMR website, where charterholders could record their continuing education activities.

John B. Neff, CFA (left), served as chair of the Advisory Council of the CFA Centre for Financial Market Integrity for 2004–2007; Fred H. Speece, Jr., CFA (right), served as ICFA chair for 1997–1998 and AIMR chair for 2000–2001.

BEST ETHICAL PRACTICES

The challenges the CFA Program faced at the beginning of its fifth decade brought it into the spotlight in a new way. It is one thing to be the professional organization for analysts and investment managers in tranquil times; it is quite another thing to speak for the profession when the financial industry is rocked by one disgrace after another. The early 2000s were, as Tom Bowman said, a "very, very unfortunate time in our profession's history."[44] Jeffrey J. Diermeier, CFA, who became president and CEO of CFA Institute in 2005, concurred: "The popular view of the ethical backbone of our industry's professionals sank to the bottom."[45] CFA charterholders could take some solace in the fact that their Code of Ethics and Standards of Professional Conduct had been in existence and followed for nearly 20 years by the time these scandals broke. Although few members were implicated, the *profession* was, according to Diermeier, "under attack."

In the wake of Enron and WorldCom, AIMR stepped forward to make a case for analyst independence, for the ethical reliability of CFA charterholders, and to influence proposed financial reform. In June 2001, and again in February and

[You] all used your influence to build highly ethical, client-focused spheres of impact on our business.

—Thomas B. Welch, CFA, CFA Institute 20th Anniversary Celebration, 2010

By 2002, the Code of Ethics and Standards of Professional Conduct had been translated into nine languages to support members around the world: Arabic, Chinese with simplified characters, Chinese with traditional characters, French, German, Hungarian, Italian, Japanese, and Spanish. By 2011, it had been translated into 16 languages.

March of 2002, CEO Tom Bowman testified before the U.S. Congress. He also spoke before officials in Canada, Hong Kong, and Singapore. In retrospect, Bowman noted, "Those times before Congress were very, very helpful in planting that flag as to what we stood for."[46] The difficulties in financial markets in the early 2000s also spurred the AIMR board toward a more forward-looking, comprehensive, and engaged advocacy effort on behalf of the profession than it had at the time. Raymond J. DeAngelo was charged with developing a new paradigm for AIMR advocacy. This new paradigm took form as the CFA Centre for Financial Market Integrity, which was established in 2004.[47]

According to Tom Bowman, in forming the Centre, the intention was to "expand the scope of our advocacy effort, which heretofore had been primarily dealing with accounting and financial reporting issues—fairly narrow, fairly esoteric issues." Without abandoning accounting and reporting—especially at a time when both had seeded scandal—CFA Program and AIMR leaders saw that "the old advocacy efforts really needed to be expanded more broadly into more core market issues." The best financial market practices were, as they had always been, the ethical ones. The CFA Program educated investment professionals about ethical practices, tested their knowledge, and expected their adherence.

LEADERSHIP IN TRANSITION

Before the new millennium was five years old, Tom Bowman had tendered his resignation as president and CEO. After 10 years in the position and 18 years serving the CFA Program, he was ready to retire. Bowman began to work for the CFA Program when the ICFA ran it. As CEO, he saw AIMR through its early years as a blended organization. When he bid goodbye in 2004, the organization had become CFA Institute. Not only had Bowman's tenure straddled name changes, but he had also witnessed and piloted the CFA Program through sea changes:

> I became president here in 1994, [when] our budget was $10 million and we had somewhere in the neighborhood of 10,000 candidates. When I left here at the end of 2004, we had a $100 million budget and 120,000 candidates, give or take.

These changes represented not simply growth but also expansion. In 1994, only a small percentage of members were from outside North America; in 2004, fully 50 percent were. When asked what his proudest accomplishment was, Bowman responded, "the absorption of the global membership." During his tenure, the organization brought in graders and curriculum and exam writers from beyond North America and recruited international members to form a more global Board of Governors. Bowman helped make CFA Institute a multinational organization with offices in London and Hong Kong.

Ironically, Tom Bowman had been somewhat reluctant to apply for the CEO position in 1993, in part because of the amount of travel involved. Remarkably, he spent the next 10 years circling the globe on behalf of the CFA Program, stopping in many more places than had his well-traveled predecessor, Alfred C. "Pete" Morley, CFA. It was an admitted challenge to handle the "huge inflow of people" that growth in the number of CFA candidates and charterholders represented. Bowman rose to the occasion.

One who worked with him for years on global outreach, Ray DeAngelo, recognized Bowman's feat:

> Tom's overriding achievement as CEO relates to globalization. He successfully navigated the waters outside of North America to help ensure that the CFA Program emerged as the dominant education and credentialing program for investment professionals worldwide. This created the cornerstone not only of our financial success but of our sterling reputation. It paved the way for us to be able to have the credibility to push for higher standards of practice by both individuals and firms.[48]

Others identified underlying strengths in Bowman that facilitated this global outreach. To the first non–North American board member and chair, Philippe A. Sarasin, CFA, Bowman's greatest quality was his openness to change. He had "an ability to go to a place of discomfort" and a "willingness to consider reengineering everything."[49] I. Rossa O'Reilly, CFA, who also chaired both organizations, cited Bowman's ability to "deal with enormous numbers of powerful, conflicting and well-argued positions . . . and come out with successful solutions."[50]

Proud of his work in bringing CFA Institute and the CFA Program into prominence throughout the world, Bowman also knew how to make an exit. Thinking of his successor, Jeff Diermeier, he planned the transition to new leadership as he had planned so many changes in his years as CFA Institute CEO, with openness and good grace:

> The worst thing that could happen is to have the old boss hanging around, looking over your shoulder, and saying, "I do not think you ought to do it that way" or "That is not the way it was done when I was here." So, I made a promise to myself that I was going to be scarce. My attitude has been: I have done my job.

He had. And he had done it well.

The Evolution of CFA Exam Grading

*T*he history of CFA exam grading began in July 1963 with five men hunched over 284 exam booklets. Then, as now, grading was done anonymously. Exam booklets were numbered, and the names of the candidates were unknown to those who evaluated the answers. Led by the first two employees of the Institute of Chartered Financial Analysts, C. Stewart Sheppard and C. Ray Smith, the initial CFA grading team included a former economist for the U.S. Federal Reserve, a professor of finance from the University of Virginia with significant business experience, and a UVA accounting professor. None, of course, had CFA charters; all were reading Level III exams.

Smith remembered that the Council of Examiners, who wrote the first exam, supplied some suggested answers—precursors to today's guideline answers and grading keys. No review by trustees was carried out for borderline exams that first year—because most of the trustees were themselves candidates. "After the first year," Smith noted, "we had a cadre of [charterholders] who were able to help in the grading."[1]

Among the early graders was Louis H. Whitehead, CFA, with whom Benjamin Graham had first discussed the need to certify security analysts. Ray Smith recalled him easily: "Louis had a big white handlebar mustache, drove a Rolls Royce, and couldn't wait to get here to grade."[2] Whitehead had a high opinion of the CFA grading process; he declared it "near perfect."[3] Those who have made incremental improvements in the grading program every year since then might take issue with Whitehead's notion of perfection, but in a sense, he was right. Standards of fairness and consistency have always been paramount.

Since the introduction of 25 multiple-choice questions on the Level I exam in 1968, exam grading has proceeded in two phases. The first involves machine scoring of all multiple-choice (also known as "selected response") questions, which now constitute all of Levels I and II and half of Level III.

CFA Program staff members, rather than the graders who come to Charlottes-

If candidates could see us at work—like a little fly on the wall—they would realize that we want the work to be right, not only because we have personal pride but also in terms of upholding the charter and making sure that everyone is treated fairly.

—Janet T. Miller, CFA, 2009

GRADER STORIES FROM CFA "SUMMER CAMP"

CFA exam graders come in all shapes and sizes, from many employment backgrounds and, since the late 1980s, from many countries. Gathering in Charlottesville in late June, graders form a weeklong community, which is often described as CFA Summer Camp. Like most campers, they receive T-shirts. Unlike true vacationers, however, they are in Charlottesville to work. Of course, as the stories that follow illustrate, they have fun too.

ville, handle this first stage of grading. Managing the scoring of tens of thousands of answer sheets in the first phase is not as simple as slipping them all into Scantron machines. Strict quality controls are necessary at every step. Every single answer sheet is examined and checked for damage. Every single answer sheet is reconciled with attendance rosters from test centers. By June 2011, that meant CFA Program staff, and the temporary workers hired to assist them, had to check more than 206,000 answer sheets (from the morning and afternoon sessions).

Once that process is complete and the answer sheets are machine scored, a random sample representing 5–10 percent of candidate answer sheets is independently hand graded, as a control on machine grading.[4] In addition, staff members review comments and complaints from candidates and must stay alert for any exam questions that have drawn similar complaints. Credit is given for questions judged by the staff to have been confusing or unfair or having more than one correct answer.

The other phase of grading begins in late June when several hundred selected charterholders arrive in Charlottesville to manually evaluate the Level III essay responses. These essays (or "constructed response" questions) are now the only part of CFA exams evaluated during grading week.

Since 1963, CFA exam graders have graded a single question on all exams rather than the entire exam of any candidate. Thus, one grader evaluated all the answers to an accounting question on the Level I exam; another evaluated the annual report question at Level II. This arrangement helped ensure consistency. It also meant that many different people looked at each exam and no single grader decided a candidate's fate. Graders were often recruited for expertise in an area or, having been assigned a topic in advance, became expert by the time they arrived.

A team of graders working in a classroom during CFA exam grading. Mike Bailey, photographer

Henry Hermann, CFA, carefully reviews a stack of exam booklets.

This 2002 grading team was assigned to grade question 2AB only in Level II. This team is wearing Hawaiian leis to celebrate the grading theme "Another Year in Paradise." Every grader has to wear a badge for security purposes. Row 1 (bottom, left to right): L. Csellak, CFA; W. Hanson, CFA; D. Junkans, CFA; S. Kwong, CFA; H. Holzer, CFA. Row 2 (left to right): S. Pitt, CFA; R. Killingsworth, Jr., CFA; C. Cox, CFA; E. Norton, Jr., CFA; C. Davila, CFA; A. Mangold-Eisthen, CFA; M. Schmidt, CFA. Row 3 (left to right): D. Patberg, CFA; T. Neale, CFA; G. Lind, CFA; M. Xu, CFA; P. Levy, CFA; D. Boecher, CFA; L. Swallen, CFA; D. Knowles, CFA. Row 4 (left to right): M. Masterson, CFA; C. Schuyler, CFA; D. Yee, CFA; P. Cretien, Jr., CFA; L. Wilson, CFA; M. Freeman, CFA; S. Nielander, CFA; R. Gray, CFA. Row 5 (left to right): N. Rahemtulla, CFA; T. Bower, CFA; J. Bobb, CFA; H. Lum, CFA; D. Erickson, CFA; K. Meeks, CFA; T. Miller, CFA; R. Burke, CFA. Photo courtesy of Gitchell Studios

When all three exams had essay questions, graders typically started their careers on one type of question at a particular level and later moved to others. As the number of candidates and the complexity of questions increased, however, one person might be able to grade only a portion of one question (Part A or B or C). Eventually the number of exams to be graded swelled so much that teams of graders were needed to grade even a single part of a single question.

GRADER STORY:
MESSAGES FROM HOME

Like many campers, graders sometimes miss their families and their homes. One remembered a long-standing conflict with family events:

"For 17 years, my sons—I have three of them—never saw me on Father's Day because grading always coincided with it. When they were little, they used to put Father's Day presents in my luggage."

—FRED H. SPEECE, JR., CFA
17-year grader, July 2010

top: Christine I. Koppel, CFA, graded for many years prior to joining CFA Institute as its first full-time designated officer for the Professional Conduct Program.

bottom: Graders confer with each other to ensure the question is graded correctly. Bottom photo, left to right: Rachel S. Siegel, CFA; Alice Tsang, CFA; and James C.G. Galloway, CFA. Mike Bailey, photographer

In effect, forming graders into teams simply standardized the way graders had been working all along. Graders had always conferred with each other to be sure they understood an answer, were evaluating it properly, and even whether they understood a candidate's handwriting correctly. John D. Richardson, CFA, a grader for more than 20 years, recently wondered if "any candidate, or for that matter any charterholder," realized "how much time we take to carefully look at the question, the suggested guideline answer, the modified guideline answer, or the remodified guideline answer."[5] If a grader raised a question about what score to give an individual paper, "multiple graders—not just two, but in some cases, three, or perhaps even four graders—[would] look at a paper," asking: "What is that word that this candidate wrote? What are those letters? What did the candidate mean?" The grading process, kept confidential for security reasons, may be a bit invisible to the relevant constituencies, but, Richardson believed, "There is so much care taken that the candidates would be significantly impressed."

Grading teams worked together to achieve consistency in grading, but they did not always agree about an answer. When that happened, someone had to arbitrate. Thomas A. Bowman, CFA, recalled that in 1986, his first year as director of Candidate Programs, he was that arbiter: "If there was a disagreement over how a question was to be graded, [settling it] was my responsibility."[6] As the number of graders increased, so did the need to settle disputes. Bowman said:

> On the first day of grading, I would have a line of graders 20, 30 deep, people wanting to get to me to talk about how they were differing, how their teams were differing on how a question ought to be graded. It was just overwhelming.

1986 graders and staff. Row 1 (bottom, left to right): G. Marshall, CFA; R. Bowman, CFA; T. Arndt, CFA; J. Olney, CFA; B. Cornyn, CFA; G. Wood, CFA; H. Butler, CFA; R. Lambourne, CFA; J. Tate, CFA; D. Upshaw, CFA; L. Hansen, CFA. Row 2 (left to right): S. Kimball, CFA; M. Fulford, CFA; J. Meneghetti, CFA; L. Benson, CFA; H. Kennedy, CFA; D. Churchill, CFA; M. Murphy, CFA; E. Hennigar, CFA; D. Fitzcharles, CFA; K. Bonding, CFA; K. Sherrerd, CFA. Row 3 (left to right): P. Slaughter; L. Cherico, CFA; J. Johnson, CFA; J. Richardson, CFA; T. Neale, CFA; D. Dunford, CFA; P. Keller, CFA; M. Joehnk, CFA. Row 4 (left to right): D. Bayston, CFA; T. Bowman, CFA; R. McLean, CFA; F. Speece, CFA; F. Goss, CFA; C. Clark, CFA; D. Harman, CFA; H. Neely, CFA; D. Burns, CFA; D. Hoffland, CFA. Row 5 (left to right): R. Wolf, CFA; J. Bace, CFA; G. Troughton, CFA; R. Wood, CFA; D. McCaslin, CFA; W. Carter, CFA; H. Dickinson, CFA; R. Frizell, CFA; H. Tutwiler, CFA; J. Cabell, CFA. Row 6 (left to right): B. Berlin, CFA; J. Vertin, CFA; T. Redmer, CFA; R. Kemp, CFA; P. Thiele, CFA; J. Galloway, CFA; M. McCowin, CFA; P. Lane, CFA; T. Trim, CFA; P. Morley, CFA; J. Crockett, CFA; C. Singleton, CFA. Row 7 (left to right): G. Mason, CFA; G. Schlarbaum, CFA; C. King, CFA; R. Bissell, CFA; T. Veit, CFA; R. Murray, CFA; L. Guin, CFA; R. Webb, CFA; D. Bush, CFA; J. Haltiner, CFA; D. Upton, CFA; F. Magiera, CFA; F. Reilly, CFA; R. Angevine, CFA; G. Wise, CFA; R. Witt, CFA; T. Sale, CFA. Photo courtesy of Gitchell Studios

GRADER STORY: FUN AND GAMES

CFA Summer Camp often involved games and physically challenging activities. One year, graders even held a "Grader Olympics." Ice skating, tennis, and soccer were also popular, and for many years, graders went hiking in the nearby Blue Ridge Mountains. The Charlottesville area has a temperate climate but impressive summer thunderstorms. One year, during just such a storm, the hiking graders became separated from each other, not everyone made it back to the buses on time, and a few spent the night on the mountain.

GRADER STORY: MISSING CANADA'S BIRTHDAY

The Canadian campers always miss celebrating Canada Day on their home turf. Luckily, they usually manage to observe the day with a hearty rendition of "O, Canada!" and a display of their flag. Canadian graders who drive to Charlottesville bring Canadian maple syrup, which has a distinctive flavor. Caterers then offer up for all graders a Canada Day breakfast with pancakes, waffles, and, of course, Canadian bacon.

"O, Canada!" Left to right: Darrin J. Erickson, CFA; Drew H. Boecher, CFA; Achille E. Desmarais, CFA; Unknown; Robert Dubé, CFA; Elizabeth M. Hamilton-Keen, CFA. Photo courtesy of William R. Warnke, CFA

Recognizing that one person could no longer do this job, Bowman recalled, was the genesis of the captain system that is still in operation today: "Each team has a veteran grader who is in charge of getting the team together and making sure that their questions are graded consistently." Each captain's team includes both veteran and first-time graders. And just as the captains oversee a team, grading coordinators oversee the entire process by monitoring for consistency. In addition, senior graders stay on for an additional week after CFA Summer Camp to review papers that fall within a certain range of the minimum passing score.

By a process known as "bubbling," temporary workers (typically college students and teachers on break) hand transfer the scores written by exam graders onto a master sheet for computer scanning. According to Cori Hord, former director of logistics and grading for the CFA Program, temporary workers hired to assist with grading support can number as high as 140 people; typically 60 or more of them work on bubbling in the scores.[7] CFA Program staff members then do a final quality control to ensure that all exam booklets have been properly scored and the score recorded correctly. [8]

"[Most] changes that have come about in grading have been a function of the volume of papers that need to be graded," Tom Bowman noted.[9] As candidate numbers began to increase exponentially in the late 1980s, the necessary number of graders likewise swelled, growing threefold in the years from 1984 to 1994 and tripling again by 1999, when 787 graders were needed. The following year, 2000, saw the highest total number of exam graders to date—978. CFA Institute staff that year remembered it as a huge logistical challenge in terms of housing, planning activities, and—most importantly—finding sufficient desk space in secure facilities.

Important to consistency are grading keys, which captains help create before grading begins. Peter B. Mackey, CFA, now head of CFA examinations, and

Sorting and maintaining exams is a methodical process involving many people. Here, Rowdy Dudley, a member of the summer staff, carefully selects a stack for a grader.

GRADER STORY: CAMPER RIOTS

Unfortunately, grader campers have been known to behave like true children. Every day, graders were served batches of "the BEST" homemade chocolate chip cookies during their afternoon break. When the woman who baked them retired, no cookies appeared that year. Evidently, graders wanted absolute consistency not only on the papers they graded but also with their treats. They staged a "We Want Cookies!" revolt. Eventually, it is rumored, the baker was coaxed out of retirement and brought back.[10]

himself a longtime grader, remembered when captains arrived on the Saturday before grading started and saw sample exams for the first time: "Having [only] a day or so to get your grading key finalized," was difficult, he conceded.[11] Now, captains are sent sample copies of representative answers ahead of time so they will have more time to review and compose the grading key. Moreover, when they arrive, they find copies made by the staff of actual exams to look at to establish quality control before actual grading begins.

Although processes have grown more sophisticated, "Quality control has always been there," as Mackey put it, "just manifested differently." To those involved in exam administration in 2011, those early procedures might look primitive, but they met the needs of the time. Even in the 1960s, according to Ray Smith, "The whole examination preparation and grading process was very heavily monitored and controlled . . . When the exams came back," they were put "in a locked room, and [staff would] process them to make sure that we had what we were supposed to have."[12] Collecting 284 booklets from 25 test centers in 1963, transporting them securely, and storing them safely during grading presented a challenge to the three-person staff of the early ICFA. When CFA Institute staff had to collect, transport, and arrange for the grading of upwards of 150,000 exam booklets, the challenges became enormous. But they have been met.

After 2000, changes in the exams themselves meant that most of the exams could be machine graded. Level I had become all multiple choice in 1996, and

GRADER STORY: CAMPER RIOTS EXPLAINED . . .

Sometimes campers wrote letters home:

Dear Editor:

I found the following letter crumpled on the floor in the lobby of the hotel during grading this past summer. The content is such that I felt obligated to pass it along to the Institute.

> Sincerely,
> C. Prewitt Lane, CFA

Dear Mom and Dad:

I have now been in Charlottesville at Camp ICFA for a week, and thought you might like to hear how it is going. This is my fifth season as a grader at the Camp, and I have to tell you that things just aren't what they used to be.

The Camp staff—Mr. Bowman, Mrs. Slaughter, and the others—are still the same. None have suffered a nervous breakdown so far, and we have high hopes that they have now turned the lobby atrium into the world's largest meat freezer. Oh, well . . . at least no one is complaining about the heat anymore.

We still work hard in the grading room, attempting to read illegible handwriting and ignoring hilarious notes to the grader. But seriously, Mom and Dad, there is *trouble* in Charlottesville. I and my fellow campers have been afflicted by a strange illness, and it is not a pretty sight. Mature investment professionals shaking uncontrollably, mumbling unintelligibly, and threatening a work stoppage. The reason is clear—lack of cookies! How can they expect us to carry out all of our camp duties without cookies at 10:00 a.m. and 3:00 p.m.? They just don't seem to understand that great minds need the stimulation of chocolate and oatmeal raisin cookies at regular intervals.

Mom, please go to Mrs. Field's right *away* and Federal Express me five pounds of their best before I fall apart completely. Once the cookies arrive, I think I'll be able to make it through the rest of the camp session.

> Love,
> I.R.A. Grader, CFA

Reprinted from *ICFA Newsletter* (October 1987).

Levels II and III went to 50 percent item sets in 2001. By 2005, only the essay portion of Level III still needed individual evaluation. The number of graders decreased, although not to earlier levels because by this time, the number of candidates sitting for Level III often equaled the total number of candidates for all three levels in the 1980s and early 1990s. In 1995, for example, 19,000 candidates sat for all three CFA exams, with 2,600 taking Level III. In 2009, 19,000 candidates took Level III alone. The number of temporary workers needed to help with exam grading has decreased some through efficiencies introduced into the system but still totals more than 100 people.

Thinking of the staff support given them, the internal audit processes that ensure consistency, and the high level of security, several longtime graders have compared CFA exam grading to a well-oiled machine. Yet, a person seeing grading for the first time might as easily compare it to a beehive of purposeful activity. Each of the hundreds of people involved has a carefully delineated role. The graders (who scrupulously evaluate the Level III essays), the temporary workers (who feed answer sheets into Scantron machines), those who check in and check out stacks of Level III exams, those who bubble scores, and of course, the CFA Program staff—all work diligently and unobtrusively to ensure smooth functioning.

Speaking to exam graders in 1996, I. Rossa O'Reilly, CFA, then the Board of Governors chair, praised them for their "ability and willingness" to take on the difficult task of "separating the intellectually distinguished from the intellectually delinquent."[13] Graders who, O'Reilly noted, are "chosen for their experience,

GRADER STORY: BEST CAMPER

Of course, a summer camp is not complete without awards. In CFA Summer Camp, the coveted prize is the Donald L. Tuttle Award for CFA Grading Excellence, which has been awarded since 2001. Thrilled to be honored in this way, Tuttle has handed out the awards every year. The first year, he presented them to Charles G. King, CFA, and James R. Vertin, CFA. Greta E. Marshall, CFA, was honored posthumously. That first year, however, Tuttle was startled to find that he was an award winner when Robert R. Johnson, CFA, handed him a trophy! The surprised Tuttle justly ranks among the greatest all-time graders at CFA Summer Camp. (A list of Tuttle Award winners appears in Appendix B.)

Tuttle Award winners gathered during 2010 CFA exam grading for a group photograph. Row 1 (bottom, left to right): Max E. Hudspeth, CFA; Lisa R. Weiss, CFA; Catherine E. Clark, CFA; James G. Jones, CFA; Donald L. Tuttle, CFA; David B. Stevens, CFA; Jacques R. Gagné, CFA; Shirley S. DeJarnette, CFA; Peter B. Mackey, CFA. Row 2 (left to right): Charles G. King, CFA; James C. Galloway, CFA; Larry D. Riley, CFA; Richard D. Frizell, CFA; Thomas J. Franckowiak, CFA; Douglas R. Hughes, CFA; Alan M. Meder, CFA; Robert B. Hardaway, Jr., CFA; Thomas B. Welch, CFA; Charles W. Brooks, Jr., CFA. Row 3 (left to right): James W. Bronson, CFA; Bradley J. Herndon, CFA; John E. Fitzgerald, CFA; Gordon T. Wise, CFA; Larry D. Guin, CFA; Frank T. Magiera, CFA; John D. Richardson, CFA; Jan R. Squires, CFA. Mike Bailey, photographer

GRADER STORY: CAMPER PRANKS

Like any beloved camp counselor, Robert M. Luck, Jr., CFA, who organized grading for years, was the subject of pranks.

"One year early on, in the late 1980s or early 1990s, [we had] a dinner meeting over at Alumni Hall. [When] we all showed up, somebody handed out all these nametags [that said] 'I'm Bob Luck: The tab is on me.' Bob got up to say something and, on cue, everybody held up a Bob Luck facemask—and he was just totally unable to make his presentation. He could not do it. That night we were all Bob Luck."

—JOSEPH T. DABNEY III, CFA
Exam Grader for 23 years, July 2009

training, and familiarity with investment practices on a global basis" take on this task purposefully and are eager to serve the profession. That many graders return year after year is remarkable, considering how exhausting the task can be. Peter B. Reid, CFA, a grader for several years, explained, "Grading is a combination of summer camp and a sea voyage. Up at 7:00 a.m., over to the grading centre for a quick breakfast, and then into grading stack after stack [of exams]." By the time it is over, he continued, "Your clothes don't fit and you're burned out, but the papers are all graded . . . [and you] can't wait 'til next year."[14]

One year the theme was "Grader Olympics," and graders participated in a hula hoop contest.

A TALE OF TWO GRADERS: CHARLES G. KING, CFA, AND RENÉE K.D. BLASKY, CFA

For 30 straight years (1974–2004), Charlie King graded CFA exams, which earned him the record for the *Most Consecutive Appearances at Grading*. To put this feat in historical context, consider that King's grading career began when the DJIA was under 900 and ended when it was over 10,000.

King started in the same grading room as some CFA Program luminaries—Don Tuttle, John L. Maginn, CFA, and Frank K. Reilly, CFA. According to King, the group "just kind of bonded," and every year, "we would come earlier and earlier—to make sure that we got that room."[15] They had a historic location, the Colonnade Hotel designed by Thomas Jefferson, which looked out at Monroe Hall—where the CFA Program began. Don Tuttle will never forget grading alongside King, who had been his student at the University of North Carolina. "Charlie was like a machine," said Tuttle. "Boom: Finished. Mark it down. Boom: Next question. Sometimes you'd just sit there in awe of Charlie."[16]

A resident of Charlottesville throughout his grading career, King was sometimes called back into service if grading was not completed. One time, King remembered, they were behind on the major portfolio management question, which that year asked candidates to manage a portfolio for a shrewd, elderly gentleman named "Sly Old Codger," who was full of ideas about what to sell and what to keep. King returned at night after work and "was grading along," when he heard a knock: "I went to the door, and this guy [was] standing there saying 'We're having a party in here tonight'." King replied, "I don't think so." But he was mistaken and "ended up in the kitchen on a couple of those metal roll-along tables—and I am grading in there and they are having this party out there." Somehow, he got the job done. When he received one of the first awards for grading excellence—named in honor of and presented by his old grading colleague Don Tuttle—Charlie King was called CFA grading's "Rock of Gibraltar."

Charles G. King, CFA.

Charlie King came to grading from right next door, but Renée Blasky came from halfway around the world. If CFA Institute kept records for the *Most Total Miles Logged Getting to Grading*, Renée Blasky might just hold the record. A grader for 14 consecutive years (so far), Blasky has traveled each time from East Africa.

Born in Minnesota and educated in Hong Kong and the United States, Renée Blasky has not called the United States home since 1985, the year she moved to Singapore. There, she obtained her CFA charter—not long after Alfred C. "Pete" Morley, CFA, and George E.K. Teo instituted the CFA Program in Singapore.

Renée Blasky, CFA.
Wendy Stone, photographer

Most charterholders tell tales about the months they spent studying for their exams, but few can claim to have done it the way Blasky did, on a 45-foot sailboat. After completing her exams, Blasky set sail for Africa on that same boat and settled in Kenya, where she has lived since 1992 (except for a one-year stay consulting in Rwanda in 2009).

Blasky began grading not only because she wanted to give something back to the profession but also because she "wanted to see how it was done, how my exam had been graded."[17] Like many first-time graders, she was impressed with the process. She also appreciated the fact that grading CFA exams enabled her "to keep up to date as to what is happening in the industry."

King and Blasky have been asked why they find CFA exam grading important. For Renée Blasky, the "most impressive" aspect is "how much care is actually taken by each individual grader to make sure that they have given that candidate a fair chance." For Charlie King, it is remembering what is at stake for each individual whose booklet passes though his hands: "You have a person whose career is involved, whose family is involved, whose job is involved, whose pride is involved . . . . So, it's *really* important to do a good job. It's not just a piece of paper. It's somebody's life."

chapter eight

The Global Standard:

2005–2010

*W*hen he became president and CEO of CFA Institute on 1 January 2005, Jeffrey J. Diermeier, CFA, stepped into an organization that had just come through a sea change of almost unimaginable growth. The CFA Program was its greatest strength and "crown jewel"—as former Board of Governors Chair Frank K. Reilly, CFA, called it.[1] Throughout its history but particularly in the prior decade and a half, the CFA Program had been scrutinized, updated, and upgraded. The result was an expertly polished jewel safely set within the investment industry's crown. Moreover, the pride felt by those associated with the signature program at CFA Institute was about to increase. In 2005, both *The Economist* and the *Financial Times* (UK) declared the CFA Program to be the "Gold Standard" of investment education—an apt phrase soon adopted by many others.[2]

To unpathed waters, undreamed shores.

—William Shakespeare, *The Winter's Tale*

Jeffrey J. Diermeier, CFA, served as president and CEO for 2005–2008.

Copyright Charles Peattie and Russell Taylor, used with permission

Yet, as the premier educational arm of the world's capital markets, the CFA Program was serving an industry barely recovered from the collapse of the technology bubble and the scandals of the early 2000s and about to take an even more perilous fall. In 2005, the subprime housing bubble was still inflating, but it would soon explode. By 2008, the second market detonation in a decade would result in greater dislocations for world economies and the investment management profession than those caused by the earlier dot-com collapse. In fact, as some of the world's largest financial institutions failed or required government bailouts, the 21st century's opening decade posed the greatest challenge to the investment industry since the Great Depression.

According to Bloomberg.com, "Financial companies [had] eliminated more than 100,000 investment jobs worldwide, including 76,670 in the Americas" by 2008.[3] By the middle of 2009, the total number of jobs lost at financial firms was estimated at 328,000. At that point, as a recent monograph put it, "Most investors had suffered serious losses and asset management firms were in survival mode."[4] The period from 2007 to 2009 has had a "profound effect on the profession," said John Rogers, CFA, who succeeded Diermeier as CEO of CFA Institute.[5]

To help CFA charterholders and candidates navigate such difficult waters, CFA Program leaders responsible for educating and certifying industry practitioners needed to ensure that all those earning the CFA charter were prepared not only to compute the duration of bonds based on given formulas but also to face the risks of Black Swan events like the subprime meltdown.[6]

NAVIGATING THE SHOALS

Diermeier, having most recently been chief global investment officer of UBS Global Asset Management, brought an appropriately global perspective to the CEO position. As a longtime volunteer on the Candidate Curriculum Committee and a governor since 2002, Diermeier also had an insider's perspective. Moreover, he had worked with Thomas A. Bowman, CFA, on the most recent five-year strategic plan as head of the Planning Committee. As CEO, Diermeier was deeply committed to the implementation of those goals. One of particular importance to him was helping transform CFA Institute from an entity that merely had members in many countries to one that was "truly a global organization."[7]

The growth in candidate registrations over the previous 10 years and their spread geographically clearly attested that the resources of CFA Institute had rightly been applied toward the CFA Program during that time. In 1994, approximately 20,000 people registered to take CFA exams. Of the 15,413 who actually sat for the exams, only 18 percent came from outside North America. By 2004, registrations had swelled to more than 115,000 for the June and December exams, and the growth in actual candidates sitting for the exam had risen to 81,125. That same year, 52 percent of sitting candidates came from outside North America.

By the time Jeff Diermeier began work at CFA Institute in January 2005, more than 70,000 individuals had earned the CFA designation. To Diermeier, the existence of that many charterholders warranted an increased focus on member issues (he dubbed the coming period "The Member Era")—especially, but not limited to, continuing education and the means of its delivery. In addition, he saw the need for enhancing relationships with societies and positioning the organization's advocacy arm—the CFA Institute Centre for Financial Market Integrity—as a thought leader in the industry, one to which regulators and government officials would turn. In the last years of the decade, as credit markets collapsed, credit-rating agencies were called into question, and credit

HISTORICAL SPOTLIGHT: TEN LARGEST JUNE EXAM CENTERS, 2010

Location	Tested Candidates
London, UK	6,999
New York, New York, USA	6,688
Hong Kong (SAR)	6,190
Shanghai, China	5,832
Beijing, China	5,315
Mumbai, India	5,267
Toronto, Ontario, Canada	5,037
Seoul, South Korea	4,144
Singapore	3,598
Boston, Massachusetts, USA	2,372

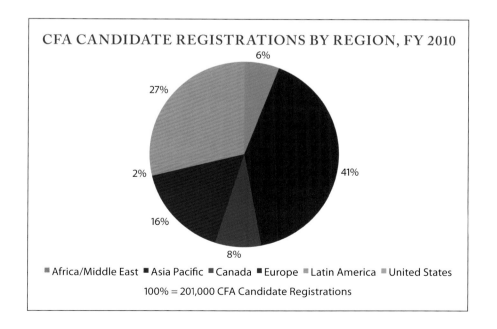

CFA CANDIDATE REGISTRATIONS BY REGION, FY 2010

6%
27%
2%
16%
8%
41%

■ Africa/Middle East ■ Asia Pacific ■ Canada ■ Europe ■ Latin America ■ United States

100% = 201,000 CFA Candidate Registrations

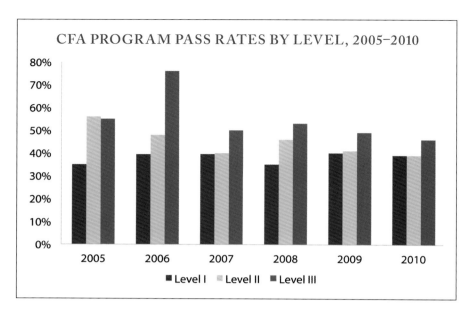

CFA PROGRAM PASS RATES BY LEVEL, 2005–2010

■ Level I　■ Level II　■ Level III

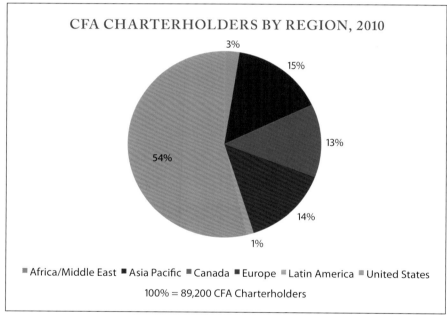

CFA CHARTERHOLDERS BY REGION, 2010

■ Africa/Middle East　■ Asia Pacific　■ Canada　■ Europe　■ Latin America　■ United States

100% = 89,200 CFA Charterholders

default swaps worked their way into the consciousness of the media, legislatures, and the public. The Centre for Financial Market Integrity was often called on to comment on these issues.

Events in troubled world financial markets also affected the CFA Program as the decade wound down, leading the program's stewards to reassess how well it was readying candidates to face unfortunate market realities. Careful scrutiny ensued. CFA Institute staff evaluated testing rubrics, analyzed candidate prepa-

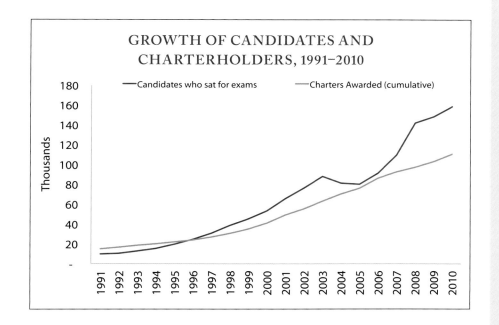

GROWTH OF CANDIDATES AND CHARTERHOLDERS, 1991–2010

Candidates who sat for exams ——— Charters Awarded (cumulative)

ration and its effect on pass rates, educated candidates to look for irrationality among investors as well as efficiency and inefficiency in markets, and ensured the relevance of the Body of Knowledge by means of continuous Practice Analysis.

NAME RECOGNITION

One institutional objective significant to the CFA Program in the mid-2000s was that of unifying the brand under the CFA banner. Renaming the governing organization CFA Institute was a crucial first step in achieving unified recognition. "Not only was this a smart marketing/branding move," according to Diermeier, but it was also "symbolic of a desire to unify the broader organization."[9] After the change of name in 2004, local societies worldwide were encouraged to retitle themselves and incorporate "CFA" into their new names.

This organizationwide renaming was accompanied by a succession of advertising campaigns (for example, "*C-F-A Spells Trust*") designed to reassure investors in a climate of lingering unease following the market woes early in the decade. Such branding ads produced instant recognition of the charter's value. The work of the organization was becoming well known; now, with the initials "CFA" in its name, efforts to benefit both the CFA Program and the organization could be streamlined. By the mid-2000s, active promotion of the CFA brand was ongoing in ad campaigns. For some people, this move came none too soon.

Advertising and publicity initiatives undertaken in the mid-2000s began with a print campaign recognizing new charterholders. Echoing the newspaper articles that appeared throughout the United States and Canada in 1963 announcing

WHAT'S IN AN INITIAL?

Some 40 years after the CFA Program began, its identifying initials were not always clear in the public's mind. One charterholder who had direct experience with this phenomenon was George J. Hauptfuhrer III, CFA, of Atlanta. In 1996, Hauptfuhrer donated money to his alma mater during an alumni fund drive. In recognition of their gifts, donors were to have a brick laid, on which their names would be inscribed. Hauptfuhrer, proud of his charter and aware of the need to "raise the visibility of the CFA designation," chose to put CFA, as well as MBA, after his name. When he eventually saw the brick on campus, however, he was dismayed to see that it read: George Hauptfuhrer, C*PA*. "This is exactly why I wanted it to say CFA," Hauptfuhrer recalled.[8] Yet, the distinction was lost on whoever prepared the copy: "Someone in the final stage of the process thought it was a typo and [that] I must be a CPA, which I am *not*." The mistake was remedied with a correctly inscribed brick.

George J
Hauptfuhrer CFA
MBA 1976

Courtesy of The University of North Carolina's Kenan-Flagler Business School

Members of the European Investors' Working Group, cosponsored by CFA Institute, discuss regulatory reform in the European Union.

the first CFA charterholders, the 2006 campaign included two-page spreads in four major newspapers congratulating new charterholders: the *Wall Street Journal* (for the United States), the *Globe and Mail* (for Canada), the *Financial Times* (for the United Kingdom), and the *South China Morning Post* (for Hong Kong). The globe-spanning ads listed the names of 3,908 new charterholders under the proud headline: "The Only Thing Harder Than Reading This List Is Getting On It."[10]

The congratulatory print campaign continued until the "number of charterholders grew larger than the size of the publications" in which ads were placed.[11] Charterholder recognition then moved online, eventually to a microsite.

A campaign extolling four charterholder virtues—rigor, analytics, tenacity, and ethics—began in 2008. It featured prominent CFA charterholders whose work exemplified the qualities, abilities, and principles characteristic of CFA charterholders. In 2010, moreover, CFA Institute began integrating social media in earnest, setting up Facebook and Twitter accounts.

Media outreach involved more than paid ads. Interviews with key staff and volunteers plus general media coverage also helped spread name recognition

Bolsa e Inversión

Entrevista Bob Johnson, viceconsejero delegado de CFA Institute

"Las pérdidas por la crisis se olvidarán, pero no la falta de ética de algunos"

Cristina Triana

MADRID. Bob Johnson, viceconsejero delegado de CFA Institute, reconoce que es la primera vez que visita España en *viaje oficial*. Este año ha sido el encargado de entregar la acreditación que otorga el instituto a los candidatos españoles que han cumplido con todos los requisitos necesarios –éticos, de conocimiento y profesionales– para obtener el *Chartered Financial Analyst*. Esta acreditación, una de las más importantes que puede lograr un experto de la industria de la inversión, es, según su viceconsejero delegado, un valor que está ganando peso por la crisis. Johnson reconoce que la actual es la peor que ha visto en su vida profesional y espera que ayude a erradicar comportamientos poco éticos. Piensa que la crisis se va a agudizar por la desconfianza originada por la falta de información y transparencia sobre los productos en los que se estaba invirtiendo.

▶ Una de las consecuencias de la crisis financiera que ha puesto al descubierto que algunas veces se ha descuidado la ética...
La crisis está revelando la importancia de la ética y el objetivo de CFA Institute es continuar profesionalizando la industria de la inversión en esa línea. Además, la confianza de los inversores se consigue con unas bases éticas. Benjamin Graham, mentor de Warren Buffet y considerado el fundador del *Value Investing*, la inversión en compañías de valor (bajos múltiplos de valoración y altas rentabilidades por dividendo), ya defendía que para ser un profesional es necesaria una serie de conocimientos, como experiencia, como un código ético. Otras profesiones, como los médi-

Sobre la regulación:
"Es necesaria, pero no se debe abusar. Ahora existe el riesgo de que se pongan límites a la innovación financiera, que no es mala, pero sí cómo se ha utilizado"

cos, se organizan en torno a la ética y es necesario que también lo haga la industria de la inversión: que se pongan los intereses de los clientes primero, que se expliquen los conflictos de interés, los acuerdos de compensación con terceros, así como todas las condiciones de los productos. CFA Institute pelea por ello y todos aquellos que obtienen el derecho a utilizar la acreditación CFA están obligados a aplicarlo. En los ciclos económicos buenos, la gente no quiere escuchar los mensajes que hablan de ética, pero ahora se reciben mejor. Mi deseo es que los profesionales se comprometan con ella, porque los mercados necesitan confianza y eso es algo que le da la transparencia.

▶ ¿Es usted partidario de la regulación o de la autorregulación?

CFA Institute, junto con otros grupos, trabajamos con varias agencias gubernamentales y regulatorias de todo el mundo. Comprendemos que es necesaria la regulación, pero entendemos que la mejor llega cuando la industria y el mercado se autorregula. A la innovación financiera ahora se la ve como a un demonio, pero no es así. Lo incorrecto es el uso que se ha hecho de ella. Las innovaciones en productos pueden ayudar a gestionar y medir el riesgo y a que las personas lo compartan y esto beneficia al mercado. El riesgo ahora es que, como se ha abusado de esa innovación, se caiga en una sobrerregulación. Reconocemos que la regulación es necesaria, pero sin abusar, no se vaya a frenar toda la innovación financiera. Lo que se debe hacer es fomentar la transparencia de los mercados, algo que sí ayudará a la gente a tomar decisiones de inversión.

▶ Los gestores de 'hedge fund' y los inversores bajistas son algunos de los 'perseguidos'... ¿cómo ve el futuro de la industria?
No creo que ninguno de ellos sean los culpables de la crisis. Pienso que los buenos gestores de fondos de inversión libres, aquellos que son éticos, sobrevivirán. En cuanto a los *short sellers* (inversores bajistas) hacen al mercado más eficiente. Lo que es necesario es que se gane transparencia, que se aporte más información detallada al mercado, como las aclaraciones que sean pertinentes. Los inversores, una vez pase la crisis, olvidarán las pérdidas ocasionadas por ella, pero no los comportamientos poco éticos. Warren Buffet lo explica muy bien. Él apunta que la reputación tarda muchos años en construirse, pero sólo cinco minutos en perderse.

▶ Habla de la importancia de la transparencia, pero ¿no cree que los cambios contables que se están aprobando, abriendo la mano a la hora de valorar los activos a precio razonable, va en su contra?
Es muy difícil para mí defender algún argumento que me haga pensar que algo diferente al sistema contable más transparente trabaja en beneficio de los inversores. CFA Institute cree en el concepto de valor razonable. La culpa de esta crisis no la tiene el *fair value*, sino la mala gestión del riesgo y una inadecuada alineación de intereses entre clientes, empleados y accionistas.

FERNANDO VILLAR

(left) Courtesy of *el Economista*

(above) As media interest in the global perspectives of CFA Institute increased, the popularity of media conferences grew. In Toronto, Canada, in 2002 (left to right) Philippe A. Sarasin, CFA, AIMR chair for 2001–2002; I. Rossa O'Reilly, CFA, AIMR chair for 1996–1997; and Emilio Gonzalez, CFA, CFA Institute chair for 2007–2008, talked about issues of analyst independence and financial reporting reform. Scott Mitchell, photographer

for the CFA Program. "Ten years ago," Tom Bowman noted in 2006, "had Enron happened, [no] representative of this organization would have been called to testify before the U.S. Congress on its standards and its code of ethics."[12] After the media coverage of Bowman's 2002 testimony and creation of the CFA Institute Centre for Financial Market Integrity in 2005, CFA Institute became a "go-to" organization exemplifying best practices for ethics, for performance presentation standards, in areas of corporate governance, and other areas. CFA Institute staff and Board of Governors members have frequently testified before U.S. lawmakers and around the globe and have often been seen on business television networks and interviewed by print media about the CFA Program. "When we talk," Bowman said, "people listen."

Media coverage of the CFA Program rose considerably in the second half of the 2000s. In 2005 alone, more than 650 stories relating to CFA Institute or the CFA Program appeared in North American, European, and Asian media outlets.[13] In 2006, candidate recruitment articles ran in global financial publications whose combined circulations totaled more than 4 million and ran online at Bloomberg.

HISTORICAL SPOTLIGHT

To commemorate the 60th anniversary of the founding, on 11 June 1947, of a professional organization for analysts, CFA Institute declared 11 June 2007 "CFA Day." It was celebrated by more than 120 societies worldwide with a variety of activities, including—in London, Toronto, and New York—CFA Institute staff and society members participating in the opening of their respective stock exchanges, which received wide media coverage.

In London, the CFA Day celebration began with the opening of the London Stock Exchange. Pictured are (left to right) Colin McLean, FSIP, president, United Kingdom Society of Investment Professionals for 2005–2007; John C. Stannard, CFA, FSIP, chair of CFA Institute for 2005–2006; Mark J.P. Anson, CFA, governor, CFA Institute for 2007–2013; Nitin M. Mehta, CFA, managing director of EMEA, CFA Institute; and Brian D. Singer, CFA, chair of CFA Institute for 2008–2009.

A CFA Day celebration was held at the Shanghai Bankers Club and included a cocktail reception and cake-cutting ceremony. Among the special guests were (left to right) Zhou Qinye, deputy manager of the Shanghai Stock Exchange; Jan R. Squires, CFA, then managing director of CFA Institute Asia Pacific Operations; Han Kang, vice director general of CSRC Shanghai; and Karl Lung, CFA, then president of the Hong Kong Society of Financial Analysts.

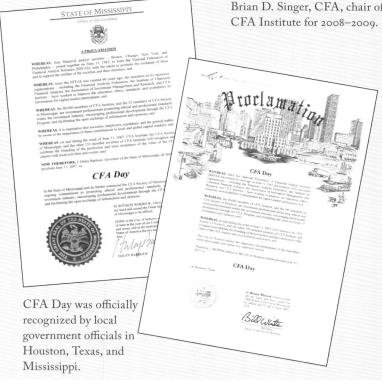

CFA Day was officially recognized by local government officials in Houston, Texas, and Mississippi.

com, Sina.com, and FT.com.[14] That same year, coverage in Zurich of the first annual conference held outside North America included television interviews on Bloomberg and CNBC. By the end of the decade, stories that covered the CFA Program had become commonplace in media outlets reaching the financial industry and investors, many outside North America.

In the first half of the 2000s, particularly in 2004 and 2005, new registrations to the CFA Program leveled off for the first time in decades. Since the beginning of the CFA Program, enrollment had generally trended upward (in both registrations and exam takers), yet occasional flat years occurred. In the 1970s, another time of turmoil in financial markets, enrollments grew at a slower pace and actually declined during two years. Not since 1979, however, had a dip in candidates taking the exam occurred, so program leaders believed the numbers in 2004 and 2005 bore looking into. According to Jeff Diermeier, they found that neither the slowdown nor the dip reflected any "disenchantment" on the part of "major plan sponsors or investment employers as regards the CFA charter. It was still highly valued."[15] If anything, the relatively flat registrations appeared to correlate most closely with employment in the financial industry, which had lagged since the market downturn that followed the dot-com bubble. Nevertheless, other possible contributing factors were examined, including candidate preparedness, low pass rates, and "concerns about relevancy, granularity, and the handling in the curriculum of the booming alternative asset class markets." As had been asked so many times in the program's history, did the CFA Program remain rigorous, comprehensive, and consistent?

Helping Candidates Prepare

"With so many candidates trying to master such a tough exam, CFA prep courses have become big business," a June 2005 *Financial Times* article noted.[16] Mindful of this development and in an effort to understand any possible relationship between lack of preparedness and declining pass rates, the CFA Institute Board of Governors assembled a CFA Preparation Task Force, which included members from three continents and was headed by Daniel S. Meader, CFA. Its charge was to investigate the manner and methods by which CFA candidates prepared for CFA exams. Some candidates, it appeared, were bypassing the curriculum and using prep courses as "shortcuts"—instead of, not in addition to, the study materials supplied by the CFA Program itself. [17]

Creating this task force marked a departure from the historical position of holding prep course providers at arm's length to avoid any real or perceived conflicts of interest. In this case, however, board members and staff were determined to find how best to support candidates through exam preparation. Task force members interviewed people at various societies (roughly half of which contracted with prep course providers), assembled candidate focus groups in key markets, and met with representatives of the largest CFA exam prep course

At a CFA Society of Mississippi charter award reception in 2009, Thomas R. Robinson, CFA (right), then head of Educational Content for CFA Institute, is shown here with new charterholder Scott R. Snively, CFA (left). Robinson later became managing director of the Education Division, which oversees the entire CFA Program.

In 2004, 15 new charterholders were recognized at the Society of Investment Analysts during Ireland's charter award ceremony at the National College of Ireland in Dublin. Robert M. Luck, Jr., CFA, then vice president, Member and Candidate Outreach (third from right), awarded the charters.

providers. They found the providers "eager to work with CFA Institute" to correct any misapprehensions or errors in their presentations.[18] The hope was for genuine collaboration to the benefit of candidates.

Reporting in May 2005, the task force made four recommendations. First, communications with candidates, societies, and preparers should be enhanced so that candidates entering the enrollment process clearly understand the extent to which success in passing is linked to serious and effective preparation—whether through study courses led by providers or on one's own. Second, CFA curriculum materials should be bundled into the enrollment process. Third, a series of voluntary guidelines should be established for prep providers. Fourth, local societies, in addition to continuing to hold charter award ceremonies, ought to consider using study groups and mock exams.

Of the task force's four recommendations, the one most readily discernible to candidates was that of bundling the curriculum into the enrollment process. As noted in Chapter 7, the CFA Program had begun developing proprietary literature in the late 1990s, and by the time of the task force report (May 2005), several proprietary titles had been published. Within a year, the CFA Program began publishing what is known as its "custom curriculum." A series of volumes containing the entire curriculum, each volume is organized into study sessions and includes assigned readings, learning outcome statements, and problem sets. According to Christopher B. Wiese, CFA, head of Candidate Products, the custom curriculum was introduced in three phases. Beginning in 2006, Level I was available; in 2007 Level II was added, and in 2008 the publication of Level III completed the series. The year 2008, Wiese noted, was "the first year we began bundling the curriculum with program registration."[19] By 2009, an eBook based on each of the three levels of the 2010 curriculum was available to candidates, and by 2011 the eBook was integrated as an alternative to print materials.

Interestingly, some of the proprietary literature initially developed for the benefit of CFA candidates is now part of the CFA Institute Investment Series, published through John Wiley & Sons, which is available publicly to college students and investment professionals. These books are updated less frequently than the custom curriculum, which is revised annually. They are also organized differently but are well suited for college courses and professional development.

Understanding the Decline in Pass Rates

Although Benjamin Graham once predicted that the level of competence needed for analyst certification would probably "be set on the low side at first and gradually raised thereafter," the Board of Trustees and staff of the Institute of Chartered Financial Analysts were justifiably proud to have held firm to high standards in the first years of the CFA Program.[20] They had failed even prominent security analysts whose work on the first several CFA exams did not pass muster. Candidates in the program's early years did pass at prodigious rates (94 percent for Level III in 1963 and an 84 percent average pass rate for all three exams in 1964), but only because they showed comprehensive knowledge of the material and had many years of professional experience. Although the Body of Knowledge for the CFA Program may have been far smaller in the 1960s than it is now, demonstrated mastery of it was still needed in order to be able to hang a low-numbered CFA charter on one's wall. Grading standards were high from the very beginning. Attainment of the CFA charter was then and is now a genuine accomplishment.

By the mid-2000s, unfortunately, earning the charter was becoming an increasingly rare accomplishment. As articles in financial journals throughout the decade attested, candidates' stress levels were going up but their pass rates were going down.[21] In the first decade of the program, the average annual pass rate for all three CFA exams hovered around 77 percent, even after the spectacular results of 1963 were factored in. From 1973 to 1982, the pass rate for all three exams averaged 71 percent; in the next 10 years, 63 percent. By 1993, the average pass rate for the CFA exams had fallen below 60 percent, and beginning in 2002

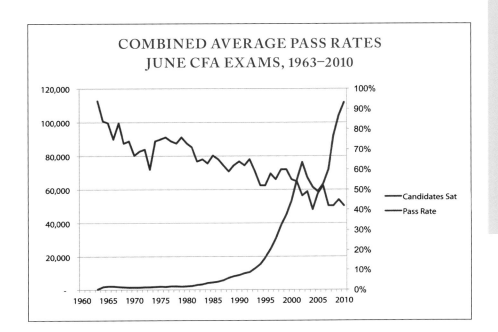

COMBINED AVERAGE PASS RATES
JUNE CFA EXAMS, 1963–2010

EXAM STORY: DISTANCE LEARNING AT ITS MOST DETERMINED

Some CFA charterholders talk about their exam preparations as if they were war stories, but Jim Boudreault's study stories actually are. Boudreault planned to take the final level of his CFA exams in 2003, but having been called to serve in the U.S. military during the Iraq War, he found himself posted to Tikrit in April of that year. Realizing that his tour of duty would end just weeks before the June 2004 CFA exams, which he was determined to take, Boudreault registered, had his wife send him curriculum materials, and began to study. "Everyone thought I was crazy," he told a reporter for *Pensions & Investments* in 2005, "but I was so close to the finish line that I was determined to go for it." Despite blazing temperatures, dust storms that coated his books with sand, and a need to watch out for both mortar rounds and venomous spiders, Jim Boudreault successfully passed his Level III exam and earned, as the *P&I* reporter phrased it, "the last of his CFA stripes."

—JAMES J. BOUDREAULT, CFA
Chicago[22]

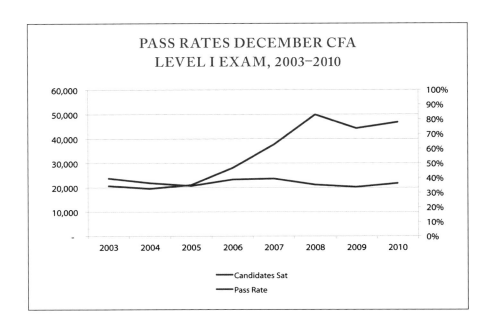

PASS RATES DECEMBER CFA
LEVEL I EXAM, 2003–2010

the pass rate for all three levels combined had fallen below 50 percent. Rates for Levels I and II were lower than those for Level III. In June 2008, for example, the individual pass rate for Level I was only 35 percent; for Level II, 46 percent; and for Level III, 53 percent.

Why such a steady—and, sometimes, steep—decline?

In September 2004, Tom Bowman wrote a brief article analyzing the problem for *CFA Magazine*. Its publication was timely: In June 2004, the pass rates were only 34 percent at Level I and 32 percent at Level II; these rates still stand, as of this writing, as the lowest for both levels in the history of the program. As noted previously, one factor significantly affecting candidate performance was the shallowness of preparation. "Over the years we have seen a steady decline in the percentage of CFA candidates who indicate they are seriously preparing for the CFA examinations," Bowman said.[23] In 2004, for example, 57 percent of Level I and 49 percent of Level II candidates indicated that they had studied fewer than 200 hours—whereas successful candidates that year had studied for 250 hours and more—and by the end of the decade, 300 hours was common.

In 2005, the board named a task force, led by Theodore R. Aronson, CFA, to continue investigating the problem to determine probable causes, within or outside the CFA Program, for the decline in pass rates. According to Jeff Diermeier, the task force "looked deeply into potential shortcomings and issues" to determine whether anything within the CFA program itself was affecting pass rates.[24] Ultimately, it confirmed that the lower pass rates were "not the result of a credentialing process that had gotten out of control." Other factors were involved. Diermeier recalled:

Theodore R. Aronson, CFA, served as CFA Institute chair for 2003–2004.

Industry market conditions, a broader knowledge base consistent with industry developments, and possibly a wider, less committed candidate pool were more likely the drivers of the lower pass rates.

From 2005 to 2010, the pass rates for the December (Level I) administrations averaged 36 percent, lower than those for the June exams (all three levels), which averaged 45 percent. The June 2006 pass rate for the three levels combined proved a bit of an anomaly at 52 percent; it was bolstered largely by a 76 percent pass rate at Level III. As might be expected, Level III exams tend to have the highest percentage of successful candidates. Overall, however, only about a fifth of those who start the CFA Program eventually hang a charter on their walls.

Fluctuations in pass rates catch the eyes of CFA program staff because care has been taken to ensure consistency in exams from year to year. Moreover, the level of difficulty for a particular year's CFA exam questions is evaluated and a state-of-the-art methodology is used to determine each year's minimum passing score (MPS).[25] Rather than carrying over an arbitrary cutoff from year to year, each year's MPS is determined through a process called "standard setting." Developed with the assistance of Timothy R. Konold, a psychometrician and head of the Research, Statistics, and Evaluation Program at the University of Virginia, CFA exam standard setting is a two-stage process. Charterholders chosen from around the world individually review the examination question by question. (In June 2007, for example, 90 charterholders from 23 countries participated, with approximately 30 members evaluating each exam level.) Each member independently arrives at an estimate of how he or she thinks a "just-qualified candidate would do on each question."[26] According to Bob Johnson, the concept of the "just-qualified candidate" is best understood by thinking about a high jumper who just clears the bar: "The bar wiggles, [but] it doesn't fall." Like that jumper who just makes it over, the just-qualified candidate is "not the great candidate or the Olympic high jumper"—but he or she does qualify.[27]

EXAM STORY: A MOST UNUSUAL STUDY GROUP

Tyler Peterson, now of San Francisco, fondly remembers sharing his preparation time for the Level III exam with some unlikely study partners:

" I took both my Level I and II tests in Washington, DC, while completing my Master's of Science in finance at George Washington University. After my graduation in August 2008, my fiancée and I moved to Kenya and lived in a canvas tent in the Masai Mara for 18 months [where] we established a fully functional and financially self-sustained wildlife conservancy, in partnership with over 800 local Masai landowners and 14 tourism camp operators.

"I did all my studying in the wild, surrounded (no exaggeration here) by up to four prides of lions, leopards, cheetah, elephant, buffalo, and the Great Migration consisting of hundreds of thousands of wildebeest, zebra, and gazelles. Often times, any number of these species would come through, usually at night. On one occasion, we had a leopard sleeping under our tent (we were on a raised platform). You can imagine trying to study while hearing lions roaring in the distance, let alone a leopard under your feet. Come test time, I traveled to Nairobi and took my Level III in May 2009. (I'm happy to say I passed all three on the first go-round.) The memory that probably stands out most was the week or two prior to the exam, studying all day while I watched elephants at the local watering hole. Trumpeting, spraying, a little pushing and shoving—all while [I was] trying to remember the difference between the Treynor and Sharpe ratios!"

—TYLER PETERSON, San Francisco

HISTORICAL SPOTLIGHT

The CFA Program has reached some significant milestones.

- In 2007, more than 100,000 candidates sat for the CFA exams for the first time.

- In 2008, the 1,000,000th CFA exam was administered, and that same year, the 100,000th charter number was awarded—to Muhammad Raza Rafiq, CFA, a native of Lahore, Pakistan.

- In 2011, roughly 200,000 people registered for CFA exams.

When I was born, there were only two graduate schools of business administration anywhere in the world, but now there are more than eight hundred. [It] would be good if we could offer each of them an opportunity to participate in the work of the Institute of Chartered Financial Analysts.

—Sir John M. Templeton, CFA, Dedication of ICFA Headquarters, 5 April 1986

The charterholders in the standard-setting review groups look at the entire exam a second time; this time, they take into account actual candidate performance and other data. As Peter B. Mackey, CFA, head of CFA Examinations, noted, "The aggregate of all standard setters' judgments on all questions on the exam can be characterized as a recommended MPS."[28] Not until exam grading is completed and this thorough standard setting is done does the MPS recommendation go to the Board of Governors. The board determines the actual MPS; in doing so, it considers the results of the standard-setting workshops, including the distribution of standard setters' individual judgments and other relevant factors.

Thomas R. Robinson, CFA, who joined the Education Division of CFA Institute in 2007, remarked that it is important to keep the complexity of standard setting in mind when looking at pass rates. Exam pass rates are based on a standard-setting process that always considers "what a qualified candidate needs to know to practice in the *current* environment."[29] It is not based on a set passing score or rate. He noted:

> While pass rates in the last decade are lower than in the early decades of the program, there is a much larger pool of candidates pursuing the designation and today's capital markets are more complex. Investment professionals need a high level of proficiency to practice in today's environment, and this is reflected in the rigorous standard-setting process.

According to Bob Johnson, "The explanation is not that the candidate pool has gotten younger or that younger candidates perform more poorly."[30] Nor is it that "more people [are] taking the exam outside of North America—as the North American and global pass rates are not statistically different." More germane is that "the field has become more complicated, so the knowledge, skills, and abilities needed to practice have advanced—and the qualities of the Just Qualified Candidate have advanced."

Perhaps the most important lesson of declining pass rates is the one pointed out by Tom Bowman in 2004 and still applicable today: "As CFA charterholders know better than anyone, there are no shortcuts to earning the CFA designation."[31] That, he concluded, is why the CFA designation "enjoys such a sterling reputation throughout the global investment community."

TRUE TEAMWORK: CFA PROGRAM PARTNERS

In his wish that universities participate in the CFA Program, the globally astute Sir John M. Templeton, CFA, was 20 years ahead of his time. The creation of CFA Program Partners, established in 2006, was just such a formal relationship. Yet, as Peter Mackey pointed out, "Since the beginning of the CFA Program, those in academe have played an important part in all of its key components."[32]

Whether as volunteers or as paid consultants, academicians (typically, also

Lingnan (University) College, Sun Yat-sen University in Guangzhou, China, was approved as a CFA Program Partner in August 2009. Pictured are (left to right): Joey Chan, CFA, director, Planning & Programme Development, CFA Institute; Rahul Keshap, head, Education Special Projects, CFA Institute; Ashvin P. Vibhakar, CFA, managing director, Asia Pacific Operations, CFA Institute; Wu Lifan, dean and professor at Lingnan (University) College, Sun Yat-sen University; Wendy (Weiyu) Guo, CFA, head, Education, CFA Institute; and Prof. Zhou Kaiguo, deputy head, Department of Finance, Lingnan (University) College, Sun Yat-sen University.

charterholders) have been involved in curriculum and exam writing, exam reviewing, grading, and more recently, standard setting. Moreover, the first three executive directors of the ICFA—C. Stewart Sheppard, W. Scott Bauman, CFA, and O. Whitfield Broome, Jr.—were all academicians. Among present CFA Program staff leaders, several are charterholders who have taught at the university level. Theirs is a unique perspective from which to view and evaluate current practices in educational testing while keeping the CFA Program true to its purpose of serving practitioners.

Despite the natural "town-and-gown" relationship between practitioners and academicians, however, until the mid-2000s, the CFA Program did not have a formal program of outreach to universities. Although several universities had adopted portions of the CFA Program in their undergraduate and graduate programs—a welcome endorsement of the soundness of the CFA curriculum— the practice was informal and not sanctioned by the program. In 2006, however, the CFA Program Partners initiative established formal relationships with universities that met certain CFA Program requirements. According to staff member Dennis W. McLeavey, CFA, one of the most important contributions the program makes to universities is "the practitioner orientation that we give," gleaned from the CFA Program practice analysis.[33] Because the CFA curriculum is based on the knowledge, skills, and abilities required for success in the investment profession, the CFA curriculum complements academic curricula, which is often more research based.

McLeavey, who taught at the University of Rhode Island, led the design effort for the CFA Program Partners initiative and signed the Saïd Business School at the University of Oxford as the first formally recognized program partner. Robert McLean, CFA, of Creighton University was hired to spearhead the program. By the time the 2006 CFA Institute Annual Report was published, 16 universities on six continents were recognized as CFA Program Partners.

To receive this designation, a university has to meet certain criteria. It has to apply to become part of the program and be visited on-site by CFA Program

THE NEXT BEN GRAHAMS?

In 2007, a program combining university outreach with global investment research made its debut in colleges and universities all over the world. The Global Investment Research Challenge launched by CFA Institute provides interested students with an opportunity to practice financial analysis and win a prize for their schools. A unique blend of university students, CFA Institute member societies, investment industry professionals, publicly traded companies, and corporate sponsors, the Global Investment Research Challenge was built on a similar program created by the New York Society of Security Analysts in 2002.

To compete, teams from various undergraduate and graduate programs work for a year analyzing a publicly traded company. They are mentored by a practicing research analyst. Each team produces a research report. According to Jeffrey J. Diermeier, CFA, who has served as a judge: "You could mix these teams' research up with professional investment research on a Wall Street desk; you wouldn't be able to tell the difference between them."[34]

Like any good college competition, the challenge, which in April 2011 was renamed the CFA Institute Research Challenge, has brackets, each of which produces a finalist. Teams first compete regionally (in New York, the Americas, EMEA, and APAC), and the winner of each bracket heads to the finals. The first global competition was won by Babson College from Wellesley, Massachusetts, USA. Subsequent victories have gone to Hong Kong Baptist University, Nanyang Technological University (Singapore), the University of the Philippines Diliman, and the Politecnico di Milano.

Politecnico di Milano of Italy won first place at the 2011 Global Investment Research Challenge. Names of students/others in this photo are (left to right) Marco Aboav, adviser; Stefano Viganò; Nicolò Rolando; Anna Belli; Francesca Claudio; Giacomo Saibene; Andrea Dal Santo, CFA, mentor, and John Rogers, CFA. Marco Cristofori, photographer

Renowned investment guru Warren Buffett (right) speaks with Robert R. Johnson, CFA (left), then senior managing director, CFA Institute, in front of an audience of students at the 2011 Global Investment Research Challenge competition in Omaha, Nebraska, USA.

staff. In addition, its courses have to cover at least 70 percent of the CFA curriculum at Level I for undergraduates and at all three levels for graduate programs. Of particular importance to CFA Institute is that participating universities cover the *Standards of Practice Handbook*. To complete the process, CFA Program staff undertake a curriculum-mapping review of each university. If all of these steps are successfully passed and the Leadership Team of CFA Institute gives its approval, the university becomes a CFA Program Partner. (The list of Program Partners can be found in Appendix C.)

By any measure, the program has been successful. In 2007, one year after its inauguration, CFA Program Partners were in place at 45 universities, among them some of the most prestigious in the world. By November 2011, the total number of partners had grown to 140, with representation from 47 leading universities in the Europe/Middle East/Africa (EMEA) region, 35 in the Asia Pacific (APAC) region, and 58 in the Americas. If Sir John Templeton were to seek a graduate business program today, he could easily find an excellent one that also conveys much of the CFA curriculum and promulgates high ethical standards.

PRACTITIONERS AT EVERY STEP OF THE PROCESS

Throughout its history, the CFA Program has existed to serve the profession of financial analysis and has, in turn, been served by practitioners of the profession. The "fingerprints of so many dedicated volunteers," as John L. Maginn, CFA, once put it, can be found on everything associated with the program.[35] In the 2000s, in particular, large numbers of charterholders have contributed by participating in standard setting, grading, and Practice Analysis, or by being a part of the numerous exam writing and curriculum reviews. As the first decade of the 2000s drew to a close, changes large and small continued to make the program better.[36] In a period when new financial instruments appeared like mushrooms after a rain, vigilance about the curriculum was important to ensure that the Candidate Body of Knowledge (CBOK) reflected not only new instruments but also the growing importance of certain disciplines. Behavioral finance, for example, had been introduced to the curriculum 20 years previously, but by this decade entire study sessions were devoted to it. The curriculum also took into account the increasing percentage of candidates involved in private wealth management. The Global Body of Investment Knowledge (GBIK) is the "comprehensive outline of knowledge for the investment profession."[37]

According to Tom Robinson, "Given the rapid pace of change in the investment profession and the need for keeping current in all educational programs, the Practice Analysis process was substantially changed in 2007."[38] Since that year, the Practice Analysis has been performed on a continuous rather than a periodic basis. Panel discussions are held in multiple cities in each global region throughout each year. A broader cross section of members and employers provides input on what is currently going on in practice and what topics are relevant for both new CFA charterholders as well as experienced practitioners. A wiki-style website was also instituted in 2008 to solicit input from investment professionals globally and is available 24/7 for members and others to critique and provide input to the bodies of knowledge. Furthermore, Robinson noted:

> An annual survey of members is now performed to further vet the input from the panel discussions and website. By the end of the decade, Practice Analysis involved thousands of contributors representing an ever-

HISTORICAL SPOTLIGHT

In 1995, only one candidate in China was enrolled in the CFA Program. Fifteen years later, more than 22,000 were enrolled.

Matthew H. Scanlan, CFA, EAC chair for 2005–2006 as well as 2008–2010 and elected governor of CFA Institute in 2011.

James G. Jones, CFA (left), COE chair (2005–2008) and governor of CFA Institute (2010–present), and Peter B. Mackey, CFA, head, CFA Program Exam and Development, CFA Institute, provided an overview of the CFA Program and its future direction at the 2008 CFA Institute Annual Conference.

broadening segment of practitioners. The input from this process is used in all educational programs—certification programs, conferences, publications, etc.

In 2007, Tom Robinson and Bob Johnson undertook the reorganization of the Education Division. The aim was to align all its elements (the CFA Program, the Continuing Education Program, and educational products) and the volunteer groups involved in content development under the aegis of the Education Advisory Committee. Perhaps the most significant change for the CFA Program at this time was the restructuring of the Candidate Curriculum Committee (CCC) and the Council of Examiners (COE). Formed as discrete bodies during the program's earliest years, these groups' workloads had been unmanageable since the mid-1990s and were increasing. Peter Mackey, who served on both committees during this period, remembered one year when he was sent textbooks to review but, like others volunteering while holding demanding jobs, found he could not "possibly do it."[39] Jan R. Squires, CFA, who, like Mackey, had served on both committees during this period, noted that the work was crowding in from all sides: "You had the job analysis pushing in a very systematic way. At the same time . . . in the late 1990s, early 2000s, we started the exam diagnostics." On both committees, the work expected from what were then groups of 15–20 volunteers had become unrealistic.

By the late 2000s, the work of curriculum and exam writing had become substantially different. Instead of 20 or fewer CCC members contributing to the formation of the curriculum, more than 100 practitioners were involved, with review and reconsideration a formal—and frequent—part of the process. Coordinating this activity was the Education Advisory Committee (EAC), which replaced the CCC. As its inaugural chair, Matthew H. Scanlan, CFA, noted that the EAC provided "oversight and guidance to the processes" by which CFA Institute develops bodies of knowledge and CFA Program curricular materials.[40] The COE, the first committee of the CFA Program, still existed, but it had the executive function of managing the writing teams that developed each level of the exam. Global exam reviews had begun in the early 2000s, but toward the middle of the decade, these reviews had increased in number and been regionalized. The COE, which for years had included members from around the world, now brought the review process to those members by holding meetings in Mumbai, Tokyo, and Dubai. In 2011, the CFA Program had a regional EMEA writing team, and in 2012, it will have a team from APAC.[41] Taking exam creation on the road presented challenges, of course, security among them, but added the benefit of having practitioners from beyond the shores of North America at every step of the process.

A history of the CFA Program understandably focuses on developments in curriculum and testing, on notable leaders and innovators, and on extraordinary worldwide growth over the past 50 years. But it would be a mistake to overlook what beats at the heart of the CFA Program: the unwavering commitment to ethics and professional conduct. No other element so defines a profession and separates it from simple work. Furthermore, in a profession that can function only if its practitioners merit the trust of their clients, neither knowledge nor innovation is sufficient: Ethical behavior is also essential.

Looking at the importance of ethics to the CFA Program, Samuel B. Jones, Jr., CFA, 2002 recipient of the Forrestal Award for Ethics and Standards of Investment Practice, noted that from its inception, the CFA Program has made a commitment to "inculcate a culture of ethics across our profession" and, generally, "to improve the integrity of the financial markets as we expanded our organization's influence beyond North America."[42]

A scholar of professions has noted that in financial professions, where the wealth of one individual is managed by another, special care is needed:

> As economists since Adam Smith have pointed out, economies depend on shared values and moral norms: good faith remains the necessary condition for all contracts, the very foundation of commerce.[43]

In 2008, reflecting on the crisis in financial markets, Jeff Diermeier said to members, "As the implications of the current credit crisis continue to unfold, I have asked myself, 'Would this have happened if CFA charterholders were at the helm making these decisions?' "[44] Charterholders, he continued, would have had the "breadth of knowledge and training to see what's coming." The principles "for which our charterholders stand" could have tempered this crisis because anyone "worthy of the CFA designation would not have engaged in the near fraudulent underwriting of mortgages" that characterized the years leading up to the crisis.

CFA charterholders, by and large, were not drawn down into the maelstrom. And, as Diermeier maintained, some saw it coming. For example, Harry M. Markopolos, CFA, a former president of the Boston Security Analysts Society, was among the first to analyze and point out the sleight of hand involved in Bernard Madoff's improbable returns. Markopolos identified Madoff's fraudulent schemes and brought them to the attention of the U.S. Securities and Exchange Commission as early as 2000.

Knowledge and foresight wedded to an ethical backbone have always meant placing clients' interests first. Analyst independence—the ability, and duty, to resist pressure to favor the bottom line over honest analysis—is essential to ethical behavior and has always been championed by CFA Institute. Such behavior

Ethical behavior is largely a voluntary outward manifestation of an inner commitment.

—Richard P. Halverson, CFA, 1994 recipient of the Forrestal Award, March 2011

Kurt N. Schacht, CFA (right), managing director, CFA Institute Standards and Financial Market Integrity in New York City, discussed with Bernard Lo (left), anchor of Bloomberg TV in Hong Kong, the Madoff scandal and the need for a hedge fund code of ethics.

Monique E.M. Gravel, CFA (left), CFA Institute chair for 2004–2005, and Vincent Duhamel, CFA (right), CFA Institute chair for 2006–2007.

is what the Code of Ethics supports and what the Standards of Practice demand. When analyst independence or other ethical precepts have been lacking, the Professional Conduct Program has stepped in to sanction as needed, revoking charters when investigations so dictate.

In 2007, CFA Institute appointed Christine I. Koppel, CFA, to be the first full-time Designated Officer, a position charged with enforcing adherence to the Code and Standards through the Professional Conduct Program. When she first took the position, Koppel conducted "benchmark analysis" to compare enforcement programs at other organizations. "We looked pretty good," she concluded, although some areas could be improved.[45] Koppel met with judges, sheriffs, and even personnel from the U.S. Department of Homeland Security in order to understand "what makes for a good enforcement program." Across the board she found two hallmarks: fairness and consistency—qualities sought in every element of the CFA Program.

Koppel developed a three-year strategic plan for the program, and given the challenges facing the industry shortly after her tenure began, such a plan was timely and welcome. The Professional Conduct Program exists for the sake of charterholders, Koppel noted: "We enforce in order to maintain and protect the integrity of the CFA designation. We work on behalf of our membership." In a decade bracketed by scandals, the strong emphasis on ethical behavior and adherence to professional standards has enabled the CFA Program to continue to shine.

THE CFA PASSPORT

> The CFA Program transcends border; it transcends language. It is portable and can go from country to country and from different parts of the industry. It has ethics at its core . . . .
>
> —Monique E.M. Gravel, CFA, 2004–2005 chair of Board of Governors, July 2009

Despite a temporary flattening of enrollments in the mid-2000s, which disappeared by 2006, the reputation of the CFA Program had been growing in prominence and its charter in desirability for years. It had truly become what the *Economist* and the *Financial Times* agreed in 2005 was "the gold standard for investment education."[46]

Why, despite the existence of dozens of other credentials offered to those working in the financial industry, is the CFA Program considered the gold standard? What sets the program apart and has enabled its dominance? The articles in the *Economist* and the *Financial Times* from 2005 delineated the program's distinctive qualities. Both identified elements unique to the program, as well as some lacking in typical graduate programs in finance.

The *Economist* article, which focused on various distance-learning programs, especially outsourced MBA programs, cited the CFA Program as the "purest example" of one that controlled its curriculum, set standards, and issued credentials uniformly and consistently. The article honed in on the program's greatest strengths. The CFA charter, it noted, "much liked by employers in financial services," is "roughly equivalent to a specialized postgraduate finance degree":

Whereas there are tens of thousands of finance degrees available around the world, ranging from the excellent to the worthless, there is only *one* CFA [charter], managed and examined by an American association of *financial professionals*, the CFA Institute.[47] [Emphasis added.]

The CFA Program is set apart because it is *one charter* the world over and because it is managed and created by *finance professionals* (practitioners) at every step of the process. Now, because of its explosive growth, what used to be simply an American qualification has become what the *Economist* termed "a global currency."

The *Financial Times* published an equally glowing analysis of the program, this one written by a journalist who was also a CFA candidate. Asking why "so many people put themselves through the rigours of the CFA programme," the article's author concluded that its consistency and portability beyond national borders had much to do with making it "the gold standard of financial training."[48] The author continued:

> Other professional schemes tend to be limited to one country, and degrees such as MBAs say little about the holder because the quality and content of courses varies widely . . . . In contrast, all CFA candidates follow the same syllabus, which is international in its scope and covers a vast array of topics, encompassing economics, statistics, professional ethics and every type of investment from real estate to derivatives.

A year earlier, two Canadian professors, Shibu Pal and his colleague Hilary Becker, both of Carleton University, also admired the program. The academicians touted the CFA Program for its homogeneity (one program, one charter worldwide) and its transportability (recognized on all continents). They also found the program's target market significant—an investment professional with three to four years of experience—and noted that its generalist curriculum was designed to provide such a person with what he or she needed to know to satisfy a firm's clients. Reporting to the Board of Governors on what these case studies found important, Bob Johnson summed it up:

> [Whether] the program is taken in Germany, the U.S., or China, candidates will be equipped with the same investment knowledge, are responsible for the same educational material, write the same examinations, and most importantly are held to the same high standards.[49]

Portability, standardization, consistency, rigor, and relevance—in a sense, these characteristics have always set the CFA Program apart from any other form of education and certification in the financial industry. They helped make it a passport recognized by financial market participants around the world. Moreover, the "fingerprints" of volunteering practitioners at every stage of the process— from curriculum development to exam creation to grading to standard setting—

In January 2011, during a speech to the Canadian Club of Toronto, Margaret E. Franklin, CFA, chair of CFA Institute for 2010–2011, called for fundamental changes to securities enforcement practice in Canada. The Canadian Club of Toronto/ Mike Hagarty

in addition to the program's central focus on ethical behavior, have made a big difference.

Emilio Gonzalez, CFA, the first Australian to serve as CFA Institute board chair (2007–2008), summarized reasons for the CFA charter's hegemony in this way: "There are a number of things that [have] attracted individuals to the CFA [Program]—its portability and its credibility and the quality of the exam."[50] To Monique E.M. Gravel, CFA, a Canadian who chaired the board in 2004–2005, the CFA Program is the only one "that really offers the international perspective, the single program that brings the financial industry into the global arena . . . ."[51] To Vincent Duhamel, CFA, also a Canadian by birth and the first chair of CFA Institute (2006–2007) located in Asia, the success of the CFA Program in the emerging economies of Asia is not difficult to understand. The "flagship educational program" of CFA Institute, he said, is distinguished by its "practical, global curriculum and its high standards of practice."[52]

ONE CHARTER FOR ONE WORLD

Interconnectedness defined the early 21st century.

—Roger Cohen, editor of the *International Herald Tribune*, 2008

When is a program truly global?

By the end of 2010, the CFA Program, propelled by swelling waves of candidates from 145 nations and with an occasional puff of publicity filling its sails, had been sailing in international waters for 25 years. Although it counted candidates and members in many countries, Jeff Diermeier believed in 2005 that it was not yet "truly a global organization." As had been true since Alfred C. "Pete" Morley, CFA, first brought the CFA Program to finance industry professionals in Asia and Europe in the mid-1980s, *journeys* abroad had to be matched by *commitment* abroad. CFA Program staff needed to be present in other countries and be drawn from the regions they served. "A firm is global when its people are global," said Louis-Vincent Gave, a participant in the organization's Vision 2012 strategy session held in Hong Kong in December 2007.[53] To begin this process, Diermeier appointed Jan Squires, a longtime CFA Program volunteer and a staff member since 1999, to head up the Asia Pacific region at the Hong Kong office beginning in 2005. A year later, Nitin M. Mehta, CFA, was hired to head up the EMEA region from the CFA Institute office in London.

Considerable outreach throughout the world soon followed. Staff members, society leaders, and some board members made numerous trips. At first, the trips were mostly to the Asia Pacific region and Europe. Soon, however, they were traveling to the Middle East, South America, and Africa. Squires and others visited four cities in China in 2006, another four in 2007. Board of Governors Chair Vincent Duhamel spoke at the second China International

The Vermont CFA Society sponsored a Leadership Program with the local Community Sailing Center to help enrich the lives of at-risk young people. The society donated funds to help pay for the Vermont CFA Society sails. Photo courtesy of Community Sailing Center

Finance Forum in Shanghai in December 2006. The Centre for Financial Market Integrity Managing Director Kurt Schacht, together with Lee Kha Loon, CFA, head of the Centre in the Asia Pacific region, discussed the work of the Centre with regulators in Hong Kong and Tokyo in 2007. In 2009, an office was opened in Brussels in recognition of the "growing influence of EU regulatory policies on the world's capital markets."[54] Beginning in 2007, visits to Latin America by CFA Program leaders grew frequent and exam registrations increased, and in 2011, a presence in Buenos Aires was established.

During this same period (2007–2011), CFA Program activities in Africa increased. In December 2009, for instance, staff member Michael G. McMillan, CFA, and CFA Program volunteer Renée K.D. Blasky, CFA, held meetings with charterholders and officials in Nairobi (Kenya) and Kigali (Rwanda). South Africa has had charterholders since the 1960s, but by the late 2000s, interest in the CFA Program was burgeoning in sub-Saharan Africa. Botswana, Ghana, Kenya, Nigeria, Uganda, and Zimbabwe, among other African nations, have shown significant increases in candidate registrations. Between fiscal years 2000 and 2010, candidate registrations in Africa grew by 304 percent. Although actual numbers are still small compared with other areas (2,956 registrations in Africa in FY2000 and 11,951 registrations there in 2011), the trend is clearly upward. According to Charles Appeadu, CFA, a staff member and native of Ghana, "The CFA Program is very attractive to young professionals in the investment industry as they see the CFA designation as the best tool to help them ascend the career ladder. The interest level among prospective candidates is very high."[55] Moreover, he added, institutions in African countries "are very friendly towards the CFA Program."

As part of the commitment abroad, Jeff Diermeier and Brian D. Singer, CFA, chair of the board in 2008, announced in the 2008 Annual Report that more staff would be based in the APAC and EMEA regions in the near future. Among them would be staff working on "alternative investments, Islamic finance, risk management and derivatives, and private wealth."[56] CFA Institute and the CFA Program, they maintained, "will not achieve truly global status until more of our staff who

EXAM STORY

One African candidate attested to the CFA charter's significance:

"I am a third level CFA candidate, and I am proud to be part of the CFA Program. Coming from Zimbabwe, a developing country, I couldn't wait to enroll for the CFA Program when I saw how it was really a diplomatic passport to those who would want to pursue a career in finance and investments. The curriculum is just globally oriented and universal. . . . I used to say I have an analytical eye, and the CFA Program really affirmed this by further improving my analytical skills. The CFA Program is synonymous with ethics, professionalism, and integrity. Now there is no longer a difference between a Zimbabwean and an American, thanks to the CFA Program."

—GODFREY MAROZVA, CFA, June 2011,
Lecturer, Investments, Finance and
Risk Management and Banking,
University of South Africa

Shown are (left to right): Raymond J. DeAngelo, managing director, Stakeholder Services, Marketing and Communications, CFA Institute; Margaret E. Franklin, CFA, chair of CFA Institute for 2010–2011; and Brian D. Singer, CFA, chair of CFA Institute for 2008–2009. Elsa Ruiz, photographer

have expertise in the key global competencies are both from and located outside of North America."

At the end of 2008, Diermeier returned to private life. As Brian Singer, who headed the search committee for his successor, noted, the search process for the next CEO was difficult: "It is always hard to fill big shoes."[57] The person they found, however, was also someone who recognized that CFA Institute and its CFA Program must function as a global organization. John Rogers, CFA, had been involved in managing global assets throughout his career. He had lived in Australia and Japan during much of his work life and knew firsthand the benefits of experience in different countries.

The global presence of the CFA Program also enabled it to be a resource to the global financial markets. Emilio Gonzalez noted that CFA Institute, "with its membership of [more than] 100,000, can quickly bring together experts in many different countries and many different fields and play a role in trying to shape the industry"—at a global level. [58]

The more the CFA Program grew around the world, the more culturally sensitive the staff and volunteers became, as illustrated by the Exam Story told by Pradeep Rajagopalan, CFA.

Exam administration staff also had to be sensitive to cultural norms in preparing test centers. In one center, for instance, a supervisor realized that men and women had been placed on the same roster for a particular room, but local customs would not allow that, so rooms were set up by gender.[59]

CONCLUSION: THE CFA PROGRAM ALONG THE NEW SILK ROAD

The great cellist Yo-Yo Ma, who was born in France to Chinese parents and grew up in the United States, tells of visiting the National Museum in Nara, Japan, and coming upon a beautiful 8th century Japanese lute called a *biwa*. *Biwas* have an interesting family history, having derived from the Chinese *pipa*, which itself comes from the Persian/Middle Eastern *oud*. They are, it would seem, an ancient, musical example of derivatives.

Painted on the front of the Nara *biwa* were an elephant, a Chinese landscape, and a Persian man. On the back, mother of pearl was inlaid, together with two beautiful red stones—stones found only in East Africa. In viewing it, one has the sense of looking at the old Silk Road, which linked Asia and the Mediterranean, epitomized in an object. This exquisite instrument gives transparent, accretive evidence of people trading their treasures, transporting beauty from one place to another, and blending bits of someone else's culture into their own.

Although any music the CFA Program makes is closer in sound to the tick of stocks trading than the strumming of a lute, it too—like African stones on

EXAM STORY: A STORY OF CULTURAL IDENTITY

This story, told by one of the society leaders, happened during the June 2009 exams in Kuwait:

"For one of the Level I candidates, there was a difference between the candidate's name in her passport and her exam registration. Asked about this, the candidate mentioned that she had [been] married during the exam registration and had used her married name to register instead of her maiden name. In the Middle East, an individual's name is fairly descriptive [and] typically contains the name of the person followed by his/her father's name, occasionally his/her grandfather's/ancestor's name, followed by the family name. Further, women do not change their name or their family name after marriage. One can thus easily relate to an individual as son or daughter of Mr. X. However, in most Western and South Asian cultures, the women take the family name of the husband after marriage, [and] tend to have much shorter names. The candidate in question was an expatriate [taking] the exam at the Kuwait Centre, so her situation would have been an oddity there.

"In this case, the candidate's passport confirmed her as, say, "Jane Smith," while the registration confirmed her as "Jane Jones." All other details including the photograph were fine. The Invigilator was puzzled and referred the case to the Supervisor in the exam hall. The Supervisor flipped through the passport for any corroborative evidence, but could not find anything specific.

"As is typical during the second half, the local society leaders had gathered outside the exam venue to display the society's banner and promote the society. The Supervisor consulted with the society leaders, who, in turn, checked with a leader from the same country as the candidate. The society leader quickly investigated and found out that the local embassy had temporarily run out of new passports and was endorsing name changes on the second-to-last page of the old passport instead of issuing new passports. True enough: For the candidate, the name change authorization was tucked away in a corner of the second-to-last page along with other stamps. During this flurry of activity, the candidate was given the exam as scheduled and undisturbed while the Supervisor was trying hard to resolve the issue. Unlike the popular misconception, the Supervisor is not a stern-faced 'meanie' out to get the candidates but is batting on the same side as the candidates, trying his best to help them."

—PRADEEP RAJAGOPALAN, CFA

the back of a Japanese lute—has ended up in some unexpected places. In 1945, did Ben Graham, nagging his fellow analysts to test themselves, ever dream that within 63 years, a million of them would? Did anyone sitting for the first CFA exam in 1963—no matter how optimistic or visionary—have the slightest idea that fewer than 50 years later, men and women would be lining up at CFA test centers in Guangzhou and Brunei, Sydney and Santiago? Could any early ICFA trustee have envisioned 200,000 registrations for CFA exams in 2010? What began as a hopeful credential for security analysts in North America—who were not even sure theirs was a profession—has grown into the gold standard of professional knowledge and ethical behavior in the financial industry. Like goods on the Silk Road, the CFA charter is portable, desirable, and difficult to attain.

The road the CFA Program has traveled over the past 50 years was paved by the efforts of volunteers, society leaders, and staff and has spanned a much

John Rogers, CFA, has been president and CEO of CFA Institute since 2009.

greater part of the globe than the old Silk Road. But like that ancient path, it has blended knowledge through trade. It has taken what was essentially a North American enterprise for the first 20 years of its existence to distant lands and Shakespeare's "undreamed shores." That journey has transformed the nature of the charter, enhancing its value in a world economy often riven by the carelessness of those who lack the ethical balance and knowledge of the CFA charterholder.

If the CFA charter is viewed at least metaphorically as an item of trade, it has a unique purchase price: upwards of 300 hours of study and 18 hours of exams, followed by a lifetime's worth of ethical behavior. "The most valuable currency is knowledge," John Rogers remarked in 2011, and no doubt charterholders would agree.[60] For those who first dreamed of financial analysis as a profession, for those who strove to make it one, and for the more than 100,000 individuals who have attained a CFA charter in the past 50 years, the knowledge gained through participation in the CFA Program as candidates, charterholders, and volunteers is currency well earned indeed.

2011 and Beyond

*T*he first 50 years of the CFA Program are a great history of vision, hard work, and perseverance. Many professions have succeeded in developing a credential, but few have experienced such worldwide demand and managed growth as well as the CFA Program. This record of achievement is a tribute to the dedication of many good people. As I consider this history, I have to ask the question: What can we do to sustain and build on this remarkable achievement?

I would observe that the need for a single, relevant, and high-quality professional accreditation in investments is more important now than ever before. With globalization, the need for high ethical standards is certain to grow, not shrink, in the future. Future generations of investment professionals seeking success on this stage will be looking for a globally recognized mark of educational and ethical achievement. The investment profession needs a "gold standard" credential.

As of this writing, some of the trends in the investment industry are easy to identify. For some time, we have been experiencing a global shift from defined-benefit to defined-contribution retirement plans. Economic growth, technology, and deregulation have hastened the shift from intermediated investing to self-directed wealth management around the world. This trend is part of a general shift from welfare safety nets to self-reliance. The change puts investment professionals increasingly on the "front lines" with investors and has major implications for the skills needed to succeed in the field.

Global economic growth patterns have broadened the dispersion of wealth, making our industry truly one without borders. Financial markets have grown in importance, as has the size of the investment profession itself. Painful market disruptions occurred in the 1997–2009 period, which led to heightened regulatory oversight in many large capital markets. Local licensing and regulatory requirements are likely to increase the complexity of the profession and increase the need for technical knowledge. These changes place great responsibility on the average investor.

If the need for the CFA Program persists and grows over the next 50 years,

If you have a memory to share of taking the CFA exams or earning the CFA charter, please send it to CFA Institute, Attn. Historian, P.O. Box 2083, Charlottesville, VA 22902, USA, or electronically to historian@cfainstitute.org.

then a very heavy responsibility rests on those of us involved in the CFA Program today and tomorrow. Not only must the CFA charter stand for the highest level of professional standards now, but as our members remind us, the program must remain relevant every day in order for the credential to hold its value for clients and employers in years to come. With the improvements in health care and life expectancy on the rise, newly minted CFA charterholders may still be practicing 50 years from now! We owe it to them to continue to advance the program and live up to their expectations.

We also have a responsibility to the entire profession and, ultimately, to society as a whole. Looking ahead another 50 years, what can we do to support the investment profession, our clients, regulators, educators, and our world? Some would no doubt say, "Carry on with persistence"—focus solely on making the designation as good as it can be. That approach contains a lot of wisdom, but with success comes the challenge of leadership. And leadership requires wrestling with the ongoing relevance and mission of CFA Institute. Perhaps we can envision the CFA Program as a means to an end, one of several initiatives that CFA Institute can sponsor over the next half century.

Finally, I would like to thank all those who brought this anniversary book to its readers—especially those who contributed their memories of taking CFA exams and earning the charter. We received many humorous and heartwarming stories, far more than we could use. All of these vignettes illustrate the determination of CFA candidates in the face of challenges even beyond the difficulty of the exams themselves. We encourage you to keep sharing these stories with us.

JOHN ROGERS, CFA
President and CEO
CFA Institute

Examination III, 15 June 1963 (Section I)

THE INSTITUTE OF CHARTERED FINANCIAL ANALYSTS, INC.

EXAMINATION III
(June 15, 1963)

Section I - 9:45 A. M. - 12:00 P. M.

Four Questions

SECTION I

Questions	Nature of Subject Matter
No. 1 (required)	Individual portfolio management
No. 2 (required)	Valuation of stocks
No. 3 (required)	Valuation of bonds
No. 4 (choice)	Selection of securities
Either . . . . bonds
or . . . . stocks

> **Candidates should accept all statistics contained in the questions as those prevailing at the time of the examination.**

Instructions to Candidate

1. Four questions must be answered. They have equal importance in grading. Arrange your time to spend, on the average, 30 minutes for each question.

2. Write legibly, and in ink.

3. Begin each question on a new page.

4. Write your Identification Number in the two spaces indicated on the front cover of your answer book. Fill in the other required information on the cover of your answer book.

Question I (required) - *Individual Portfolio Management*

Mr. Joseph Cartman is 55 years old and now earns a salary of approximately $62,000 annually as an executive of a leading chemical company. He has been earning in excess of $25,000 per year for the past 10 years and during this time has accumulated a portfolio of securities as follows:

	Number Shares	Per Share Cost	Per Share Current Mkt.	1963 Estimated Earnings	1963 Estimated Dividend
Avco Corp.	200	$ 25	$ 26	$1.80	$ .80
Bobbie Brooks	100	27	25	1.05	.40
Brunswick	250	40	16	1.25	.60
Crysler	200	35 (1)	53	6.00	1.00
Dupont	50	102	247	9.20	7.50
"	50	160	"	"	"
"	50	175	"	"	"
"	50	202	"	"	"

(1) Adjusted for 2 for 1 stock split in 1963

The above stocks were purchased between 1953 and the time of your analysis. Mr. Cartman subscribes to several "investment services" and has based his stock purchases on recommendations from these services.

Mr. Cartman is married and has two daughters in college. His salary and the income from the stocks listed above constitute the total of the family's annual income. He has adequate life insurance and liquid savings amounting to $16,000. His pension benefits at age 65 will amount to $12,000 per year.

At the close of 1953, the Dow-Jones Industrial Average was 275.04.

Following are selected market and yield statistics prevailing at the time of your analysis:

Dow-Jones Industrial Average	717.16
Standard and Poor's Index of 425 Industrials	73.19
Dividend Yield on Dow-Jones Industrial Average	3.25
Yield on municipal bonds	3.21
Yield on high grade corporate bonds	4.20
Yield on high grade preferred stocks	4.34
Yield on "growth" stocks	1.71

QUESTION: Mr. Cartman is dissatisfied with the results of this portfolio and has come to you for advice.

Assume Mr. Cartman's investment objective is maximum long-term after-tax return consistent with a reasonable degree of safety of principal. Outline briefly your advice to Mr. Cartman regarding his portfolio.

1

Question II (required) - Valuation of Stocks

"Retained earnings have value to stockholders only as a source of future dividends; thus, dividends, and not earnings, should be capitalized to arrive at stock valuations."

QUESTIONS:

1. Would the capitalization of dividends usually lead to a different valuation of a stock than the capitalization of earnings? Explain briefly.

2. If the capitalization of dividends leads to a different value than the capitalization of earnings, explain briefly the possible reasons for the difference.

Question III (required) - Valuation of Bonds

In determining the investment grade of bonds, it is common to use financial ratios for an industry and compare the bond under consideration with these ratios. Select a particular industry and give examples of at least three financial ratios for the industry. List and explain briefly the advantages and limitations of the ratios you have selected.

Question IV - Selection of Securities (Choice of either (a) bonds or (b) stocks)

N. B. Answer only (a) or (b)

(a) Bonds

Following are selected data pertaining to two public utility bond issues:

Cincinnati Gas & Electric Co. 1st 2 3/4's 1975
Offered at 101 on October 18, 1945

	1959	1960	1961	1962
Interest and other fixed charge coverage after taxes	5.40	5.15	4.72	5.45

$45,500,000 outstanding   Callable at $102\frac{1}{4}$

Price range 1962-1963   82-$86\frac{1}{2}$ Present Price $85\frac{1}{4}$ Bid

Yield to maturity 4.18

S & P's rating AAA   Moody's rating Aaa

2

Texas Electric Service Co. 1st 4½'s 1988
Offered at 101 5/8 on October 28, 1958

	1959	1960	1961	1962
Interest and other fixed charge coverage after taxes	5.71	5.63	4.11	4.52

$10,000,000 outstanding   Callable at 105.31

Price range 1962-1963   99 3/4 - 103 1/2   Present Price   103 Bid

Yield to maturity 4.25

S & P's rating AAA   Moddy's rating Aa

Standard and Poor's Utility Bond Yields
   AAA = 4.30   AA = 4.34   A = 4.42

QUESTION: Based on the information given, which of the two bonds described above would you recommend for holding by a private financial institution with a sizable investment in public utility bonds? Explain briefly the basis for your selection.

(b) Stocks

Following are selected data pertaining to Ginn & Co. (NYSE GNN)

Current Price = 27¼
Dividend   = .65
Yield   = 2.4%

1962-1963 Price Range
16 3/8-32 3/8
Dow-Jones Industrial Average 717.16
Price-Earnings Ratio for Dow-Jones
Industrial Average 19.7
Yield on Dow-Jones Industrial Average 3.25

Revenue & Earnings Statistics

	Net Sales (000)	Net Income (000)	Per Share (1) Earnings	Per Share (1) Dividend
1962	$32,953	$3,406	$1.20	$ .53
1961	32,665	3,179	1.12	.42
1960	27,088	2,468	.83	.30
1959	26,385	2,299	.82	.20
1958	25,710	1,666	.58	.20
1957	23,152	1,507	.52	.17
1956	20,141	1,296	.44	.17
1955	18,315	1,190	.39	.17

(1) Adjusted for 35-1 stock split in October, 1960.

3

Balance Sheet Statistics	1962
Current Assets	$23,089,000
Current Liabilities	7,340,000
Net Working Capital	$15,749,000

Long-term debt -- None
Book value per common share $7.23
Common stock outstanding 2,835,745 Shares ($1 par)

Approximately 12½% of the outstanding common stock is owned by officers and directors.

Background Information

The company is one of the largest publishers of textbooks and related educational materials. Sales of the company are particularly strong at the elementary and high school levels with these institutions accounting for approximately 95% of the sales volume.

The staff of the college department has been increased and greater emphasis is being placed on the college market.

Within the past two years the company has entered the fields of standardized educational testing and audio-visual aids.

Sales representatives are used in the distribution of the company's products.

There are approximately 5,200 stockholders and 700 employees.

Finances

817,391 shares of common stock were offered on November 29, 1960, at $24.50, with 644,091 shares being sold for certain stockholders and the remaining shares representing new financing.

Industry Outlook

Projections are for an expanding enrollment at all educational levels during the next decade. This increase in school enrollment should be reflected in increased textbook sales.

QUESTION: Mr. Robert Jones, 30 years of age, married and two children, has inherited a $50,000 portfolio from his father. These securities consist of $15,000 Government bonds, $25,000 in municipal bonds, and $10,000 in American Telephone and Telegraph common stock. Mr. Jones earns a salary of $12,000 per year. He is considering selling the $15,000 Government bonds and purchasing $15,000 of Ginn & Company common stock.

Based on the information given, would you recommend the purchase of Ginn & Company stock for Mr. Jones? Explain briefly the reasons for your recommendation.

* * *

4

Donald L. Tuttle Award for CFA Grading Excellence Recipients

2001   Donald L. Tuttle, CFA
Greta E. Marshall, CFA
James R. Vertin, CFA
Charles G. King, CFA

2002   Larry D. Guin, CFA
Jules A. Huot, CFA
Jamsheed A. Khan, CFA
George H. Troughton, CFA

2003   Catherine E. Clark, CFA
Douglas R. Hughes, CFA
John D. Richardson, CFA
Tom S. Sale III, CFA

2004   James C. Galloway, CFA
Peter B. Mackey, CFA
Lisa R. Weiss, CFA
Gordon T. Wise, CFA

2005   Shirley S. DeJarnette, CFA
Alan M. Meder, CFA

2006   James W. Bronson, CFA
Richard D. Frizell, CFA
Robert B. Hardaway, Jr., CFA
Thomas B. Welch, CFA

2007   Bradley J. Herndon, CFA
Frank T. Magiera, CFA
Thomas J. Franckowiak, CFA

2008   Charles W. Brooks, Jr., CFA
Larry D. Riley, CFA
John E. Fitzgerald, CFA

2009   Jan R. Squires, CFA
Thomas J. O'Loughlin, CFA
Max E. Hudspeth, CFA

2010   Jacques R. Gagné, CFA
David B. Stevens, CFA
James G. Jones, CFA

2011   Renée K. D. Blasky, CFA
Marilyn J. Ettinger, CFA
Michelle E. Laux, CFA

CFA Program Partners

THE AMERICAS—CENTRAL AMERICA

- *Instituto Centroamericano de Administración de Empresas (INCAE)* (Alajuela, Costa Rica)
  MBA Program, Finance Concentration

THE AMERICAS—NORTH AMERICA

Canada

- *Concordia University, John Molson School of Business* (Montreal, Quebec, Canada)
  Goodman Institute of Investment Management MBA Program

- *HEC Montréal* (Montreal, Quebec, Canada)
  Bachelor in Business Administration, Finance Specialization
  D.E.S.S. en professions financiers (Specialized Graduate Diploma in Financial Professions)

- *Queen's University* (Kingston, Ontario, Canada)
  MBA; Master of Science in Finance; Bachelor of Commerce; Master of Management in Finance

- *Université Laval* (Quebec City, Quebec, Canada)
  Bachelor of Administration with Finance Major; MBA Finance

- *Université de Sherbrooke* (Sherbrooke, Quebec, Canada)
  M.Sc. Finance

- *University of Alberta* (Edmonton, Alberta, Canada)
  Bachelor of Commerce

- *University of British Columbia* (Vancouver, British Columbia, Canada)
  Bachelor of Commerce (BCom); MBA with Specialization in Finance

- *University of Toronto* (Toronto, Ontario, Canada)
  Bachelor of Commerce (B.Com.)

- *University of Western Ontario* (London, Ontario, Canada)
  Honors Bachelor of Arts in Business Administration (HBA)
  Masters in Business Administration (MBA)
- *York University* (Toronto, Ontario, Canada)
  Master of Finance Program

Mexico

- *Instituto Tecnológico Autónomo de México (ITAM)* (Mexico City, Mexico)
  B.A. in Business Administration; Master in Finance
- *Instituto Tecnológico y de Estudios Superiores de Monterrey (ITESM)—Monterrey Campus* (Monterrey, Mexico)
  Master in Finance; Bachelor in Financial Management

United States

- *Baruch College, The City University of New York* (New York City, New York, USA)
  Executive MS in Financial Statement Analysis
- *Boston University, School of Management* (Boston, Massachusetts, USA)
  M.Sc. in Finance
- *Cornell University* (Ithaca, New York, USA)
  MBA Program at the Johnson School of Management
- *Creighton University* (Omaha, Nebraska, USA)
  Master of Security Analysis and Portfolio Management
- *Fordham University* (New York City, New York, USA)
  Bachelor of Science in Finance
  Master of Business Administration: Finance and Business Economics
  Concentration with Investment Management Specialization
- *Georgia Institute of Technology* (Atlanta, Georgia, USA)
  Master of Business Administration
- *Howard University* (Washington, DC, USA)
  MBA in Finance; BBA in Finance
- *Louisiana State University* (Baton Rouge, Louisiana, USA)
  Master of Science in Finance; Bachelor of Science in Finance
- *Marquette University* (Milwaukee, Wisconsin, USA)
  Applied Investment Management Program, Undergraduate
- *Michigan State University* (East Lansing, Michigan, USA)
  Bachelor of Arts in Finance; MBA Program
- *New York University* (New York City, New York, USA)
  MBA with a Specialization in Finance
- *Ohio State University* (Columbus, Ohio, USA)
  MBA in Finance; BSBA in Finance

- *Rutgers University* (Newark and New Brunswick, New Jersey, USA)
  MBA Program at the Rutgers Business School—Newark and New Brunswick
  B.S. in Finance at the Rutgers Business School—Newark and New Brunswick

- *Saint Louis University* (St. Louis, Missouri, USA)
  Bachelor of Science in Finance, Financial Analyst Track

- *Texas A&M University* (College Station, Texas, USA)
  MBA; MS in Finance; BBA in Finance

- *Texas Tech University* (Lubbock, Texas, USA)
  Bachelor of Business Administration, Finance Major with Investment Emphasis

- *Tulane University* (New Orleans, Louisiana, USA)
  Master of Finance (New Orleans campus)
  Bachelor of Science in Management, Finance Major

- *University of California, Irvine* (Irvine, California, USA)
  MBA

- *University of Florida* (Gainesville, Florida, USA)
  Bachelor of Science in Business Administration with a Major in Finance
  Master of Science in Finance (MSF)

- *University of Illinois at Urbana-Champaign* (Urbana-Champaign, Illinois, USA)
  Master of Science in Finance

- *University of Iowa* (Iowa City, Iowa, USA)
  MBA, Finance

- *University of Kansas* (Lawrence, Kansas, USA)
  Bachelor of Science in Business, Major in Finance

- *University of Maryland* (College Park, Maryland, USA)
  Bachelor of Science in Business Administration with a Major in Finance

- *University of Minnesota* (Minneapolis, Minnesota, USA)
  MBA

- *University of Missouri at Columbia* (Columbia, Missouri, USA)
  Bachelor of Business Administration, Concentration in Finance

- *University of Nebraska at Lincoln* (Lincoln, Nebraska, USA)
  B.S. in Business Administration, CFA Track within the Finance Major

- *University of North Carolina at Chapel Hill* (Chapel Hill, North Carolina, USA)
  MBA—Investment Management

- *University of Pittsburgh* (Pittsburgh, Pennsylvania, USA)
  MBA with Concentration in Finance Program
  BS in Business Administration with Major in Finance

- *University of Rhode Island* (Kingston, Rhode Island, USA)
  Bachelor of Science, Major in Finance

- *University of Richmond* (Richmond, Virginia, USA)
  BS in Finance

- *University of San Francisco* (San Francisco, California, USA)
  MS in Financial Analysis
- *University of Southern California* (Los Angeles, California, USA)
  MBA; BS in Business Administration
- *University of Virginia, Darden Graduate School of Business Administration* (Charlottesville, Virginia, USA)
  MBA
- *University of Virginia, McIntire School of Commerce* (Charlottesville, Virginia, USA)
  B.S. in Commerce with a Concentration in Finance
- *University of Wisconsin-Madison* (Madison, Wisconsin, USA)
  MBA—Applied Securities Analysis Program
- *Virginia Tech* (Blacksburg, Virginia, USA)
  Bachelor of Science in Finance

THE AMERICAS—SOUTH AMERICA

- *Insper* (São Paulo, Brazil)
  Bachelor in Business Administration; Bachelor in Economics
- *Instituto de Estudios Superiores de Administración (IESA)* (Caracas, Venezuela)
  Maestría de Finanzas
- *Pontifícia Universidad Católica de Chile* (Santiago, Chile)
  Master in Finance
- *Pontifícia Universidade Católica do Rio de Janeiro* (Rio de Janeiro, Brazil)
  Bachelor of Arts Degree in Economics
- *Universidad Adolfo Ibáñez* (Santiago, Chile)
  Magister en Finanzas
- *Universidad del CEMA* (Buenos Aires, Argentina)
  Maestria en Finanzas
- *Universidad del Pacifico* (Lima, Peru)
  Master in Finance with Specialization in Portfolio Management
- *Universidad de San Andres, Faculty of Management* (Buenos Aires, Argentina)
  Masters in Finance
- *Universidad Torcuato Di Tella* (Buenos Aires, Argentina)
  Master's in Finance

ASIA-PACIFIC REGION

- *Aoyama Gakuin University* (Tokyo, Japan)
  MBA Program
- *Asian Institute of Management* (Manila, Philippines)
  Master of Business Administration/Finance Area of Excellence

- *Chinese University of Hong Kong* (Hong Kong)
  Bachelor of Science in Quantitative Finance
- *Chulalongkorn University-Sasin* (Bangkok, Thailand)
  Master of Business Administration (MBA)
  Bachelor of Business Administration International Program, International Business Management Major, Financial Analysis and Investment Track
- *Fudan University* (Shanghai, China)
  Master of Finance
- *Hitotsubashi University* (Tokyo, Japan)
  MBA program in Finance Strategy
- *Hong Kong University of Science and Technology, School of Management* (Hong Kong)
  M.Sc. in Financial Analysis; M.Sc. in Investment Management
- *Institute of Business Administration (IBA) Karachi* (Karachi, Pakistan)
  BBA; MBA; MS (Finance)
- *Korea Advanced Institute of Science and Technology (KAIST)* (Seoul, Korea)
  Finance MBA
- *Korea University* (Seoul, Korea)
  Undergraduate Program (BBA) Finance MBA
- *Lahore University of Management Sciences (LUMS)* (Lahore, Pakistan)
  B.Sc. (Honours) in Accounting and Finance (ACF)
- *Nanyang Technological University* (Singapore)
  Bachelor of Business in Banking and Finance
- *National Chengchi University* (Taipei City, Taiwan)
  B.S. in Finance
- *National Institute of Development Administration* (Bangkok, Thailand)
  M.Sc. in Financial Investment and Risk Management
- *National Taiwan University* (Taipei, Taiwan)
  Master of Business Administration (MBA)
  Bachelor of Business Administration (BBA)
- *National University of Singapore* (Singapore)
  Bachelor of Business Administration, Specialization in Finance
- *Peking University* (Beijing, China)
  Master of Science in Finance
- *Shanghai Jiao Tong University* (Shanghai, China)
  MBA Program in Finance
- *Shanghai University* (Shanghai, China)
  Global Finance MBA Degree Program – GFMBA
- *Singapore Management University* (Singapore)
  Bachelor of Business Management (Finance Major)
  Master of Science in Applied Finance; Master of Science in Applied Finance (China)
  Master of Science in Wealth Management

- *Sun Yat-sen University (aka Zhongshan University)* (Guangzhou, China)
  Master of Finance; Bachelor of Finance

- *Tsinghua University* (Beijing, China)
  Master of Finance

- *Waseda University* (Tokyo, Japan)
  MBA Program in Finance

- *Yonsei University* (Seoul, Korea)
  Finance MBA; MS in Finance; Bachelor of Business Administration

AUSTRALIA/NEW ZEALAND

- *Australian National University* (Canberra, Australian Capital Territory, Australia)
  Bachelor of Finance (BFIN) with a Major in Corporate Finance and Investment Management

- *La Trobe University* (Melbourne, Victoria, Australia)
  Master of Financial Analysis

- *Macquarie University, Applied Finance Center* (Sydney, New South Wales, Australia)
  Masters in Applied Finance

- *Massey University* (Auckland, New Zealand)
  Bachelor of Business Studies (Finance)

- *Monash University* (Melbourne, Victoria, Australia)
  Bachelor of Business; Bachelor of Business (Banking and Finance)

- *University of Adelaide* (Adelaide, South Australia, Australia)
  Master of Applied Finance; Master of Accounting and Finance

- *University of Auckland* (Auckland, New Zealand)
  Bachelor of Commerce, Finance Major

- *University of Melbourne* (Melbourne, Victoria, Australia)
  Master of Finance; Bachelor of Commerce (Major in Finance)

- *University of Otago* (Dunedin, New Zealand)
  Bachelor of Commerce in Finance

- *University of Sydney* (Sydney, New South Wales, Australia)
  Bachelor of Commerce (BCom) with a major in Finance
  Bachelor of Economics (BEc) with a major in Finance

- *University of Technology, Sydney* (Sydney, New South Wales, Australia)
  Bachelor of Business with a major in Finance
  Master of Business in Finance (MBus)

EUROPE/MIDDLE EAST/AFRICA REGION

Africa

- *University of Cape Town* (Cape Town, South Africa)
  Bachelor of Business Science-Finance (Chartered Accountant (CA) Option)
  Bachelor of Business Science-Finance (Non-CA Option)

- *University of Pretoria* (Pretoria, South Africa)
  Bachelor of Commerce in Investment Management
  BCom (Hons) Finance Management Sciences, Investment Management option
- *University of Stellenbosch* (Stellenbosch, South Africa)
  Bachelor of Commerce (Investment Management)

Europe

- *ALBA Graduate Business School* (Vouliagmeni, Greece)
  MSc in Finance
- *Bilkent University* (Ankara, Turkey)
  MBA; MS in Finance; Undergraduate degree: BS
- *Bocconi University* (Milan, Italy)
  M.Sc. in Finance- CLEFIN-LS
  Corso di Laurea in Economia e Finanza, CLEF (Bachelor of Economics and Finance, CLEF)
  Bachelor of International Economics, Management and Finance (BIEMF), major in Finance
- *Cass Business School, City University London* (London, UK)
  MSc in Banking and International Finance; MSc in Finance
  MSc in Finance and Investment (part-time); MSc in International Accounting and Finance
  MSc in Investment Management
- *Durham Business School* (Durham, UK)
  MSc Programme in Economics and Finance
  MSc Finance; MSc Finance and Investment; MSc Corporate and International Finance
  MSc International Money, Finance and Investment; MSc International Banking and Finance
  MSc Economics and Finance; MSc Accounting and Finance
- *Ecole des Hautes Etudes Commerciales* (EDHEC) (Nice, France)
  M.Sc. in Finance
- *ESADE Business School* (Barcelona, Spain)
  MSc Finance
- *ESCP Europe* (Paris, France)
  Master in Management
- *ESSEC* (Paris, France)
  Specialized Master's in Financial Techniques; ESSEC MBA Finance Track
- *European Business School* (Oestrich-Winkel, Germany)
  Bachelor of Science in General Management
- *Goethe University Frankfurt* (Frankfurt, Germany)
  Executive Master of Finance and Accounting
- *Hautes Etudes Commerciales* (HEC) (Paris, France)
  MS in Management, Finance Major

- *IE Business School (Instituto de Empresa)* (Madrid, Spain)
  Master in Finance; Master in Advanced Finance
- *Imperial College* (London, UK)
  M.Sc. in Finance
- *INSEAD* (Fontainebleau, France)
  MBA (France/Singapore)
- *Koç University* (Istanbul, Turkey)
  Master of Science in Finance
- *Lancaster University* (Lancaster, UK)
  M.Sc. in Accounting and Financial Management and the M.Sc. in Finance
  BA (Hons) Accounting & Finance; BS (Hons) Accounting & Finance
  BSc (Hons) Finance
- *London Business School* (London, UK)
  Masters in Finance
- *Manchester Business School* (Manchester, UK)
  BA Econ (Accounting); BA Econ (Finance); BSC Management
  BA International Business Finance and Economics; MSc Accounting
  and Finance
  MSc Finance
- *Reims Management School: Sup de Co* (Reims, France)
  M.Sc. in Management (CFA Track)
- *RSM Erasmus University* (Rotterdam, The Netherlands)
  M.Sc in Business Administration
- *State University-Higher School of Economics* (Moscow, Russia)
  MBA in Investment Management
- *Tilburg University* (Tilburg, The Netherlands)
  MSc in Finance; MSc Accounting
- *Trinity College, Dublin* (Dublin, Ireland)
  BBS, Finance Concentration; M.Sc. in Finance
- *Universidade Catolica Portuguesa* (Lisbon, Portugal)
  Master in Finance
- *Universität Mannheim* (Mannheim, Germany)
  Bachelor of Science in Business Administration (Betriebswirtschaftslehre)
- *Université Paris 1 Panthéon Sorbonne* (Paris, France)
  Master 2 Professionnel Banque Finance
- *Université Paris-Dauphine* (Paris, France)
  Master in Asset Management; Master in Banking and Finance
  Master in Corporate Finance and Financial Engineering
  Master in Investment Banking and Markets
  Master in Security Markets, Commodity Markets and Risk Management
  Master in Economic Engineering; Master in Economics, Banking, Finance
  and Insurance
  Master in Financial and Monetary Economics; Master of Finance

- *University of Amsterdam* (Amsterdam, The Netherlands)
  Master of International Finance (MIF)

- *University of Cambridge* (Cambridge, UK)
  Master of Finance

- *University College Dublin* (Dublin, Ireland)
  MSc in Finance

- *University of Edinburgh Business School* (Edinburgh, Scotland, UK)
  M.Sc. in Finance and Investment; M.Sc. in Accounting and Finance

- *University of Exeter, Xfi Centre for Finance and Investment* (Exeter, UK)
  M.Sc. in Finance in Financial Analysis and Fund Management

- *University of Lausanne* (Lausanne, Switzerland)
  MSc in Finance specialized in financial engineering

- *University of Leicester* (Leicester, UK)
  M.Sc. in Financial Economics

- *University of Oxford's Saïd Business School* (Oxford, UK)
  M.Sc. in Financial Economics

- *University of Reading, ICMA Centre* (Reading, UK)
  MS. in Investment Management

- *University of St. Gallen* (St. Gallen, Switzerland)
  Master of Arts in Banking and Finance (MBF)

- *University of Stirling* (Stirling, Scotland, UK)
  M.Sc. in Investment Analysis

- *University of Warwick* (Coventry, UK)
  M.Sc. in Economics and Finance; M.Sc. in Finance; B.Sc. in Accounting and Finance

- *Vlerick Leuven Gent Management School* (Ghent, Belgium)
  Masters in Financial Management

- *Wrocław University of Economics* (Wrocław, Poland)
  Bachelor in Finance; Master in Finance

Middle East

- *American University of Beirut* (Beirut, Lebanon)
  B.B.A. with Emphasis in Finance

- *American University of Sharjah* (Sharjah, UAE)
  Bachelor of Science in Finance

As of November 2011

Past Presidents and Chairs

Institute of Chartered Financial Analysts

A. Moyer Kulp, CFA	1961–1964	Robert W. Morrison, CFA	1982–1983
David D. Williams, CFA	1964–1965	Charles D. Ellis, CFA	1983–1984
M. Dutton Morehouse, CFA	1965–1966	Paul E. Vawter, Jr., CFA	1984–1985
E. Linwood Savage, Jr., CFA	1966–1967	John L. Maginn, CFA	1985–1986
Raymond W. Hammell, CFA	1967–1968	James N. von Germeten, CFA	1986–1987
David G. Watterson, CFA	1968–1969	Daniel J. Forrestal III, CFA	1987–1988
Leonard E. Barlow, CFA	1969–1970	Eugene C. Sit, CFA	1988–1989
Edmund A. Mennis, CFA	1970–1972	Gary P. Brinson, CFA	1989
Frank E. Block, CFA	1972–1973	Eugene H. Vaughan, Jr., CFA	1989
Mary Petrie, CFA	1973–1974	Frederick L. Muller, CFA	1990–1991
Robert D. Milne, CFA	1974–1975	Michael L. McCowin, CFA	1991–1992
Robert E. Blixt, CFA	1975–1976	I. Rossa O'Reilly, CFA	1992–1993
Walter P. Stern, CFA	1976–1977	Eliot P. Williams, CFA	1993–1994
Philip P. Brooks, Jr., CFA	1977–1978	Brian F. Wruble, CFA	1994–1995
C. Roderick O'Neil, CFA	1978–1979	Abby Joseph Cohen, CFA	1995–1996
William A. Cornish, CFA	1979–1980	Frank K. Reilly, CFA	1996–1997
Alfred C. Morley, CFA	1980–1981	Fred H. Speece, Jr., CFA	1997–1998
James R. Vertin, CFA	1981–1982	Philippe A. Sarasin, CFA	1998–1999

Association for Investment Management and Research 1990–2004

Eugene H. Vaughan, Jr., CFA	1990–1991	Abby Joseph Cohen, CFA	1997–1998
James K. Dunton, CFA	1991–1992	Frank K. Reilly, CFA	1998–1999
Frederick L. Muller, CFA	1992–1993	R. Charles Tschampion, CFA	1999–2000
Charles D. Ellis, CFA	1993–1994	Fred H. Speece, Jr., CFA	2000–2001
John L. Maginn, CFA	1994–1995	Philippe A. Sarasin, CFA	2001–2002
Thomas L. Hansberger, CFA	1995–1996	Dwight D. Churchill, CFA	2002–2003
I. Rossa O'Reilly, CFA	1996–1997	Theodore R. Aronson, CFA	2003–2004

CFA Institute 2004–2012

Monique E.M. Gravel, CFA	2004–2005
John C. Stannard, CFA, FSIP	2005–2006
Vincent Duhamel, CFA	2006–2007
Emilio Gonzalez, CFA	2007–2008
Brian D. Singer, CFA	2008–2009
Thomas B. Welch, CFA	2009–2010
Margaret E. Franklin, CFA	2010–2011
Daniel S. Meader, CFA	2011–2012

Notes

PROLOGUE

1   The quotations of an SEC commissioner are those of Jack M. Whitney II in a speech to the Financial Analysts Federation on 15 May 1963:3.

2   Youssef Cassis, *Capitals of Capital: The Rise and Fall of International Financial Centres, 1780–2009* (Cambridge: Cambridge University Press, 2007):204.

ONE: FROM IDEA TO INSTITUTE

1   Howard Gardner and Lee S. Schulman, "The Professions in America Today: Crucial but Fragile," *Daedalus*, vol. 134, no. 3 (Summer 2005):14; also discussed in John C. Bogle, *Enough: True Measures of Money, Business, and Life* (Hoboken, NJ: John Wiley & Sons, 2009):121.

2   William Sullivan, "Markets vs. Professions: Value Added?" *Daedalus,* vol. 134, no. 3 (Summer 2005):25.

3   Lucien Hooper, *The Best of Times* (Old Tappan, NJ: Hewitt House, 1973):90.

4   Jason Zweig and Rodney N. Sullivan, eds., *Benjamin Graham, Building a Profession*: *The Early Writings of the Father of Security Analysis* (Charlottesville, VA: CFA Institute, 2010):9–10.

5   Janet Lowe, *Benjamin Graham on Value Investing* (New York: Penguin Group, 1996):127; first published by Dearborn Financial Publishing in 1994.

6   Lowe, *Benjamin Graham on Value Investing*:127.

7   Charles D. Ellis, "Ben Graham: Ideas as Mementos," *Financial Analysts Journal* (July-August 1982):41.

8   Hooper, *The Best of Times*:52.

9   Kennard Woodworth, "The National Federation of Financial Analysts' Societies," *The Analysts Journal* (4th quarter 1947):52.

10 Woodworth, "The National Federation of Financial Analysts' Societies":52.

11 This and the next quotation are from Investment Analysts Society of Chicago, "A Brief History of the Investment Analysts Society, 1925–1975," unpublished (1975).

12 M. Harvey Earp, letter to the author dated 2 July 1985.

13 FAF, *From Practice to Profession: A History of the Financial Analysts Federation and the Investment Profession* (Charlottesville, VA: Association for Investment Management and Research, 1997):25.

14 This and the next quotation are from John Steele Gordon, *The Great Game: The Emergence of Wall Street as a World Power, 1653–2000* (New York: Scribner, 1999):258.

15 Lowe, *Benjamin Graham on Value Investing*:56.

16 From Charles D. Ellis and James Vertin, eds., *Classics: An Investor's Anthology,*

Anniversary Edition (Homewood, IL: Business One Irwin, 1989):741.

17 *The Exchange* (March 1953).

18 Whitehead, speech to prospective CFA candidates, New York, 1967.

19 Hooper, *The Best of Times*:54–55.

20 Zweig and Sullivan, *Benjamin Graham*:10.

21 Graham, *The Analysts Journal* (January 1945):37.

22 Hooper, *The Best of Times*:55.

23 Unless otherwise noted, the arguments of Graham and Hooper appeared in the January 1945 issue of *The Analysts Journal*.

24 This and the following quotations in the next two paragraphs are from Zweig and Sullivan, *Benjamin Graham*:2.

25 Nicholas Molodovsky, "Editor's Notes," *Financial Analysts Journal* (January-February 1964):7.

26 This and the following quotation are from "A Brief History of the Investment Analysts Society of Chicago, 1925–1975."

27 This and the following quotation are from Woodworth, first NFFAS president, "The National Federation of Financial Analysts' Societies."

28 David D. Williams, letter to the author dated 1 July 1985.

29 Nancy Regan, *The Institute of Chartered Financial Analysts: A Twenty-Five Year History* (Charlottesville, VA: Institute of Chartered Financial Analysts):6.

30 NYSSA Executive Committee Report (9 April 1952):1.

31 Quotations and information in this paragraph are from Regan, *The Institute of Chartered Financial Analysts*:7.

32 This and the following quotation are from the "Report of the Subcommittee on Certified Security Analyst Proposal" (31 March 1953).

33 "A Brief History of the Investment Analysts Society of Chicago, 1925–1975."

34 Davis, Report of PES Committee dated 30 April 1954.

35 The quotations in this paragraph are from Regan, *The Institute of Chartered Financial Analysts*:10.

36 Smith interview with Tom Bowman, December 2008.

37 Naess letter to the author dated 20 June 1985.

38 Smith interview with Tom Bowman, December 2008.

39 This and the following quotation are from the Report of the Subcommittee on Certification (22 April 1954).

40 Regan, *The Institute of Chartered Financial Analysts*:12.

41 Norby letter to the author dated 4 June 1985.

42 The quotations in this and the next paragraph are from the Minutes of the Directors Annual Meeting (1 May 1958).

43 Williams, letter to the author dated 1 July 1985.

44 Ray Smith interview with Tom Bowman, December 2008.

45 These quotations and those in the next paragraph are from Regan, *The Institute of Chartered Financial Analysts*:13–15.

46 Solomon Proposal:5.

47 Regan, *The Institute of Chartered Financial Analysts*:29–30.

48 NFFAS Executive Committee (December 1959):2.

49 Regan, *The Institute of Chartered Financial Analysts*:34.

50 A. Moyer Kulp, "National Federation to Set Professional Standards," *Financial Analysts Journal*, vol. 16, no. 4 (July–August 1960):11.

51 Regan, *The Institute of Chartered Financial Analysts*:37.

52 Regan, *The Institute of Chartered Financial Analysts*:38.

53 This and the following quotations are from an interview with Ray Smith given to Tom Bowman, December 2008.

54 Hansen interview with The Winthrop Group, 9 January 1998.

55 Ray Smith interview given to Tom Bowman, December 2008.

56 Sheppard interview with the author in April 1985.

57 Regan, *The Institute of Chartered Financial Analysts*:39–40.

58 The quotations from Ray Smith in this paragraph come from a December 2008 interview conducted by Thomas Bowman.

59 Regan, *The Institute of Chartered Financial Analysts*:41.

60 Regan, *The Institute of Chartered Financial Analysts*:42.

61 Ray Smith interview given to Tom Bowman, December 2008.

62 Hooper, *The Best of Times*:91.

63 Letter to Peggy Slaughter dated 25 January 1992.

64 This and following quotations are from an interview with Hansen by The Winthrop Group on 11 January 1996.

65 This quotation is from a letter written by Fred Young, CFA, to Peggy Slaughter dated 25 February 1992.

66 This quotation is from a letter written by Thomas N. Mathers, CFA, to Peggy Slaughter dated 25 February 1992.

67 This quotation is from a letter written by George H. Norton, Jr., CFA, to Peggy Slaughter dated 18 March 1992.

68 Interview conducted by Michelle Armentrout with Robert Larson, on 12 August 2009.

69 This quotation is from a letter written by Harold Dulan, to Peggy Slaughter dated 10 April 1962.

70 The quotations in the paragraph are from Regan, *The Institute of Chartered Financial Analysts*:44.

71 This and following quotation from Ray Smith are from a letter to the author dated 4 June 1985.

72 Ray Smith interview given to Tom Bowman, December 2008.

73 Correspondence of Ray Smith with the author dated 13 October 2010.

TWO: ESTABLISHING STANDARDS

1   Quotations in this and the next paragraph are from the ICFA Annual Meeting Report (27 April 1964):2, 4.

2   Nancy Regan, *The Institute of Chartered Financial Analysts: A Twenty-Five Year History* (Charlottesville, VA: Institute of Chartered Financial Analysts, 1987):49.

3   ICFA Annual Meeting Report (27 April 1964):5.

4   Speech to the National Association of Accountants, Washington, DC, on 23 June 1964.

5   *Chicago Tribune* (22 September 1963):D-3.

6   John H. Allan, "Stock Analysis Gaining Status," *New York Times* (25 September 1963):50, 61.

7   Kulp, ICFA Annual Meeting (27 April 1964):5.

8   This and the following quotation are from an interview with Ray Smith given to Tom Bowman in December 2008.

9   Sheppard, "Reflections on a Profession." Unpublished material (15 July 1985):9.

10 Smith, interview with Tom Bowman (December 2008).

11 The quotations in this paragraph are from Regan, *The Institute of Chartered Financial Analysts*:56.

12 These quotations of Sheppard are from "The Professionalization of the Financial Analyst," *Financial Analysts Journal*, vol. 23, no. 6 (November/December 1967):39.

13 See *The Analysts Journal* (January 1945):44.

14 Watterson, letter to Pete Morley dated 27 June 1985.

15 This and the next quotations are from Regan, *The Institute of Chartered Financial Analysts*:51.

16 Unless otherwise noted, all the CFA exam stories in this book were generously shared by their authors in response to requests from Wendi

Ruschmann, historian and archivist, CFA Institute.

17 Charles Ellis, "Notes on CFA Institute History," unpublished material (2010):7.

18 Regan, *The Institute of Chartered Financial Analysts*:79–80.

19 Regan, *The Institute of Chartered Financial Analysts*:80.

20 This and the quotation in the next paragraph are from correspondence of John G. Gillis with the author dated 25 May 2010:6.

21 Regan, *The Institute of Chartered Financial Analysts*:96.

22 Canadian charterholders, whose regulation was at the provincial government, not national, level, faced different challenges. Harvey Earp has noted, however, that "our Canadian members were consulted for their ideas" in regard to regulations, although to his knowledge, no cases involving Canadians came forward during those years (from Earp correspondence with the author dated 17 October 2010).

23 Quotations of Gillis are from correspondence with the author dated 26 May 2010:8.

24 Bauman, memoir of ICFA, submitted to the author on 9 July 1985:7.

25 Gillis correspondence with the author dated 26 May 2010:9.

26 Bauman, memoir of ICFA:7.

27 This and the following quotations are from Gillis correspondence with the author dated 26 May 2010:10.

28 Earp quotations are from correspondence with the author dated 18 July 2010.

29 Quotations of Bauman are from his memoirs:10.

30 Bauman, memoirs:20.

31 Williams to NYSSA on 2 February 1979.

32 Regan, *The Institute of Chartered Financial Analysts*:115.

33 ICFA Board Minutes (16 September 63):3.

34 Sheppard, "Reflections on a

Profession," unpublished material (15 July 1985):3.

35 ICFA Board Minutes (16 September 1963):3.

36 Smith interview with Tom Bowman (December 2008).

37 These quotations of Whitehead are from an address made to candidates on 10 February 1967:6.

38 This and the quotation in the next paragraph are from a Mike McCowin interview given to Bob Johnson on 1 July 2009.

39 Quotations of Tuttle are from his interview with the author on 23 September 2009.

40 Tom Bowman, correspondence with the author dated 27 July 2010.

41 This and following quotations are from the Smith interview with Tom Bowman (December 2008); the comments were expanded in correspondence with the author of 2 March 10.

42 Van Dyke-Cooper, interview with Christina Grotheer conducted on 10 November 2009.

43 In this profile, the quotation from Mennis is from "*Financial Analysts Journal*: Marrying the Academic and Practitioner Worlds," *Financial Analysts Journal*, vol. 61, no. 3 (May/June 2005):6; Smith's words are from the interview with Tom Bowman (December 2008); the Earp quotations are from his unpublished material titled "Notes on Ed Mennis" and dated May 2010; Treynor is quoted from his unpublished correspondence with the author titled "Remembering Ed Mennis" dated 13 May 2010; the quotations of Greenspan are from his unpublished correspondence with the author dated 24 November 2010. Information on Mennis's later years is from Gerald Musgrave's article "In Memoriam: Edmund A. Mennis," *Business Economics*, vol. 44 (July 2009):130–131.

44 *The Analysts Journal* (January 1945): 40.

45 Report of the Board of Trustees (May 1966):2.

46 McCowin interview (1 July 2009).

47 *New York Times* (17 June 1963).

48 Sheppard, First Annual Meeting of the ICFA (27 April 1964):2.

49 Smith, correspondence with the author dated 21 October 2009.

50 The quotations of Whitehead are from his address:4, 8.

51 Report of the Board of Trustees of the Institute of Chartered Financial Analysts (24 April 1967):1.

52 Smith interview with Tom Bowman (December 2008).

53 Report of the Board of Trustees of the Institute of Chartered Financial Analysts (undated; probably September 1965):1.

54 Dulan, letter to Peggy Slaughter dated 10 April 1992.

55 Smith, interview with Tom Bowman (December 2008).

56 Quotation from "Grading the CFA Examination," AIMR, ESI Productions on DVD (undated).

57 Smith, letter to Pete Morley dated 6 June 1985:1.

58 These and the following quotations are from Sheppard, "Reflections on a Profession" (15 July 1985):4–5.

59 Sheppard, *The Making of a Profession: The CFA Program* (Charlottesville, VA: Association for Investment Management and Research, 1992):7.

60 Ketchum, "Is Financial Analysis a Profession?" *Financial Analysts Journal*, vol. 23, no. 6 (November/December 1967):35.

61 The quotations in this paragraph are from the Smith interview with Tom Bowman (December 2008).

62 Maginn, interview with Bob Johnson on 1 July 2010.

63 Report to the ICFA Board of Trustees (12 September 1966):2.

64 Smith, interview with Tom Bowman (December 2008).

65 This and the following quotation are from ICFA Board of Trustees Minutes (14 March 1964):7.

66 Sheppard, *The Making of a Profession*: 9.

67 Sheppard to the ICFA Annual Meeting, Boston (5 May 1968):4.

68 Regan, *The Institute of Chartered Financial Analysts*:65–66.

69 Regan, *The Institute of Chartered Financial Analysts*:67.

70 ICFA Annual Meeting Minutes (5 May 1968):4.

71 This quotation and material on the R&P Committee report are from Regan, *The Institute of Chartered Financial Analysts*:69.

72 Smith, interview with Tom Bowman (December 2008).

73 Regan, *The Institute of Chartered Financial Analysts*:73.

74 Regan, *The Institute of Chartered Financial Analysts*:72.

75 Regan, *The Institute of Chartered Financial Analysts*:118.

76 Quotations in this paragraph are from Earp, letter to the author dated 2 July 1985:1.

77 Ketchum, letter to the author dated 28 June 1985.

78 Regan, *The Institute of Chartered Financial Analysts*:125.

79 This and the next quotation are from Vawter, letter to the author dated 4 February 1986.

80 Regan, *The Institute of Chartered Financial Analysts*:125.

81 Regan, *The Institute of Chartered Financial Analysts*:126.

82 Quotations of Maginn are from an interview with Bob Johnson (1 July 2010) or correspondence with author dated 7 February 2011; quotations of Tuttle are from an interview with Bob Johnson (29 March 2010) or correspondence with the author dated 6 February 2011; quotations of Maginn and Tuttle may also be from a joint interview with Bob Johnson (1 July 2010). Johnson's quotation comes from the joint interview of 1 July 2010. Quotations of Hughes are from an interview with Bob Johnson (2 July 2009). Vertin quotations come from an interview with Tom Bowman (17 February 2010), and the Bowman quotations are from an interview with Wendi Ruschmann (18 December 2006). The Vaughan quotations are from an interview with Tom Bowman (13 January 2010).

83 Tuttle interview with the author (23 September 2009).

84 Maginn and Tuttle, interview with Bob Johnson on 1 July 2010.

85 Progress Report on Possible Joint Venture Publication (22 January 1981):1.

86 Tuttle, interview with the author on 23 September 2009.

87 Johnson, interview questions for Tuttle in February 2010.

THREE: SETTING THE PACE

1 Charles R. Geisst, *Wall Street: A History from Its Beginnings to the Fall of Enron* (New York: Oxford University Press, 1997):328.

2 Quotations of Morley in this and the next paragraph are from a letter to the author dated 5 November 1985.

3 Peter L. Bernstein, *Capital Ideas: The Improbable Origins of Modern Wall Street* (New York: Free Press, 1992):3.

4 Tom Bowman, correspondence with the author of April 2010.

5 Vertin, correspondence with the author of 19 May 2010.

6 Bowman, correspondence with the author dated 15 May 2010.

7 Dudley, interview with Bowman in December 2008.

8 Bowman, conversation with the author in July 2010.

9 Morley, April 1980, quoted in Nancy Regan, *The Institute of Chartered Financial Analysts: A Twenty-Five Year History* (Charlottesville, VA: Institute of Chartered Financial Analysts, 1987):148.

10　Regan, *The Institute of Chartered Financial Analysts*:149.

11　Regan, *The Institute of Chartered Financial Analysts*:152.

12　"Institute of Chartered Financial Analysts[:] Strategic Issues and Opportunities 1983–1986," a report of the Strategic Planning Committee, submitted September 1983:4.

13　Vertin, interview with Derik Rice on 26 May 2000.

14　This and the following quotation are from Regan, *The Institute of Chartered Financial Analysts*:55.

15　Quotations of Vawter here are from e-mail correspondence with Wendi Ruschmann, CFA Institute historian and archivist, dated 27 November 2007.

16　This and the next material are from Bowman to the author (30 April 2010).

17　Bowman, interview with Ruschmann on 18 December 2006.

18　Correspondence from Vawter to the author dated 4 February 1986.

19　Correspondence from Bowman to the author dated 30 April 2010.

20　Correspondence with Wendi Ruschmann dated 19 November 2007.

21　The quoted material is from Youssef Cassis, *Capitals of Capital: The Rise and Fall of International Financial Centres, 1780–2009* (Cambridge: Cambridge University Press, 2007):249.

22　The quotation of Yeung is from correspondence with the author dated 23 December 2010. Morley's remarks are from "Looking Back," *Communicating* (an AIMR staff newsletter) (27 June 1990). Quotations of Bowman, correspondence with the author dated 30 April 2010 or from an interview given to Wendi Ruschmann (18 December 2006). Maginn quotations are from a joint interview with Donald L. Tuttle, given to Bob Johnson (1 July 2010). Vertin quotations are from correspondence with the author dated 2 May 2010. Staff quotations were compiled by Wendi

Ruschmann in November 2010. Quotations of Yura are from correspondence with the author dated 5 October 2010 and 13 April 2011.

23　The Cornish quotations are from the annual address of Cornish to members that was printed in the *CFA Newsletter* (August 1980):4–6.

24　Regan, *The Institute of Chartered Financial Analysts*, quoting C. Roderick O'Neil, CFA:134.

25　Kulp, Report to Members (24 April 1964):5.

26　*CFA Digest* (Inaugural Issue 1971):1.

27　Vertin, interview of 26 May 2000.

28　Regan, *The Institute of Chartered Financial Analysts*, quoting the report:140.

29　Vertin, interview of 17 February 2010:3.

30　Regan, *The Institute of Chartered Financial Analysts*.

31　Ellis, Notes on CFA Institute History (22 July 2010):7.

32　Tuttle, correspondence with the author dated 28 September 10.

33　Vertin, interview of 17 February 2010.

34　*The CFA Newsletter* (July 1985):1.

35　ICFA Board Minutes (14 May 1989):4.

36　Bowman, interview of 18 December 2006.

37　This and next quotation are from Vawter's letter to the author dated 4 February 1986:4.

38　ICFA Board Minutes (5 August 1984):2.

39　Quotations in this and the following two paragraphs are from the Report to the ICFA Board of Trustees of the Select Committee to Review and Evaluate the CFA Candidate Program (September 1984):1–2.

40　A psychometrician is an expert skilled in the administration and interpretation of testing.

41　These quotations are from Don Tuttle's Memo to the ICFA Board (2 January 1985):2.

42　These quotations are from Daniel Forrestal, Gary Brinson, and Eugene Sit, "Institute of Chartered Financial Analysts Strategic Plan" (5 November 1985):5.

43　Material from Bowman is from a conversation with the author of 12 July 2010.

44　All the Mikuni quotations are from an interview given to John Rogers on 17 November 2009.

45　Gentaro Yura, interview with Tom Bowman in September 2009.

46　Memo to ICFA Board of Trustees (2 December 1987):2.

47　The quotations from Smith are from an interview given to Bowman in December 2008.

48　Earp, letter to the author dated 2 July 1985.

49　Johnson, Admissions Committee discussion paper (20 September 1979).

50　*CFA Newsletter* (February 1982):1.

51　Minutes of the annual meeting (10 May 1982):2.

52　Regan, *The Institute of Chartered Financial Analysts*:145.

53　Charles D. Ellis, "Coming of Age: A Brief History of the Changing Role of the Securities Analyst." *The Investment Professional: The Journal of NYSSA*, vol. 2, no. 1 (2009):3.

54　Board Minutes (16 June 1986):5–6.

55　This quotation and the next two are from the ICFA Board Minutes (17 September 1986):5, 6.

56　Candidate Programs Report (20 December 1986):1.

57　ICFA Board Minutes (17 September 1986):6.

58　This and the next quotation are from the 1986 ICFA Annual Report:8.

59　Bowman, interview (18 December 2006).

60　Candidate Programs Report (20 December 1986):1.

61　ICFA Board Minutes (8 September 1989):8.

62　This and the following quotations are from the annual meeting minutes (15 May 1989):1.

63　Bowman memo to the ICFA Board of Trustees (22 April 1988):2.

64　Memo of 30 April 1987:1.

65　Memo of 30 April 1987:2.

66 This and the following quotation are from the memo of 30 April 1987:7.

67 Memo of 30 April 1987:2.

68 Recommended changes here and in the next paragraph are from the ICFA Board Minutes (10 May 1987):15.

69 This and the following quotation are from the Bowman Memo to ICFA Trustees (2 December 1987):1.

70 This and the next quotation are from a memo from Pete Morley to the ICFA Board of Trustees on the Review of the ICFA Curriculum and Examination Program (16 December 1988):5.

71 Bowman conversation with the author of 12 July 2010.

72 ICFA Board Minutes (10 May 1987):15.

73 Report to the board (12 December 1987):3.

74 Cassis, *Capitals of Capital*:248.

75 Bowman, correspondence with the author dated 30 June 2010.

76 Correspondence with the author dated 10 September 2010.

77 This and the next two quotations are from Bowman, interview (18 December 2006).

78 Kulp, Report to the Members (7 April 1964):5.

79 Vawter, letter to the author dated 4 February 1986.

80 Vawter, Report on International Strategy (1987):4.

81 Quotations from Teo in this paragraph are from Teo, "CFA Program in Singapore," unpublished material (August 2010):1–2.

82 *CFA Newsletter* (April 1987):2.

83 This and the next quotation are from Yura correspondence with the author dated 9 October 2010.

84 ICFA Board Minutes (19 January 1988):7.

85 Correspondence with the author dated 9 July 2010.

86 Bowman, interview (18 December 2006).

87 Maginn and Tuttle, interview with Bob Johnson of 1 July 2010.

88 ICFA Board Minutes (17 January 1989):5.

89 International Strategy Report (January 1987):1.

FOUR: THE MERGER YEARS

1 Hardaway, "AIMR through the Eyes of a Fifty-Year Local Society Member," speech given in 2002:1.

2 Nancy Regan, *The Institute of Chartered Financial Analysts: A Twenty-Five Year History* (Charlottesville, VA: Institute of Chartered Financial Analysts, 1987):103.

3 ICFA Board Minutes (26 January 73):4.

4 The Ellis quotations in this paragraph are from his "Notes on CFA Institute History," unpublished (22 July 2010): 1, 4.

5 These quotations of Muller are from a Muller memo to the author dated 29 June 2010:2.

6 Murphy, conversation with the author on 14 June 2010.

7 Murphy, letter to FAF delegates dated 7 April 1989.

8 Quotations of Hardaway in this paragraph are from "AIMR through the Eyes of a Fifty-Year Local Society Member":2–3.

9 Quotations of Ellis in this paragraph are from his "Notes on CFA Institute History":1.

10 In 1987, the great majority of these societies (49) were located in the United States, while 8 were in Canada. One—the International Society of Financial Analysts—represented analysts in many countries and was based in Charlottesville. Another, founded that year and a true harbinger of things to come, was in Asia—the Singapore Society of Financial Analysts.

11 ICFA Board Minutes (15 September 1987):4.

12 Quotations of Sit in this paragraph are from ICFA Board Minutes (10 May 1987):5.

13 This and the next quotation are from Gary P. Brinson, ICFA Board Minutes (2 August 1987):10, 11.

14 This and the next quotation are from Paul E. "Jay" Vawter, ICFA Board Minutes (2 August 1987):14.

15 The quotations of Vertin in this section are from ICFA Board Minutes (2 August 1987):12.

16 Noyes, ICFA Board Minutes (2 August 1987):16.

17 Brinson, ICFA Board Minutes (10 May 1987):6.

18 Forrestal, ICFA Board Minutes (15 September 1987):4.

19 Bowman correspondence with the author dated 2 September 2010.

20 ICFA Board Minutes (10 May 1987):5, 9.

21 Ellis, "Notes on CFA Institute":1.

22 Morley, ICFA Board Minutes (2 August 1987):9.

23 Vaughan, ICFA Board Minutes (2 August 1987):17.

24 ICFA Board Minutes (15 September 1987):5.

25 These quotations of Muller are from his correspondence with the author dated 7 February 2011.

26 Because this book deals with the history of the CFA Program, the FAF point of view on the merger is discussed only briefly. For some further detail, including a profile of the lead negotiators, Dan Forrestal and B. Millner, see *From Practice to Profession: A History of the Financial Analysts Federation and the Investment Profession* (Charlottesville, VA: Association for Investment Management and Research, 1997).

27 Murphy, conversation with the author on 14 June 2010.

28 Sit, ICFA Board Minutes (18 September 1987):4.

29 McCowin letter to William S. Gray, dated 18 June 2002.

30 Diana Henriques, "Analysts, Unite!" *Barron's* (24 April 1989):24.

31 Muller, correspondence with Wendi Ruschmann dated 8 November 2010.

32 Vaughan, notes for a Keynote Address for the 20th Anniversary Dinner, CFA Institute, dated 13 January 2010; also conversations with John G. Gillis on 13 January 2010.

33 This and next two quotations are from the Vaughan interview with Bowman (13 January 2010).

34 This and next quotation are from Bowman, interview with Wendi Ruschmann (18 December 2006); also, Bowman, correspondence with Ruschmann dated 17 November 2007.

35 The quotations of Forrestal are from ICFA Board Minutes (13 March 1989):5.

36 Bowman, correspondence with Ruschmann, no date.

37 These quotations of Vaughan are from the interview with Bowman (13 January 2010).

38 Quotations of Vaughan in this paragraph and the next are from the Vaughan interview with Bowman (13 January 2010).

39 These quotations of Vaughan are from his notes for a Keynote Address and conversations with John G. Gillis, both 13 January 2010).

40 Morley, memo to ICFA Board of Trustees dated 1 September 1989:1.

41 Vaughan, interview with Bowman (13 January 2010).

42 Noyes, correspondence with Wendi Ruschmann dated 7 November 2010.

43 These quotations of Vertin are from the interview with Tom Bowman (17 February 2010).

44 Vaughan, notes for a Keynote Address (13 January 2010).

FIVE: FACING NEW REALITIES

1 This and the following quotation are from Ruschmann correspondence with the author dated 25 August 2010.

2 Tom Welch, speech at the AIMR 20th anniversary dinner (13 January 2010):1.

3 All the quotations in this paragraph are from Morley, AIMR board meeting (19 May 1990):2.

4 Charles R. Geisst, *Wall Street: A History from its Beginnings to the Fall of Enron* (New York: Oxford University Press, 1997):362.

5 Youssef Cassis, *Capitals of Capital: The Rise and Fall of International Financial Centres, 1780–2009* (Cambridge: Cambridge University Press, 2007):248.

6 The quotations of McCowin are from an interview of Tom Bowman and McCowin by the author (July 2009).

7 Muller, correspondence with the author dated 17 November 2010.

8 Muller, correspondence with the author dated 29 June 2010:2.

9 Vaughan, interview with Tom Bowman (13 January 2010).

10 Vertin, interview with Derik Rice (26 May 2000).

11 Muller, correspondence with the author dated 29 June 2010:2.

12 "Report of Task Force" to ICFA trustees (15 January 1991).

13 This description is from Bowman, memo to Ted Muller dated 10 April 1990.

14 Bowman, correspondence with the author dated 2 September 2010.

15 Tuttle, interview with the author (23 September 2009).

16 Geisst, *Wall Street*:368.

17 Muller, correspondence with the author dated 17 November 2010.

18 These quotations of Speece are from an interview with the author (7 July 2010).

19 Bowman, correspondence with the author dated 22 September 2010.

20 ICFA Board Minutes (5 February 1991):2.

21 Speece, interview with the author (7 July 2010).

22 Muller, correspondence with the author dated 29 June 2010:2.

23 This and the following quotation are from Troughton correspondence with the author dated 31 August 2010 and 27 October 2010.

24 Interview of Jan R. Squires, Tom Bowman, and Peter Mackey with the author (24 September 2009).

25 Bowman, conversation with the author on 29 September 2010.

26 ICFA Board Minutes (19 May 1991):11.

27 ICFA Board Minutes (5 February 1992):5.

28 Tom Bowman, memo to the ICFA board dated 29 July 1993:1.

29 1990 AIMR Annual Report:7.

30 Professional Conduct Committee Report (7 October 1991):1; also, correspondence between Professional Conduct Program staff and the author dated 22 September 2010.

31 Quotations of Vaughan are from the 1990 AIMR Annual Report:1.

32 Quotations of Morley are from Diana Henriques, "Analyst Who Criticized Trump Is Ousted," *New York Times* (27 March 1990):D2.

33 1991 AIMR Annual Report:12.

34 John Markoff, "Dismissed in Trump Case, Analyst is Awarded $750,000," *New York Times* (6 March 1991):D1.

35 All quotations in this section are from Templeton's acceptance speech at the AIMR Annual Conference of 21 May 1991:3–6.

36 This and the following quotation are from Bowman, interview with Ruschmann (18 December 2006).

37 Muller, correspondence with the author dated 22 September 2010:2.

38 Muller, "Foreword" to the Report of the Performance Presentation Standards Implementation Committee (December 1991):2.

39 The total number of charters awarded since 1963 was 16,602, but some members were deceased or inactive.

40 Bowman, memo to Ted Muller dated 10 April 1990:1.

41 Quotations of Crutchfield in this section are from her correspondence with the author dated 3 March 2010.

42 *The CFA Accreditation Program,* undated brochure, circa 1987:1.

43 Quotations of Bowman in this section

are from his correspondence with the author dated 8 March 2010.

44 This and the information from Gillis are from ICFA Board Minutes (4 February 1992):2.

45 This and the following quotation are from ICFA Board Minutes (4 August 1992):2.

46 These quotations of Tuttle are from an interview with Bob Johnson (29 March 2010).

47 Cassis: *Capitals:*241.

48 Muller, ICFA Board Minutes (8 October 1991):10.

49 Bayston, ICFA Board Minutes (5 February 1991):5.

50 Morley, ICFA Board Minutes (5 February 1991):5.

51 Tom Bowman, interview with Ruschmann (18 December 2006).

52 Bowman, memo to ICFA trustees dated 5 January 1990:1.

53 Bowman, correspondence with the author dated 25 September 2010.

54 ICFA Board Minutes (5 February 1991):6.

55 Tuttle, correspondence with the author dated 16 November 2010.

56 This and the following quotation are from ICFA Board Minutes (5 February 1991):5.

57 Jim Vertin, ICFA Board Minutes (5 February 1991):9.

58 Tom Bowman, memo to ICFA trustees dated 4 January 1988:1.

59 Quotations of Bowman in this and the next two paragraphs are from his interview with Ruschmann (18 December 2006).

60 AIMR 1990 Annual Report:21.

61 Yura, interview given to Tom Bowman (September 2010).

62 ICFA Board Minutes (9 August 1992):5.

63 SAAJ website: www.saa.or.jp/english/about_saa/objectives.html.

64 ICFA Board Minutes (9 August 1992):5.

65 These quotations are from a conversation between Yura and Tom Bowman on 6 July 2010:2.

66 Cassis, *Capitals:*267.

67 AIMR Board Minutes (23 May 1993):7.

68 Bowman, interview with Ruschmann (18 December 2006).

69 Yura, interview with Bowman (6 July 2010).

70 Gentaro Yura, correspondence with the author dated 9 October 2010:2.

71 Bowman, correspondence with the author dated 18 November 2010.

72 Troughton, correspondence with the author dated 15 November 2010. The authors mentioned are Franco Modigliani and Merton Miller.

73 Troughton, interview given to the author (29 September 2009).

74 Eliot Williams, memo to AIMR board dated 21 September 1993; also Gentaro Yura, interview given to Tom Bowman (6 July 2010).

75 This and the next quotation are from an interview given to Tom Bowman (December 2008).

76 Tuttle, correspondence with the author dated 16 November 10.

77 Eugene Sit, International Committee Report (1 August 1990):3.

78 Bowman, correspondence with the author dated 26 September 2010.

79 ICFA Board Minutes (4 February 1992):5.

80 Troughton, correspondence with the author dated 15 November 10.

81 Quotations in this paragraph are from Bowman, interview with Ruschmann (18 December 2006).

82 Quotations in this profile are as follows: LeBaron, correspondence with the author dated 11 February 2011; Sherrerd, correspondence with the author dated 5 January 2011; Bowman, interview with Wendi Ruschmann (18 December 2006); Vertin, correspondence with the author dated 4 March 2011 and interview with Tom Bowman (17 February 2010).

83 Quotations of Bowman in this and the next paragraph are from his interview with Ruschmann (18 December 2006).

84 Charles D. Ellis, "Notes on CFA Institute History," unpublished (July 2010):7.

SIX: EXPANDING THE INFRASTRUCTURE

1 The quotations of Churchill in this and the next paragraph are from his letter to Maginn dated 4 May 1994:1–3.

2 Singleton, ICFA Board Minutes (15 May 1994):3.

3 See Benjamin Graham and Lucien O. Hooper, "Should Security Analysts Have a Professional Rating?" *The Analyst's Journal*, vol. 1, no. 1 (January 1945):43.

4 All quotations in this and the next paragraph are from J. Clay Singleton, ICFA Board Minutes (15 May 1994):3, 5–6.

5 DeAngelo, interview with the author (29 August 2009).

6 The quotations and three points in this paragraph are from Tom Bowman's report "Synthesis of Major Points/Conclusions Reached at Education Summit" (12 January 1994):1; also, Bowman's report at the ICFA Board Meeting (15 May 1994):2.

7 Churchill, ICFA Trustees Meeting (15 May 1994):3.

8 In subsequent years, the GBOK became known as the Global Body of Investment Knowledge (GBIK) and represented broad knowledge for the profession, including specialist knowledge; the CFA Program Candidate Body of Knowledge (CBOK) represented the subset of that knowledge required for a new charterholder.

9 This and the next quotation are from Bowman, correspondence with Wendi Ruschmann and others dated 10 November 2009.

10 Youssef Cassis, *Capitals of Capital: The Rise and Fall of International Financial Centres, 1780–2009* (Cambridge: Cambridge University Press, 2007):256.

11 Charles R. Geisst, *Wall Street: A History from Its Beginnings to the Fall of Enron*

(New York: Oxford University Press, 1997):337.

12 Nancy Regan, *The Institute of Chartered Financial Analysts: A Twenty-Five Year History* (Charlottesville, VA: Institute of Chartered Financial Analysts, 1987):101.

13 All quotations of Vertin in this sidebar are from his correspondence with the author dated 4 May 2010.

14 This and next quotations are from Sherrerd, correspondence with Wendi Ruschmann dated 12 April 2011.

15 "Industry Trendsetter Gary P. Brinson, CFA, Shares His Views on an Ever-Evolving Global Profession," *AIMR Exchange* (July/August 1999):18.

16 Sherrerd, interview with the author (3 September 2010).

17 CFA Institute website: www.cfainstitute.org/about/foundation.

18 Quotations in this paragraph are from Tuttle, ICFA Board Minutes (21 May 1995):4.

19 Quotations of Tuttle in this paragraph are from an interview with the author (23 September 2009).

20 AIMR Annual Report 1995:7.

21 Information in this section and Tuttle quotations are from ICFA Board Minutes (4 August 1994):6.

22 Quotations of Muller are from AIMR Board Minutes (18 May 1991). Vertin quotations from an interview with Derik Rice (26 May 2000) or an interview with Tom Bowman (17 February 2010). The Bernstein quotations come from his book *Capital Ideas: The Improbable Origins of Modern Wall Street* (New York: Free Press, 1992). Quotations of Ellis are from correspondence with the author dated 7 February 2011. The Speece quotation is from an interview with the author (24 February 2011), and the Sherrerd quotation is from correspondence with the author dated 5 January 2011.

23 This and the quotations in the next paragraph are from a memo from Tuttle to the ICFA Board of Trustees (25 January 1995).

24 This discussion is from ICFA Board Minutes (21 May 1995):2–3.

25 See Johnson, Squires, Mackey, and Lamy, *The CFA Program* (undated):3.

26 From the 1999 AIMR Annual Report:25.

27 All Churchill quotes here are from correspondence with the author dated 26 December 2010.

28 Johnson, interview with the author (14 October 2009).

29 Johnson, interview with Jessica Galehouse (December 2006).

30 In this and the next paragraph, Bowman quotations are from a memo to the ICFA trustees (24 July 1995):2–3.

31 Johnson, interview with the author (14 October 2009).

32 See Johnson, Squires, Mackey, and Lamy, *The CFA Program*:5.

33 ICFA Board Minutes (7 September 1995):4.

34 This and the next quotation are from Wruble correspondence with Wendi Ruschmann dated 5 July 2010.

35 Quotations of Johnson in this paragraph are from an interview with the author (14 October 2009).

36 Quotations of Luck in this paragraph are from an interview with the author (28 September 2009).

37 According to Nancy Dudley, then head of Exam Administration & Security, a total of 30 scores (out of 11,000) were changed from fail to pass once this scanner error was discovered.

38 Singleton, ICFA Board Minutes (7 September 1995):2.

39 Quotations of Singleton in this paragraph are from the "Report of the Council of Examiners" (21 August 1995):2.

40 Quotations of Tuttle in this paragraph are from an interview with the author (23 September 2009).

41 Quotations of Gentaro Yura in this paragraph are from his correspondence with the author dated 14 April 2011.

42 Reilly, interview with the author (9 March 2011).

43 Specialization Committee Background Report (September 1995):2.

44 Tuttle, ICFA Board Minutes (6 February 1997):6.

45 ICFA Board Minutes (18 September 1997):7.

46 Education Committee Minutes (8 January 1998).

47 ICFA Board Minutes (6 February 1998):7.

48 ICFA Board Minutes (7 September 1995):7.

49 ICFA Board Minutes (7 September 1995):6.

50 Bowman, interview with Wendi Ruschmann (18 December 2006).

51 Bowman, memo to ICFA trustees (21 August 1995):1.

52 Tschampion, correspondence with the author dated 13 December 2010.

53 Maginn, interview with Johnson (1 July 2010).

54 Ray DeAngelo, interview with the author (28 August 2009).

55 Bob Johnson, interview with Galehouse (December 2006).

56 Sarasin, interview with Bob Johnson (April 2009).

57 Bowman, interview with Wendi Ruschmann (18 December 2006).

58 Speece quotations in this and the next paragraph are from an interview with the author (7 July 2010).

59 All the Sarasin quotations in this section are from the interview with Bob Johnson (April 2009).

SEVEN: BEST PRACTICES

1 Rogers, correspondence with the author dated 31 March 2011.

2 Stannard, interview with Bob Johnson (14 January 2010).

3 Smith, interview with Tom Bowman (December 2008).

4 Welch, correspondence with Wendi Ruschmann (15 December 2010).

5 Here as elsewhere in this book, a

cited number of candidates per year refers only to those who actually sat for the CFA exam, not the number who registered to take it. The number who register is typically 25 percent higher than the number who attend on exam days. When the number who registered is cited, that number is specifically called "registrations" or "enrollments," not candidates.

6   Minutes of Joint Session of AIMR Governors and ICFA Trustees (16 May 1998):11.

7   This and the following quotations of Mackey are from an interview with the author (10 November 2010).

8   Mackey, correspondence with the author dated 31 March 2011.

9   AIMR 2000 Annual Report:3.

10 Dudley, interview with Tom Bowman (23 December 2008).

11 Johnson, interview with the author (14 October 2009).

12 Remington, correspondence with Wendi Ruschmann dated 22 October 2010.

13 Tuttle, conversation with the author (21 December 2010).

14 2002 AIMR Annual Report:15.

15 "Proprietary literature" refers to original work commissioned by the CFA Program on topics specifically designed to serve its curriculum.

16 This and the next quotation are from Tuttle, interview with Bob Johnson (29 March 2010).

17 This and the next quotation of Tuttle are from an interview with Bob Johnson (29 March 2010).

18 HOKT information is from an e-mail by Tom Robinson to the author dated 24 February 2010.

19 This and the next Squires quotation are from an interview with the author (24 September 2009).

20 Johnson, interview with Jessica Galehouse (December 2006).

21 Tuttle, interview with Bob Johnson (29 March 2010).

22 McCowin, interview with Bob Johnson (1 July 2009).

23 Churchill, correspondence with the author dated 26 December 2010.

24 Squires, interview with the author (24 September 2009).

25 This quotation is from the 2001 AIMR Annual Report (unpaged).

26 Dudley, interview with Tom Bowman (23 December 2008).

27 *AIMR Exchange*, November/December 2001:9.

28 Miller, AIMR Board Minutes (20 September 2001):3.

29 Bowman, correspondence with the author dated 10 October 2010.

30 Johnson, Squires, Mackey, and Lamy, *The CFA Program: Our Fifth Decade* (undated):3.

31 Jerome L. Valentine and Edmund A. Mennis, *Quantitative Techniques for Financial Analysis*. Revised edition (Homewood, IL: Richard D. Irwin, 1980).

32 John L. Maginn and Donald A. Tuttle, *Managing Investment Portfolios: A Dynamic Process* (Boston: Warren, Gorham & Lamont, 1983).

33 Johnson, interview with the author (14 October 2009).

34 Richard A. Defusco, Dennis W. McLeavey, Jerald E. Pinto, and David E. Runkle, *Quantitative Methods for Investment Analysis* (Charlottesville, VA: CFA Institute, 2004).

35 John D. Stowe, Thomas R. Robinson, Jerald E. Pinto, and Dennis W. McLeavey, *Equity Asset Valuation* (Hoboken, NJ: Wiley, 2007).

36 Johnson, interview with the author (14 October 2009).

37 This and the next quotation are from Mackey correspondence with the author dated 31 March 2011.

38 Maginn, interview with Bob Johnson (1 July 2010).

39 Sherrerd, AIMR Board Minutes (4 February 2000):5.

40 All quotations of Sherrerd in these two paragraphs are from an interview with the author (3 September 2010).

41 James M. Cudahy, "Members Make Adjustment to Model CE Program," *AIMR Exchange* (November/December 2000):1, 16.

42 All the quotations of Speece in this paragraph are from an interview with the author (7 July 2010).

43 Gravel, interview with Bob Johnson (30 July 2009).

44 Bowman, interview with Wendi Ruschmann (18 December 2006).

45 This and the following quotation of Diermeier are from his unpublished "Reflections on CFA Institute, 2005–2008":11.

46 Quotations of Bowman in this and the next section are from an interview with Wendi Ruschmann (18 December 2006).

47 DeAngelo, correspondence with the author dated 31 March 2011.

48 DeAngelo, correspondence with the author dated 8 March 2011.

49 Sarasin, comments presented to Tom Bowman upon his retirement in December 2004 (available on DVD in the CFA Institute archives).

50 O'Reilly, comments presented to Tom Bowman upon his retirement in December 2004 (available on DVD in the CFA Institute archives).

INTERLUDE: THE EVOLUTION OF CFA EXAM GRADING

1   Smith, correspondence with the author dated 29 December 2010.

2   All quotations of Smith in this paragraph are from an interview with Tom Bowman (December 2008).

3   Whitehead, speech to CFA candidates, New York City (1967):2.

4   Robert R. Johnson, Jan R. Squires, Peter B. Mackey, and Bobby Lamy, *The CFA Program: Our Fifth Decade* (Charlottesville, VA: CFA Institute, undated): www.cfainstitute.org/cfaprogram/ Documents/the_cfa_program_our_ fifth_decade.pdf#curr_dev.

5   All quotations of Richardson are from an interview with Bob Johnson (2 July 2009).

6   All quotations of Bowman are from an interview with Wendi Ruschmann (18 December 2006).

7   Information in this section comes from Cori Hord, conversation with the author (13 May 2011).

8   For additional details on the grading process, see Johnson et al., *The CFA Program*, on the CFA Institute website.

9   Bowman, interview with Ruschmann (18 December 2006).

10 Informal grader conversations with the author (2 July 2009).

11 Mackey, interview with the author (9 November 2010).

12 Smith, interview with Tom Bowman (December 2008).

13 This and the next quotation are from I. Rossa O'Reilly, "The Success of Grading," *AIMR Newsletter* (September/October 1996):10.

14 Reid, "Why I'm a Grader," *AIMR Newsletter* (October/November 1994):4.

15 All quotations of King are from an interview with the author (5 February 2011).

16 Tuttle, interview with the author (23 September 2009).

17 All quotations of Blasky are from an interview with Bob Johnson (2 July 2009).

EIGHT: THE GLOBAL STANDARD

1   Frank K. Reilly, "The Guarding of AIMR's 'Crown Jewel'," *AIMR Exchange* (March/April 1999):2.

2   "Free Degrees to Fly," *The Economist* (26 February 2005):68; Matthew Richards, "Inside View of the Chartered Financial Analyst Exams: A Tale of Dedication, Suffering, Sleeplessness and Pain," *Financial Times* (20 June 2005):4.

3   Ian Katz, "46% of 33,449 Level 2 Passed: CFA Institute Says Passing Rate Climbed for Certification Exam," Bloomberg.com (19 August 2008): www.analystforum.com/phorums/read.php?12,815832.

4   Frank J. Fabozzi, Sergio M. Focardi, and Caroline Jonas, *Investment Management after the Global Financial Crisis* (Charlottesville, VA: Research Foundation of CFA Institute, 2010):vii.

5   Rogers, conversation with the author (8 March 2011).

6   Information on previous speculative bubbles, such as the Dutch tulip bubble, had been in the curriculum for many years. "Black Swan" events are those occurrences that are so rare as to seem impossible, as was the existence of black swans at one time. See Nassim Nicholas Taleb, *The Black Swan: The Impact of the Highly Improbable* (New York: Random House, 2007).

7   Diermeier, 2005 Annual Report:4.

8   Quotations of Hauptfuhrer are from correspondence with Wendi Ruschmann dated 25 March 2011.

9   Diermeier, 2005 Annual Report:5.

10 Quoted in "Congratulating New Charterholders in a Worldwide Forum," *CFA Magazine* (March/April 2006):12.

11 Jennifer Taylor, correspondence with the author dated 25 March 2011.

12 Bowman, interview with Wendi Ruschmann (18 December 2006).

13 2005 Annual Report:9.

14 2006 Annual Report:6.

15 This and next quotation of Diermeier are from his unpublished reflections on CFA Institute (2010):7.

16 Richards, "Inside View of Chartered Financial Analysts Exams":4.

17 2005 Annual Report:8.

18 Final report summary, CFA Preparation Task Force (7 May 2005):5.

19 Information and quotation of Wiese are from correspondence with Wendi Ruschmann dated 12 April and 5 May 2011.

20 Graham, *The Analysts Journal* (January 1945):40.

21 In addition to the June 2005 *Financial Times* article (Richards, "Inside View of Chartered Financial Analysts Exams"), see also, for example, "Scarcity Increases the Value of a Rigorous Qualification," *Financial Times* (16 June 2008); "How Not to Unwind after Work," *The Economist* (7 June 2008); "Mettle Detector," *Canadian Business* (7 July–13 August 2006); "The Grueling Test of Finance Professionals," *The Times* of London (21 August 2009).

22 Mark Bruno, "And Beware of Venomous Camel Spiders," *Pensions and Investments* (12 December 2005):8.

23 Bowman, "Pass Rates Tell the Story: No Shortcuts," *CFA Magazine* (September/October 2004):6.

24 Quotations here of Diermeier are from his unpublished reflections:9.

25 The process of arriving at the MPS, briefly touched on here, is thoroughly explained in Johnson, Squires, Mackey, and Lamy, *The CFA Program: Our Fifth Decade* (undated).

26 Johnson et al., *The CFA Program*:10.

27 Johnson, interview with the author (14 October 2009).

28 Mackey, correspondence with the author dated 3 May 2011.

29 This and the next quotation of Robinson are from correspondence with the author dated 31 March 2011.

30 Quotations in this paragraph are Johnson, correspondence with the author dated 30 March 2011.

31 This and the next Bowman quotations are from "Pass Rates Tell the Story":6.

32 Mackey, correspondence with the author dated 2 May 2011.

33 McLeavey, correspondence with the author dated 1 April 2011.

34 Diermeier, in "First Global Investment Research Challenge," *CFA Magazine* (July/August 2007):25.

35 Maginn interview with Bob Johnson, 1 July 2010.

36 Johnson, correspondence with the author dated 31 March 2011.

37 Johnson et al., *Our Fifth Decade*:4.

38 This and the following quotations of Robinson are from correspondence with the author dated 16 May 2011.

39 Mackey and Squires quotations are from an interview with the author (24 September 2009).

40 Scanlan, Education Advisory Committee Report (14 July 2008):1.

41 Johnson, correspondence with the author dated 30 March 2011.

42 Jones, correspondence with Wendi Ruschmann dated 24 March 2011.

43 William M. Sullivan, "Markets vs. Professions: Value Added?" *Daedalus* (Summer 2005):22.

44 Quotations of Diermeier in this paragraph are "CFA Charterholders Are in a League of their Own," *CFA Magazine* (May/June 2008):4.

45 Quotations of Koppel in this and next paragraph are from conversation with the author (17 November 2009).

46 Phrase quoted is from a CFA Institute strategic planning memo dated 3 January 2005.

47 "Free Degrees to Fly."

48 This and next quotation are from Richards, "Inside View of the Chartered Financial Analysts Exams":4.

49 Johnson, memo to AIMR board (26 April 2004):3.

50 Gonzalez, interview given to Jeff Diermeier (22 July 2009).

51 Gravel, interview with Bob Johnson (22 July 2009).

52 Duhamel, "Chairman's Message," 2006 Annual Report:2.

53 Jan Squires quoting Louis Gave, internal staff report (9 May 2008):3.

54 2009 Annual Report:15.

55 Quotations of Appeadu in this paragraph are from his "Africa Report" (July 2008):4.

56 Diermeier and Singer, 2008 Annual Report:4.

57 Singer, interview with Jeff Diermeier (22 July 2009).

58 Gonzalez, interview with Bob Johnson (22 July 2009).

59 Aimée Rhodes, interview with the author (November 2010).

60 Rogers, correspondence with the author dated 1 April 2011.

Sources

In preparing this book, the author relied on many interviews and unpublished materials, as documented in the endnotes. In addition, the following published works were consulted:

Bernstein, Peter L. *Capital Ideas: The Improbable Origins of Modern Wall Street.* New York: Free Press, 1992.

Bogle, John C. *Enough: True Measures of Money, Business and Life.* Hoboken, NJ: John Wiley and Sons, 2009.

"A Brief History of the Investment Analysts Society of Chicago, 1925–1975." Chicago, IL: Investment Analysts Society of Chicago, 1975.

Cassis, Youssef. *Capitals of Capital: The Rise and Fall of International Financial Centres, 1780–2009.* Cambridge, U.K.: Cambridge University Press, 2007.

Ellis, Charles D. "Ben Graham: Ideas as Mementos," *Financial Analysts Journal*, vol. 38, no. 4 (July/August 1982):51–54.

Ellis, Charles D. "Coming of Age: A Brief History of the Changing Role of the Securities Analyst." *The Investment Professional: The Journal of NYSSA*, vol. 2, no. 1 (2009).

Ellis, Charles D., and James R. Vertin, editors. *Classics: An Investor's Anthology.* Homewood, IL: Business One Irwin, 1988.

Ellis, Charles D., and James R. Vertin, editors. *Classics II: An Investor's Anthology.* Homewood, IL: Business One Irwin, 1991.

Fabozzi, Frank, Sergio M. Focardi, and Caroline Jonas. *Investment Management after the Global Financial Crisis.* Charlottesville, VA: Research Foundation of CFA Institute, 2010.

"Free Degrees to Fly." *Economist* (26 February 2005):68.

From Practice to Profession: A History of the Financial Analysts Federation and the Investment Profession. Charlottesville, VA: Association for Investment Management and Research, 1997.

Gardner, Howard, and Lee S. Schulman. "The Professions in America Today: Crucial but Fragile." *Daedalus: Journal of the American Academy of Arts and Sciences*, vol. 134, no. 3 (Summer 2005):13–18.

Geisst, Charles R. *Wall Street: A History from Its Beginnings to the Fall of Enron.* New York: Oxford University Press, 1997.

Gillis, John G. "Federal Regulation of Analysts." *Financial Analysts Journal*, vol. 33, no. 4 (July/August 1977):10–11, 54, 69.

Gordon, John Steele. *The Great Game: The Emergence of Wall Street as a World Power, 1653–2000.* New York: Scribner, 1990.

Graham, Benjamin, and David Dodd. *Security Analysis: The Classic 1934 Edition.* New York: McGraw-Hill, 1996; other editions are also available as reprints.

Graham, Benjamin, and Lucien O. Hooper. "Should Security Analysts Have a Professional Rating?" *The Analyst's Journal*, vol. 1, no. 1 (January 1945).

Hayes, Douglas A. "Potential for Professional Status." *Financial Analysts Journal*, vol. 23, no. 6 (November/December 1967):29–31.

Henriques, Diana B. "Analyst Who Criticized Trump Casino Is Ousted." *New York Times* (27 March 1991):D2.

Henriques, Diana B. "Analysts, Unite!" *Barron's* (April 1989):16, 24.

Johnson, Robert R., Jan R. Squires, Peter B. Mackey, and Bobby Lamy. *The CFA Program: Our Fifth Decade*. Charlottesville, VA: CFA Institute, undated (www.cfainstitute.org/cfaprogram/Documents/the_cfa_program_our_fifth_decade.pdf#curr_dev).

Kahn, Irving, and Robert D. Milne. *Benjamin Graham: The Father of Financial Analysis*. Occasional Paper No. 5, Financial Analysts Research Foundation, 1977.

Khunara, Rakesh. *From Higher Aims to Hired Hands: The Social Transformation of American Business Schools and the Unfulfilled Promise of Management As a Profession*. Princeton, NJ: Princeton University Press, 2007.

Lambourne, Richard W. "The Security Analyst: Growth of a Profession." *The Exchange*. New York Stock Exchange (March 1953).

Lowe, Janet. *Benjamin Graham and Values Investing: Lessons from the Dean of Wall Street*. Dearborn, MI: Dearborn Financial Publishing, 1994.

Markoff, John. "Dismissed in Trump Case, Analyst Is Awarded $750,000." *New York Times* (6 March 1991):D1.

Mennis, Edmund A. "*Financial Analysts Journal*: Marrying the Academic and Practitioner Worlds." *Financial Analysts Journal*, vol. 61, no. 3 (May/June 2005).

Molodovsky, Nicholas. "Editor's Notes." *Financial Analysts Journal*, vol. 20, no. 1 (January/February 1964):7.

Muller, Frederick L. "Equity Security Analysis in the U.S." *Financial Analysts Journal*, vol. 50, no. 1 (January/February 1994):6–9.

Musgrave, Gerald. "In Memoriam: Edmund A. Mennis." *Business Economics*, vol. 44, no. 3 (July 2009):130–131.

Previts, Gary John, and Barbara Dubis Merino. *A History of Accountancy in the United States: The Cultural Significance of Accounting*. Columbus, OH: Ohio State University Press, 1998.

Regan, Nancy. *The Institute of Chartered Financial Analysts: A Twenty-Five Year History*. Charlottesville, VA: Institute of Chartered Financial Analysts, 1987.

Richards, Matthew. "Inside View of the Chartered Financial Analysts Exams: A Tale of Dedication, Suffering, Sleeplessness and Pain." *Financial Times* (20 June 2005):4.

Sheppard, Stewart. *The Making of a Profession: The CFA Program*. Charlottesville, VA: Association for Investment Management and Research, 1992.

Sheppard, Stewart. "The Professionalization of the Financial Analyst." *Financial Analysts Journal*, vol. 23, no. 6 (November/December):39–41.

Sullivan, William M. "Markets vs. Professions: Value Added?" *Daedalus*, vol. 134, no. 3 (Summer 2005):19–26.

The New York Times: The Complete Front Pages, 1851–2008. New York: Black Dog and Leventhal, 2008.

Zweig, Jason, and Rodney N. Sullivan. *Benjamin Graham, Building a Profession: The Early Writings of the Father of Security Analysis*. New York: McGraw-Hill, 2010.

Index

globalization. *See* financial markets; global investing, Templeton on; international growth of the CFA Program

Gonzalez, Emilio, *231*, 246, 248, 270

Goss, F., *217*

graders

 See also grading of CFA exams; *and specific individuals*

 1960s graders, 32–33, 59–60, *61*, *62*, 213

 CFA Summer Camp, 214–22, *215*, *217*, *222*

 by charterholders, 59, 213, 214

 disagreements, 216, 218

 employment agreements, 198

 number needed, 163, 218, 220

 from outside North America, 95–96, 156, 170, 183–84, 210

 profiles, 223

 Tuttle Award, 221, *221*, 259

 workload and hours, 60–61

grading of CFA exams

 See also graders

 anonymous grading, 213

 changes driven by volume, 178, 213, 218, 219–20

 first exam, 32–33, 59–60, 213

 grading process, 59–61, 72, 213–20, *219*

 location, in early years, 223

 machine grading, 213–14, 219–20

 not curved, 60

 standards, 32–33, 58–62, 213, 235, 237–38

Graham, Benjamin, *4*, *5*

 certification first proposed, 3–9, 249

 considered for ICFA director, 20–21

 on exam difficulty, 58, 235

 Graham-Hooper debate, 6–8, 16–17, 44–45, 58, 117

 Templeton a student of, 4, 143

Graham-Hooper debate, 6–8, 16–17, 44–45, 58, 117

"grandfathering" issue, 13–14, 16–18, 25, 32, 99

Gravel, Monique E.M., 84, 209, *244*, 246, 270

Graves, William W., Jr., 35

Gray, Allan W.B., *108*

Gray, Eugene H., 35

Gray, M. Mallory, 35

Gray, R., *215*

Gray, William S., III, 71

Great Britain

 See also Society of Investment Analysts

 AIMR's London office, 207, 246

 CFA Day, *232*

 exam center statistics, 166, 197, 227

 International Education Summit (London, 1997), 184

Greenspan, Alan, 57

Greer, Raymond C.L., Jr., 52

Gregory, Arthur W., Jr., 35

Guin, Larry D., *217*, 221, 259

Guo, Wendy (Weiyu), *239*

Gutman, Walter K., 11

Haeringer, Stephen, 112

Haladyna, Thomas, 201

Hall, J. Parker, III, 12, 31

Hall, John R., 35, *42*

Haltiner, J., *217*

Halverson, Richard P., *134*

Hamilton-Keen, Elizabeth M., *218*

Hammell, Raymond W., 35, 57, 269

Han Kang, *232*

Hansberger, Thomas L., 270

Hansen, George M., 22

 early committee membership, 10

 file cabinet purchased, 38

 first CFA Charter received, *29*, 30, 34

 on ICFA board, *26*, 57

 NFFAS vote tabulated, 19

 on the NYSSA certification proposal, 11

 Sheppard Award, 51

 UVA suggested as ICFA seat, 21

Hansen, Lea B., 101, *101*, *217*

Hanson, W., *215*

Hardaway, Robert B., Jr., 115, 118, 221, 259

Harlow, W. Van, III, 136

Harman, D., *217*

Harper, Allen D., 34

Harter, Raymond J., 35

Hasse, Richard D., 35

Hauptfuhrer, George J., III, 229

Hausmann, Frank W., Jr., 34

Haverstick, Edward E., Jr., 35

Hayes, Douglas A., 20, 22–23, 45, 57, *62*

Heer, William D., Jr., 34

Heimer, Gordon L., 35

Held, William P., 11–12, 13

Hellawell, George A., 35

Hennigar, E., *217*

Henriques, Diana, 124

Hermann, Henry, *214*

Herndon, Bradley J., *221*, 259

Hesse, Frederick A., 35

Higher Order Knowledge Team (HOKT), 201–3

Hinkle, John, 35

Hinze, Arno F.W., 35

Hitchman, Thomas N., 34

Hoffland, D., *217*

Holloway, John W., 34

Holzer, H., *215*

Homans, Alan, 34, *42*

Hong Kong

 AIMR (CFA Institute) office, *184*, 187, *187*, 246

 exam center statistics, 160, 166, 197, 227

Hong Kong Baptist University, 240

Hooper, Lucien O., *6*

 charter awarded (1963), 30, 35

 death, 124

 Graham-Hooper debate, 6, 8–9, 16–17, 44–45, 58, 117

 test preparation, 30, 38, 40

Hopkins, Samuel, 34

Hord, Cori, 218

Horton, Roland P., 35

Hoskin, Charles A., 34, *42*

Houston, Robert W., 34

"How Ethical Are Businessmen?" (Baumhart), 45

Howard, Bion B., 34, 51, 64

Howard, E. Douglas, II, 35

Howe, Winthrop K., Jr., 35

Huber, Bernhard, *112*

Hudspeth, Max E., *221*, 259

Huff, M. Aimée, 180

Hughes, Douglas R., 45, 58, 73, *221*, 259

Hume, R. Austin, 35, *57*

Hunter, Herbert Davis, 34

Huot, Jules A., 259

Hyre, John E., 35

IASC. *See* Investment Analysts Society of Chicago

ICFA. *See* Institute of Chartered Financial Analysts

index funds, 172

India, 110–11, 152, *194*, 227, 242

Indonesia, 150

Information Central (call center), 165, 183, 194